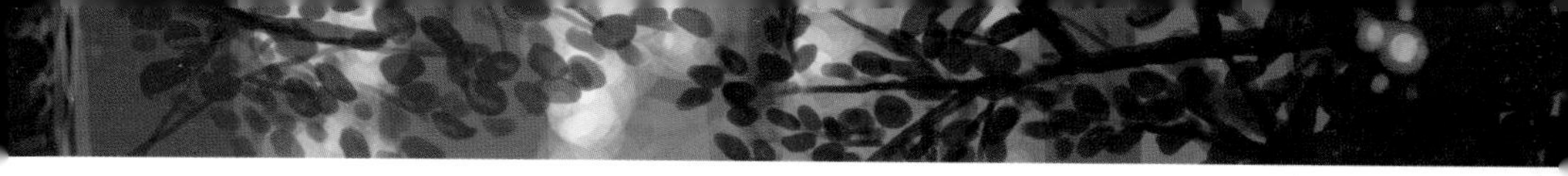

INVERLOCH

VOLUME 1

ART & STORY BY
SARAH ELLERTON

INVERLOCH

First published online at www.seraph-inn.com

Publisher: Seven-Seas Entertainment

Visit us online at www.gomanga.com

ISBN: 1-933164-13-1

Printed in Canada

First printing: April, 2006

10 9 8 7 6 5 4 3 2 1

INVERLOCH
VOLUME 1

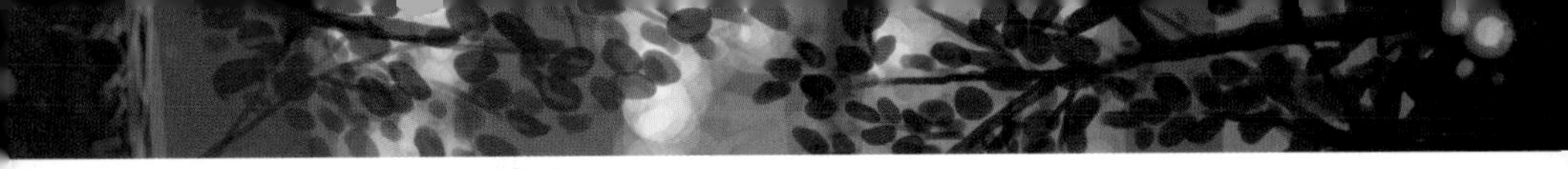

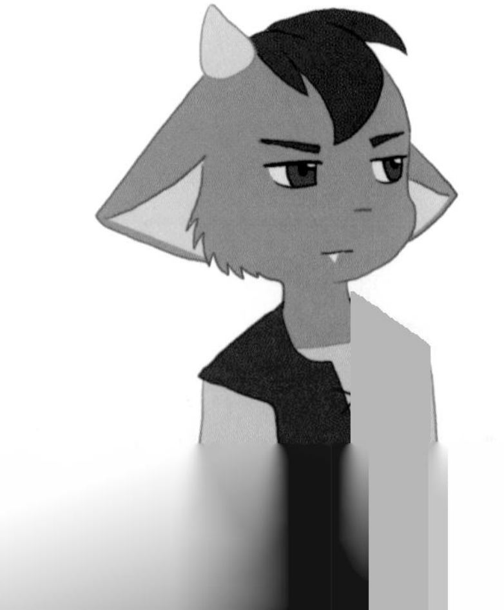

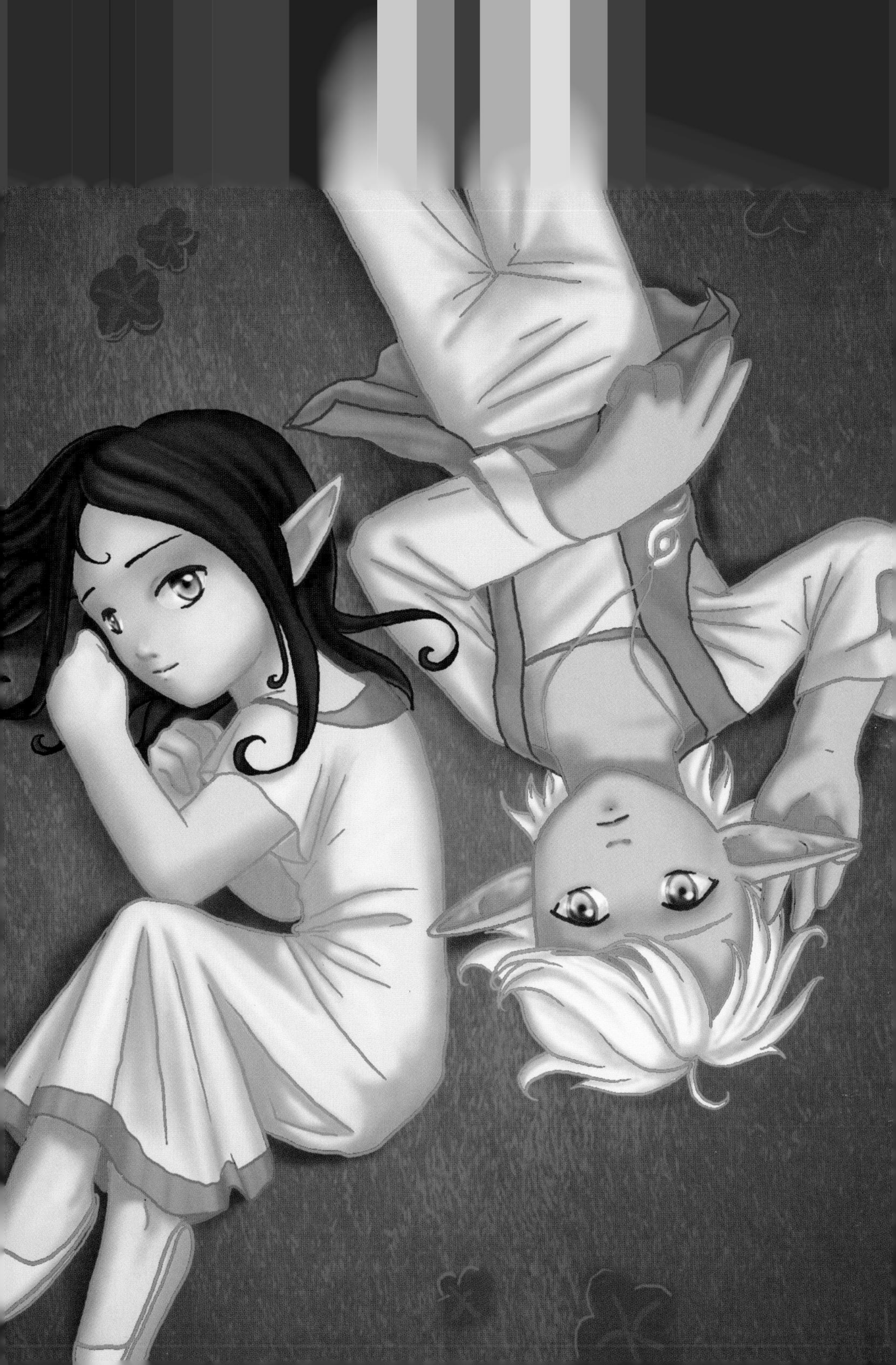

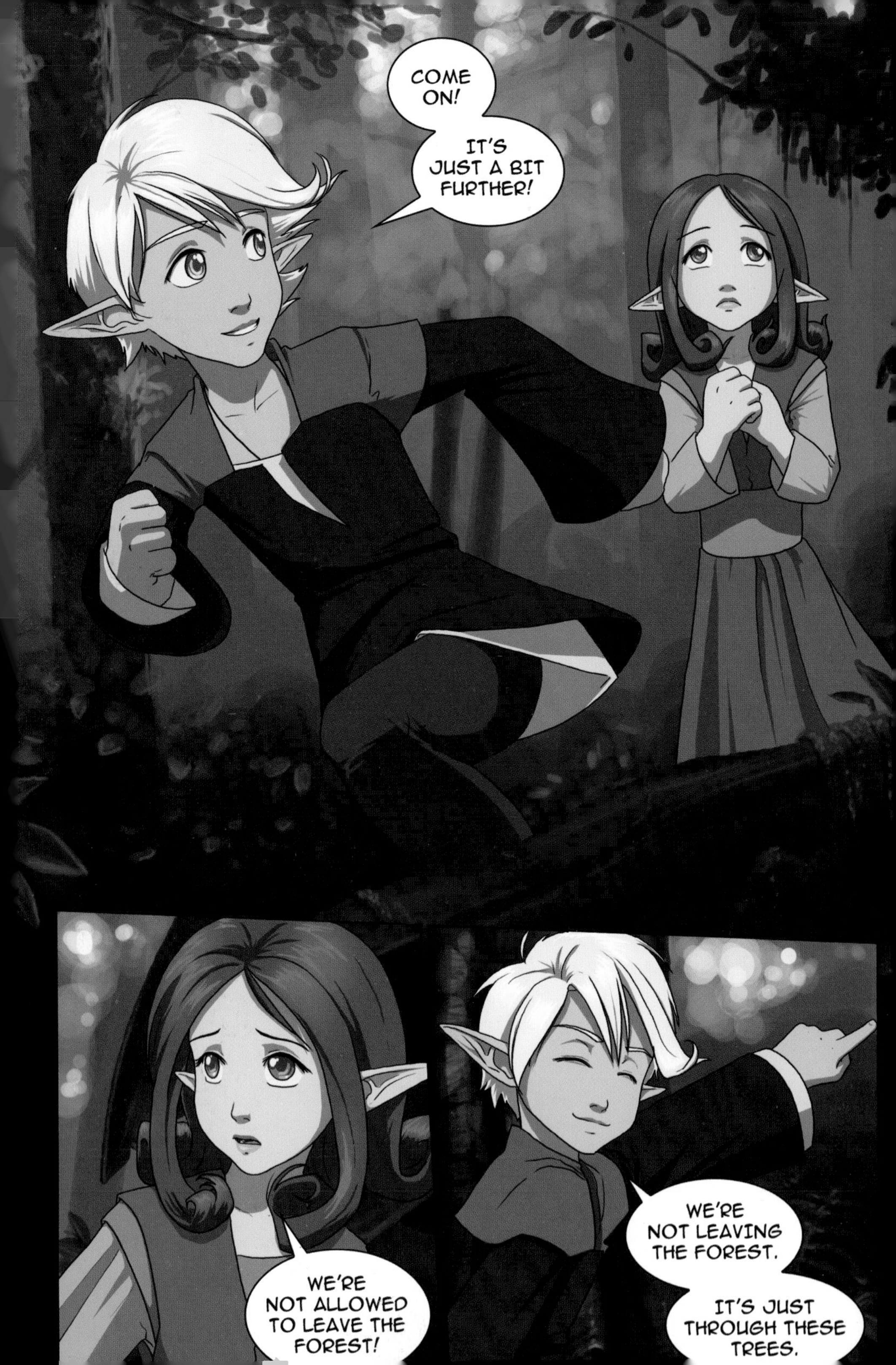
COME ON!
IT'S JUST A BIT FURTHER!
WE'RE NOT ALLOWED TO LEAVE THE FOREST!
WE'RE NOT LEAVING THE FOREST.
IT'S JUST THROUGH THESE TREES.

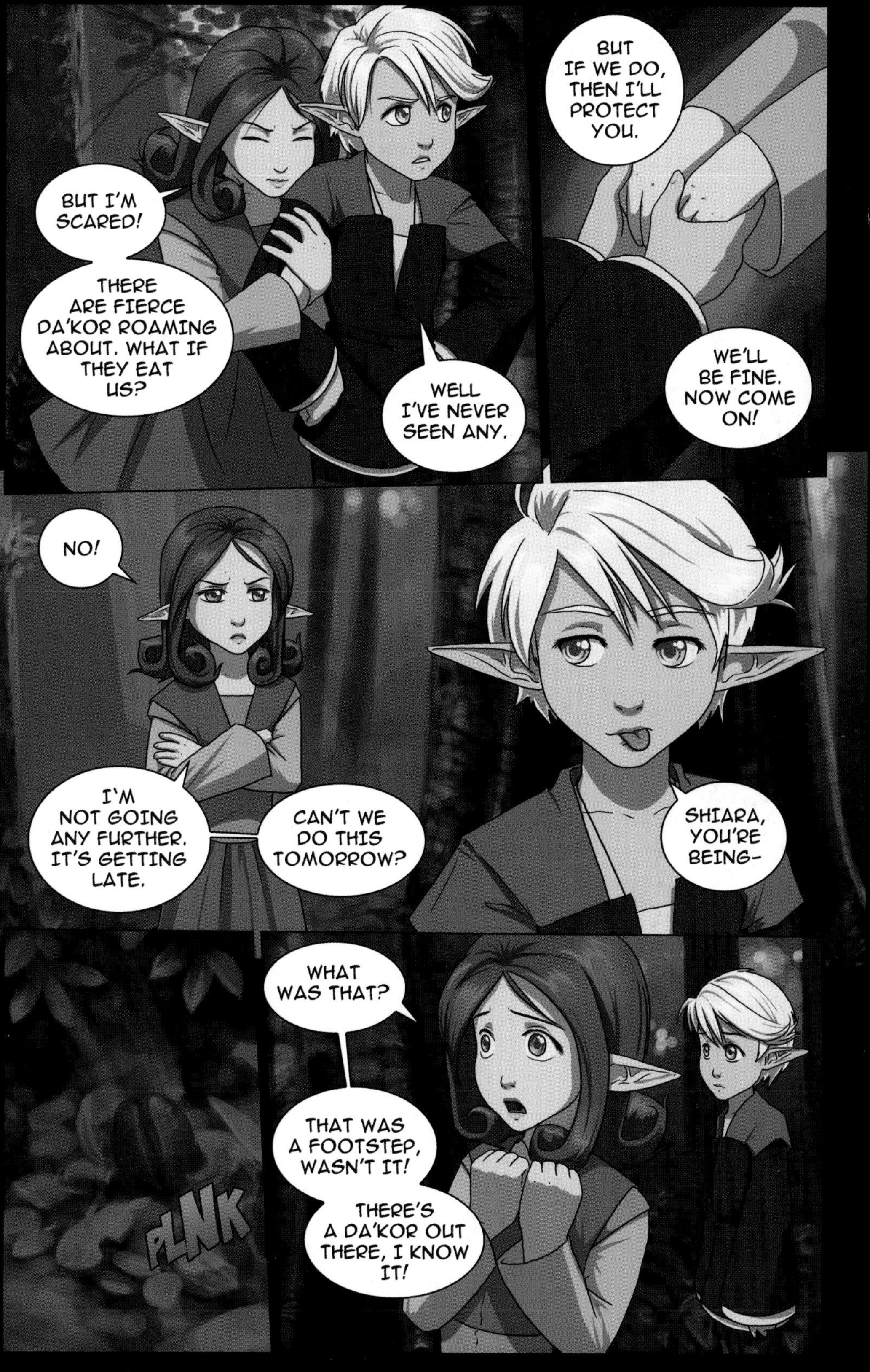
BUT I'M SCARED!
THERE ARE FIERCE DA'KOR ROAMING ABOUT. WHAT IF THEY EAT US?
WELL I'VE NEVER SEEN ANY.
BUT IF WE DO, THEN I'LL PROTECT YOU.
WE'LL BE FINE. NOW COME ON!
NO!
I'M NOT GOING ANY FURTHER. IT'S GETTING LATE.
CAN'T WE DO THIS TOMORROW?
SHIARA, YOU'RE BEING-
PLNK
WHAT WAS THAT?
THAT WAS A FOOTSTEP, WASN'T IT!
THERE'S A DA'KOR OUT THERE, I KNOW IT!

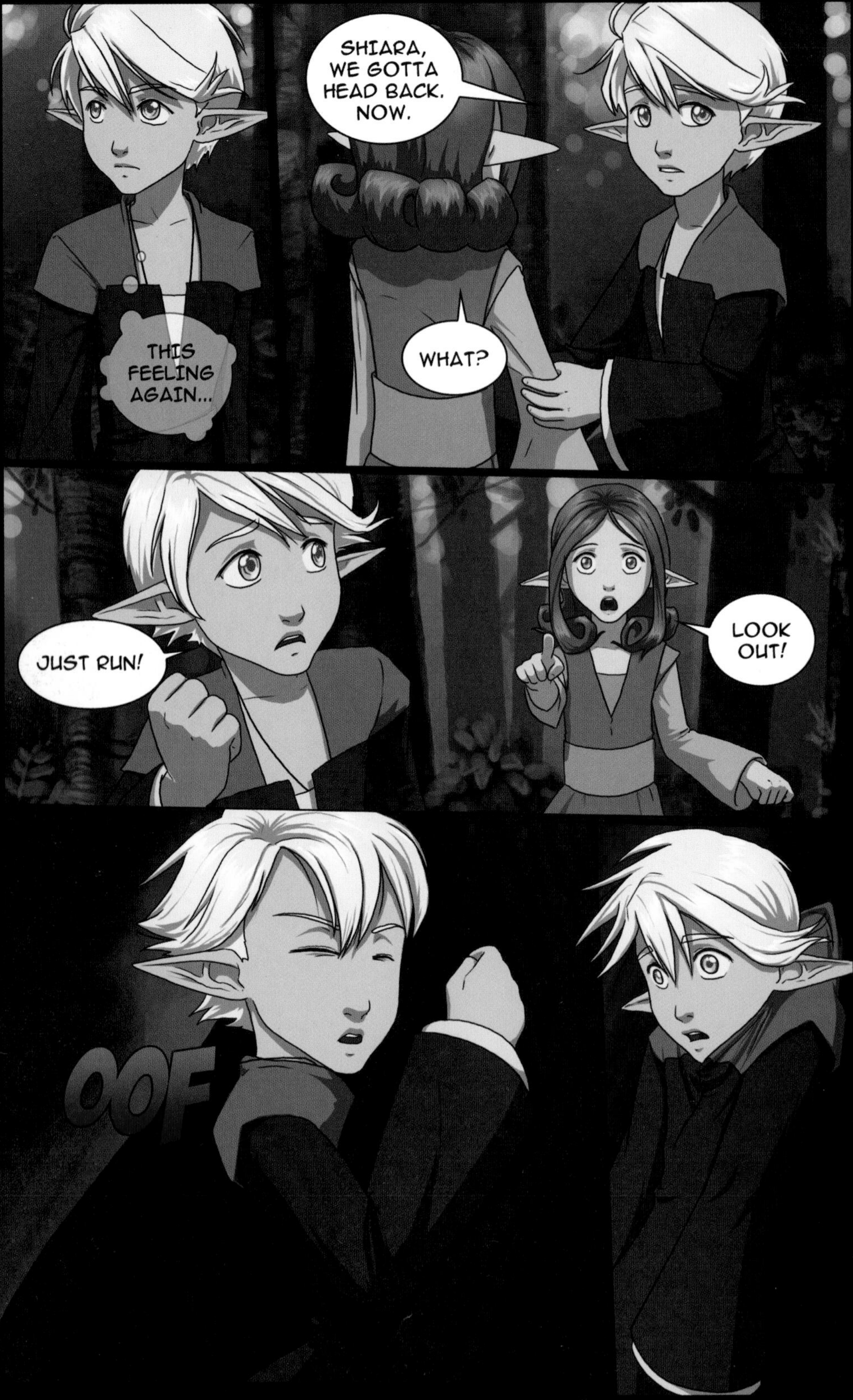
THIS FEELING AGAIN...
SHIARA, WE GOTTA HEAD BACK. NOW.
WHAT?
JUST RUN!
LOOK OUT!
OOF

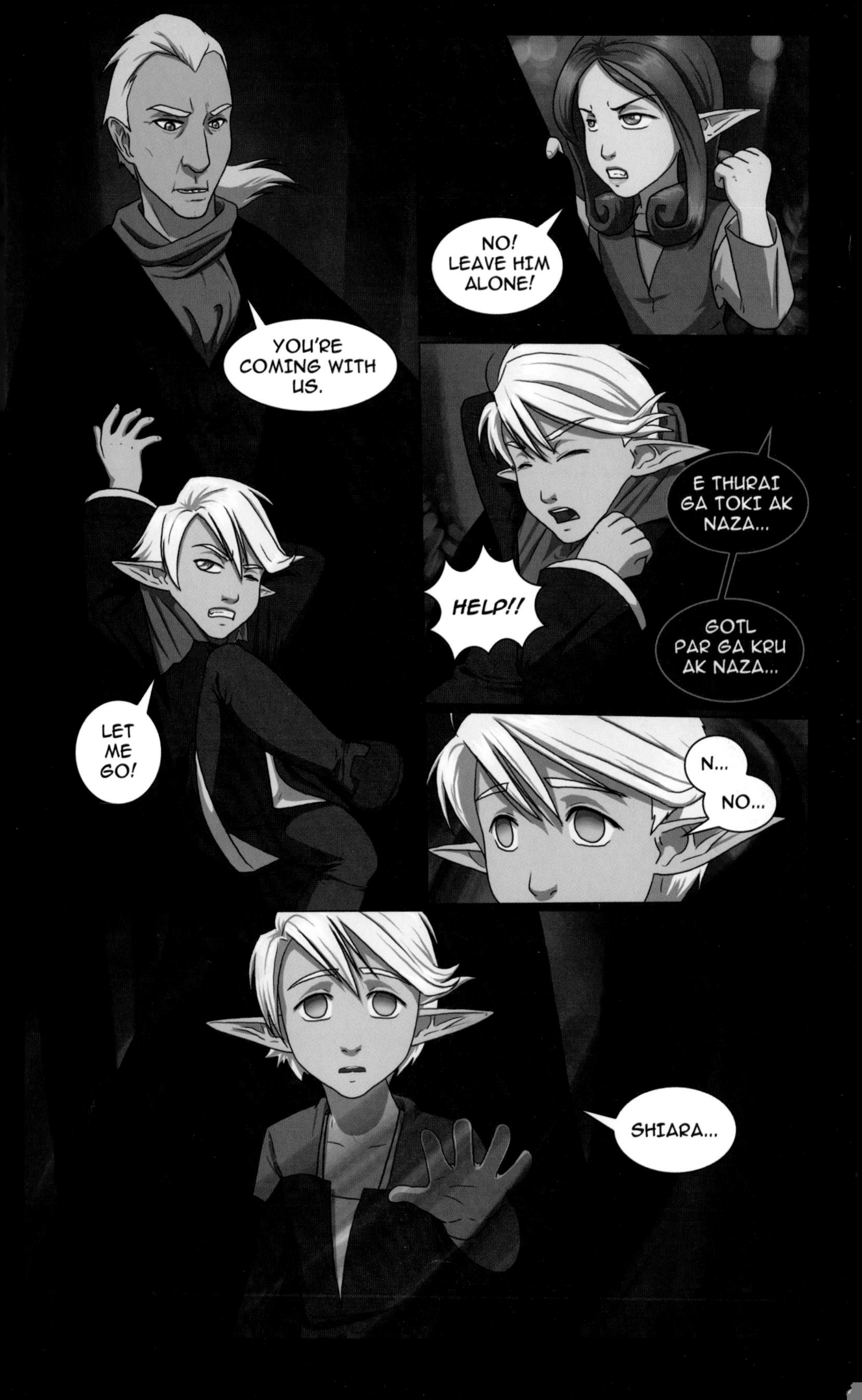
YOU'RE COMING WITH US.
NO! LEAVE HIM ALONE!
LET ME GO!
E THURAI GA TOKI AK NAZA...
GOTL PAR GA KRU AK NAZA...
HELP!!
N...
NO...
SHIARA...

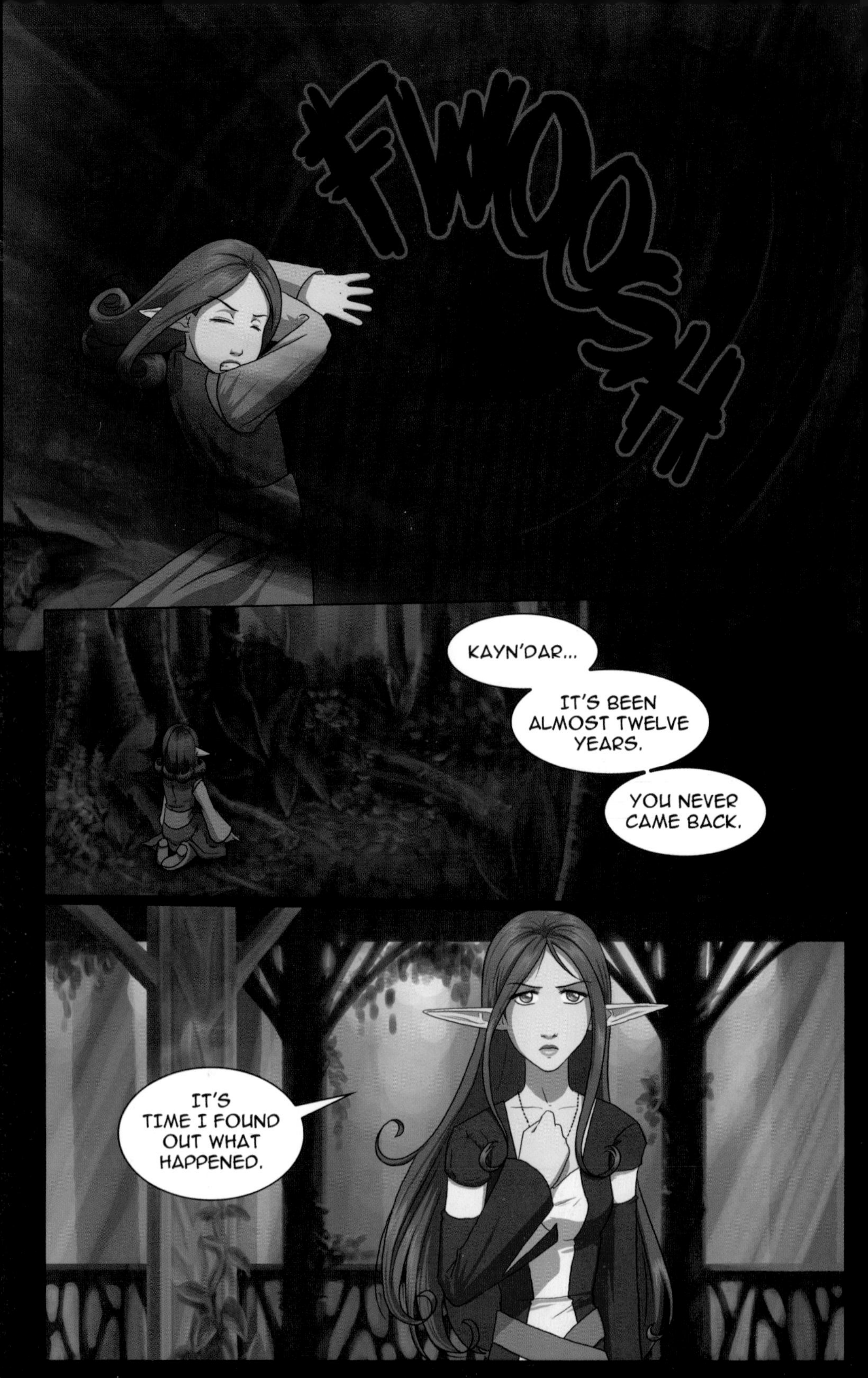
FWOOSH
KAYN'DAR...
IT'S BEEN ALMOST TWELVE YEARS.
YOU NEVER CAME BACK.
IT'S TIME I FOUND OUT WHAT HAPPENED.

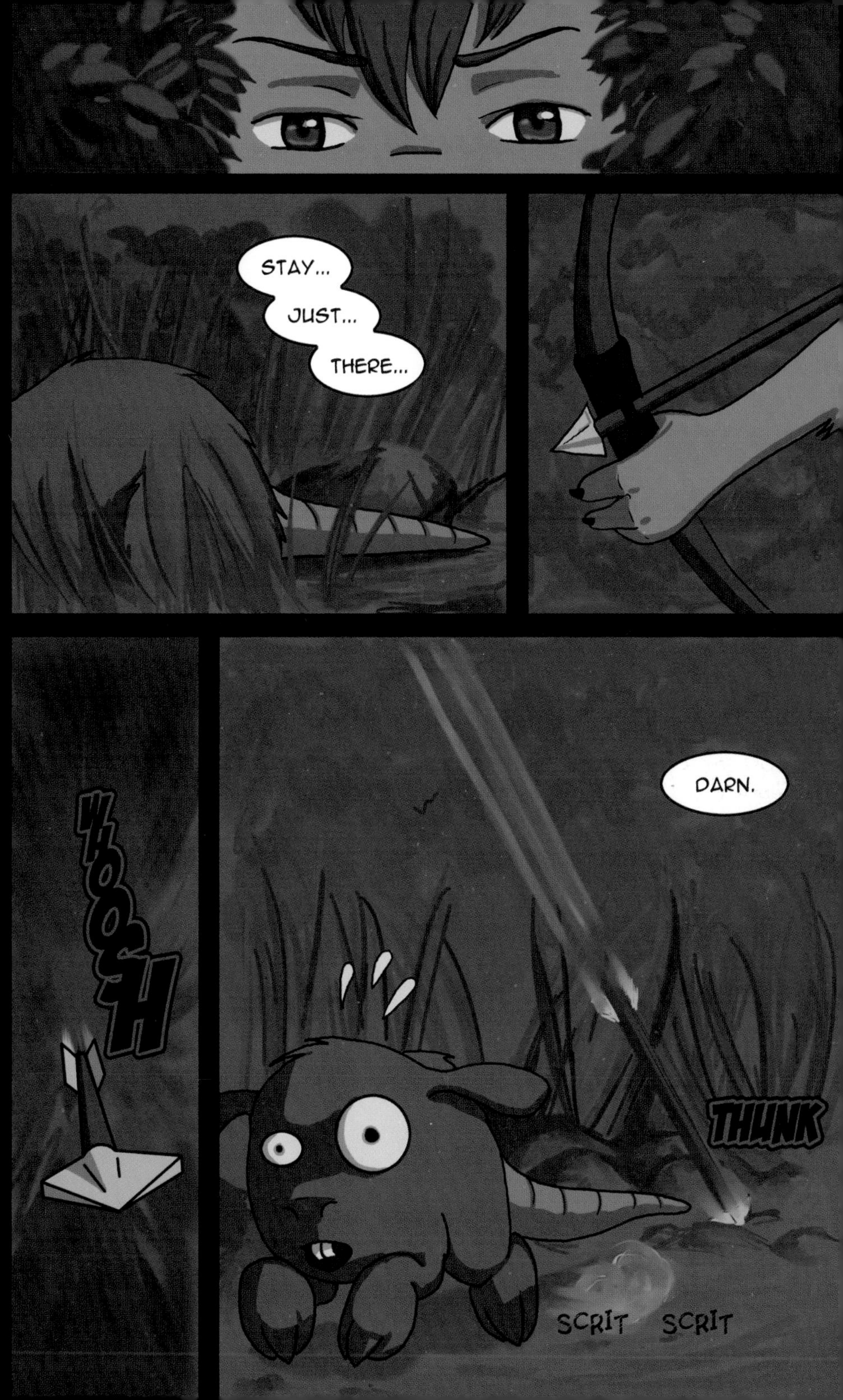
STAY...
JUST...
THERE...
WHOOSH
DARN.
THUNK
SCRIT SCRIT

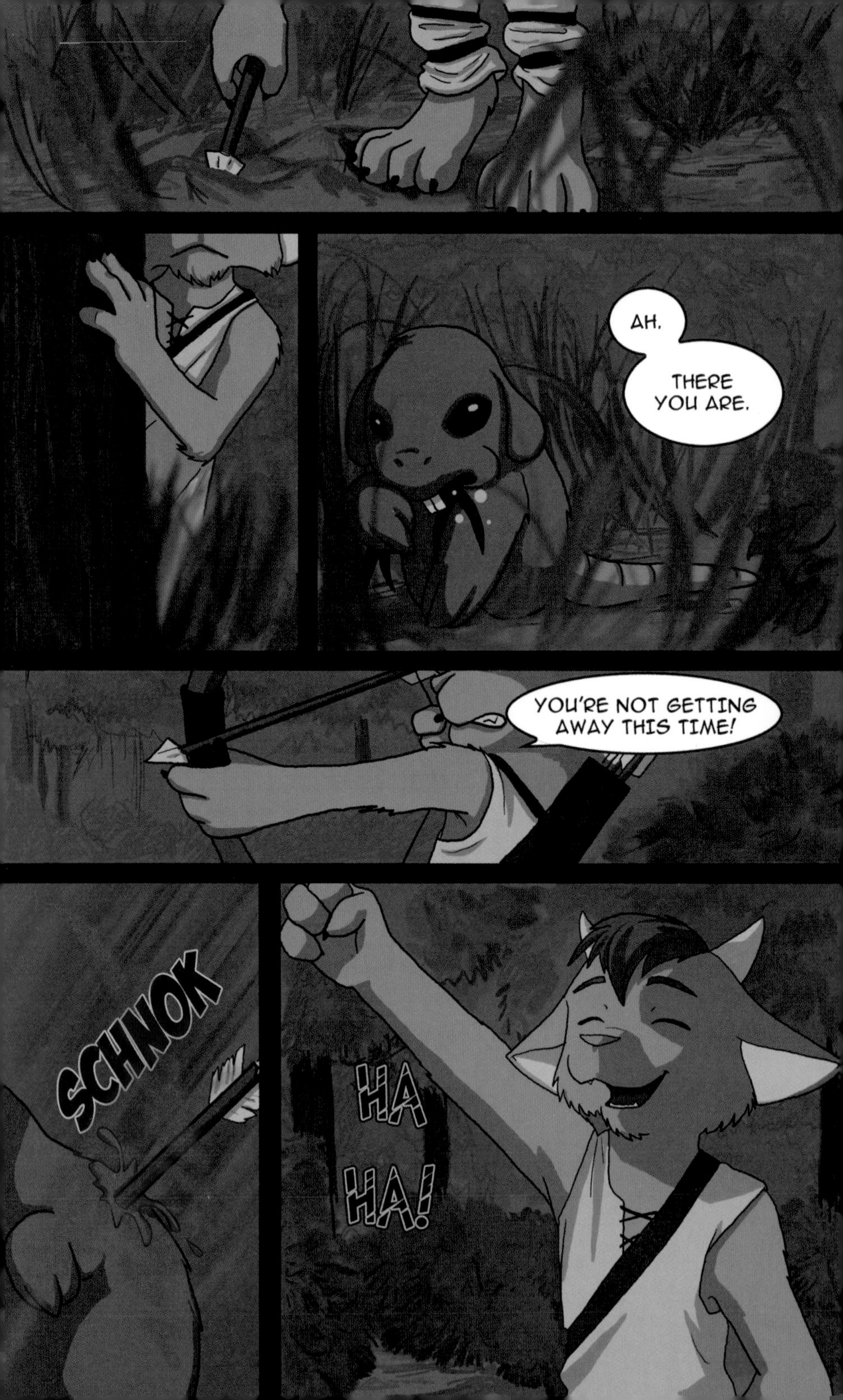
AH.
THERE YOU ARE.
YOU'RE NOT GETTING AWAY THIS TIME!
SCHNOK
HA HA!

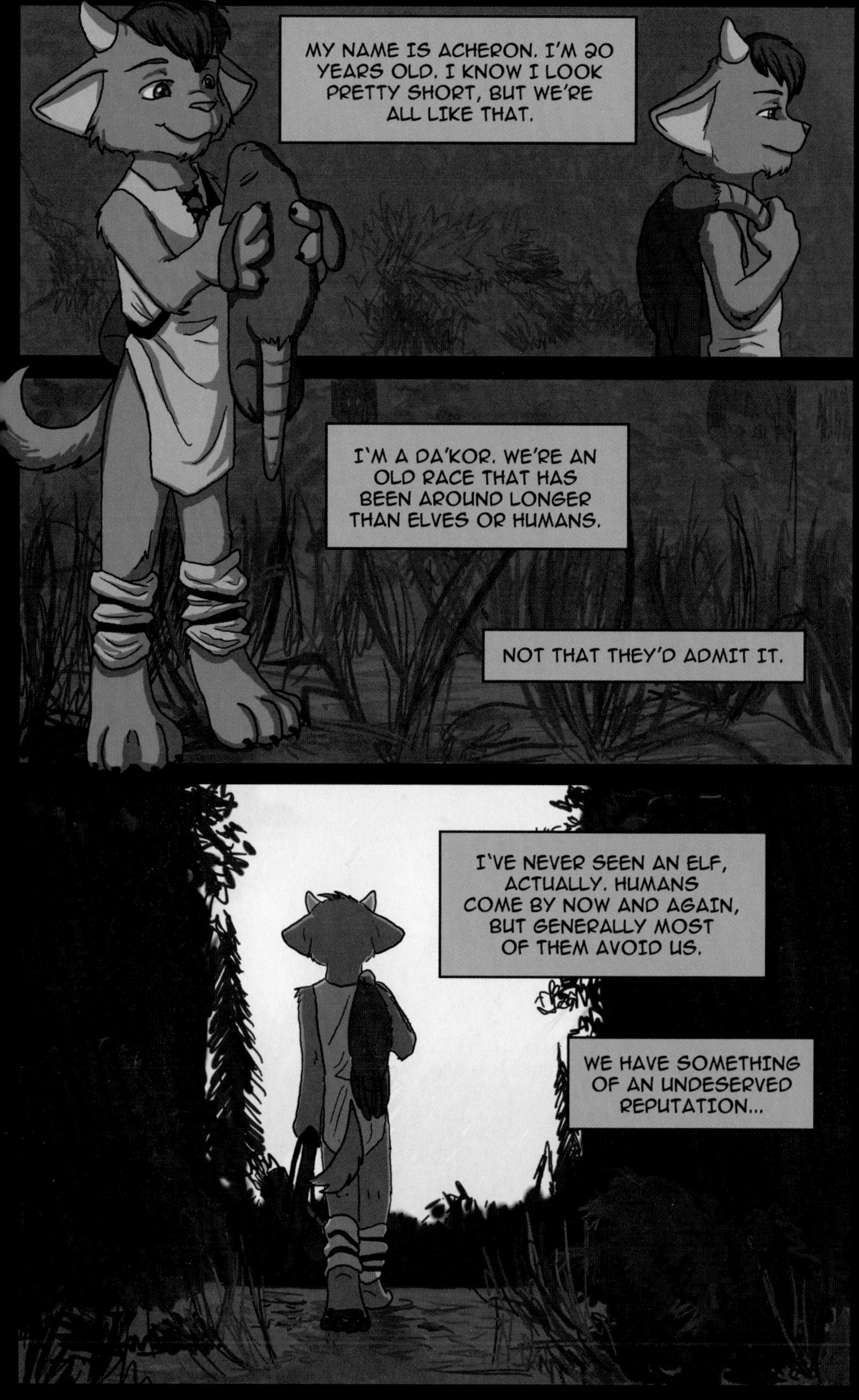
MY NAME IS ACHERON. I'M 20 YEARS OLD. I KNOW I LOOK PRETTY SHORT, BUT WE'RE ALL LIKE THAT.
I'M A DA'KOR. WE'RE AN OLD RACE THAT HAS BEEN AROUND LONGER THAN ELVES OR HUMANS.
NOT THAT THEY'D ADMIT IT.
I'VE NEVER SEEN AN ELF, ACTUALLY. HUMANS COME BY NOW AND AGAIN, BUT GENERALLY MOST OF THEM AVOID US.
WE HAVE SOMETHING OF AN UNDESERVED REPUTATION...

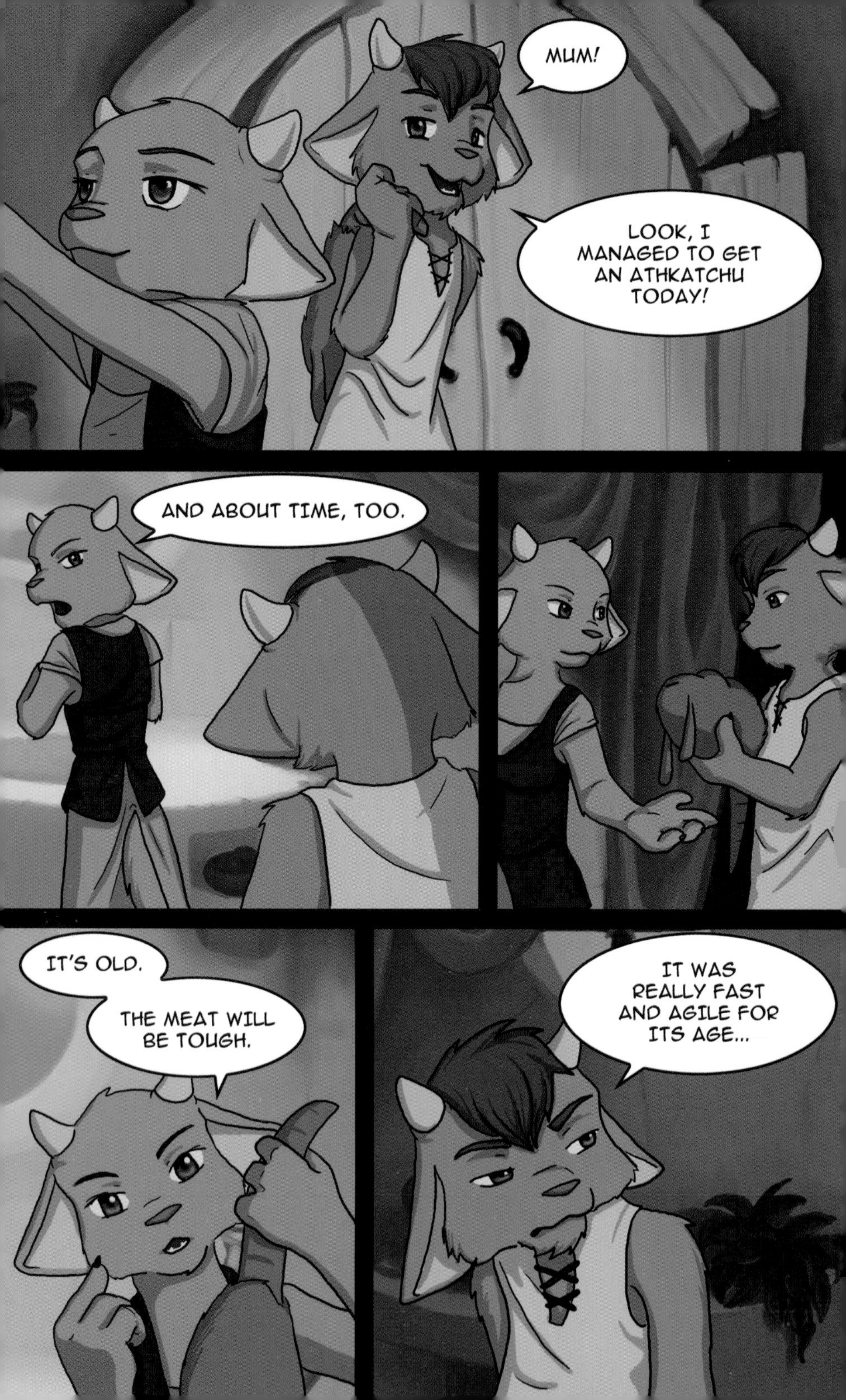
MUM!
LOOK, I MANAGED TO GET AN ATHKATCHU TODAY!
AND ABOUT TIME, TOO.
IT'S OLD.
THE MEAT WILL BE TOUGH.
IT WAS REALLY FAST AND AGILE FOR ITS AGE...

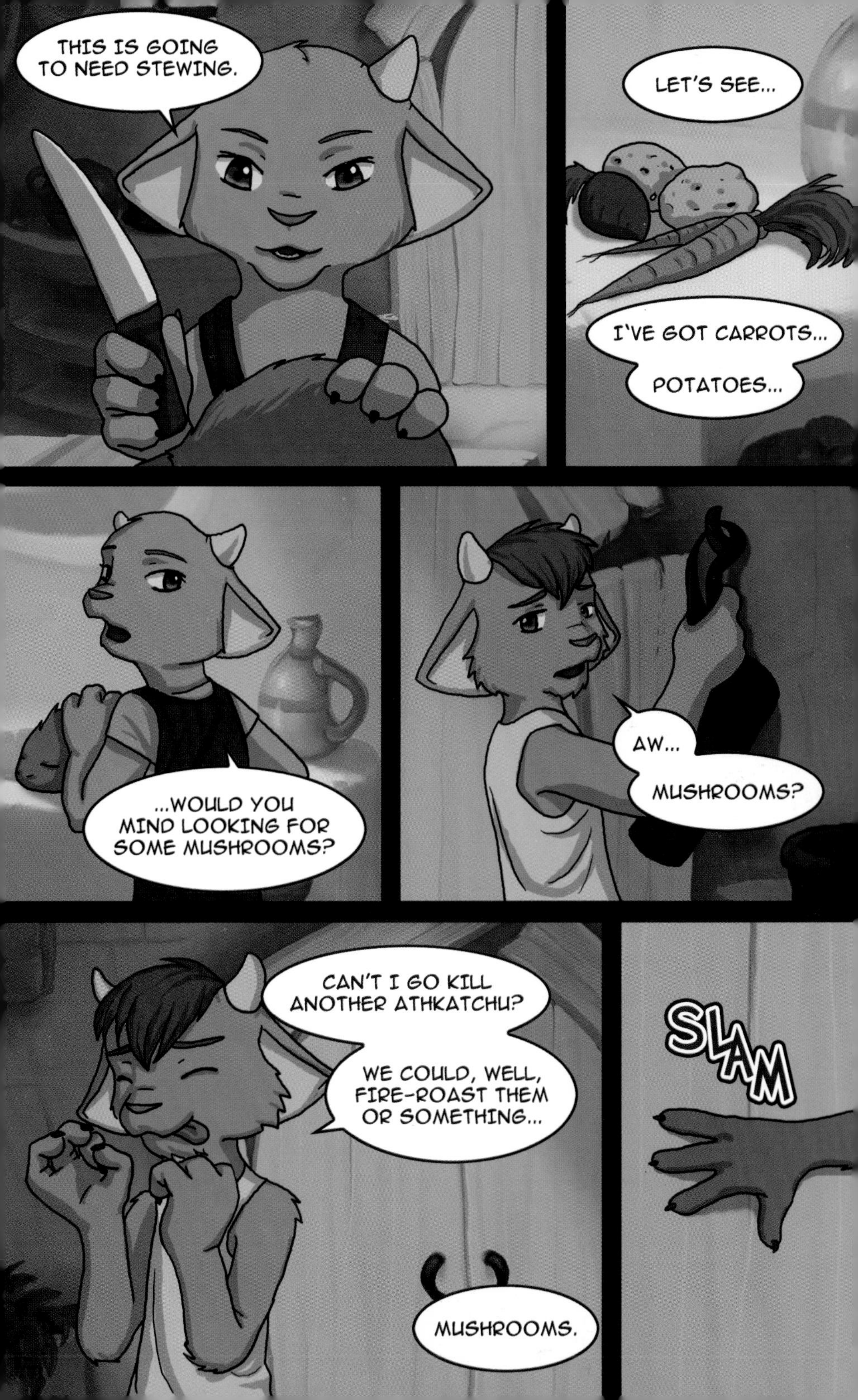
THIS IS GOING TO NEED STEWING.
LET'S SEE...
I'VE GOT CARROTS...
POTATOES...
...WOULD YOU MIND LOOKING FOR SOME MUSHROOMS?
AW...
MUSHROOMS?
CAN'T I GO KILL ANOTHER ATHKATCHU?
WE COULD, WELL, FIRE-ROAST THEM OR SOMETHING...
MUSHROOMS.
SLAM

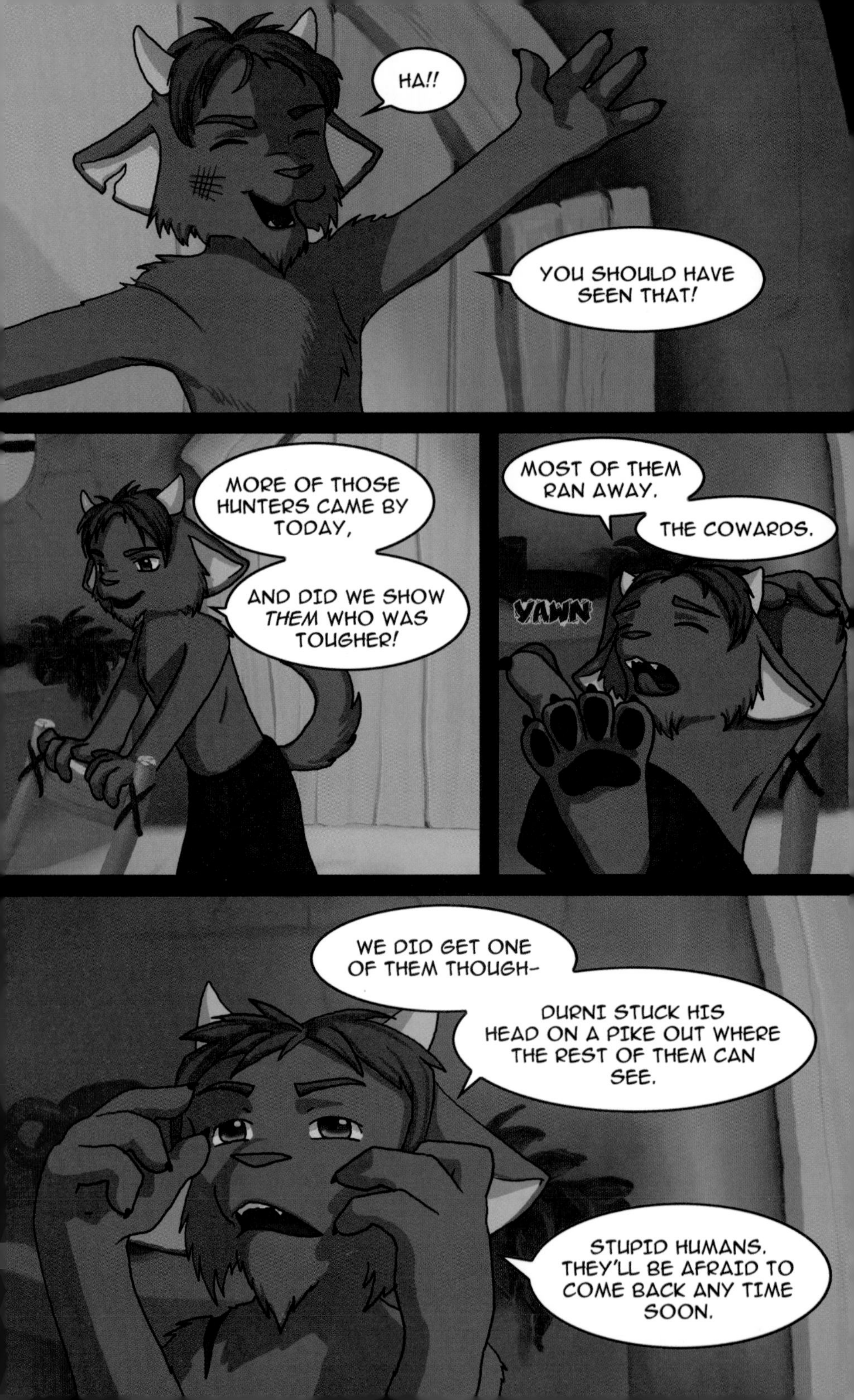
HA!!
YOU SHOULD HAVE SEEN THAT!
MORE OF THOSE HUNTERS CAME BY TODAY,
AND DID WE SHOW *THEM* WHO WAS TOUGHER!
MOST OF THEM RAN AWAY.
THE COWARDS.
YAWN
WE DID GET ONE OF THEM THOUGH-
DURNI STUCK HIS HEAD ON A PIKE OUT WHERE THE REST OF THEM CAN SEE.
STUPID HUMANS. THEY'LL BE AFRAID TO COME BACK ANY TIME SOON.

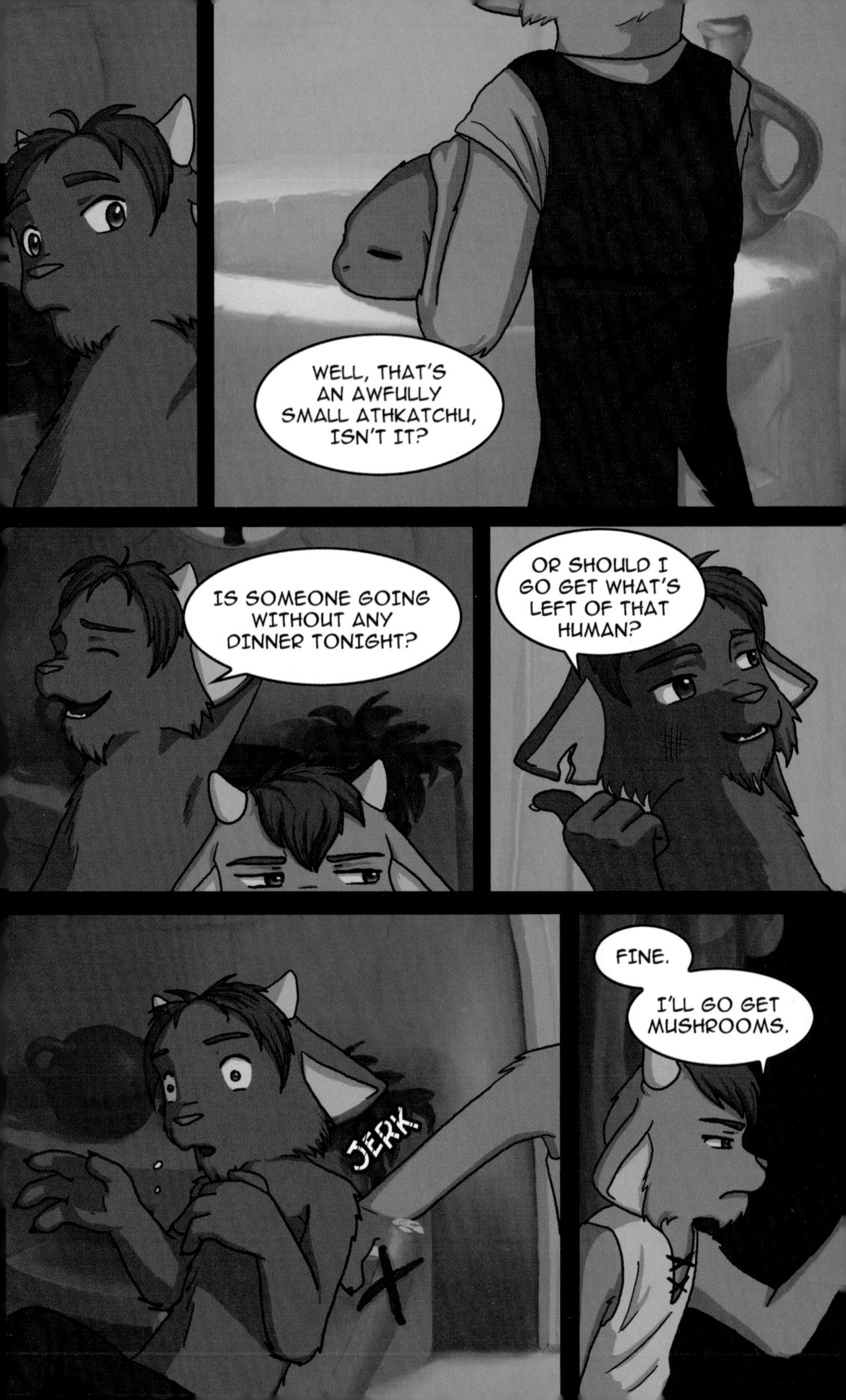
WELL, THAT'S AN AWFULLY SMALL ATHKATCHU, ISN'T IT?
IS SOMEONE GOING WITHOUT ANY DINNER TONIGHT?
OR SHOULD I GO GET WHAT'S LEFT OF THAT HUMAN?
JERK
FINE.
I'LL GO GET MUSHROOMS.

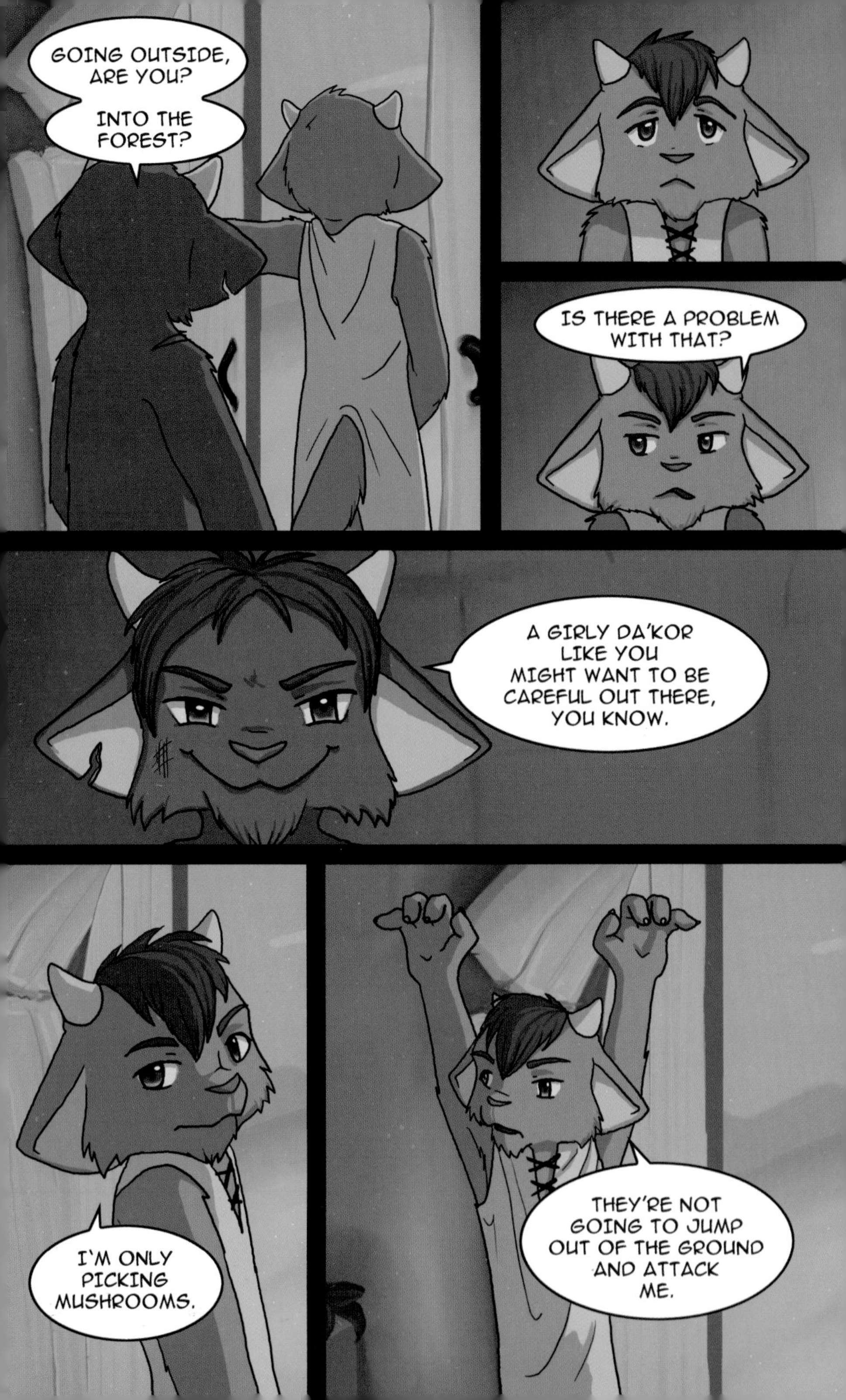
GOING OUTSIDE, ARE YOU?
INTO THE FOREST?
IS THERE A PROBLEM WITH THAT?
A GIRLY DA'KOR LIKE YOU MIGHT WANT TO BE CAREFUL OUT THERE, YOU KNOW.
I'M ONLY PICKING MUSHROOMS.
THEY'RE NOT GOING TO JUMP OUT OF THE GROUND AND ATTACK ME.

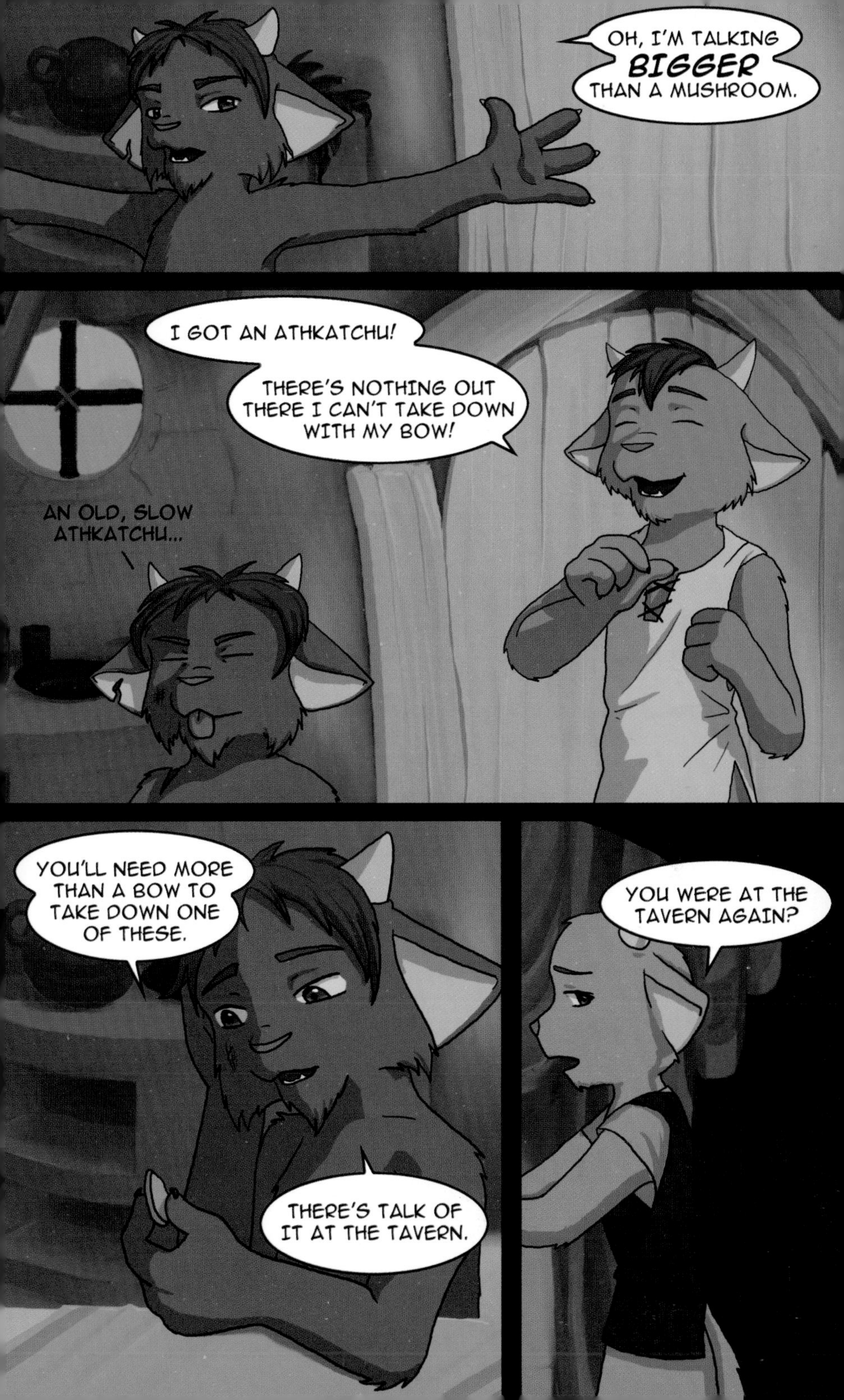
OH, I'M TALKING **BIGGER** THAN A MUSHROOM.
I GOT AN ATHKATCHU!
THERE'S NOTHING OUT THERE I CAN'T TAKE DOWN WITH MY BOW!
AN OLD, SLOW ATHKATCHU...
YOU'LL NEED MORE THAN A BOW TO TAKE DOWN ONE OF THESE.
THERE'S TALK OF IT AT THE TAVERN.
YOU WERE AT THE TAVERN AGAIN?

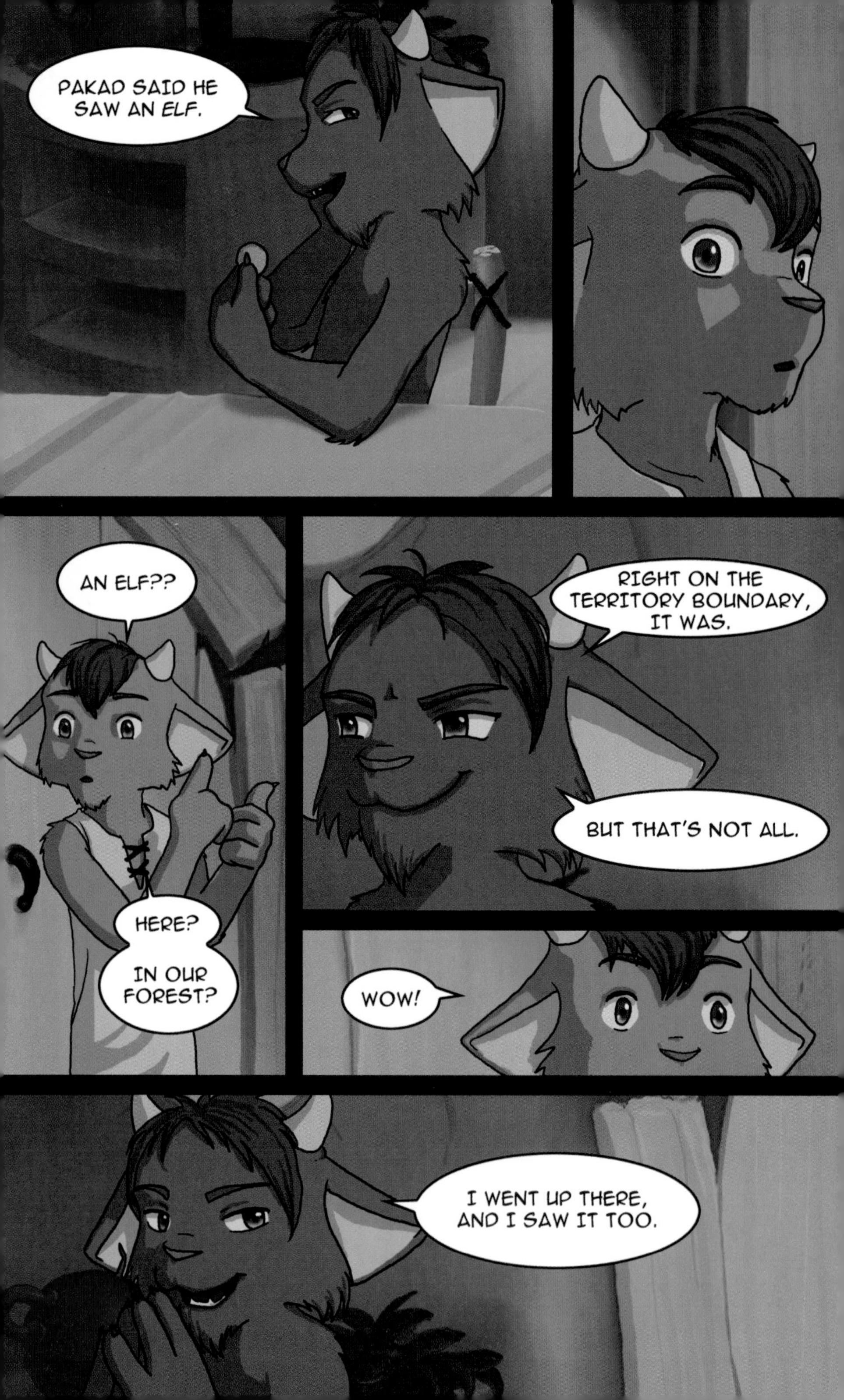
PAKAD SAID HE SAW AN *ELF*.
AN ELF??
HERE?
IN OUR FOREST?
RIGHT ON THE TERRITORY BOUNDARY, IT WAS.
BUT THAT'S NOT ALL.
WOW!
I WENT UP THERE, AND I SAW IT TOO.

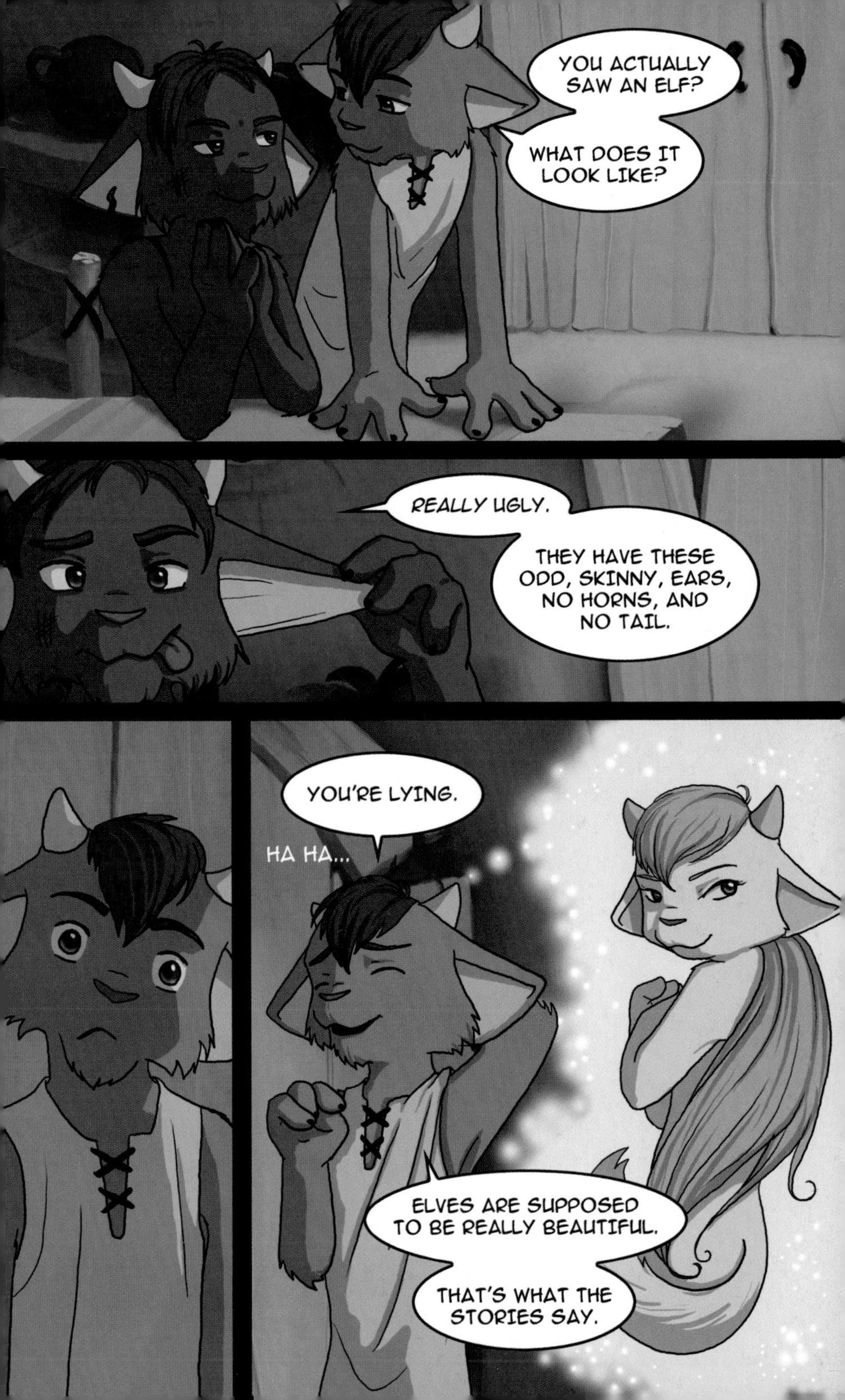
YOU ACTUALLY SAW AN ELF?
WHAT DOES IT LOOK LIKE?
REALLY UGLY.
THEY HAVE THESE ODD, SKINNY, EARS, NO HORNS, AND NO TAIL.
YOU'RE LYING.
HA HA...
ELVES ARE SUPPOSED TO BE REALLY BEAUTIFUL.
THAT'S WHAT THE STORIES SAY.

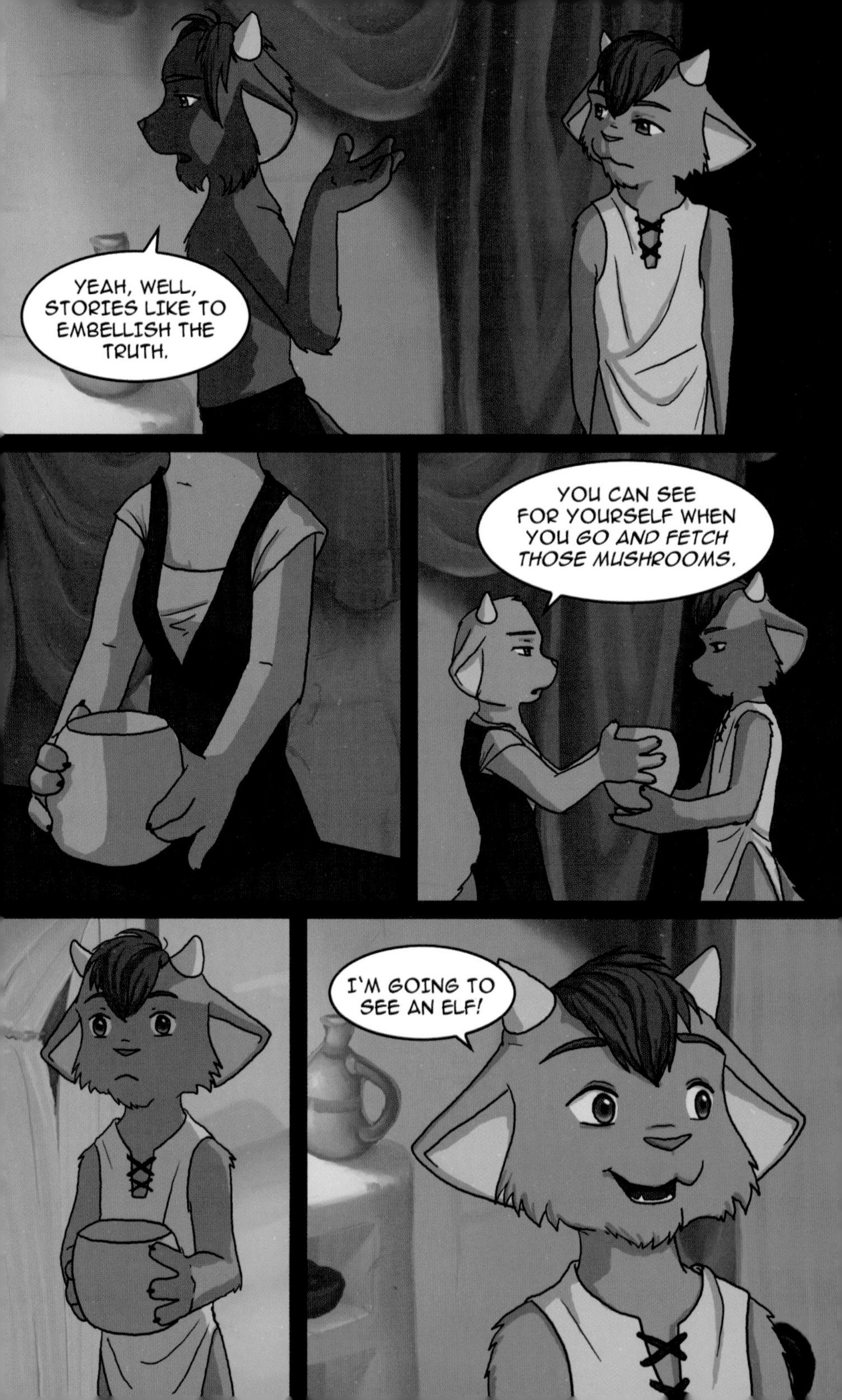
YEAH, WELL, STORIES LIKE TO EMBELLISH THE TRUTH.
YOU CAN SEE FOR YOURSELF WHEN YOU *GO* AND FETCH THOSE MUSHROOMS.
I'M GOING TO SEE AN ELF!

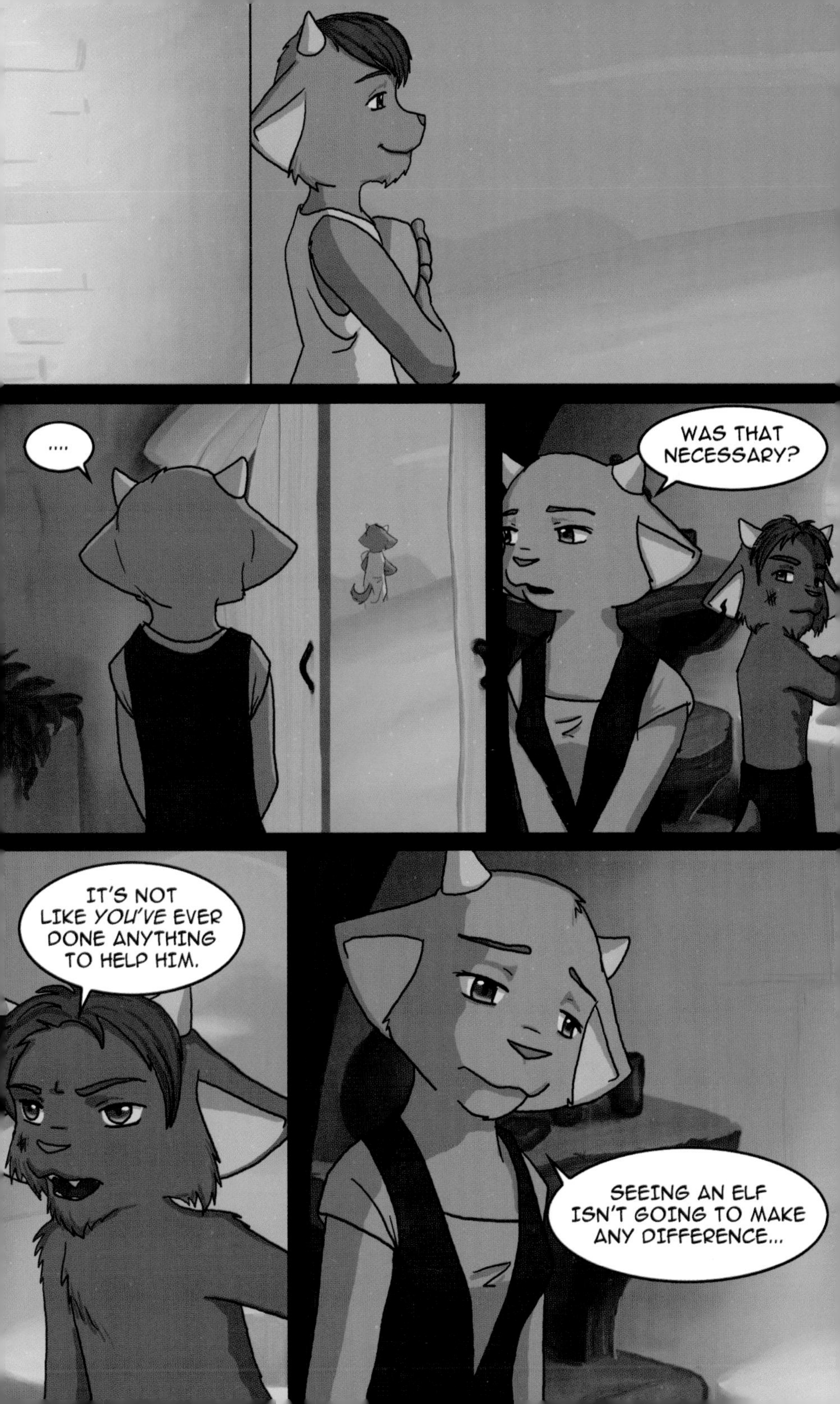
....
WAS THAT NECESSARY?
IT'S NOT LIKE *YOU'VE* EVER DONE ANYTHING TO HELP HIM.
SEEING AN ELF ISN'T GOING TO MAKE ANY DIFFERENCE...

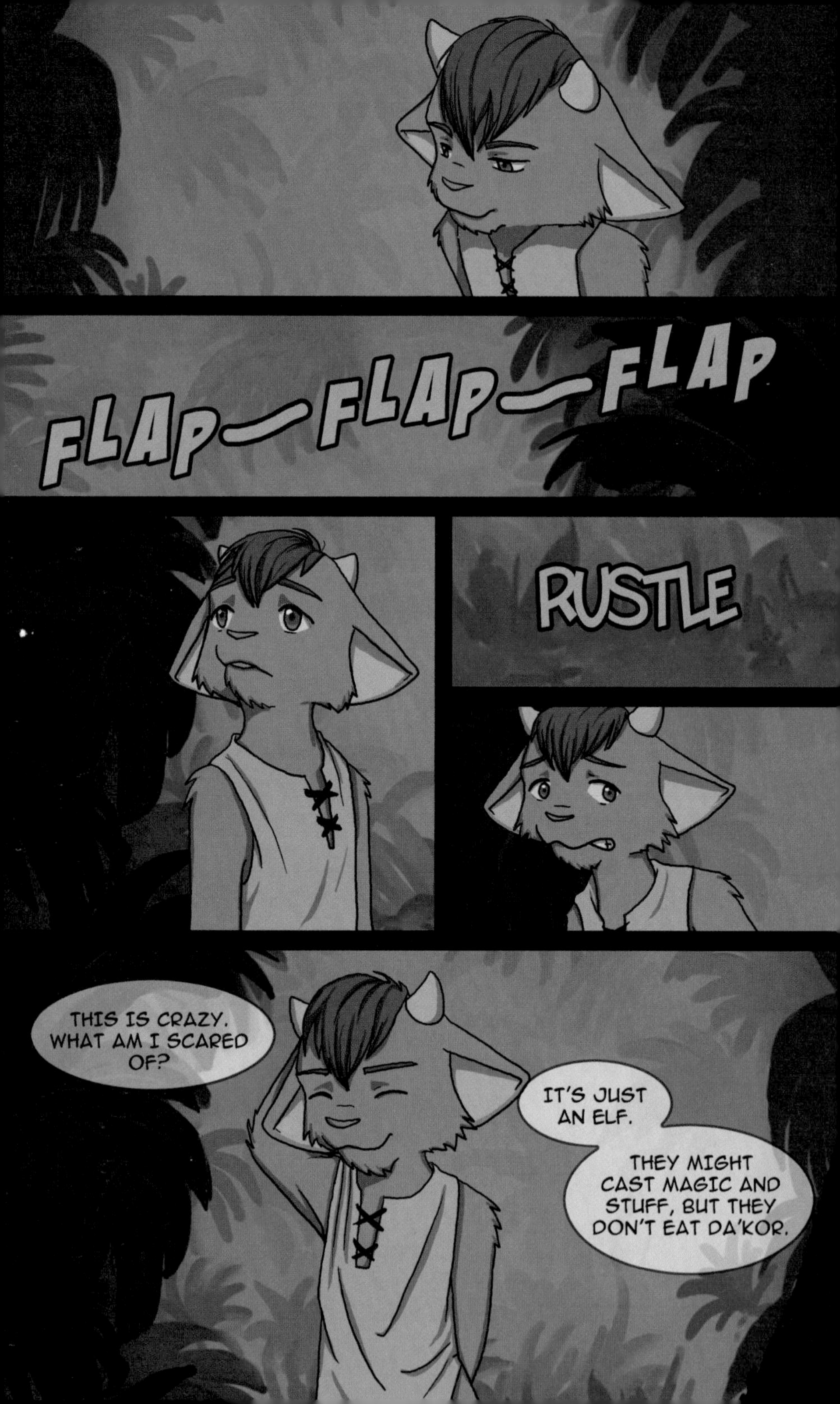
FLAP—FLAP—FLAP
RUSTLE
THIS IS CRAZY. WHAT AM I SCARED OF?
IT'S JUST AN ELF.
THEY MIGHT CAST MAGIC AND STUFF, BUT THEY DON'T EAT DA'KOR.

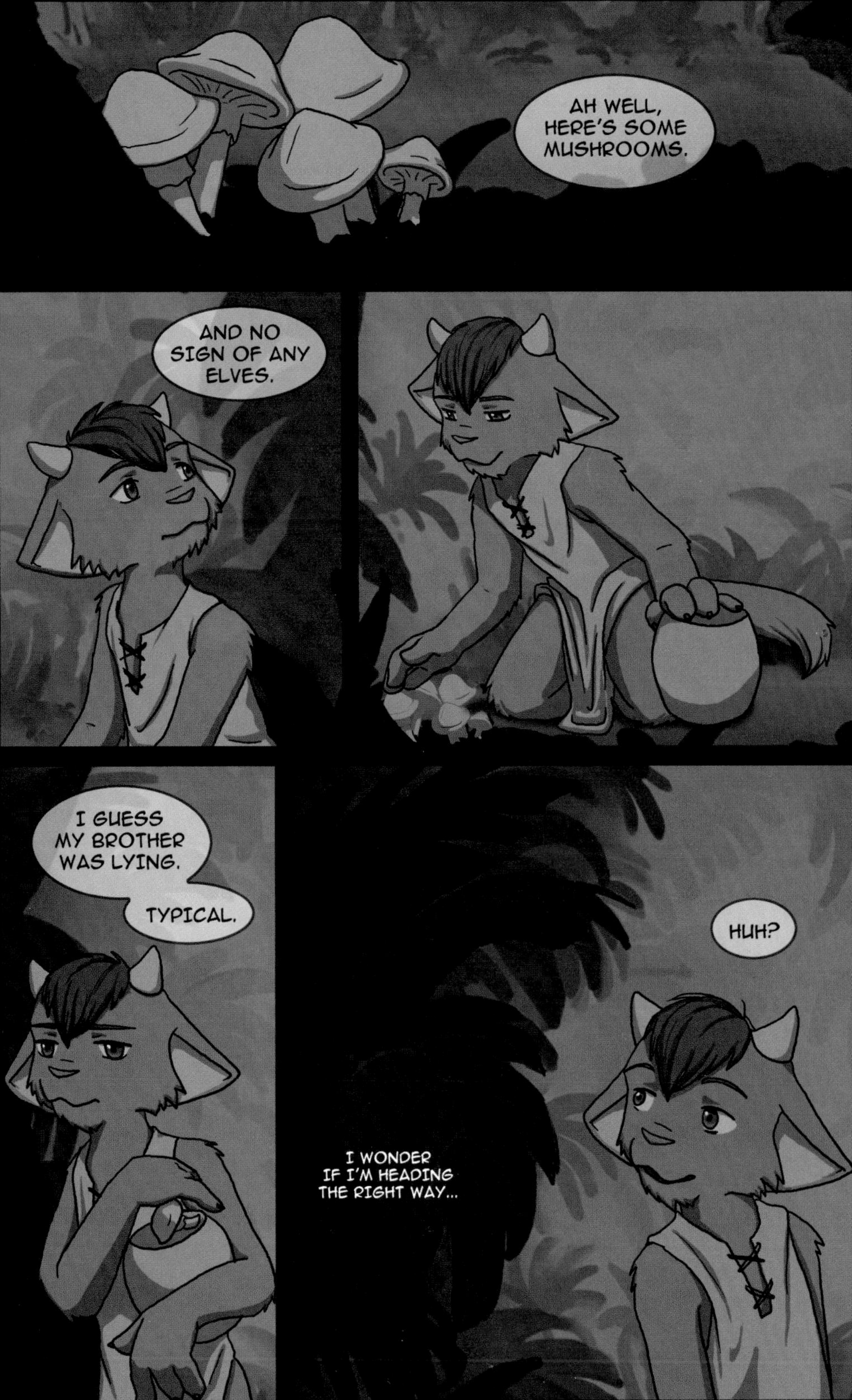
AH WELL, HERE'S SOME MUSHROOMS.
AND NO SIGN OF ANY ELVES.
I GUESS MY BROTHER WAS LYING.
TYPICAL.
I WONDER IF I'M HEADING THE RIGHT WAY...
HUH?

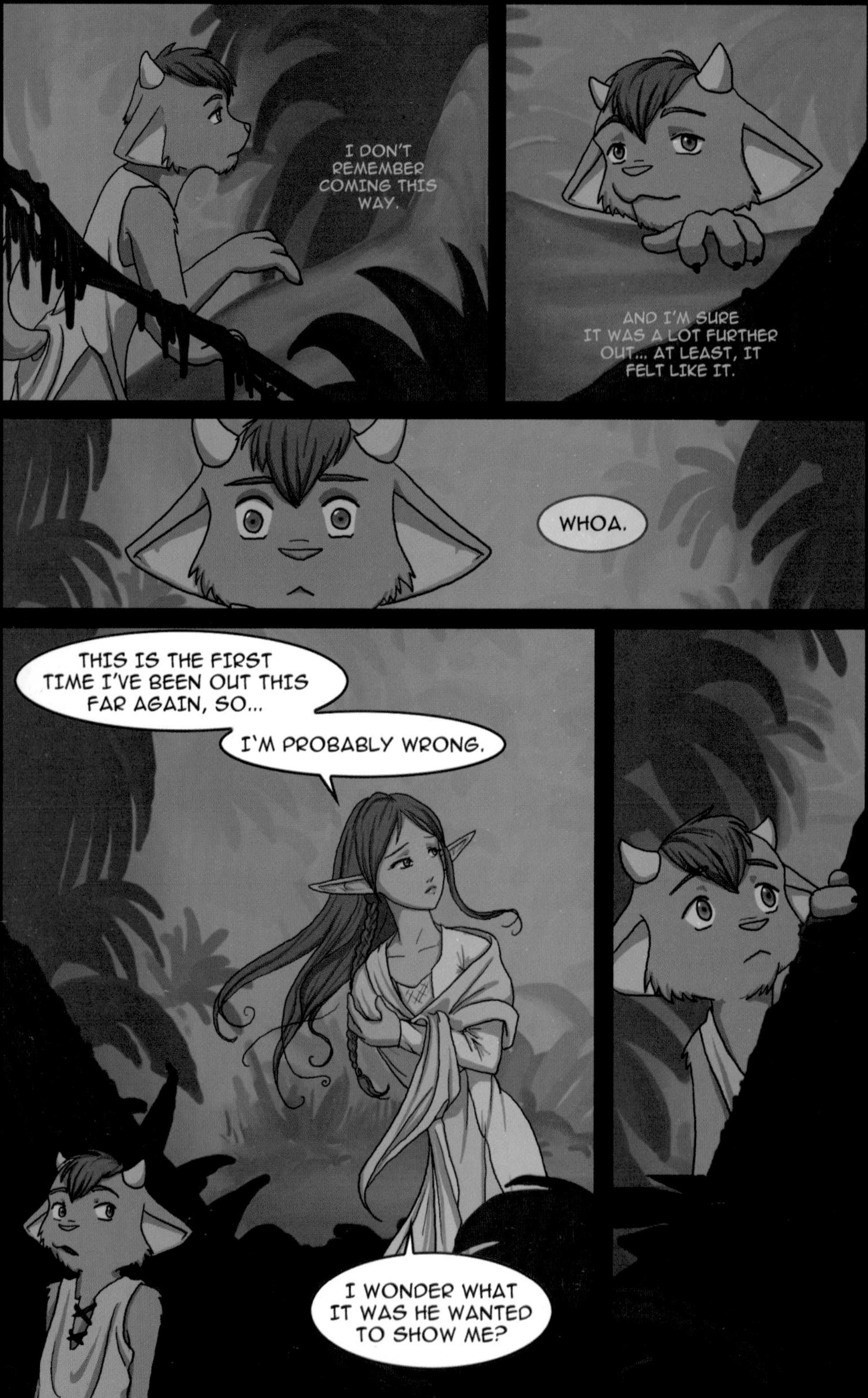
I DON'T REMEMBER COMING THIS WAY.
AND I'M SURE IT WAS A LOT FURTHER OUT... AT LEAST, IT FELT LIKE IT.
WHOA.
THIS IS THE FIRST TIME I'VE BEEN OUT THIS FAR AGAIN, SO...
I'M PROBABLY WRONG.
I WONDER WHAT IT WAS HE WANTED TO SHOW ME?

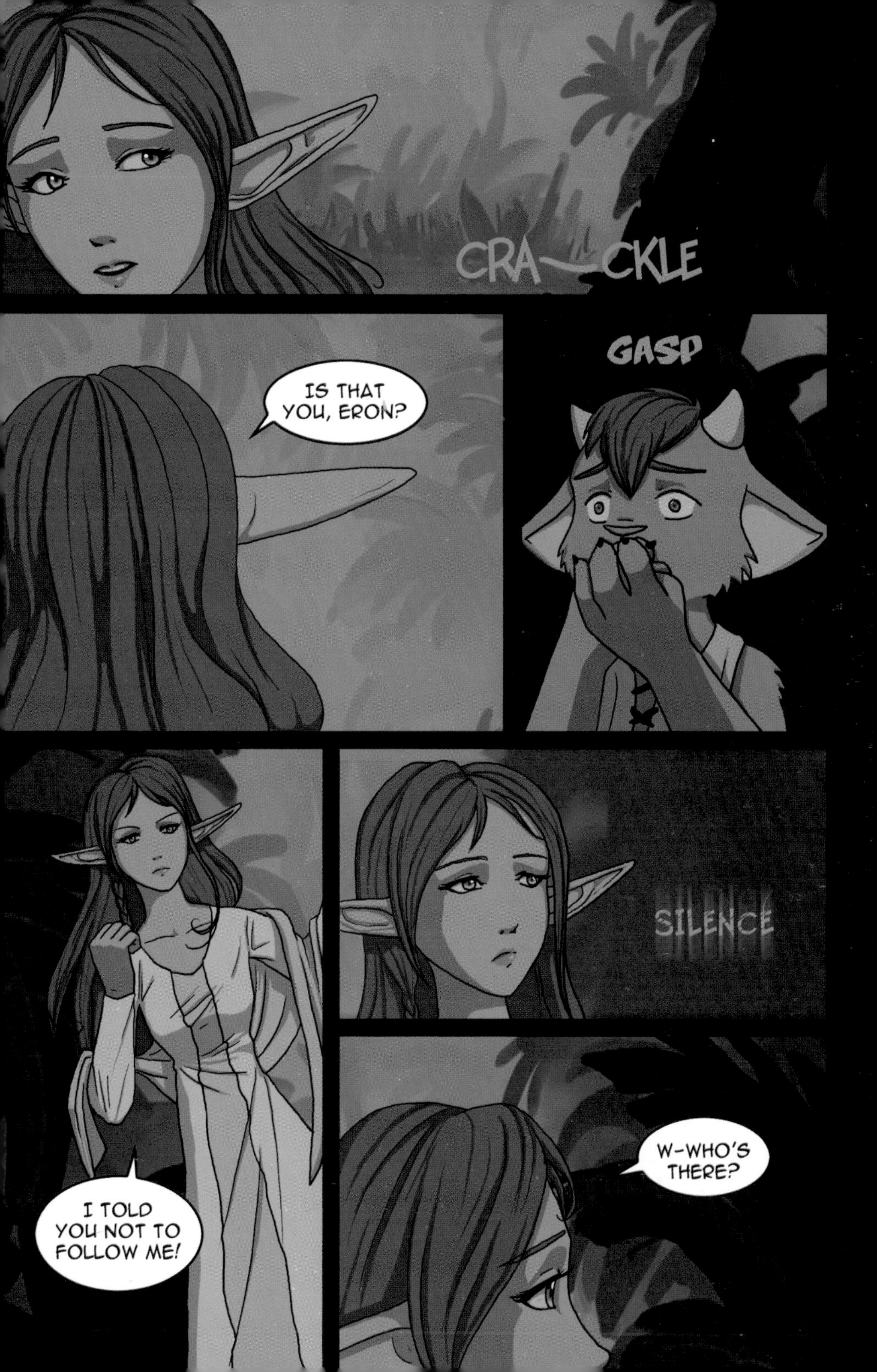
CRA-CKLE
IS THAT YOU, ERON?
GASP
SILENCE
I TOLD YOU NOT TO FOLLOW ME!
W-WHO'S THERE?

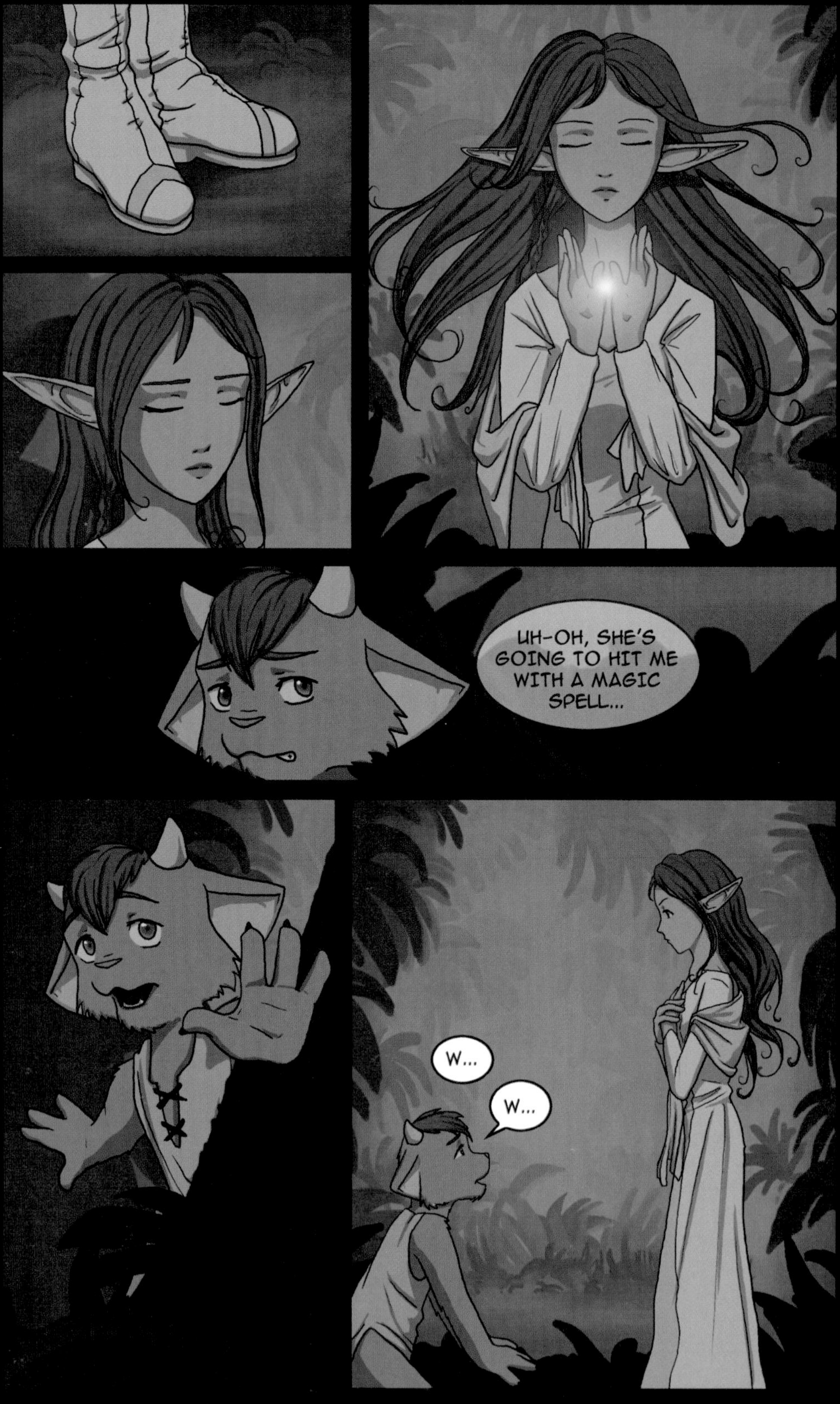
UH-OH, SHE'S GOING TO HIT ME WITH A MAGIC SPELL...
W...
W...

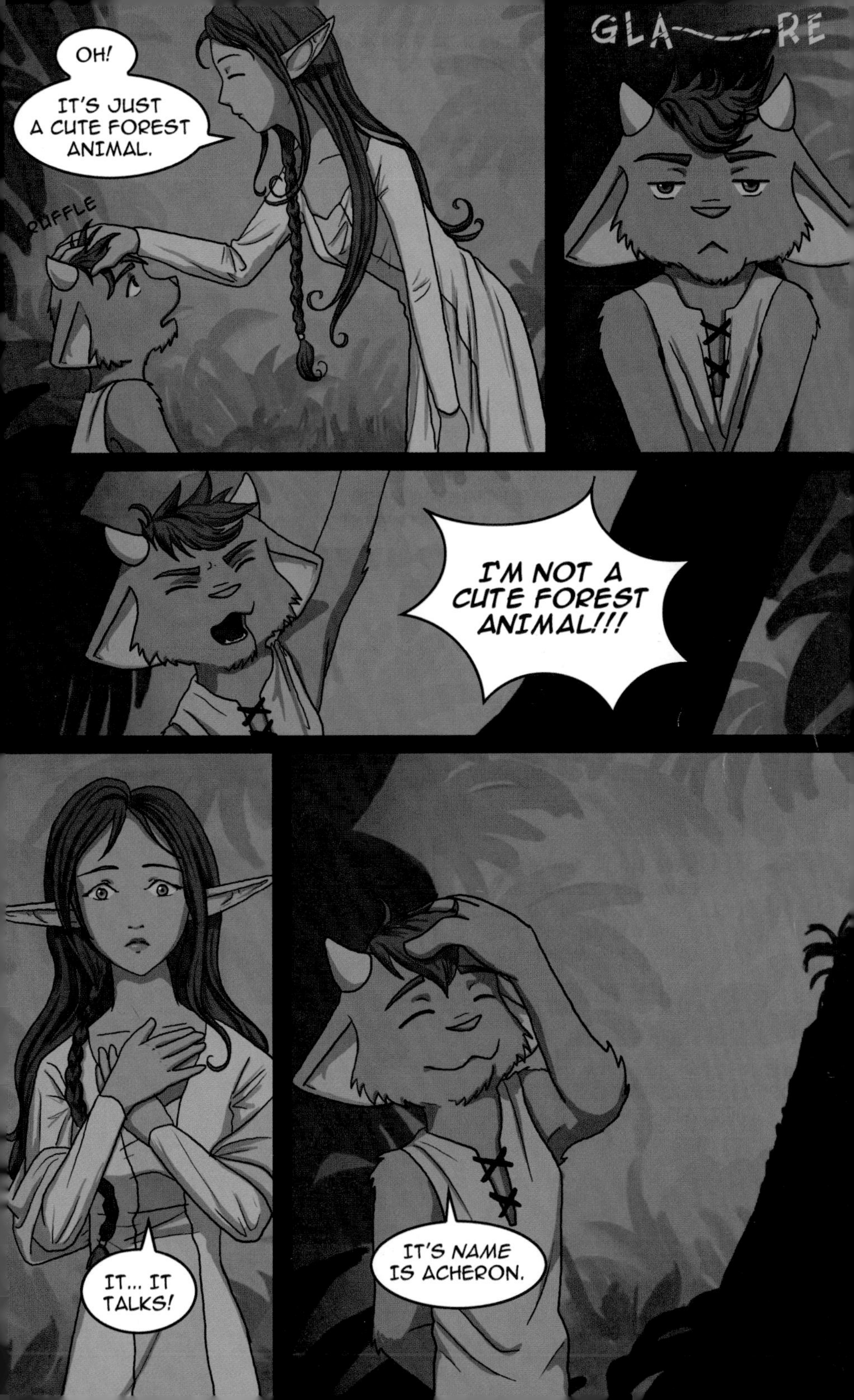
OH!
IT'S JUST A CUTE FOREST ANIMAL.
RUFFLE
GLA——RE
I'M NOT A CUTE FOREST ANIMAL!!!
IT... IT TALKS!
IT'S NAME IS ACHERON.

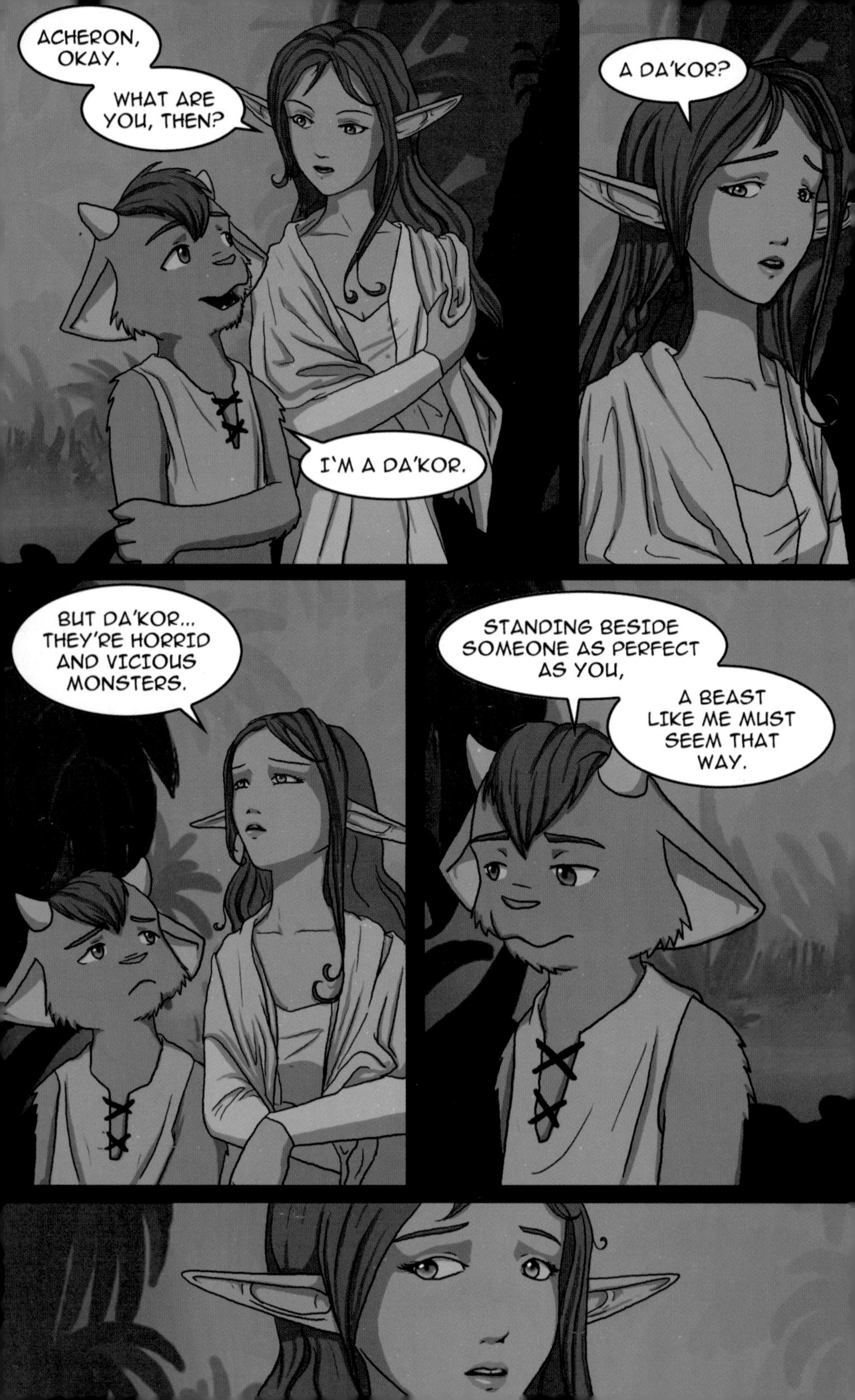
ACHERON, OKAY.
WHAT ARE YOU, THEN?
I'M A DA'KOR.
A DA'KOR?
BUT DA'KOR... THEY'RE HORRID AND VICIOUS MONSTERS.
STANDING BESIDE SOMEONE AS PERFECT AS YOU,
A BEAST LIKE ME MUST SEEM THAT WAY.

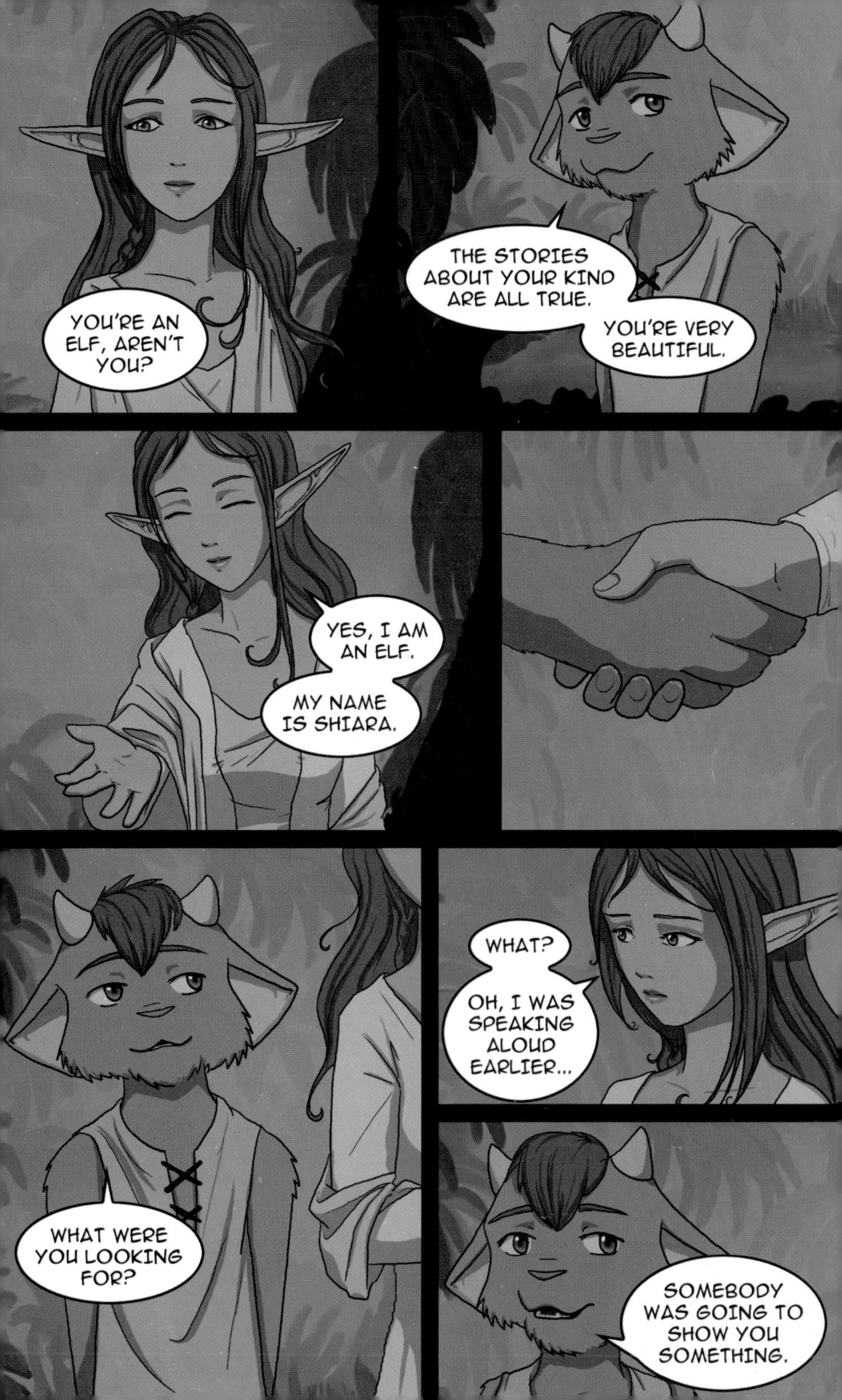
YOU'RE AN ELF, AREN'T YOU?
THE STORIES ABOUT YOUR KIND ARE ALL TRUE.
YOU'RE VERY BEAUTIFUL.
YES, I AM AN ELF.
MY NAME IS SHIARA.
WHAT WERE YOU LOOKING FOR?
WHAT?
OH, I WAS SPEAKING ALOUD EARLIER...
SOMEBODY WAS GOING TO SHOW YOU SOMETHING.

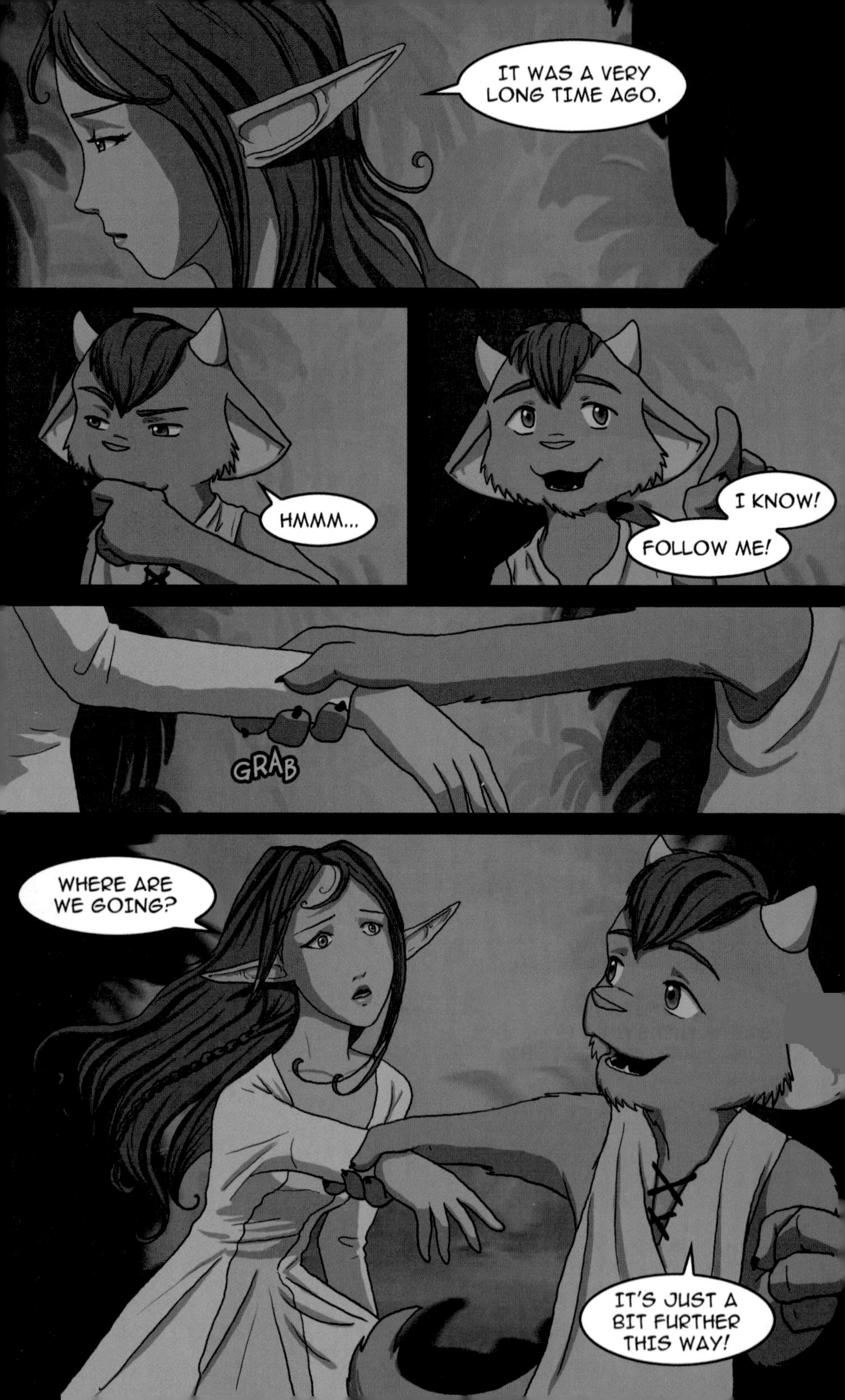
IT WAS A VERY LONG TIME AGO.
HMMM...
I KNOW!
FOLLOW ME!
GRAB
WHERE ARE WE GOING?
IT'S JUST A BIT FURTHER THIS WAY!

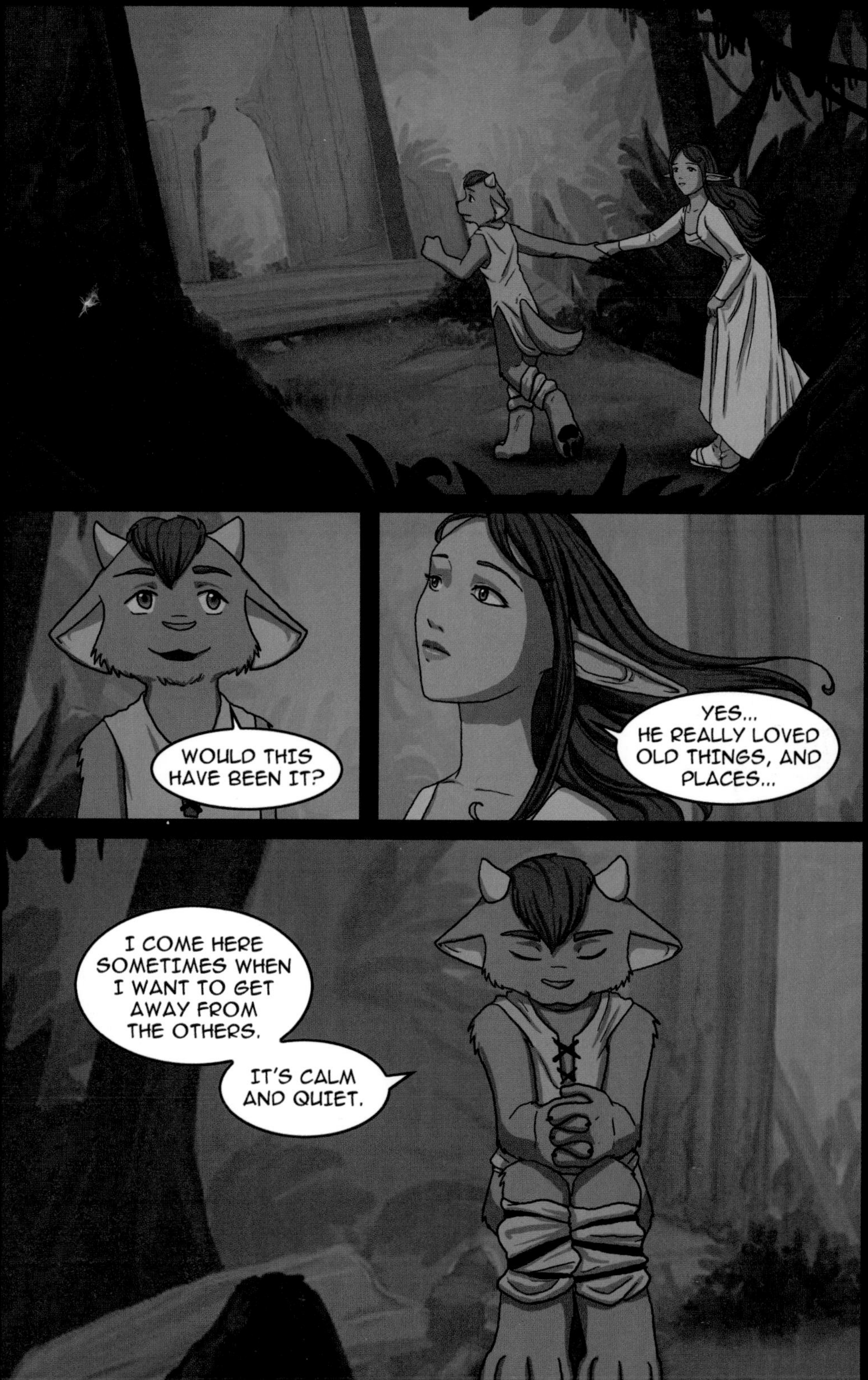
WOULD THIS HAVE BEEN IT?
YES... HE REALLY LOVED OLD THINGS, AND PLACES...
I COME HERE SOMETIMES WHEN I WANT TO GET AWAY FROM THE OTHERS.
IT'S CALM AND QUIET.

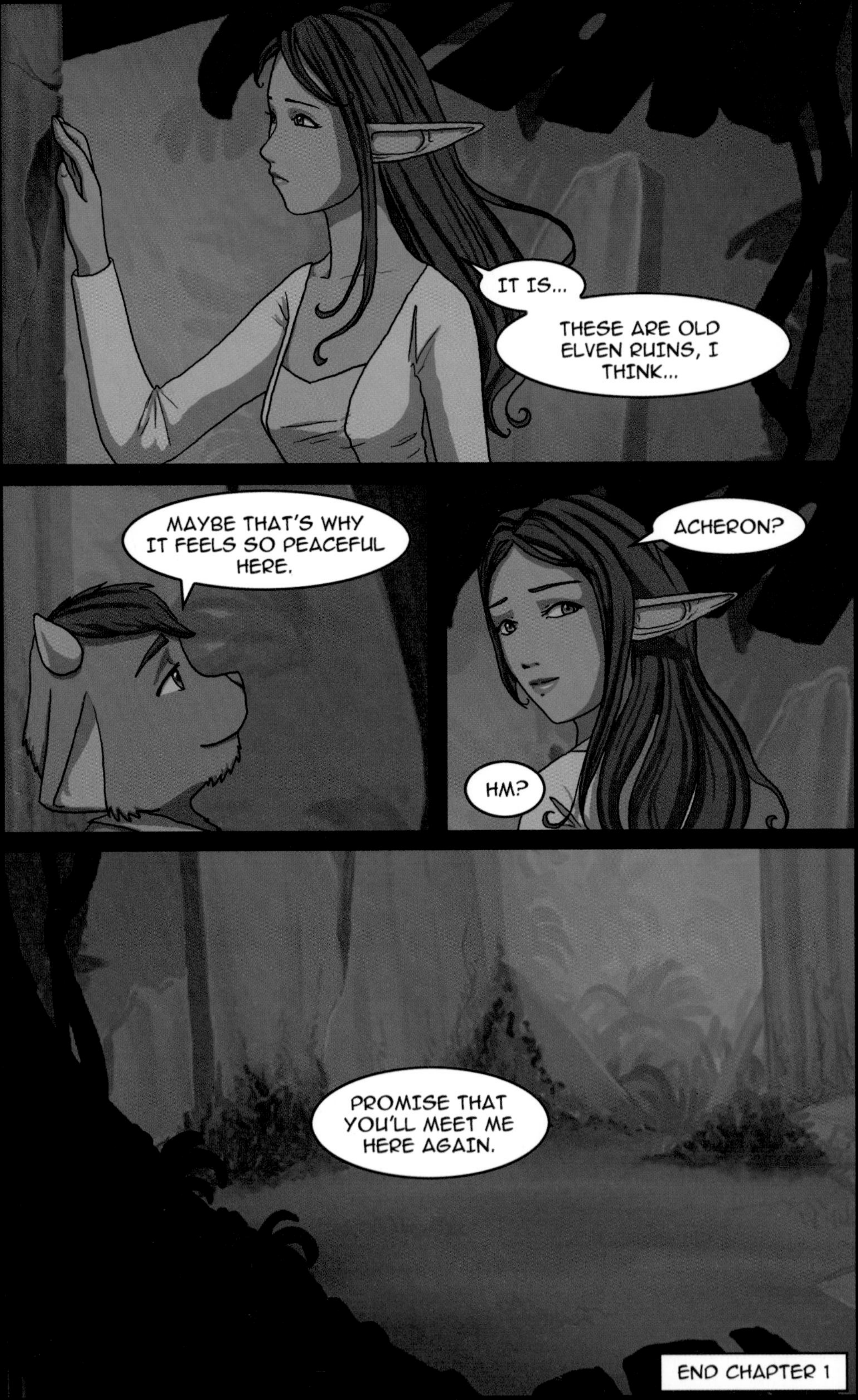
IT IS...
THESE ARE OLD ELVEN RUINS, I THINK...
MAYBE THAT'S WHY IT FEELS SO PEACEFUL HERE.
ACHERON?
HM?
PROMISE THAT YOU'LL MEET ME HERE AGAIN.
END CHAPTER 1

CHAPTER 2 :A PAST REVEALED

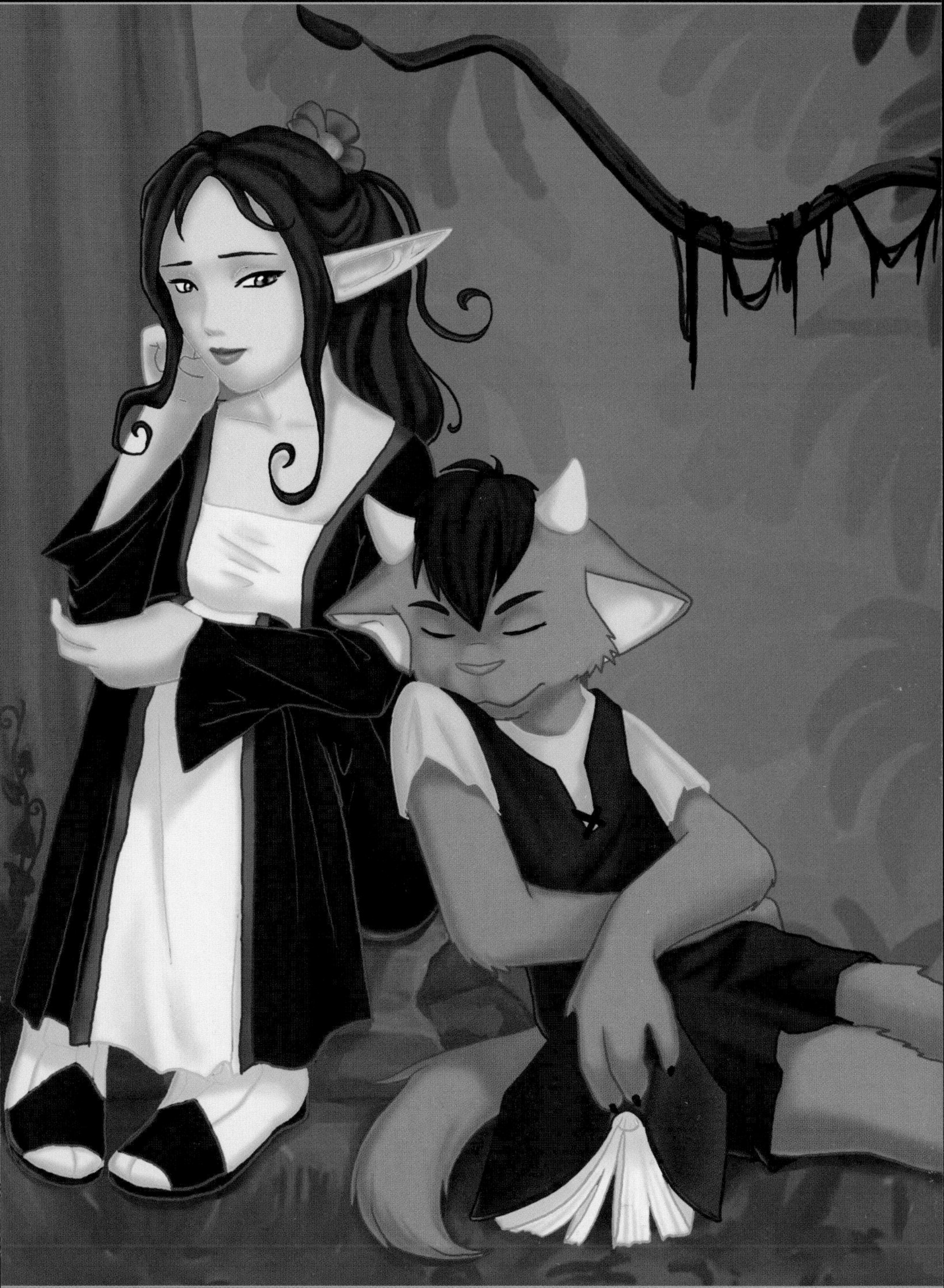

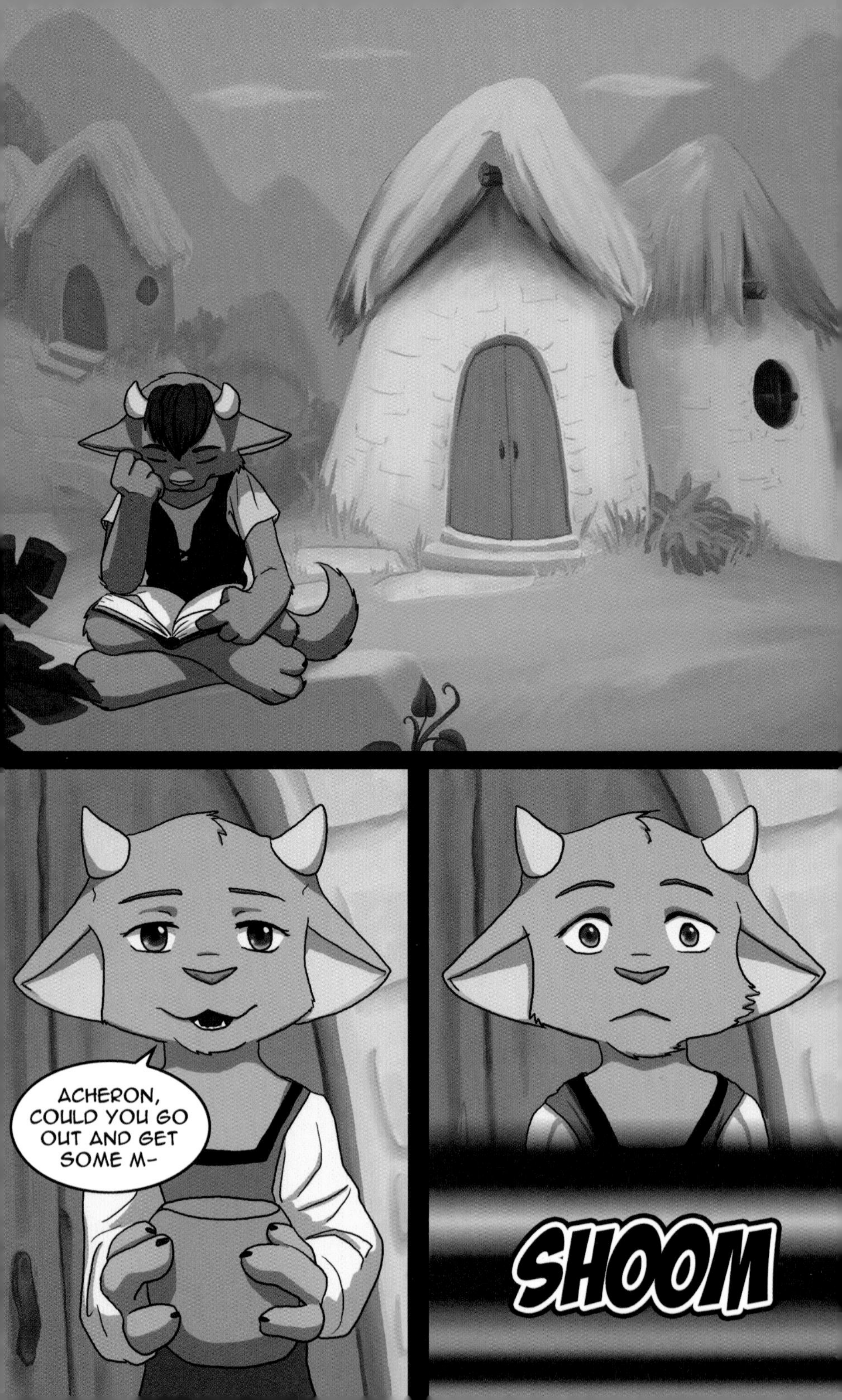
ACHERON, COULD YOU GO OUT AND GET SOME M-
SHOOM

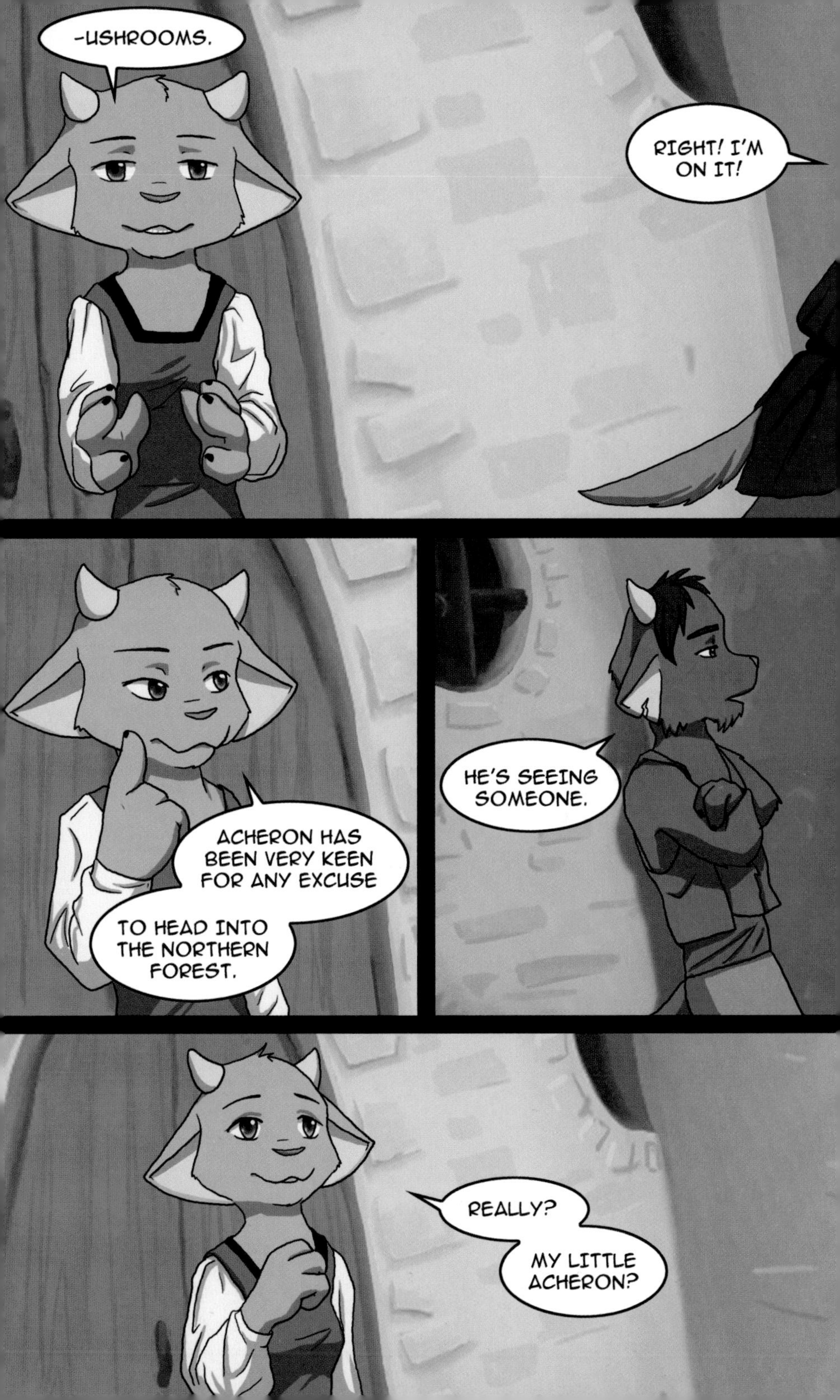
-USHROOMS.
RIGHT! I'M ON IT!
ACHERON HAS BEEN VERY KEEN FOR ANY EXCUSE
TO HEAD INTO THE NORTHERN FOREST.
HE'S SEEING SOMEONE.
REALLY?
MY LITTLE ACHERON?

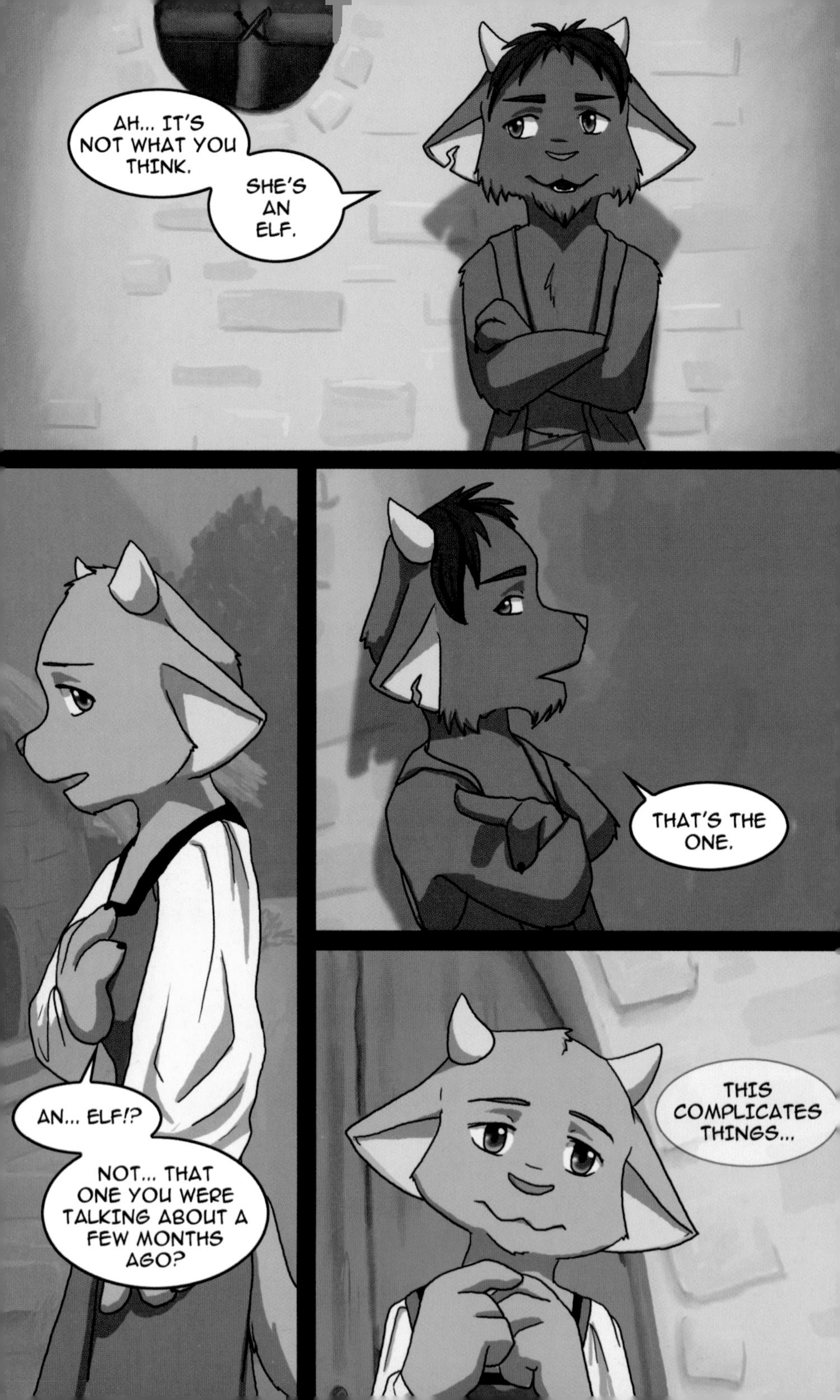
AH... IT'S NOT WHAT YOU THINK.
SHE'S AN ELF.
AN... ELF!?
NOT... THAT ONE YOU WERE TALKING ABOUT A FEW MONTHS AGO?
THAT'S THE ONE.
THIS COMPLICATES THINGS...

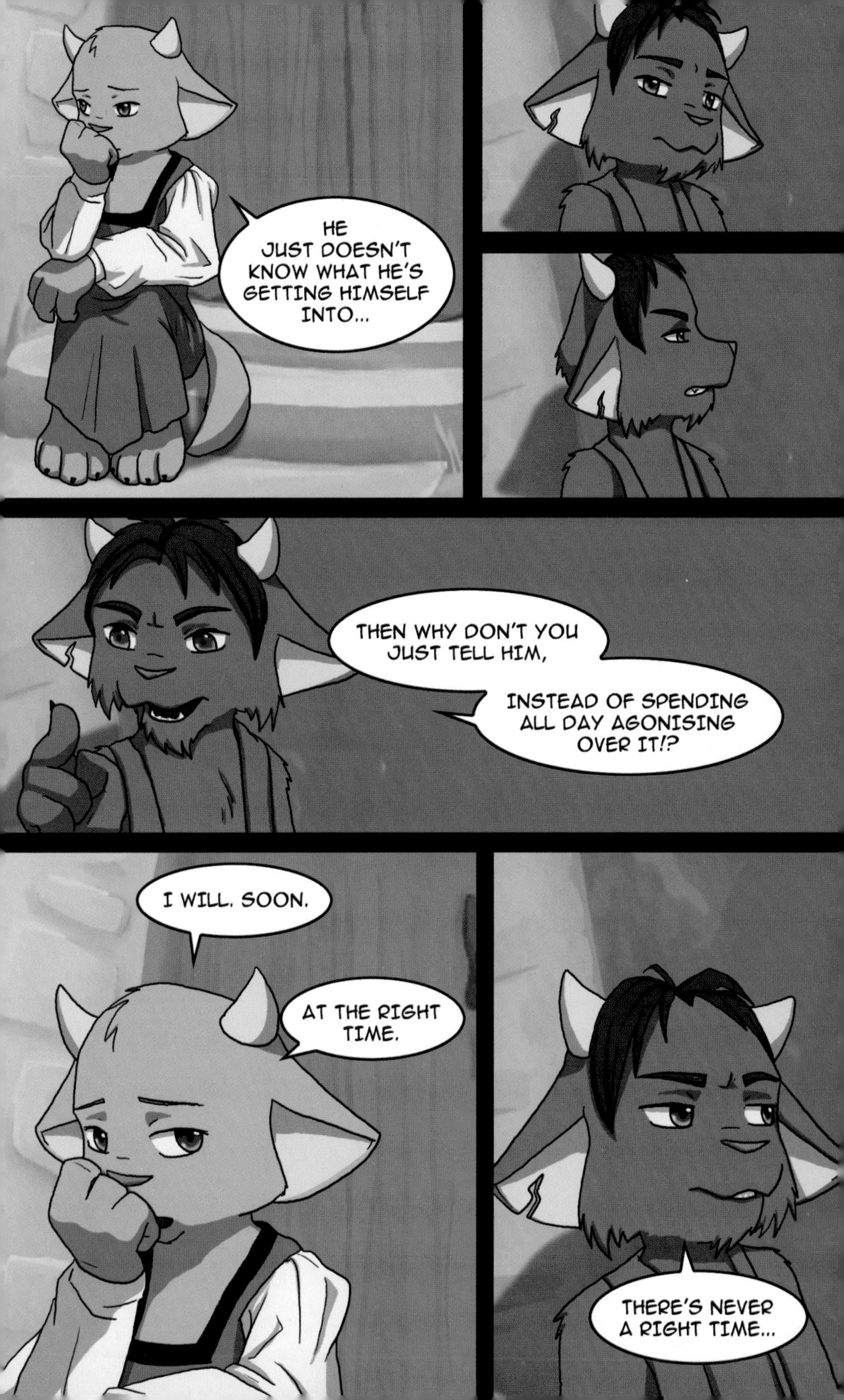
HE JUST DOESN'T KNOW WHAT HE'S GETTING HIMSELF INTO...
THEN WHY DON'T YOU JUST TELL HIM,
INSTEAD OF SPENDING ALL DAY AGONISING OVER IT!?
I WILL. SOON.
AT THE RIGHT TIME.
THERE'S NEVER A RIGHT TIME...

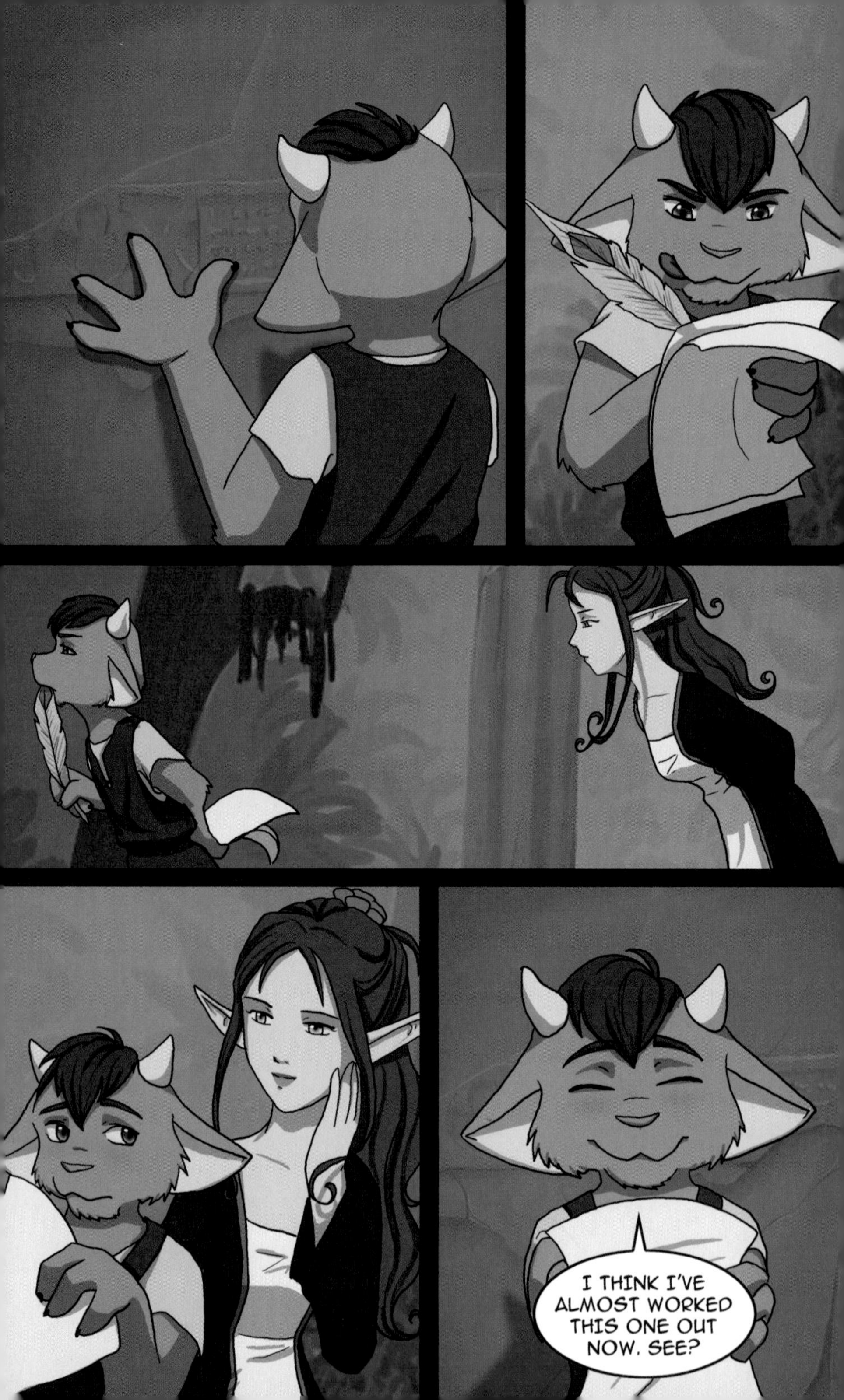
I THINK I'VE ALMOST WORKED THIS ONE OUT NOW. SEE?

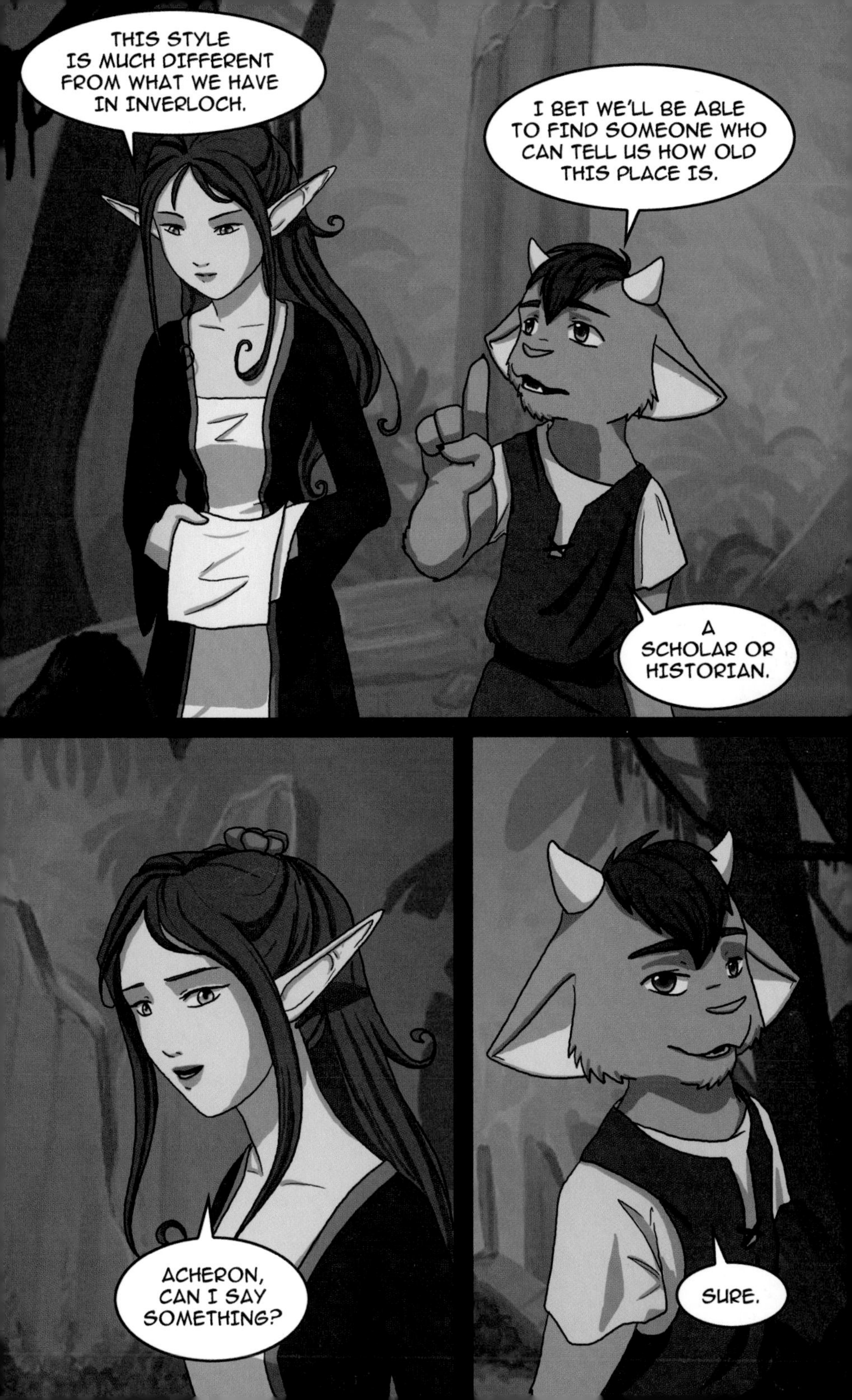
THIS STYLE IS MUCH DIFFERENT FROM WHAT WE HAVE IN INVERLOCH.
I BET WE'LL BE ABLE TO FIND SOMEONE WHO CAN TELL US HOW OLD THIS PLACE IS.
A SCHOLAR OR HISTORIAN.
ACHERON, CAN I SAY SOMETHING?
SURE.

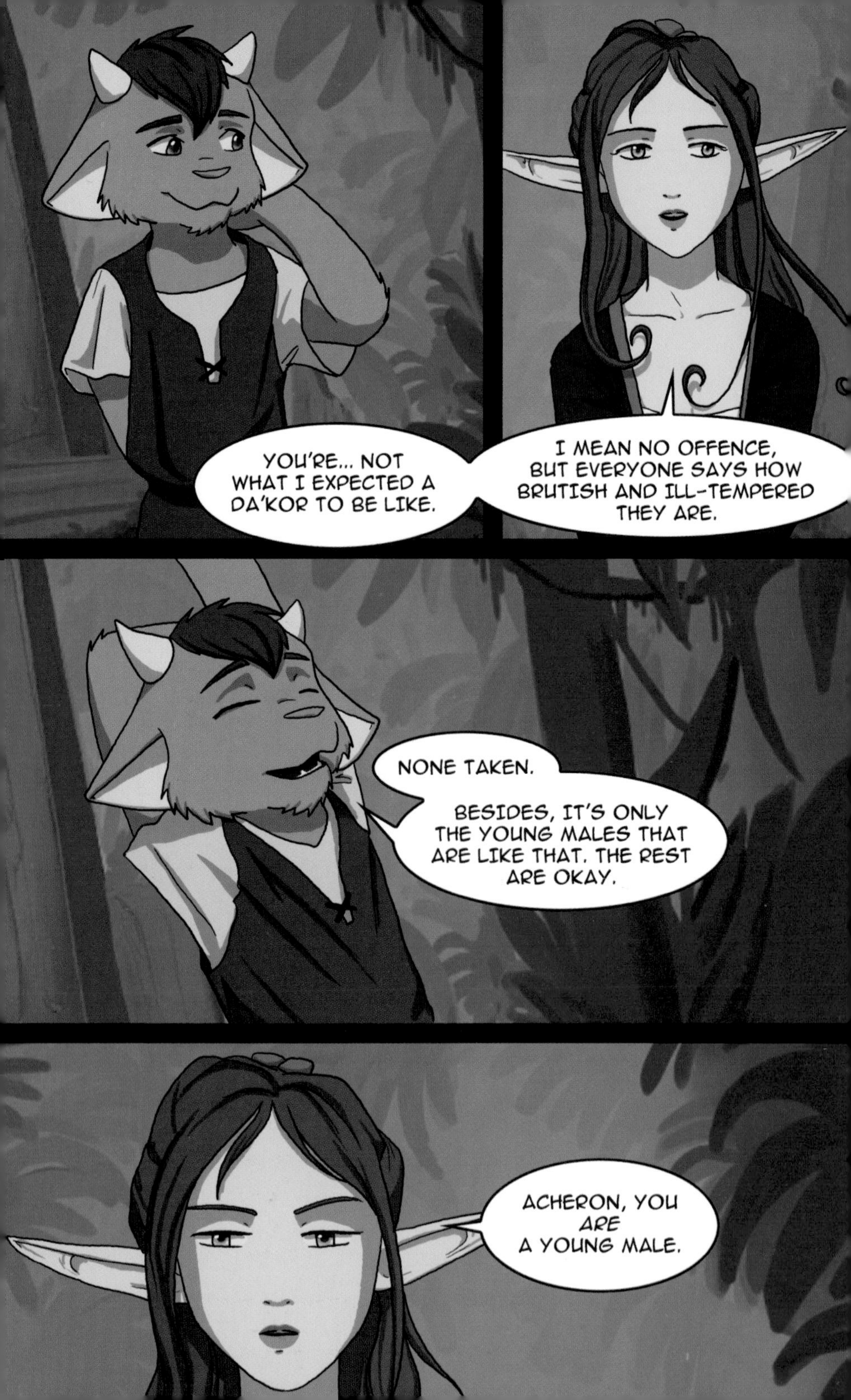
YOU'RE... NOT WHAT I EXPECTED A DA'KOR TO BE LIKE.
I MEAN NO OFFENCE, BUT EVERYONE SAYS HOW BRUTISH AND ILL-TEMPERED THEY ARE.
NONE TAKEN.
BESIDES, IT'S ONLY THE YOUNG MALES THAT ARE LIKE THAT. THE REST ARE OKAY.
ACHERON, YOU *ARE* A YOUNG MALE.

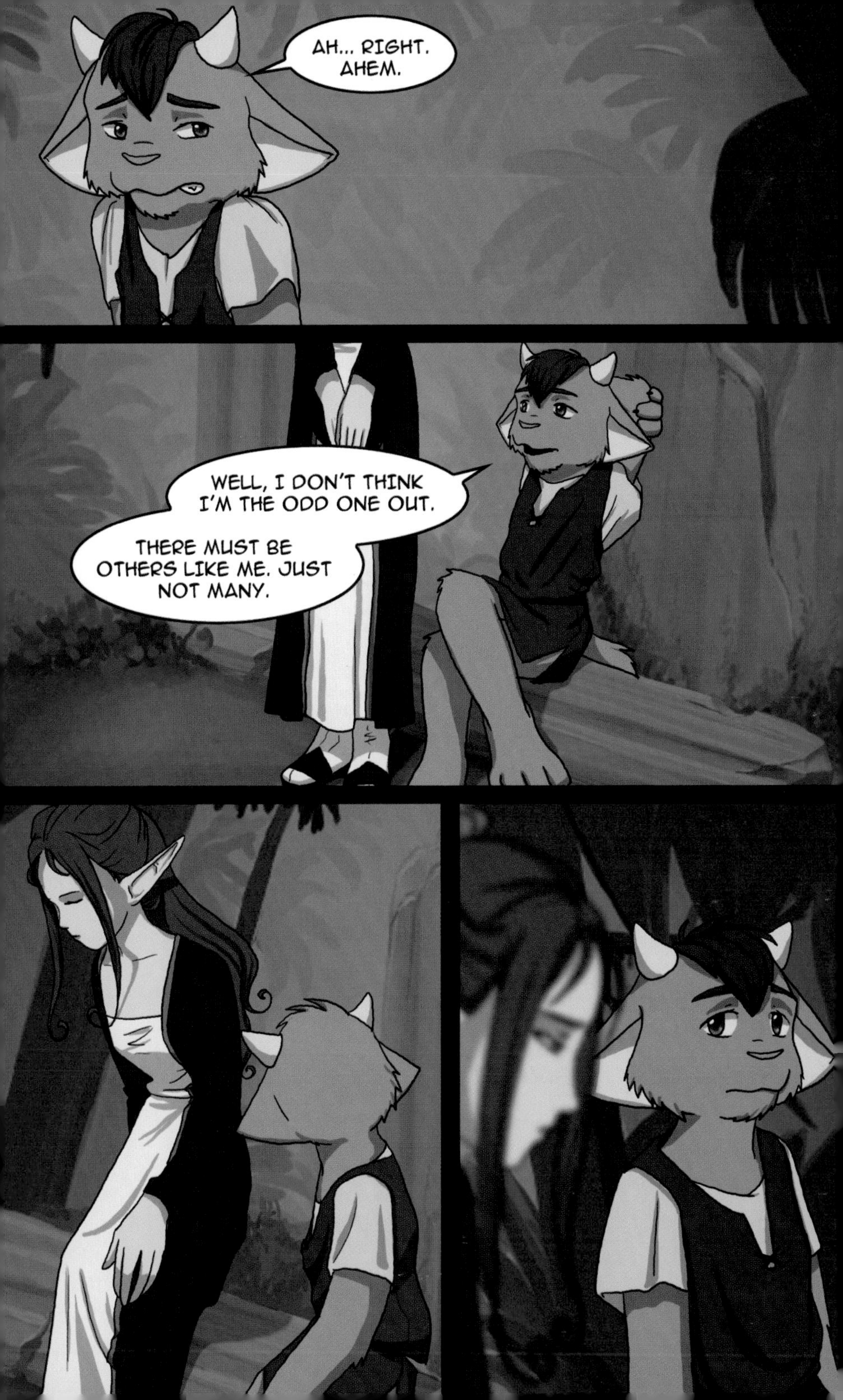
AH... RIGHT. AHEM.
WELL, I DON'T THINK I'M THE ODD ONE OUT.
THERE MUST BE OTHERS LIKE ME. JUST NOT MANY.

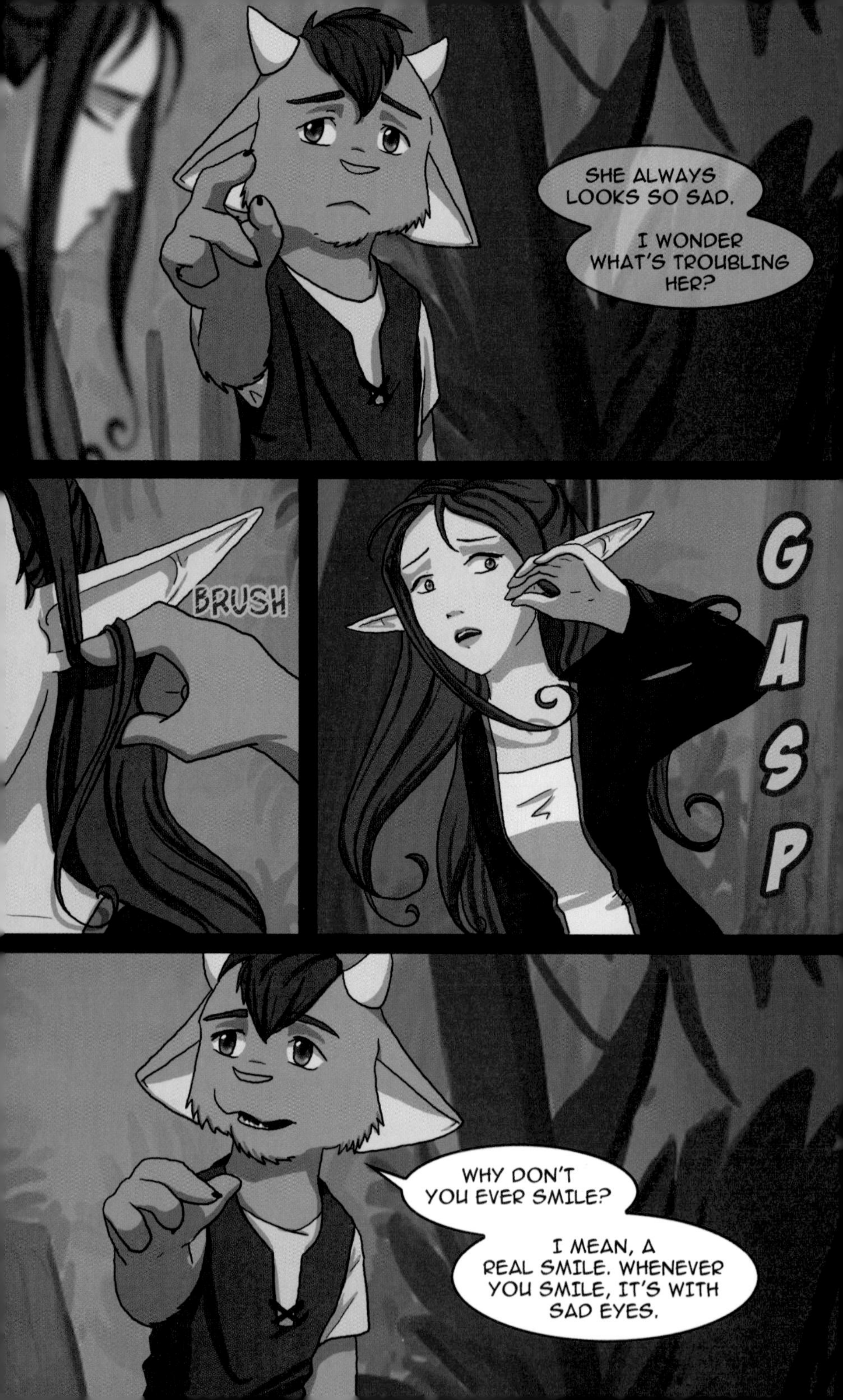
SHE ALWAYS LOOKS SO SAD.
I WONDER WHAT'S TROUBLING HER?
BRUSH
GASP
WHY DON'T YOU EVER SMILE?
I MEAN, A REAL SMILE. WHENEVER YOU SMILE, IT'S WITH SAD EYES.

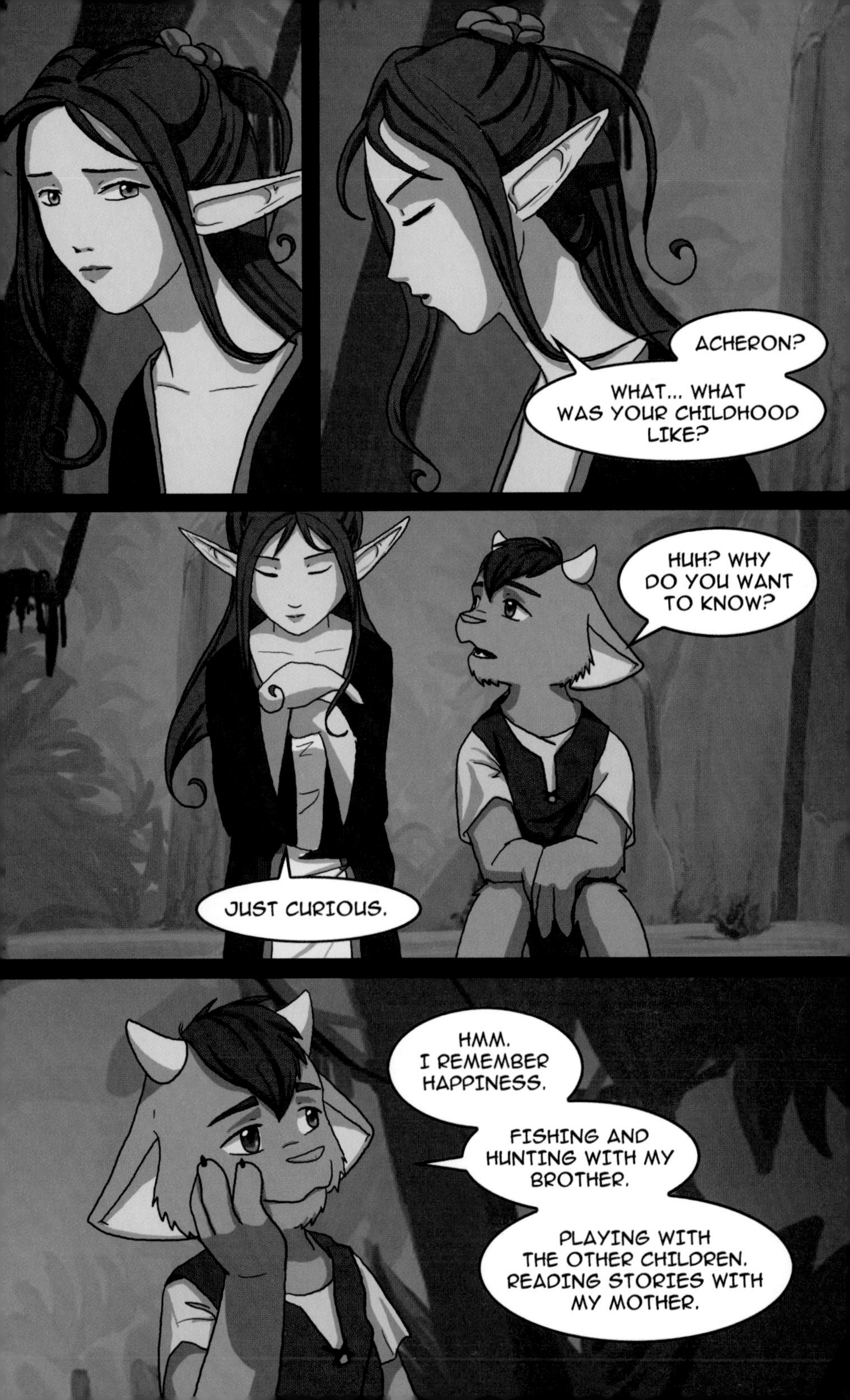
ACHERON?
WHAT... WHAT WAS YOUR CHILDHOOD LIKE?
HUH? WHY DO YOU WANT TO KNOW?
JUST CURIOUS.
HMM. I REMEMBER HAPPINESS.
FISHING AND HUNTING WITH MY BROTHER.
PLAYING WITH THE OTHER CHILDREN. READING STORIES WITH MY MOTHER.

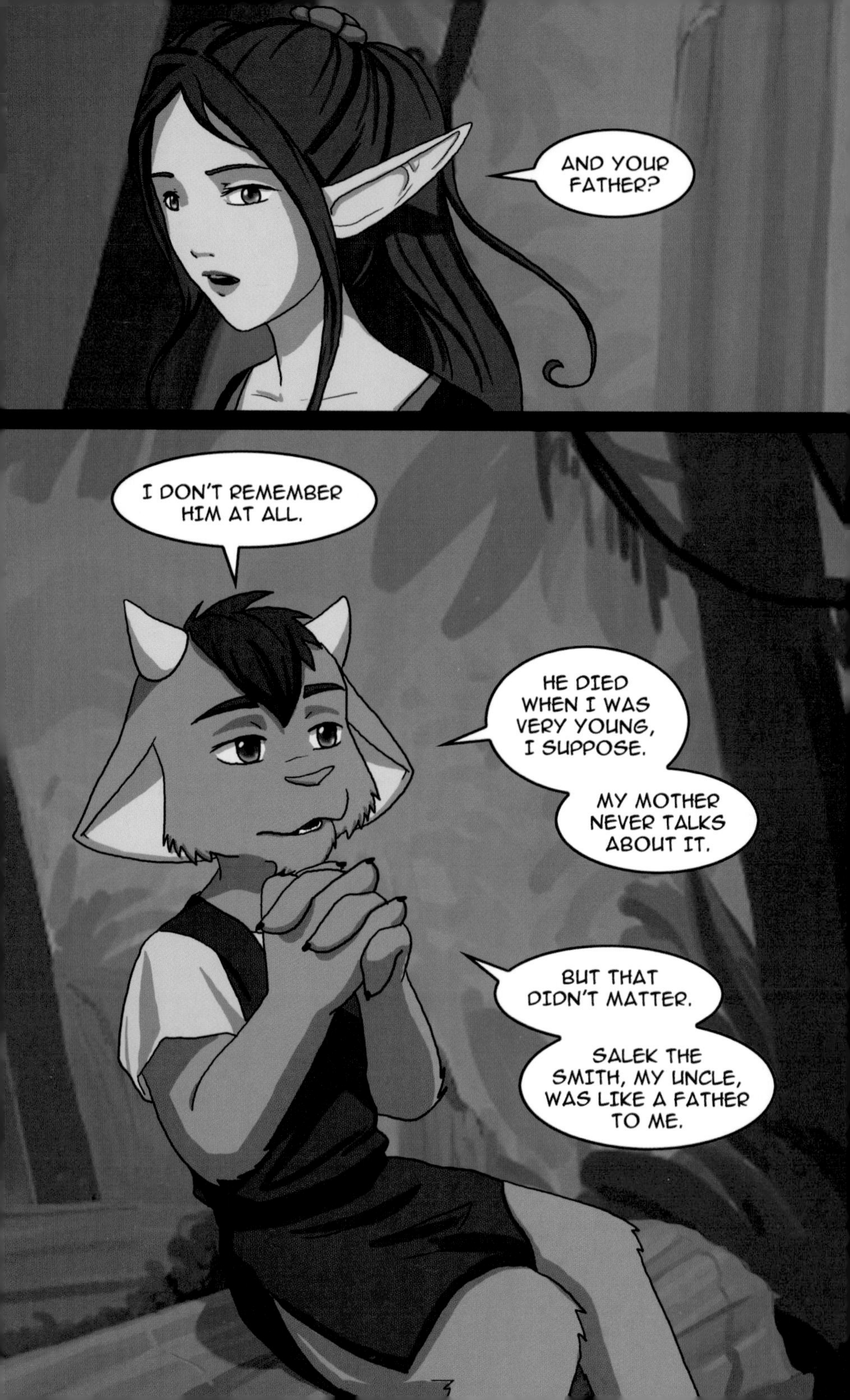
AND YOUR FATHER?
I DON'T REMEMBER HIM AT ALL.
HE DIED WHEN I WAS VERY YOUNG, I SUPPOSE.
MY MOTHER NEVER TALKS ABOUT IT.
BUT THAT DIDN'T MATTER.
SALEK THE SMITH, MY UNCLE, WAS LIKE A FATHER TO ME.

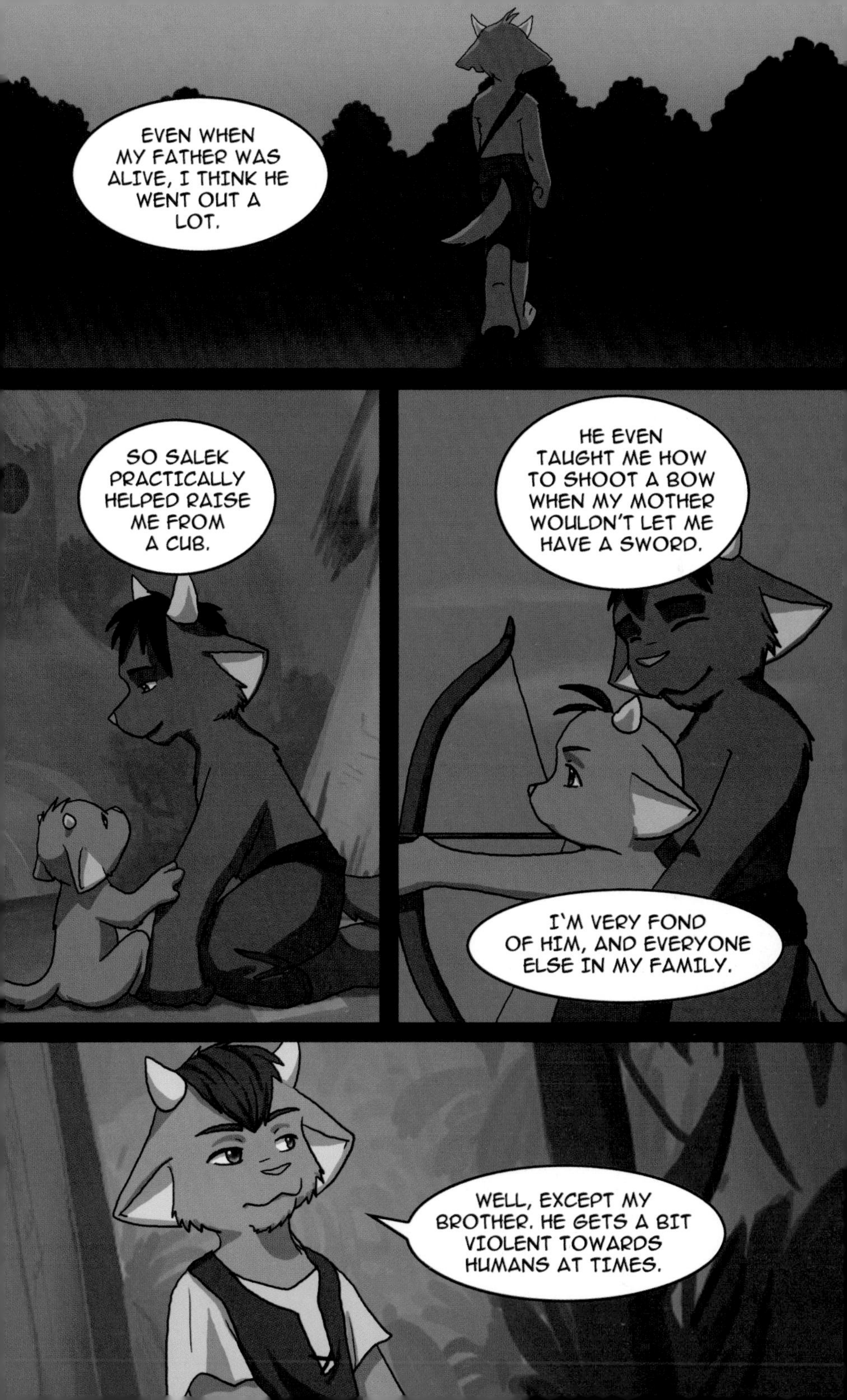
EVEN WHEN MY FATHER WAS ALIVE, I THINK HE WENT OUT A LOT.
SO SALEK PRACTICALLY HELPED RAISE ME FROM A CUB.
HE EVEN TAUGHT ME HOW TO SHOOT A BOW WHEN MY MOTHER WOULDN'T LET ME HAVE A SWORD.
I'M VERY FOND OF HIM, AND EVERYONE ELSE IN MY FAMILY.
WELL, EXCEPT MY BROTHER. HE GETS A BIT VIOLENT TOWARDS HUMANS AT TIMES.

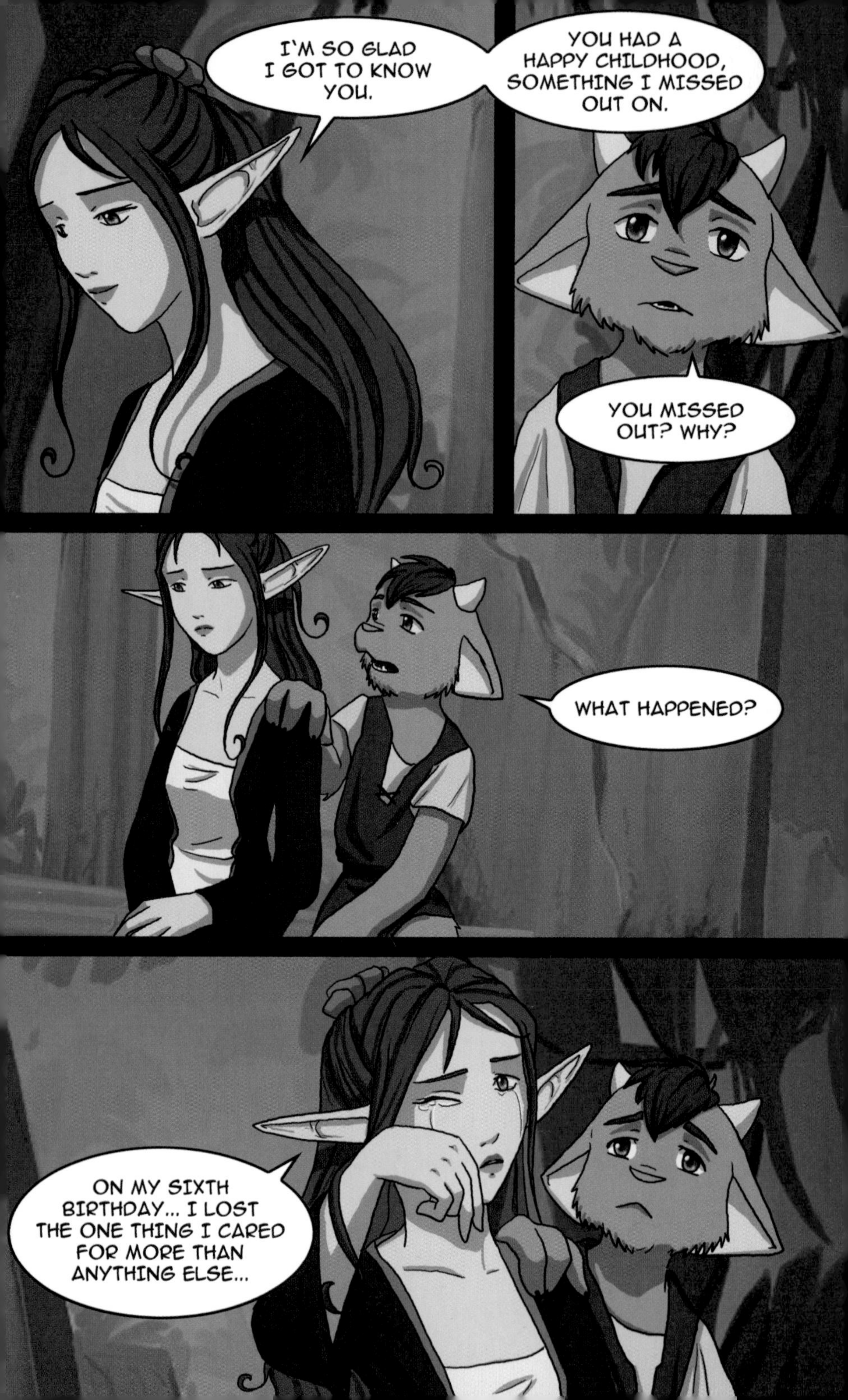
I'M SO GLAD I GOT TO KNOW YOU.
YOU HAD A HAPPY CHILDHOOD, SOMETHING I MISSED OUT ON.
YOU MISSED OUT? WHY?
WHAT HAPPENED?
ON MY SIXTH BIRTHDAY... I LOST THE ONE THING I CARED FOR MORE THAN ANYTHING ELSE...

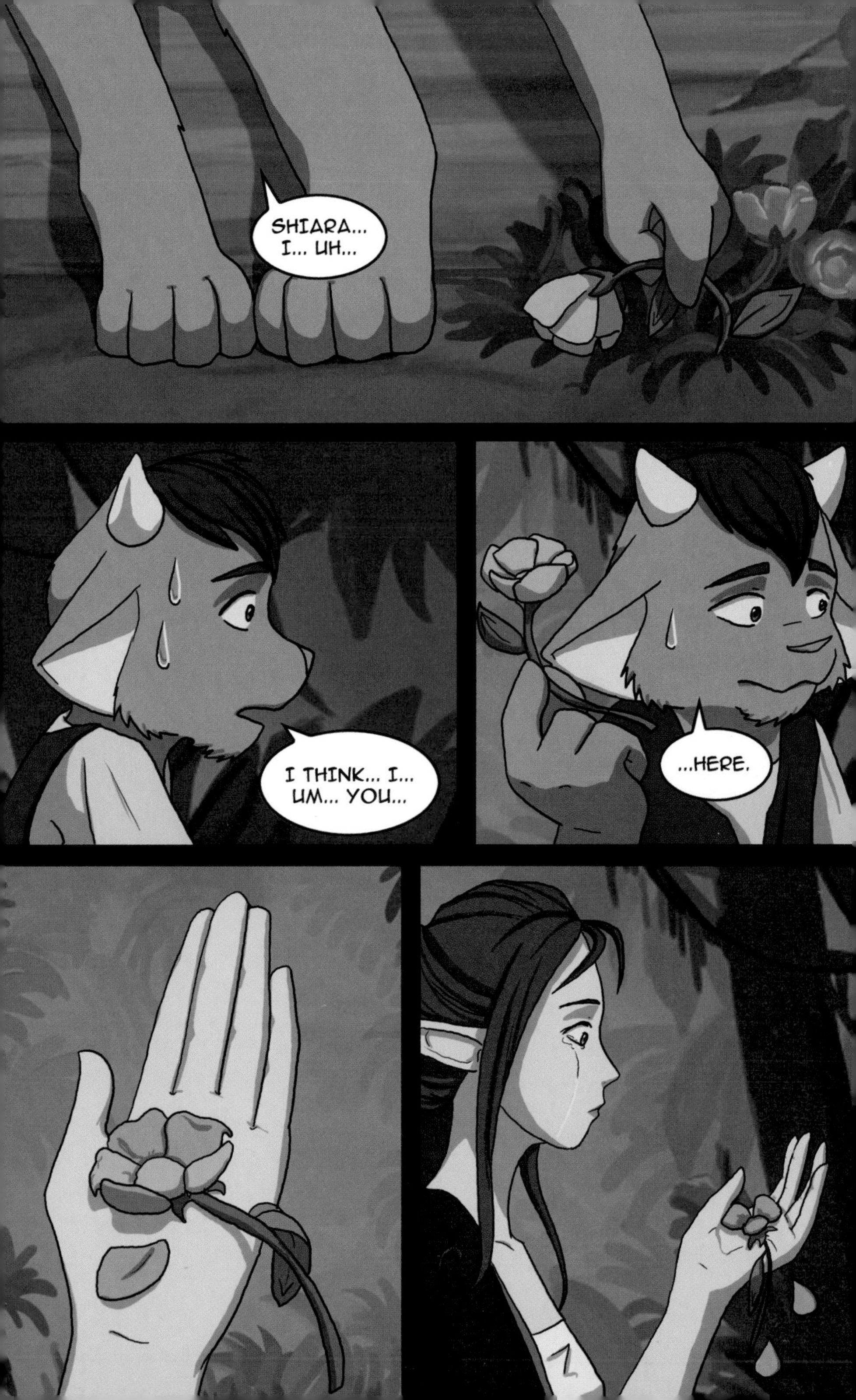
SHIARA...
I... UH...
I THINK... I...
UM... YOU...
...HERE.

ACHERON, I... I'M SORRY...

SHIARA! PLEASE COME BACK!

WHY?

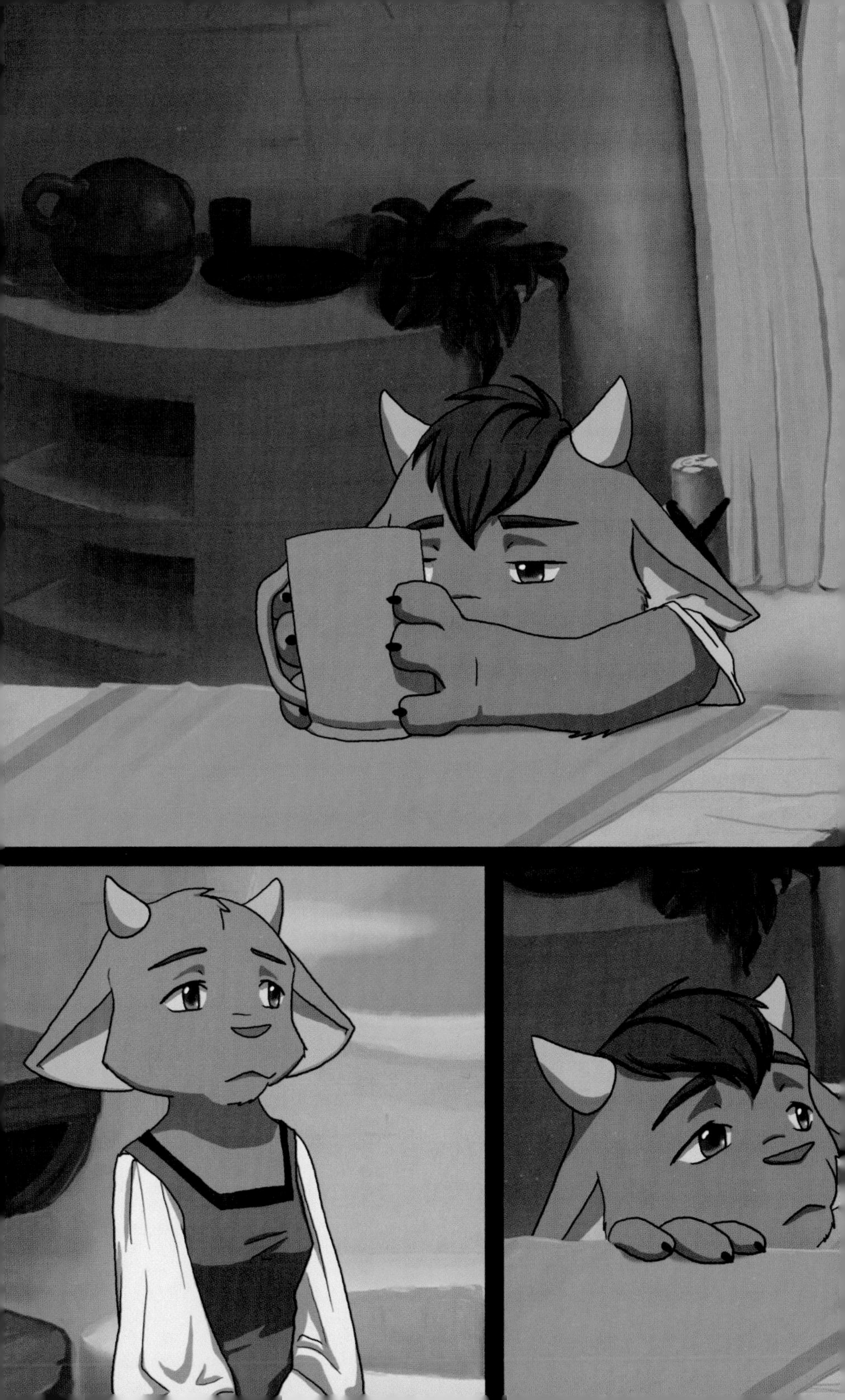

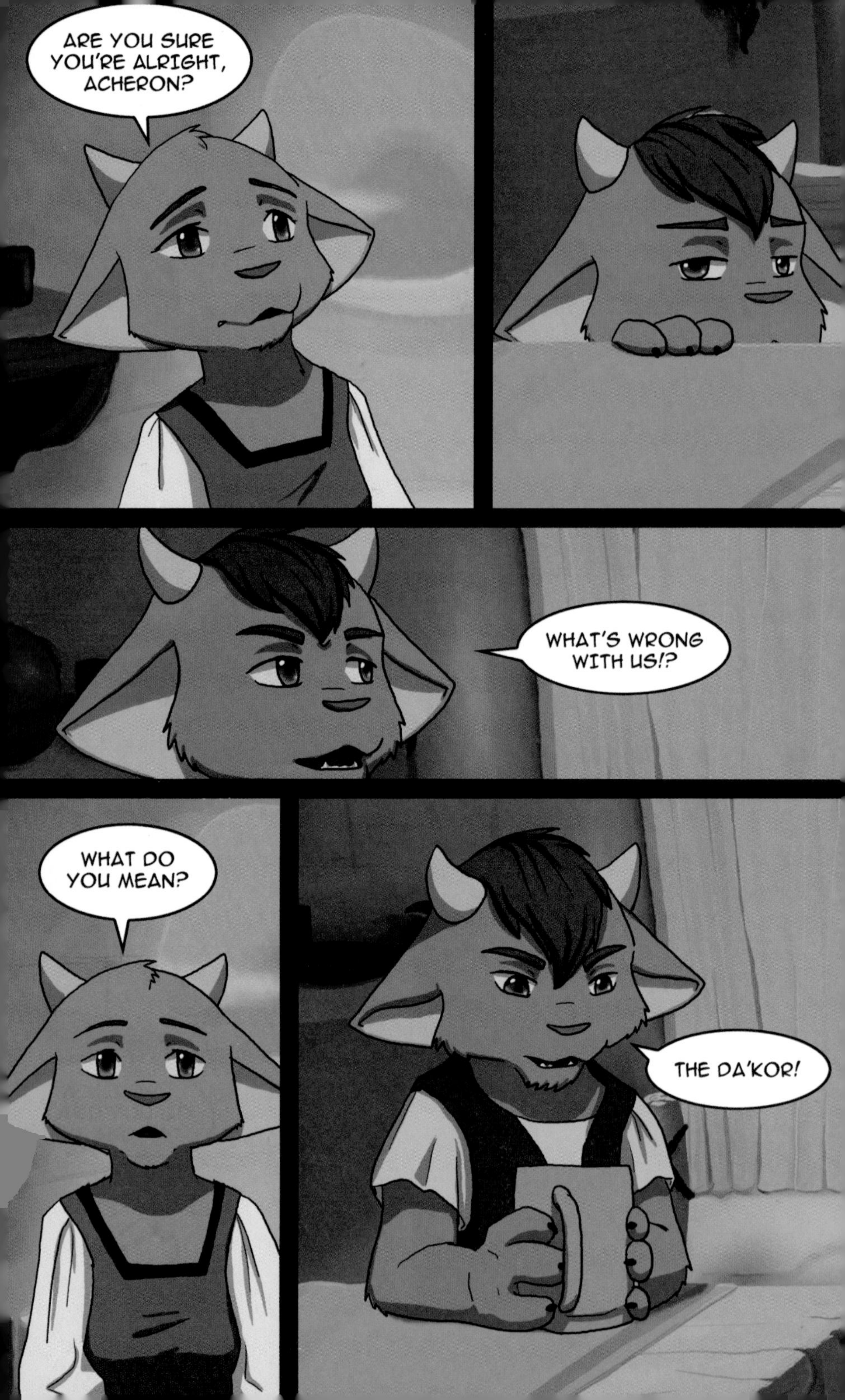
ARE YOU SURE YOU'RE ALRIGHT, ACHERON?
WHAT'S WRONG WITH US!?
WHAT DO YOU MEAN?
THE DA'KOR!

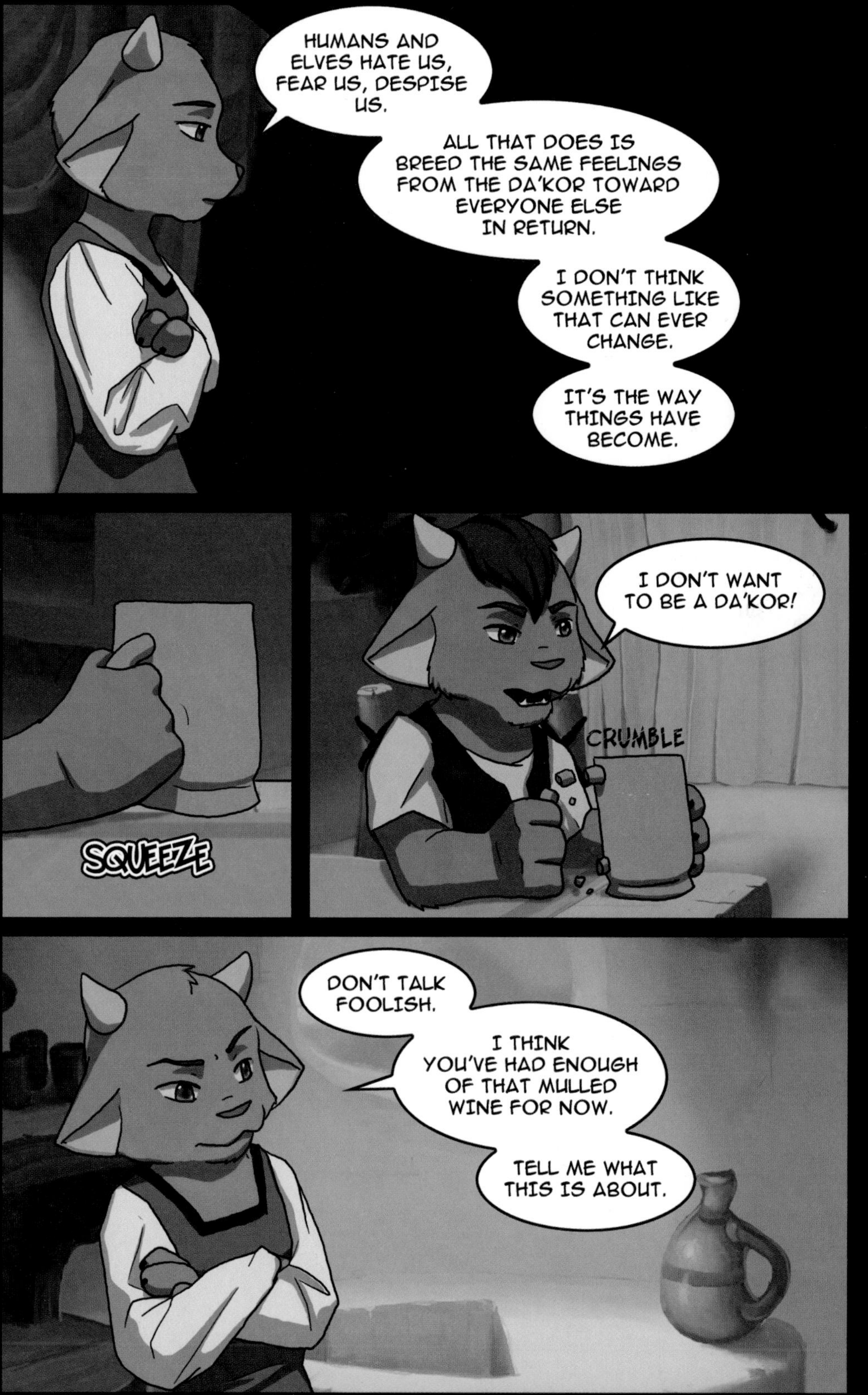

HUMANS AND ELVES HATE US, FEAR US, DESPISE US.
ALL THAT DOES IS BREED THE SAME FEELINGS FROM THE DA'KOR TOWARD EVERYONE ELSE IN RETURN.
I DON'T THINK SOMETHING LIKE THAT CAN EVER CHANGE.
IT'S THE WAY THINGS HAVE BECOME.
SQUEEZE
I DON'T WANT TO BE A DA'KOR!
CRUMBLE
DON'T TALK FOOLISH.
I THINK YOU'VE HAD ENOUGH OF THAT MULLED WINE FOR NOW.
TELL ME WHAT THIS IS ABOUT.

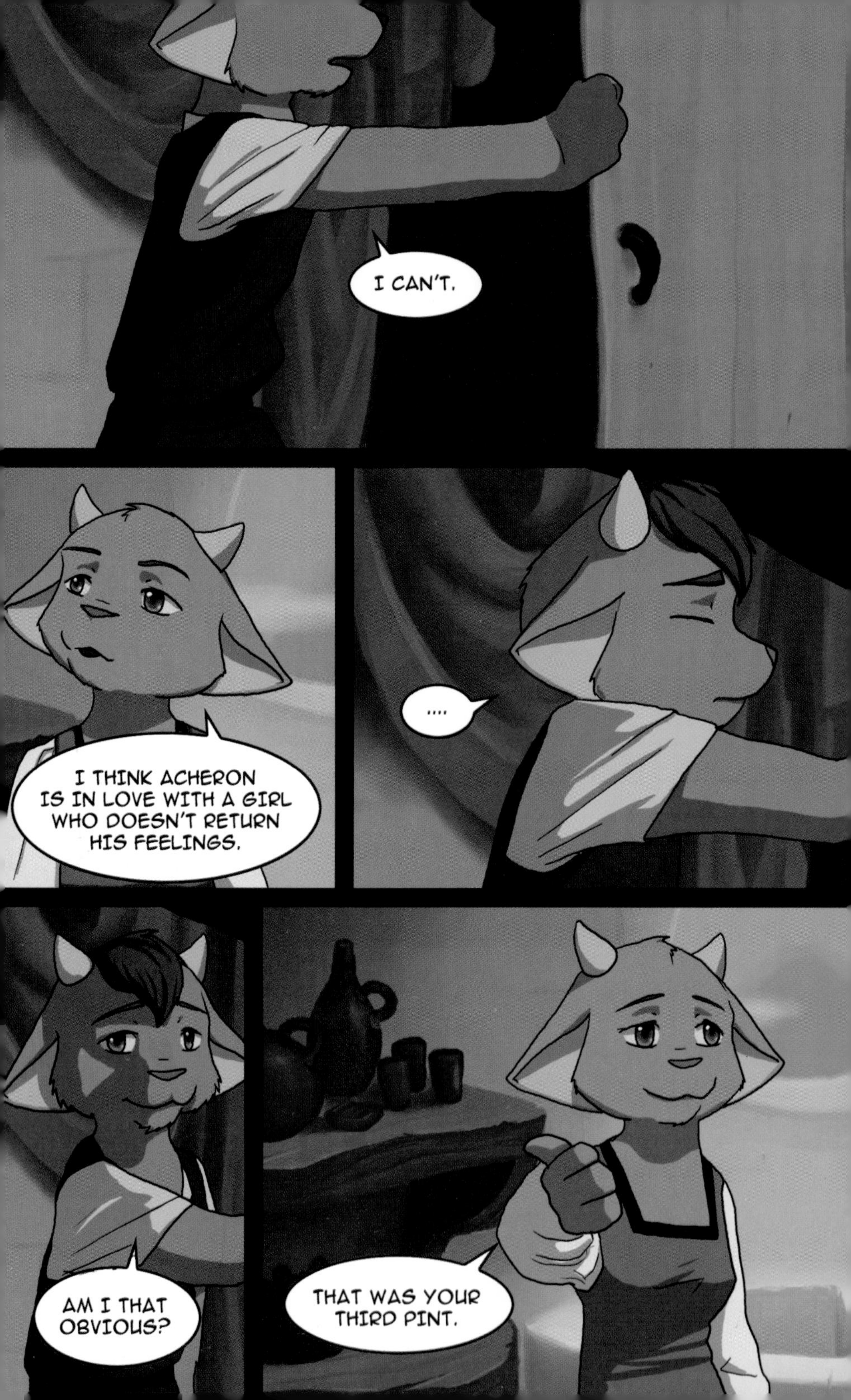
I CAN'T.
I THINK ACHERON IS IN LOVE WITH A GIRL WHO DOESN'T RETURN HIS FEELINGS.
....
AM I THAT OBVIOUS?
THAT WAS YOUR THIRD PINT.

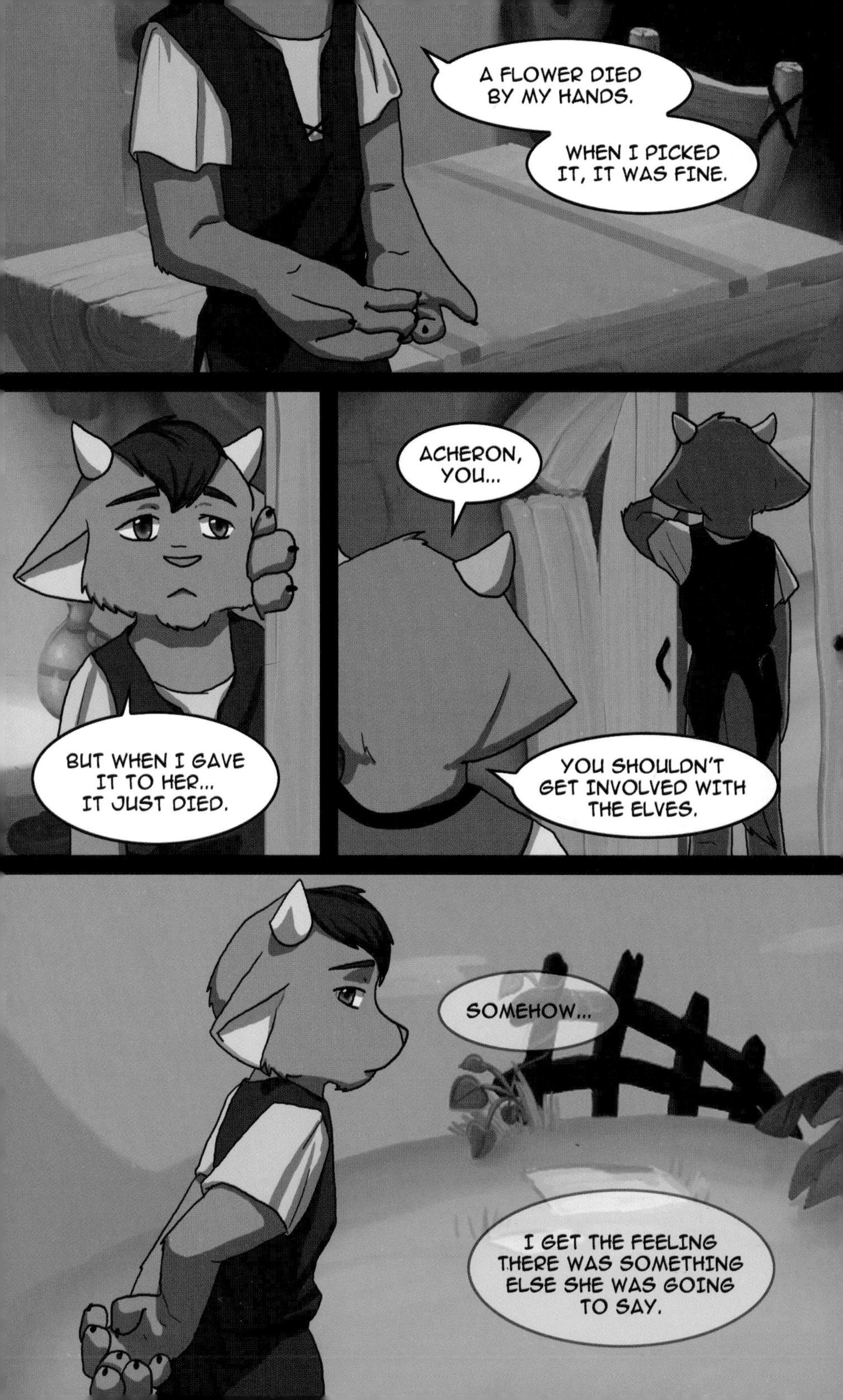
A FLOWER DIED BY MY HANDS.
WHEN I PICKED IT, IT WAS FINE.
BUT WHEN I GAVE IT TO HER... IT JUST DIED.
ACHERON, YOU...
YOU SHOULDN'T GET INVOLVED WITH THE ELVES.
SOMEHOW...
I GET THE FEELING THERE WAS SOMETHING ELSE SHE WAS GOING TO SAY.

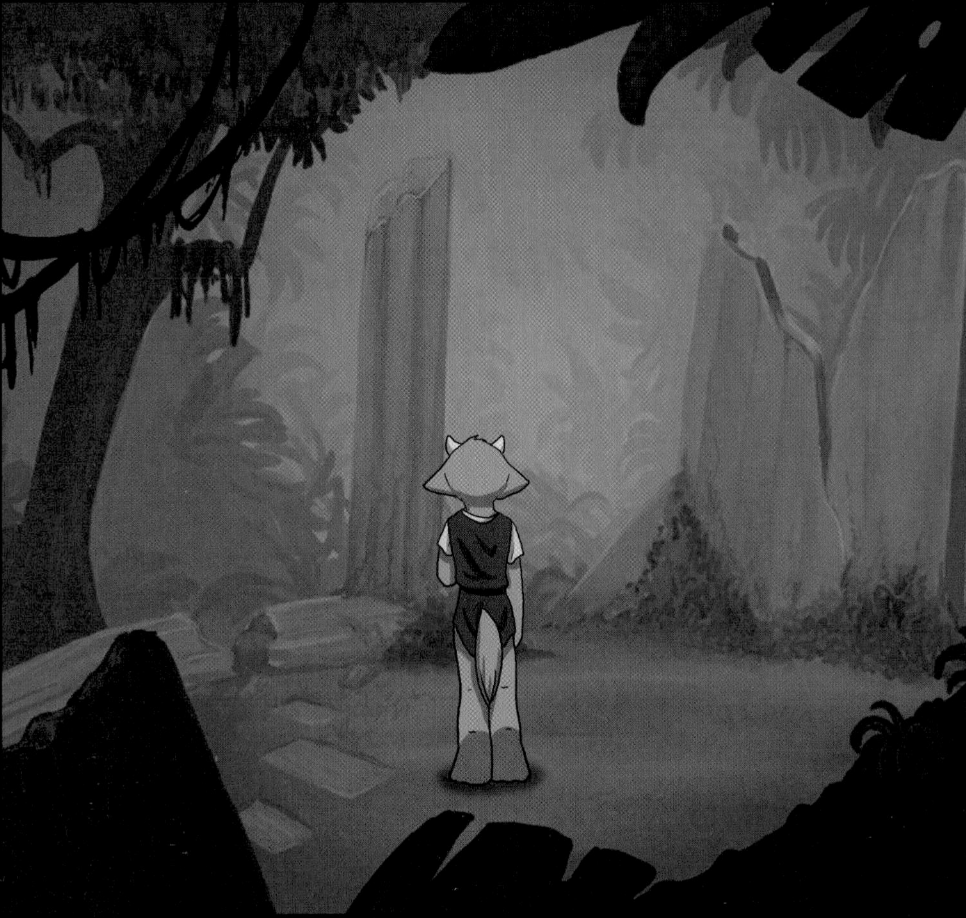

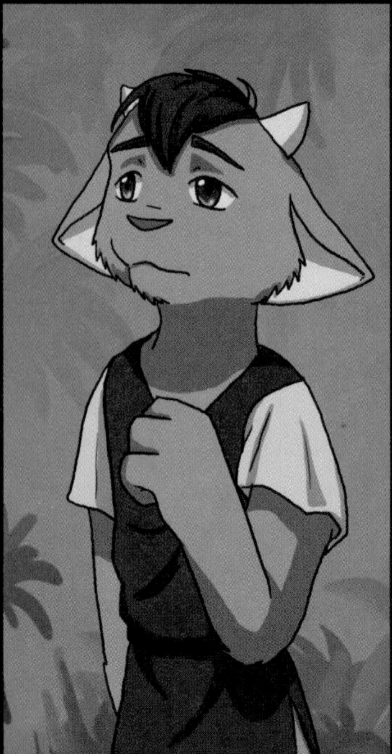

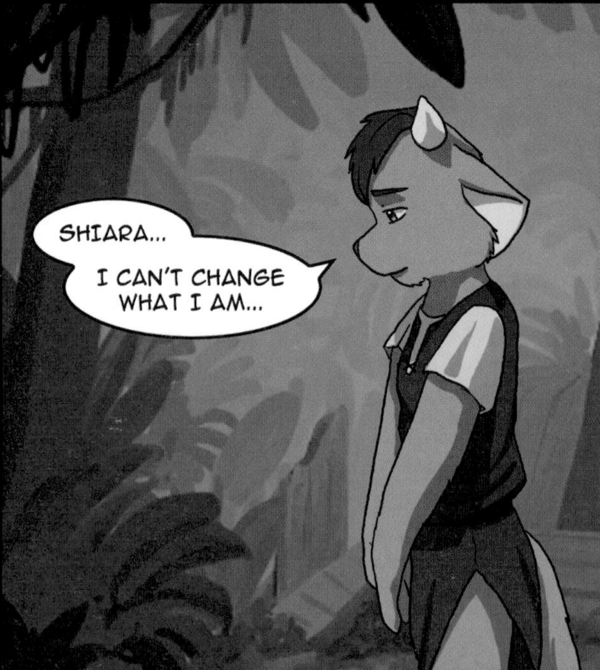
SHIARA...
I CAN'T CHANGE WHAT I AM...

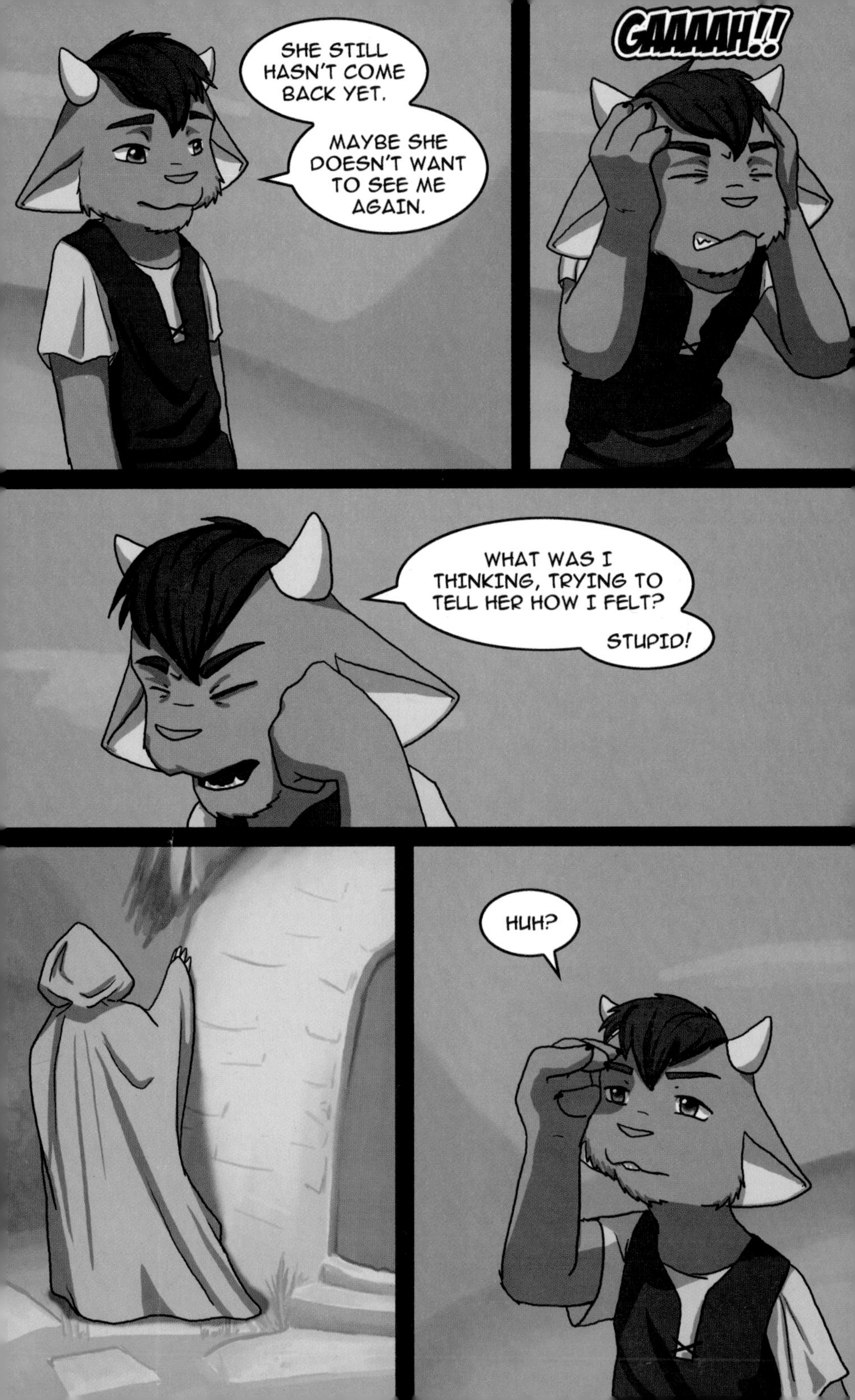
SHE STILL HASN'T COME BACK YET.
MAYBE SHE DOESN'T WANT TO SEE ME AGAIN.
GAAAAH!!
WHAT WAS I THINKING, TRYING TO TELL HER HOW I FELT?
STUPID!
HUH?

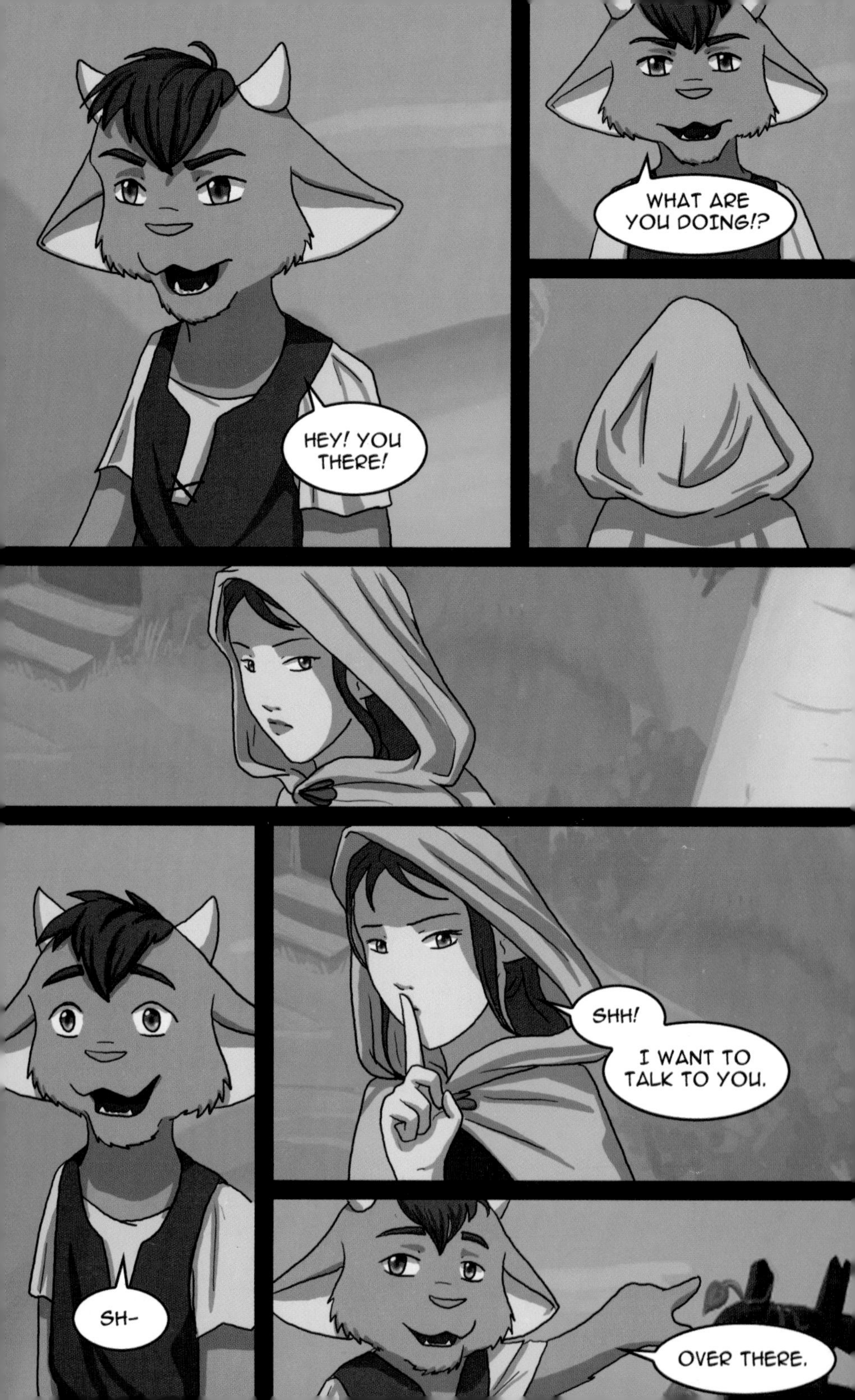
HEY! YOU THERE!
WHAT ARE YOU DOING!?
SH-
SHH!
I WANT TO TALK TO YOU.
OVER THERE.

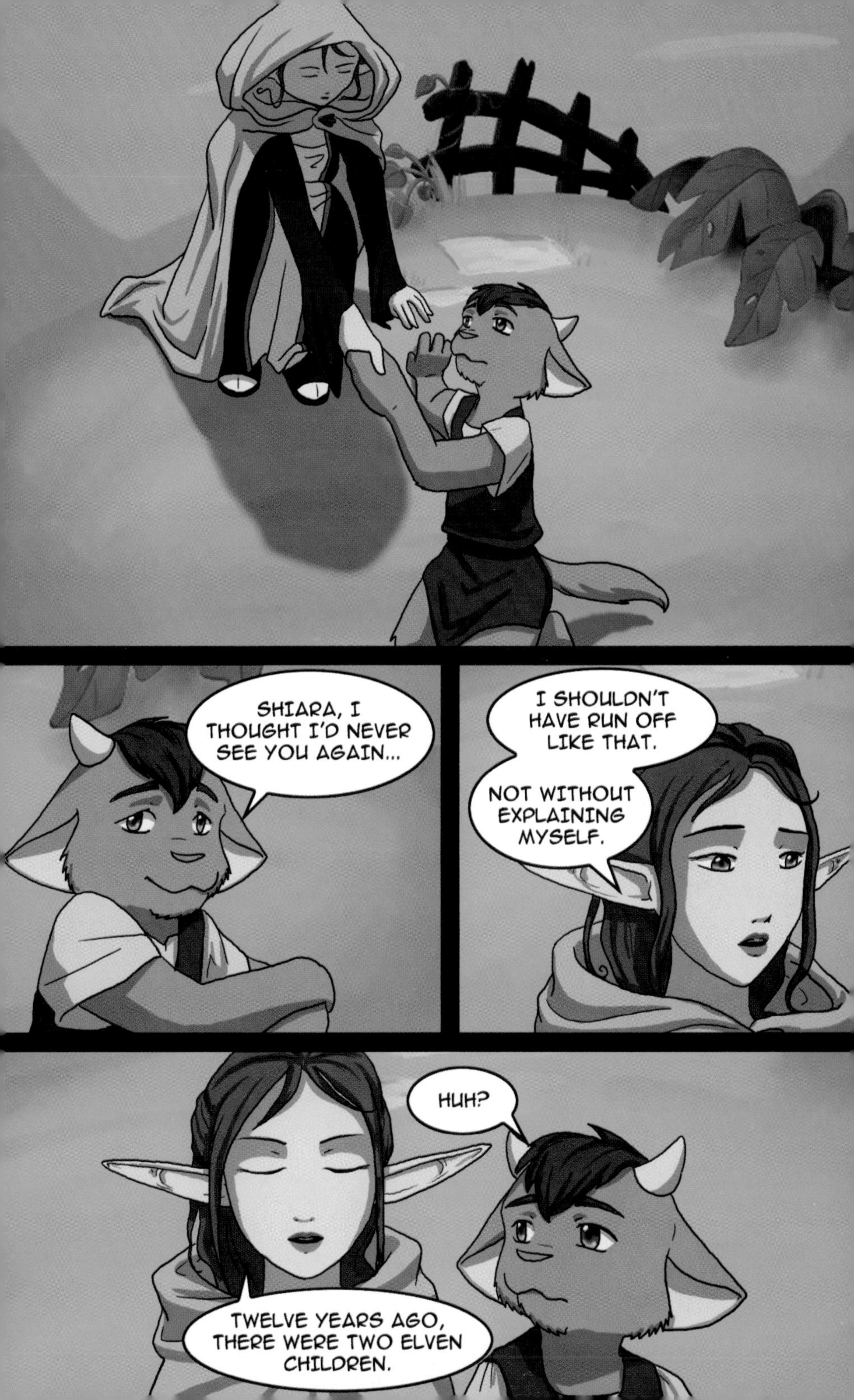

SHIARA, I THOUGHT I'D NEVER SEE YOU AGAIN...
I SHOULDN'T HAVE RUN OFF LIKE THAT.
NOT WITHOUT EXPLAINING MYSELF.
HUH?
TWELVE YEARS AGO, THERE WERE TWO ELVEN CHILDREN.

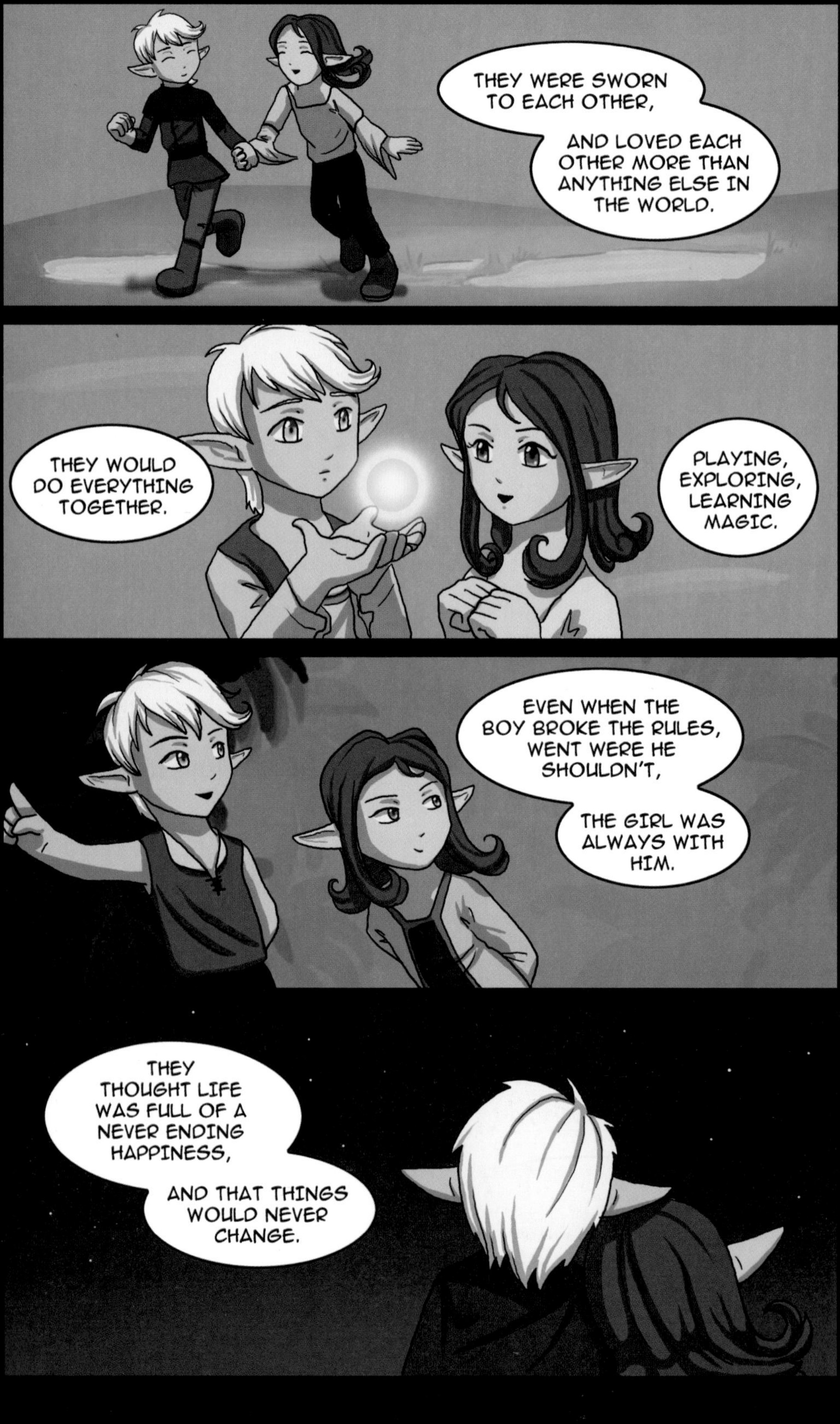
THEY WERE SWORN TO EACH OTHER,
AND LOVED EACH OTHER MORE THAN ANYTHING ELSE IN THE WORLD.
THEY WOULD DO EVERYTHING TOGETHER.
PLAYING, EXPLORING, LEARNING MAGIC.
EVEN WHEN THE BOY BROKE THE RULES, WENT WERE HE SHOULDN'T,
THE GIRL WAS ALWAYS WITH HIM.
THEY THOUGHT LIFE WAS FULL OF A NEVER ENDING HAPPINESS,
AND THAT THINGS WOULD NEVER CHANGE.

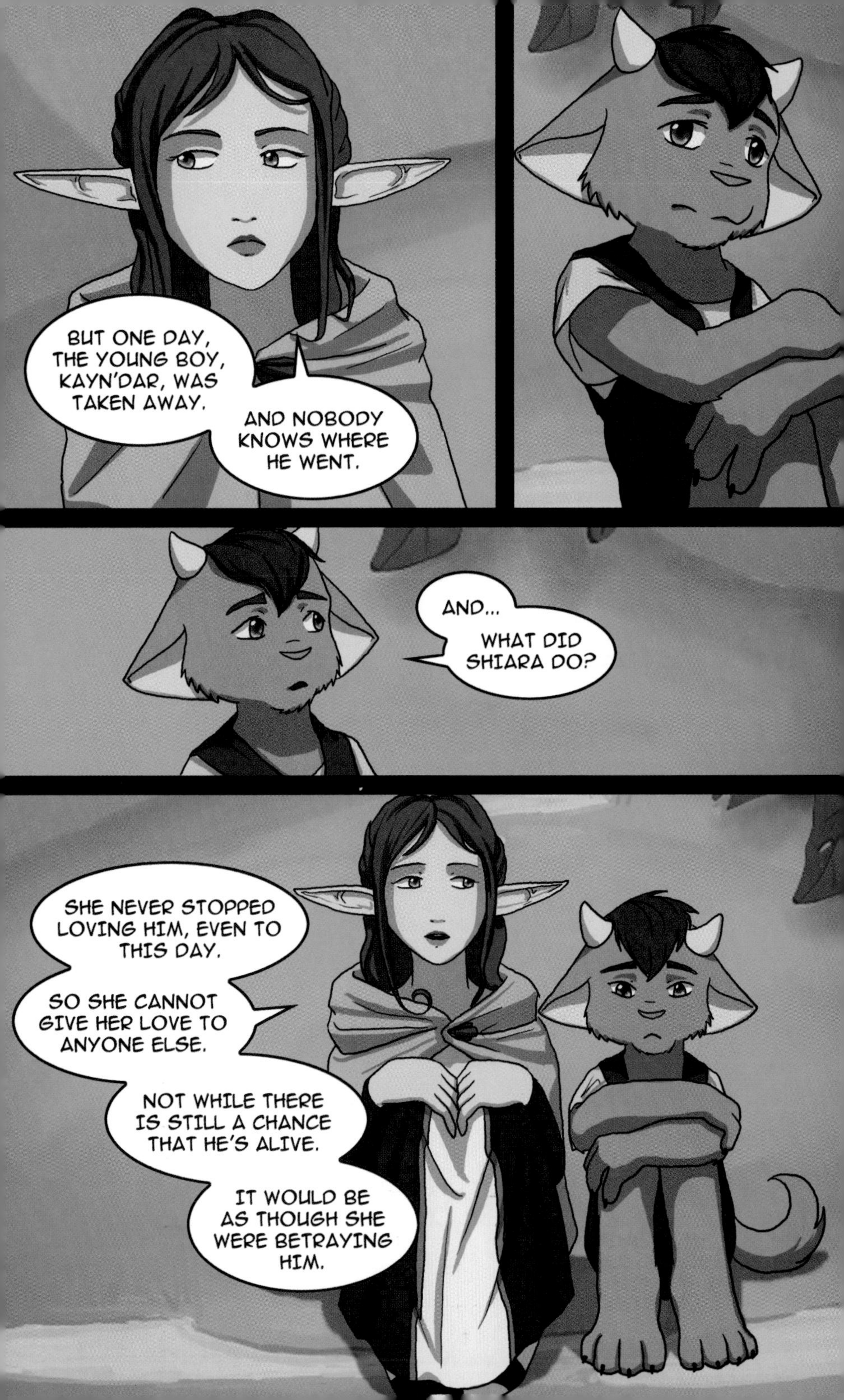
BUT ONE DAY, THE YOUNG BOY, KAYN'DAR, WAS TAKEN AWAY.
AND NOBODY KNOWS WHERE HE WENT.
AND... WHAT DID SHIARA DO?
SHE NEVER STOPPED LOVING HIM, EVEN TO THIS DAY.
SO SHE CANNOT GIVE HER LOVE TO ANYONE ELSE.
NOT WHILE THERE IS STILL A CHANCE THAT HE'S ALIVE.
IT WOULD BE AS THOUGH SHE WERE BETRAYING HIM.

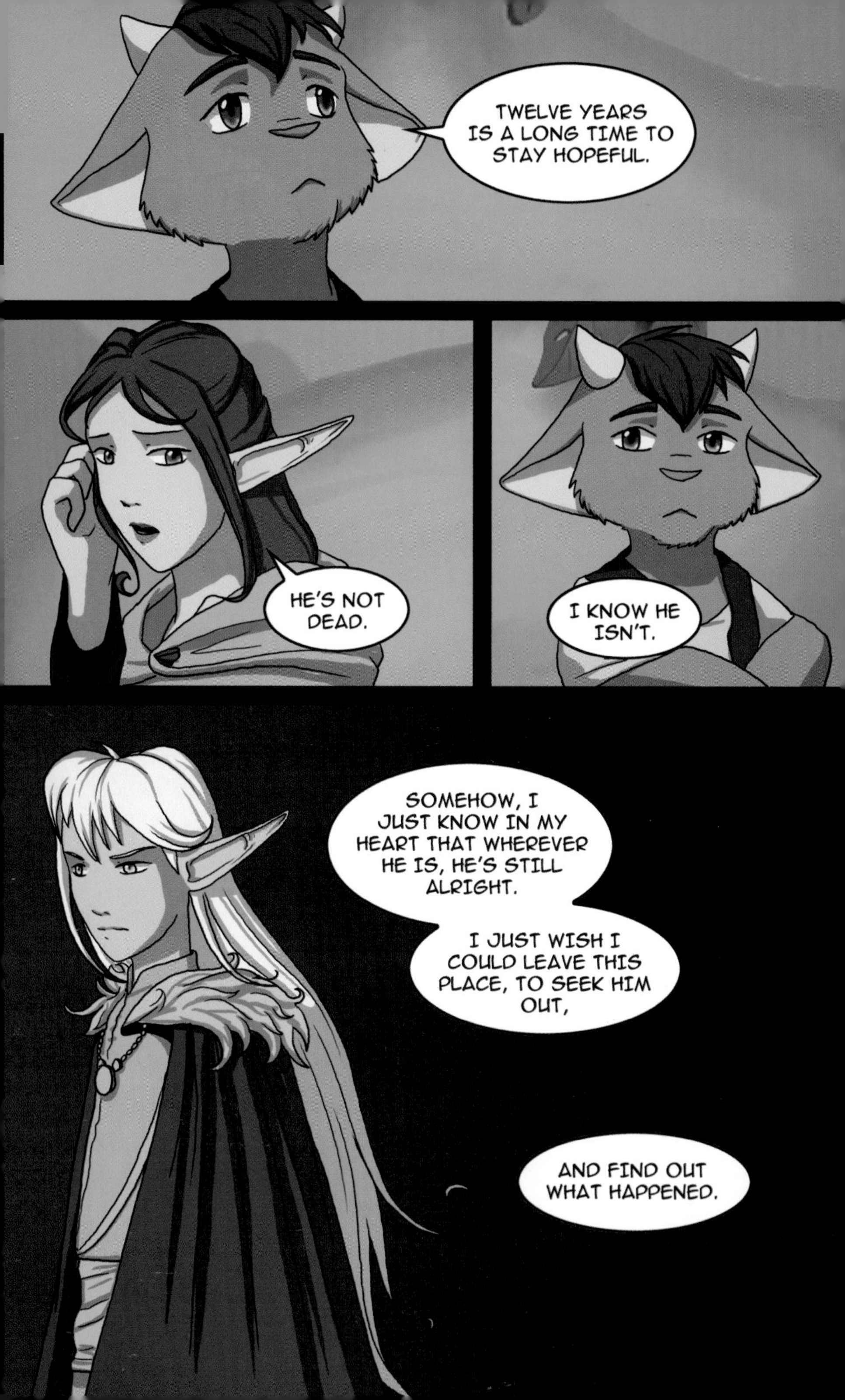
TWELVE YEARS IS A LONG TIME TO STAY HOPEFUL.
HE'S NOT DEAD.
I KNOW HE ISN'T.
SOMEHOW, I JUST KNOW IN MY HEART THAT WHEREVER HE IS, HE'S STILL ALRIGHT.
I JUST WISH I COULD LEAVE THIS PLACE, TO SEEK HIM OUT,
AND FIND OUT WHAT HAPPENED.

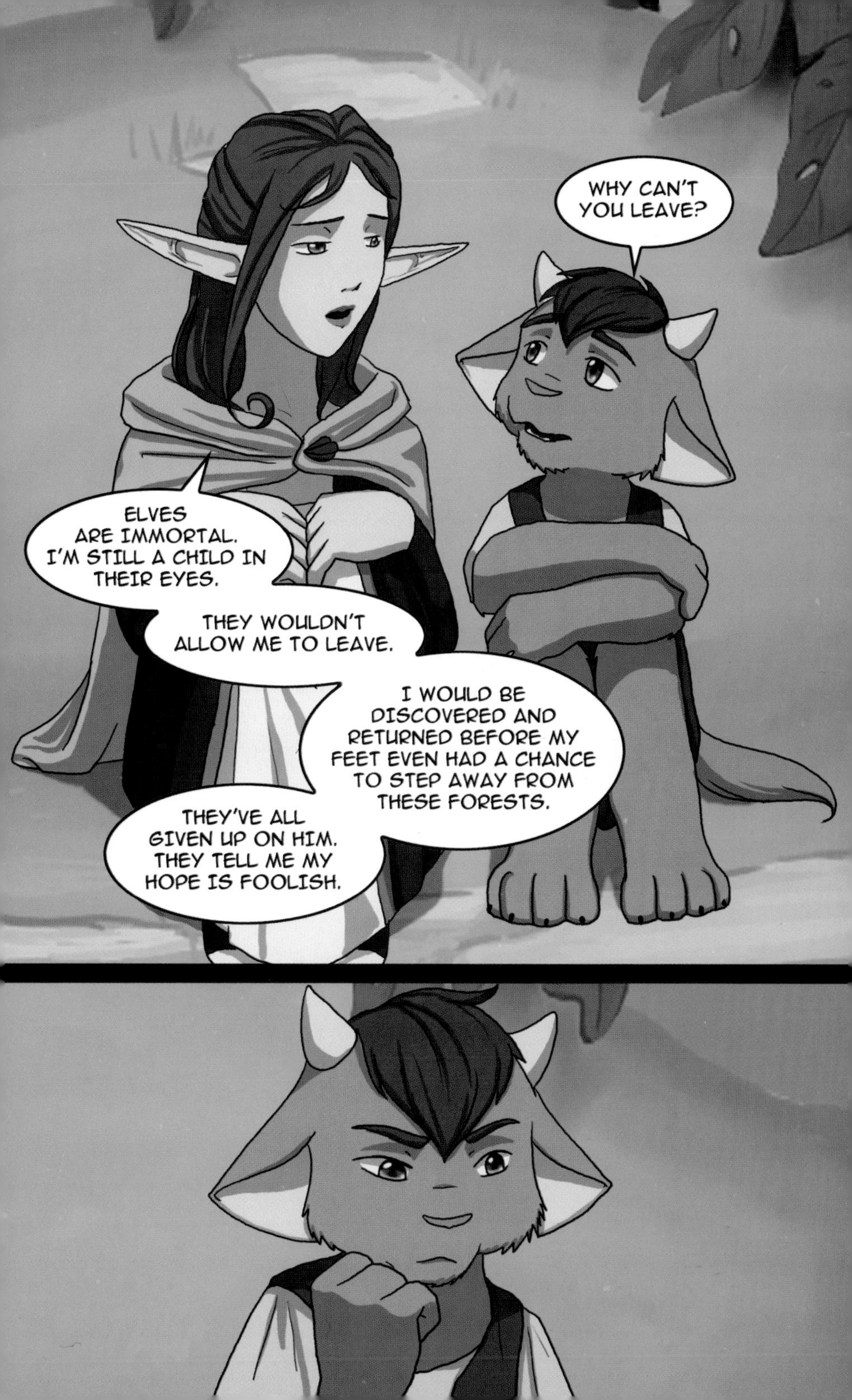
WHY CAN'T YOU LEAVE?
ELVES ARE IMMORTAL. I'M STILL A CHILD IN THEIR EYES.
THEY WOULDN'T ALLOW ME TO LEAVE.
I WOULD BE DISCOVERED AND RETURNED BEFORE MY FEET EVEN HAD A CHANCE TO STEP AWAY FROM THESE FORESTS.
THEY'VE ALL GIVEN UP ON HIM. THEY TELL ME MY HOPE IS FOOLISH.

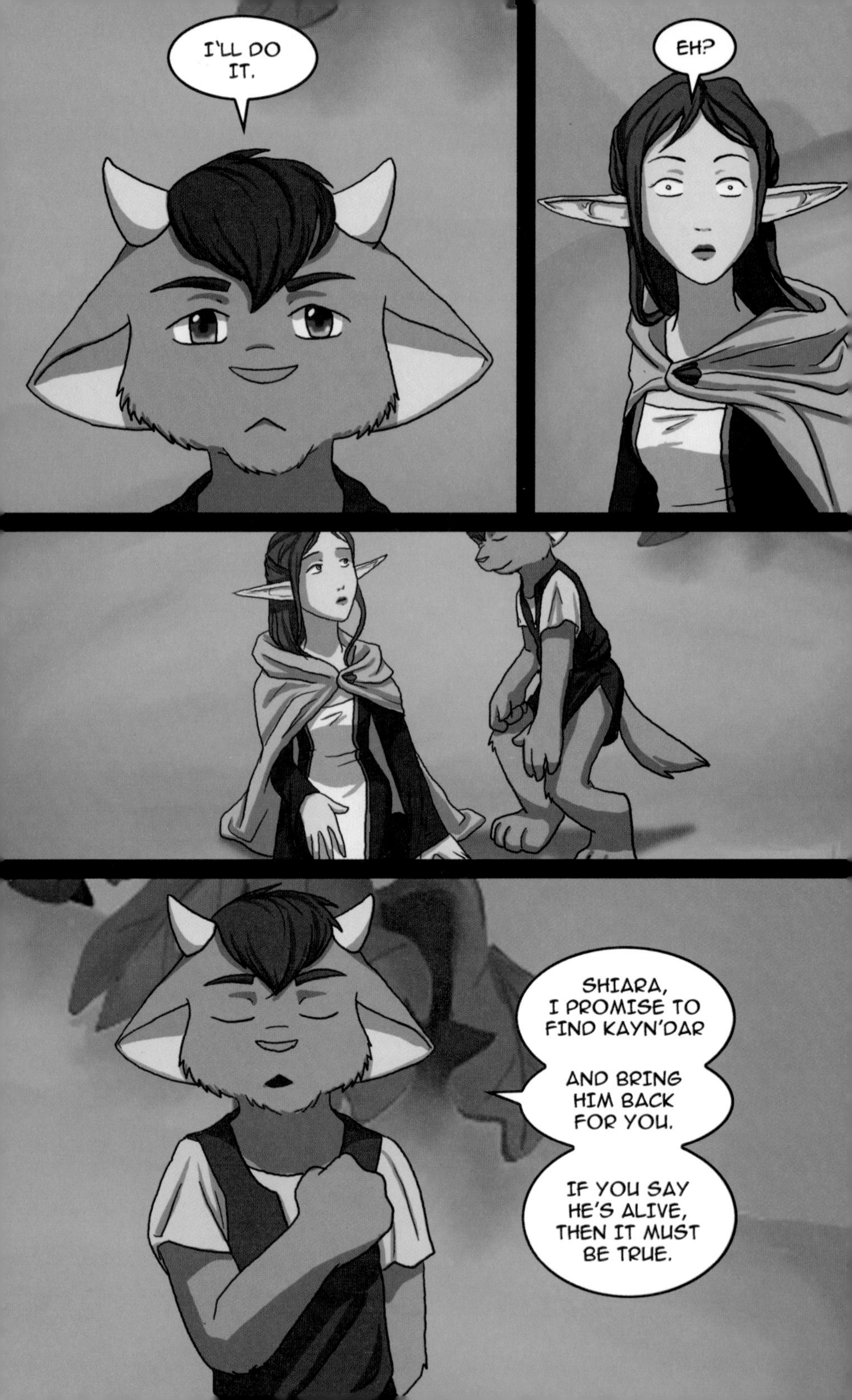
I'LL DO IT.
EH?
SHIARA, I PROMISE TO FIND KAYN'DAR
AND BRING HIM BACK FOR YOU.
IF YOU SAY HE'S ALIVE, THEN IT MUST BE TRUE.

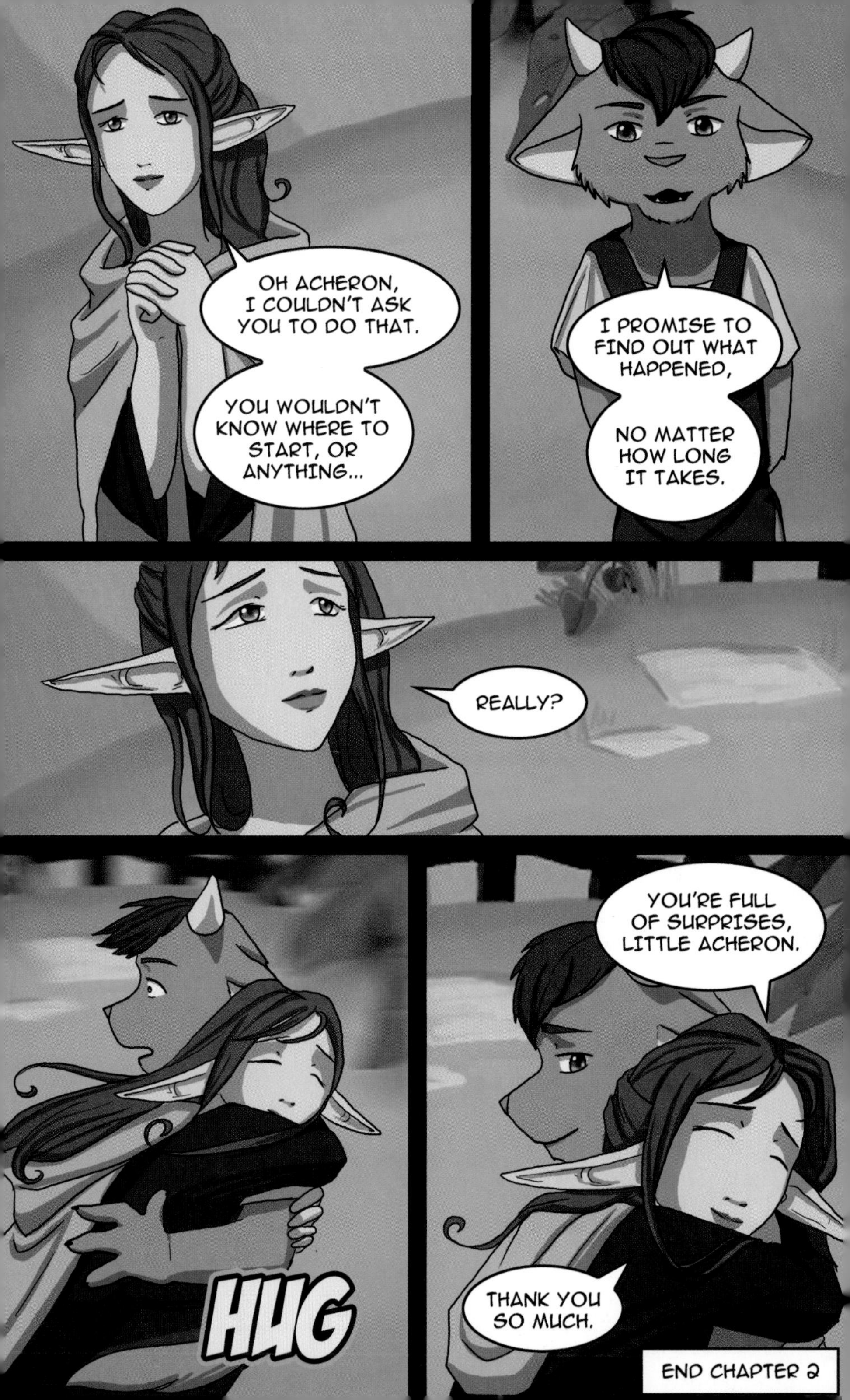
OH ACHERON, I COULDN'T ASK YOU TO DO THAT.
YOU WOULDN'T KNOW WHERE TO START, OR ANYTHING...
I PROMISE TO FIND OUT WHAT HAPPENED,
NO MATTER HOW LONG IT TAKES.
REALLY?
HUG
YOU'RE FULL OF SURPRISES, LITTLE ACHERON.
THANK YOU SO MUCH.
END CHAPTER 2

CHAPTER 3 :ALL THAT IS LEFT BEHIND

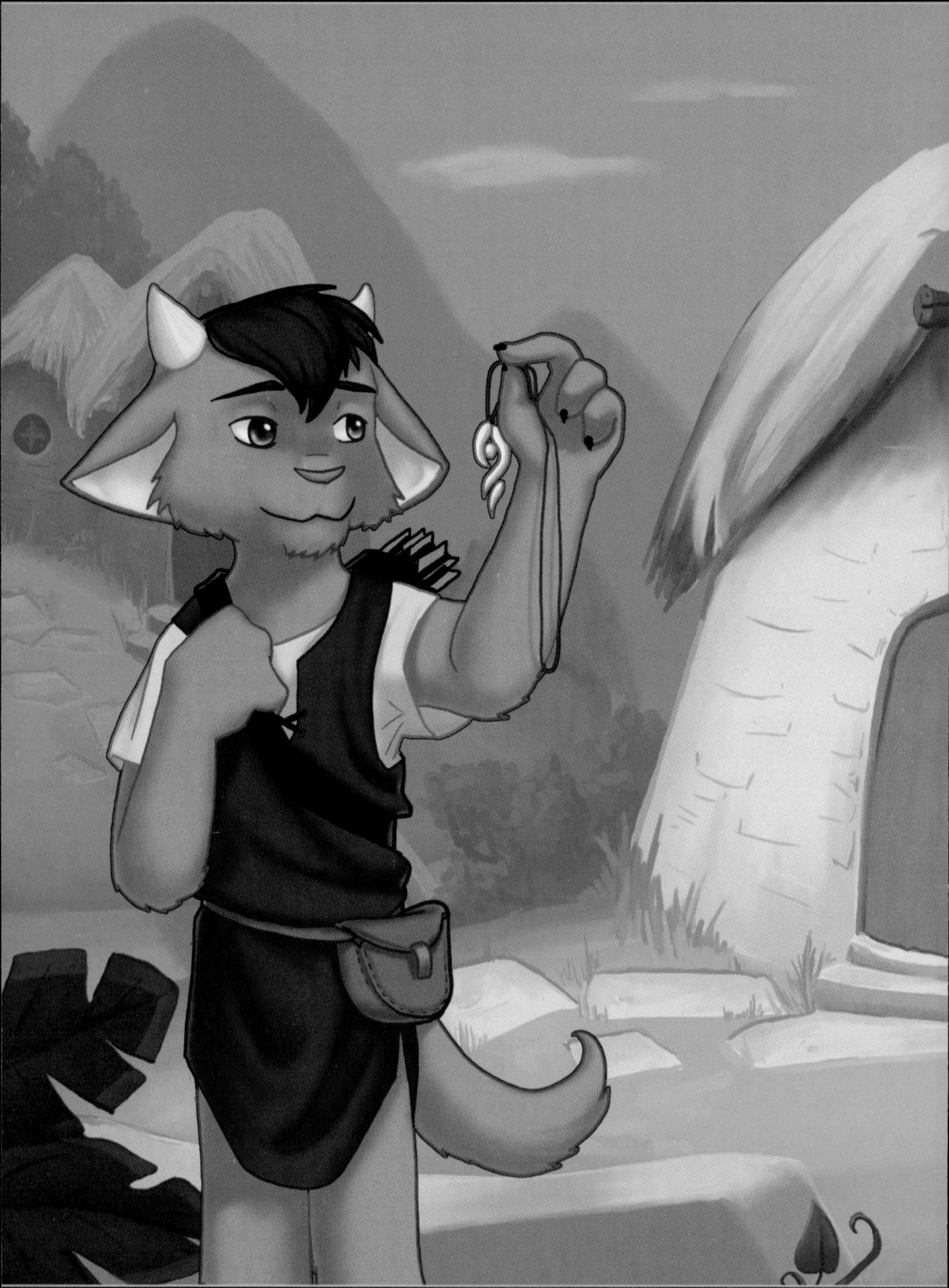

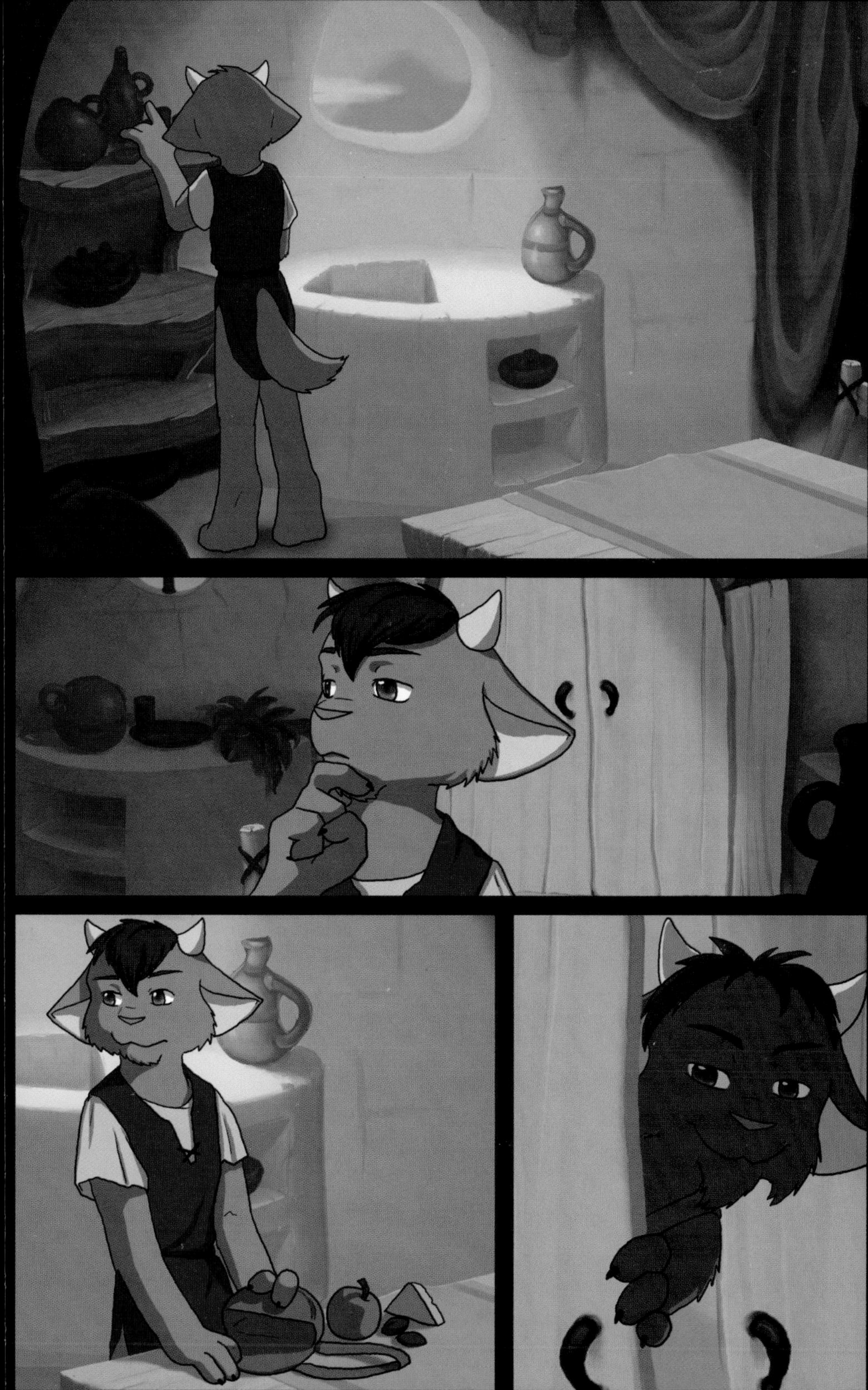

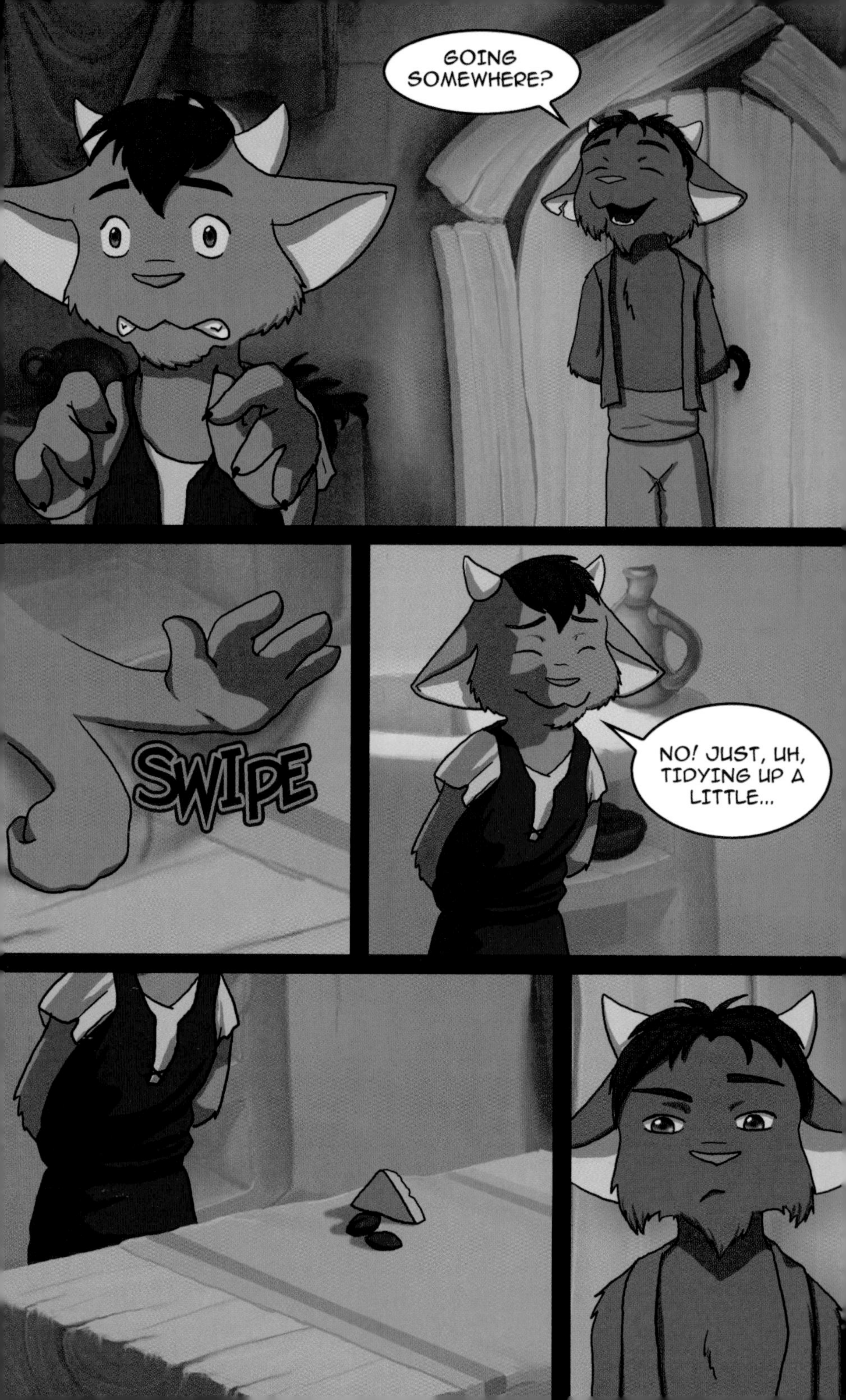
GOING SOMEWHERE?
SWIPE
NO! JUST, UH, TIDYING UP A LITTLE...

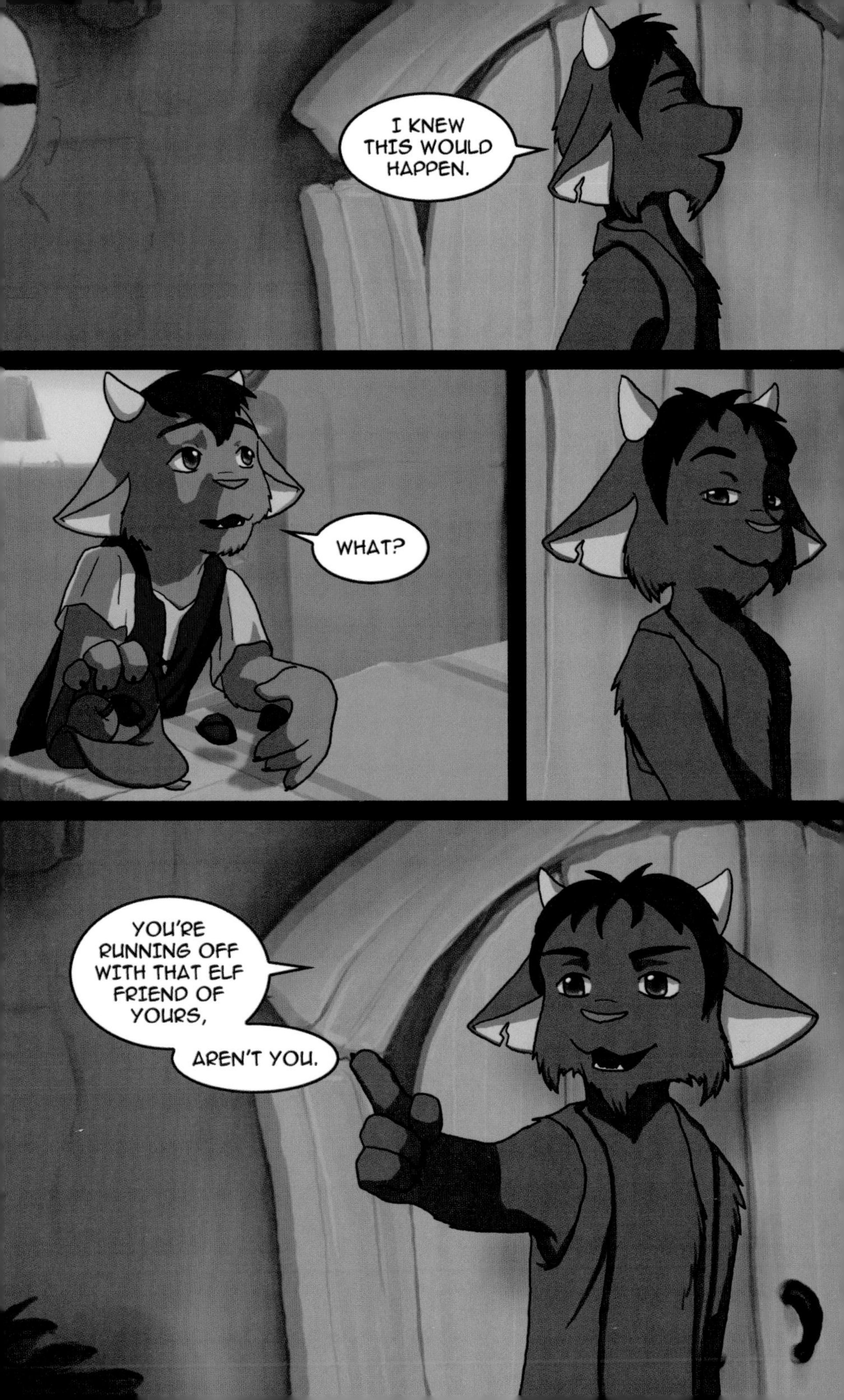
I KNEW THIS WOULD HAPPEN.
WHAT?
YOU'RE RUNNING OFF WITH THAT ELF FRIEND OF YOURS,
AREN'T YOU.

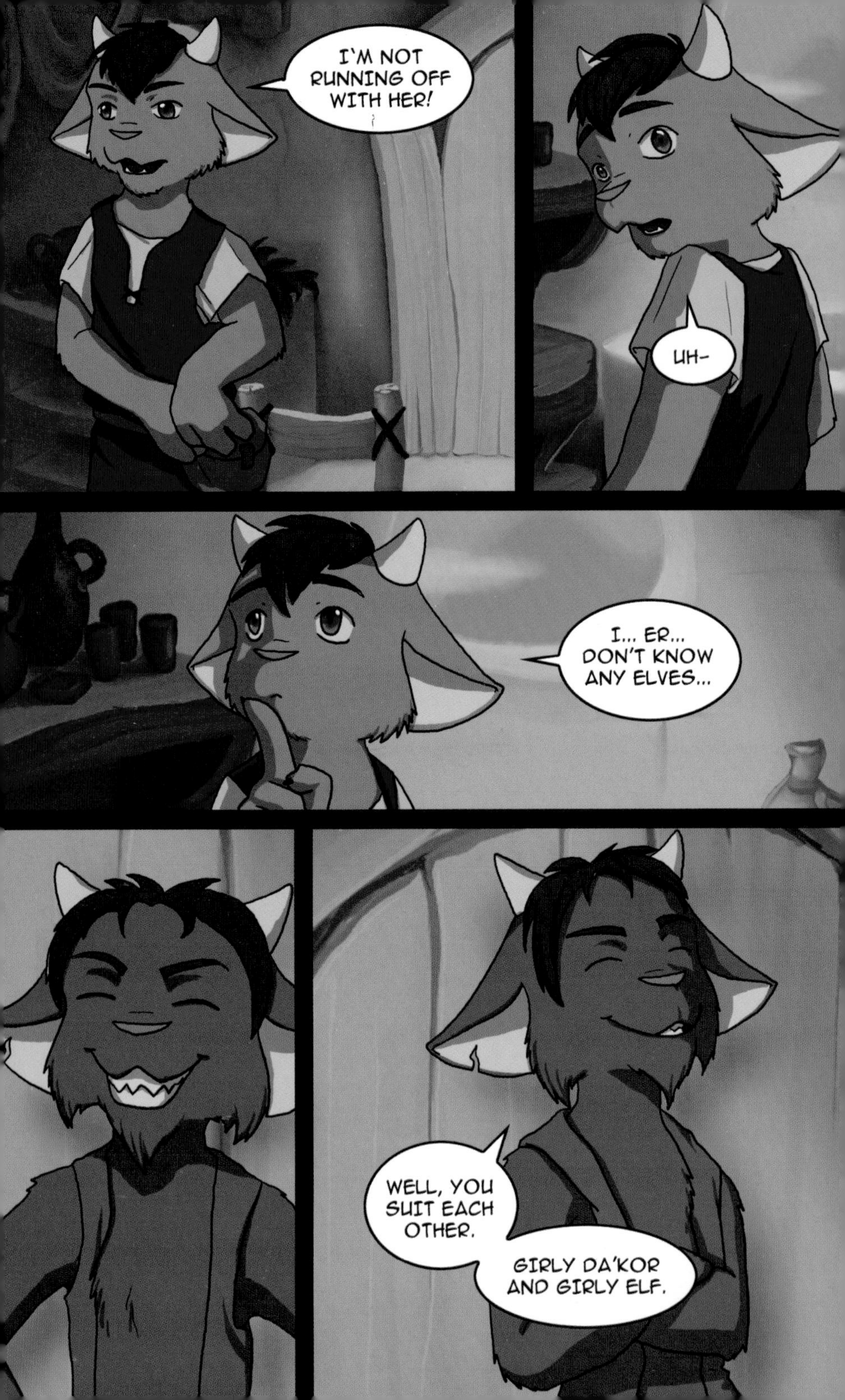
I'M NOT RUNNING OFF WITH HER!
UH-
I... ER... DON'T KNOW ANY ELVES...
WELL, YOU SUIT EACH OTHER.
GIRLY DA'KOR AND GIRLY ELF.

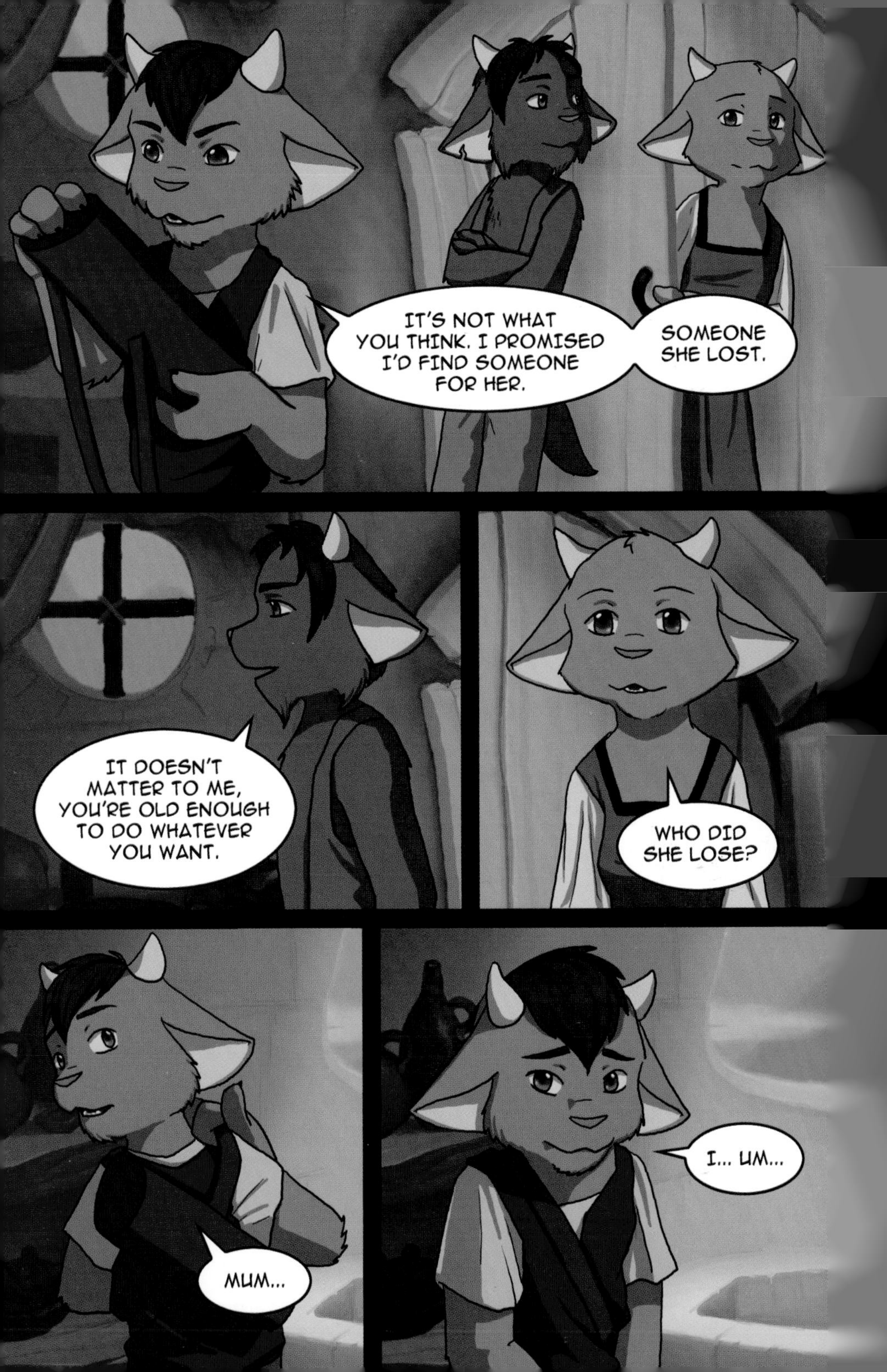
IT'S NOT WHAT YOU THINK. I PROMISED I'D FIND SOMEONE FOR HER.
SOMEONE SHE LOST.
IT DOESN'T MATTER TO ME, YOU'RE OLD ENOUGH TO DO WHATEVER YOU WANT.
WHO DID SHE LOSE?
MUM...
I... UM...

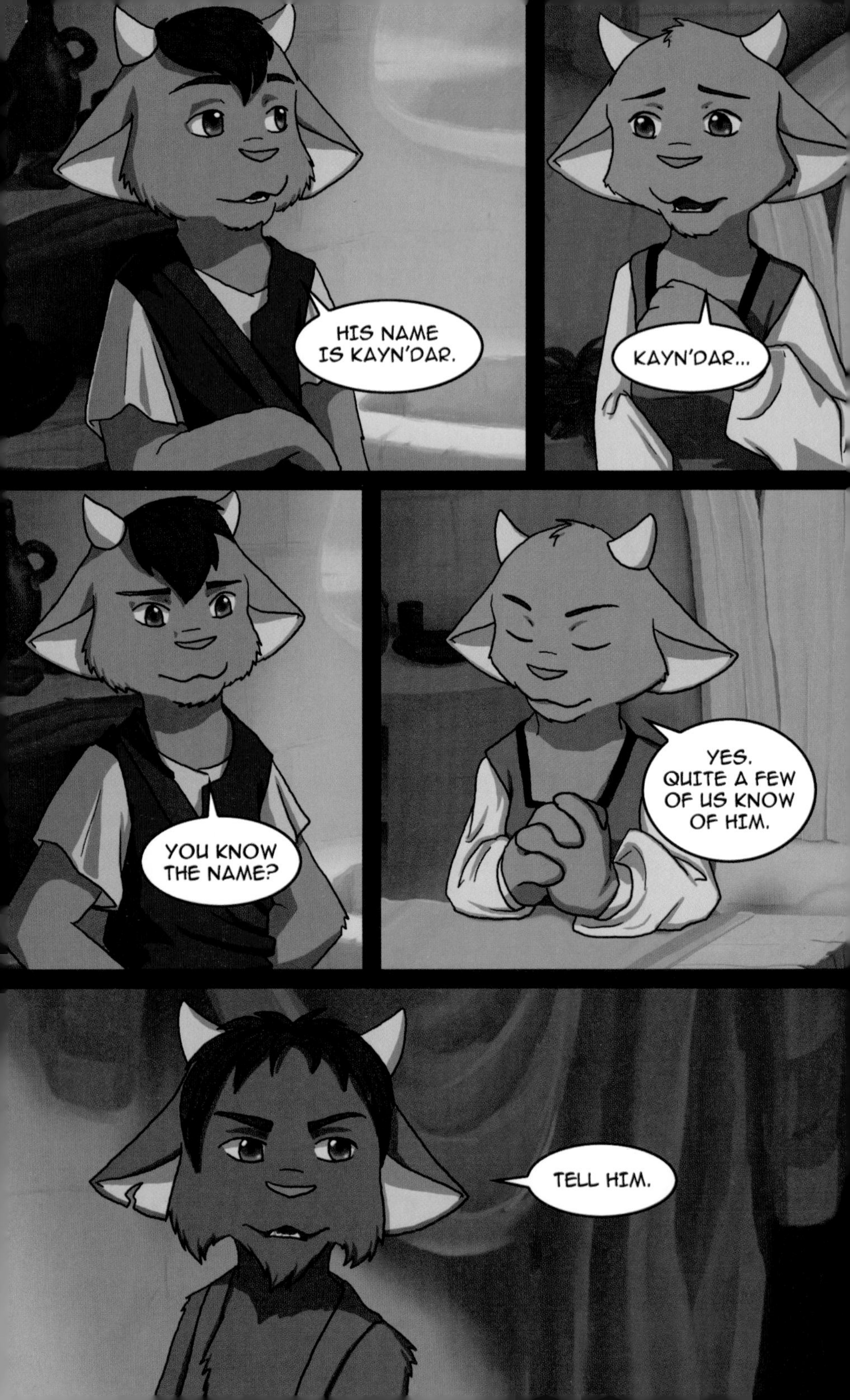
HIS NAME IS KAYN'DAR.
KAYN'DAR...
YOU KNOW THE NAME?
YES. QUITE A FEW OF US KNOW OF HIM.
TELL HIM.

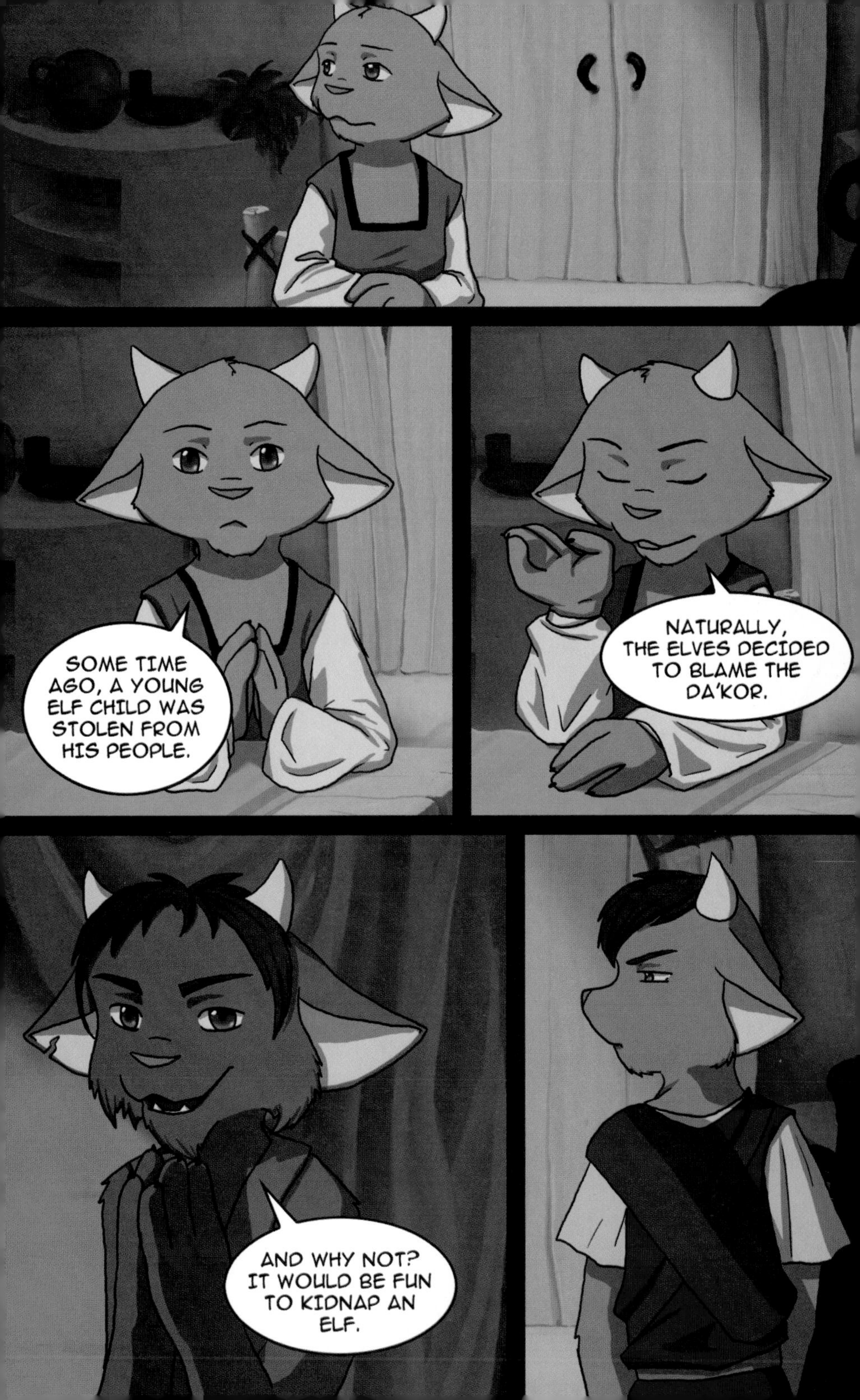
SOME TIME AGO, A YOUNG ELF CHILD WAS STOLEN FROM HIS PEOPLE.
NATURALLY, THE ELVES DECIDED TO BLAME THE DA'KOR.
AND WHY NOT? IT WOULD BE FUN TO KIDNAP AN ELF.

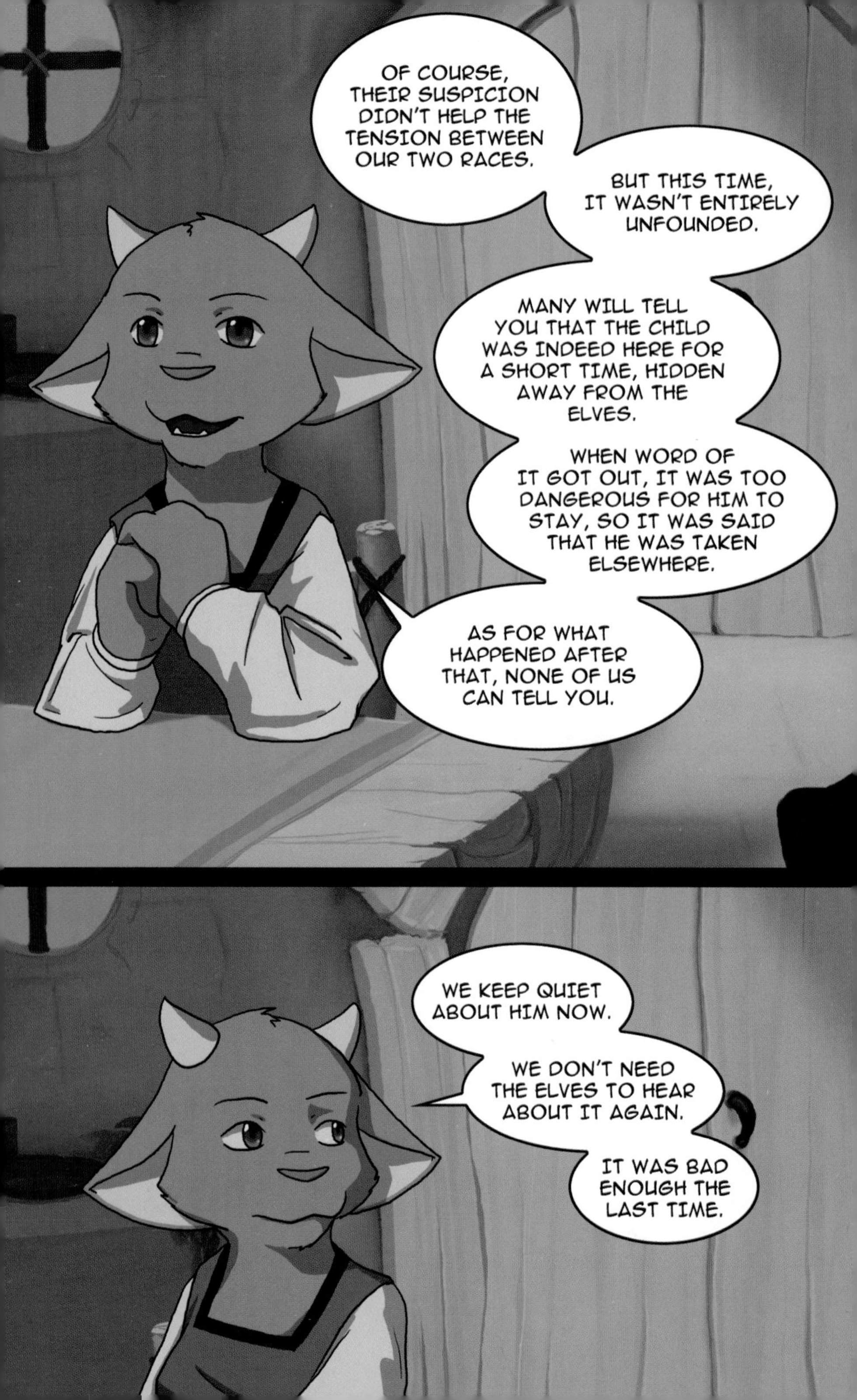
OF COURSE, THEIR SUSPICION DIDN'T HELP THE TENSION BETWEEN OUR TWO RACES.
BUT THIS TIME, IT WASN'T ENTIRELY UNFOUNDED.
MANY WILL TELL YOU THAT THE CHILD WAS INDEED HERE FOR A SHORT TIME, HIDDEN AWAY FROM THE ELVES.
WHEN WORD OF IT GOT OUT, IT WAS TOO DANGEROUS FOR HIM TO STAY, SO IT WAS SAID THAT HE WAS TAKEN ELSEWHERE.
AS FOR WHAT HAPPENED AFTER THAT, NONE OF US CAN TELL YOU.
WE KEEP QUIET ABOUT HIM NOW.
WE DON'T NEED THE ELVES TO HEAR ABOUT IT AGAIN.
IT WAS BAD ENOUGH THE LAST TIME.

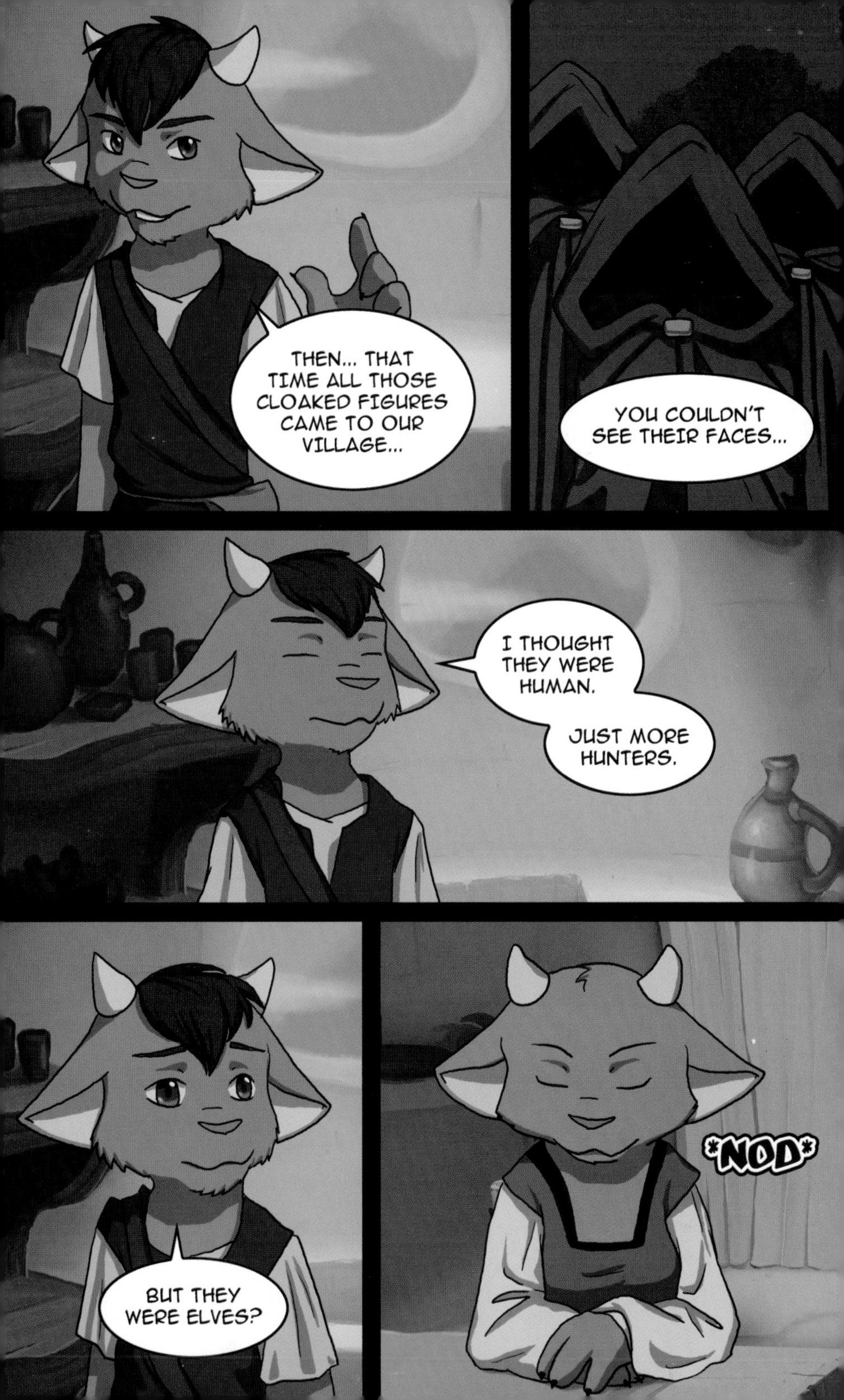
THEN... THAT TIME ALL THOSE CLOAKED FIGURES CAME TO OUR VILLAGE...
YOU COULDN'T SEE THEIR FACES...
I THOUGHT THEY WERE HUMAN.
JUST MORE HUNTERS.
BUT THEY WERE ELVES?
NOD

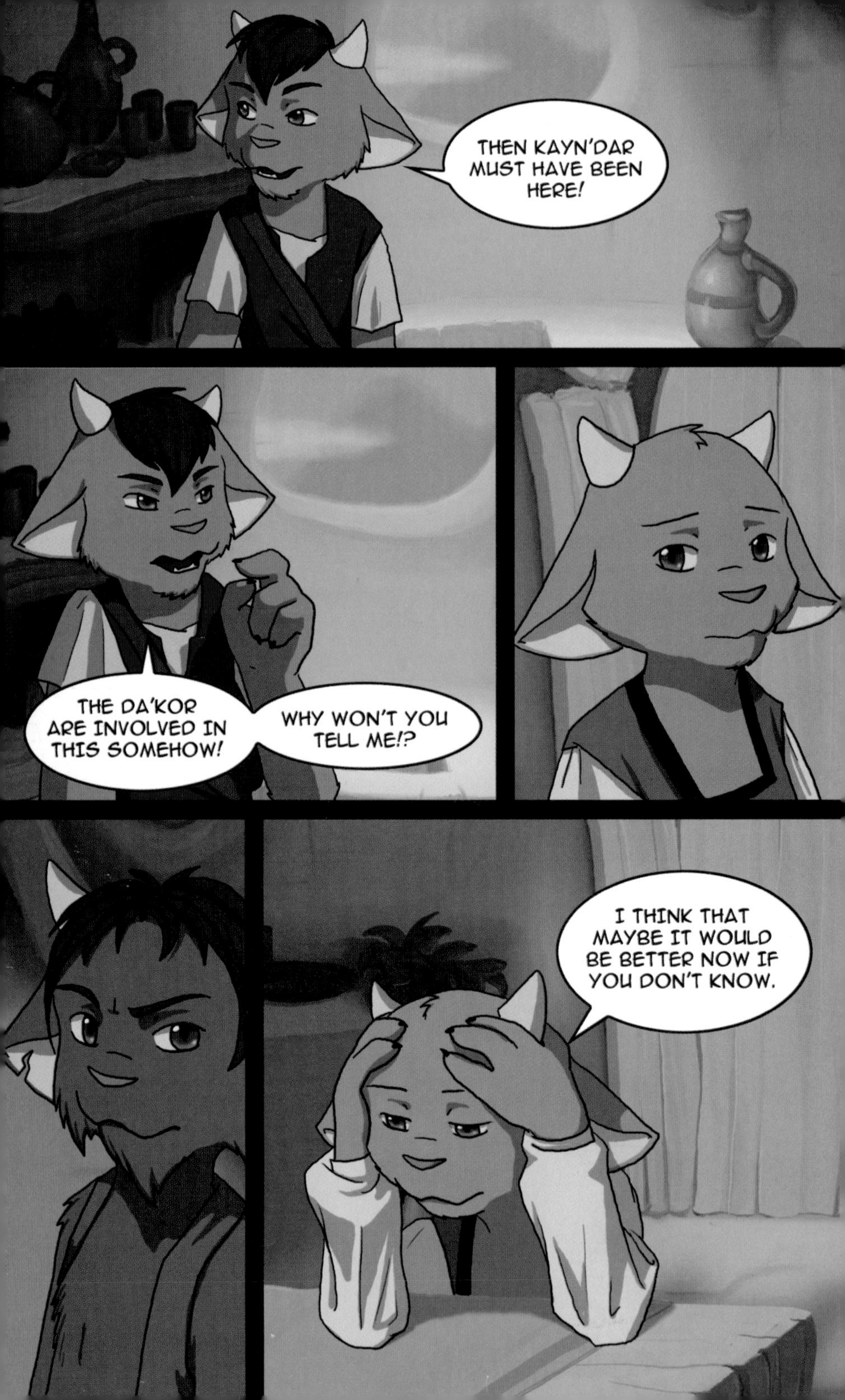
THEN KAYN'DAR MUST HAVE BEEN HERE!
THE DA'KOR ARE INVOLVED IN THIS SOMEHOW!
WHY WON'T YOU TELL ME!?
I THINK THAT MAYBE IT WOULD BE BETTER NOW IF YOU DON'T KNOW.

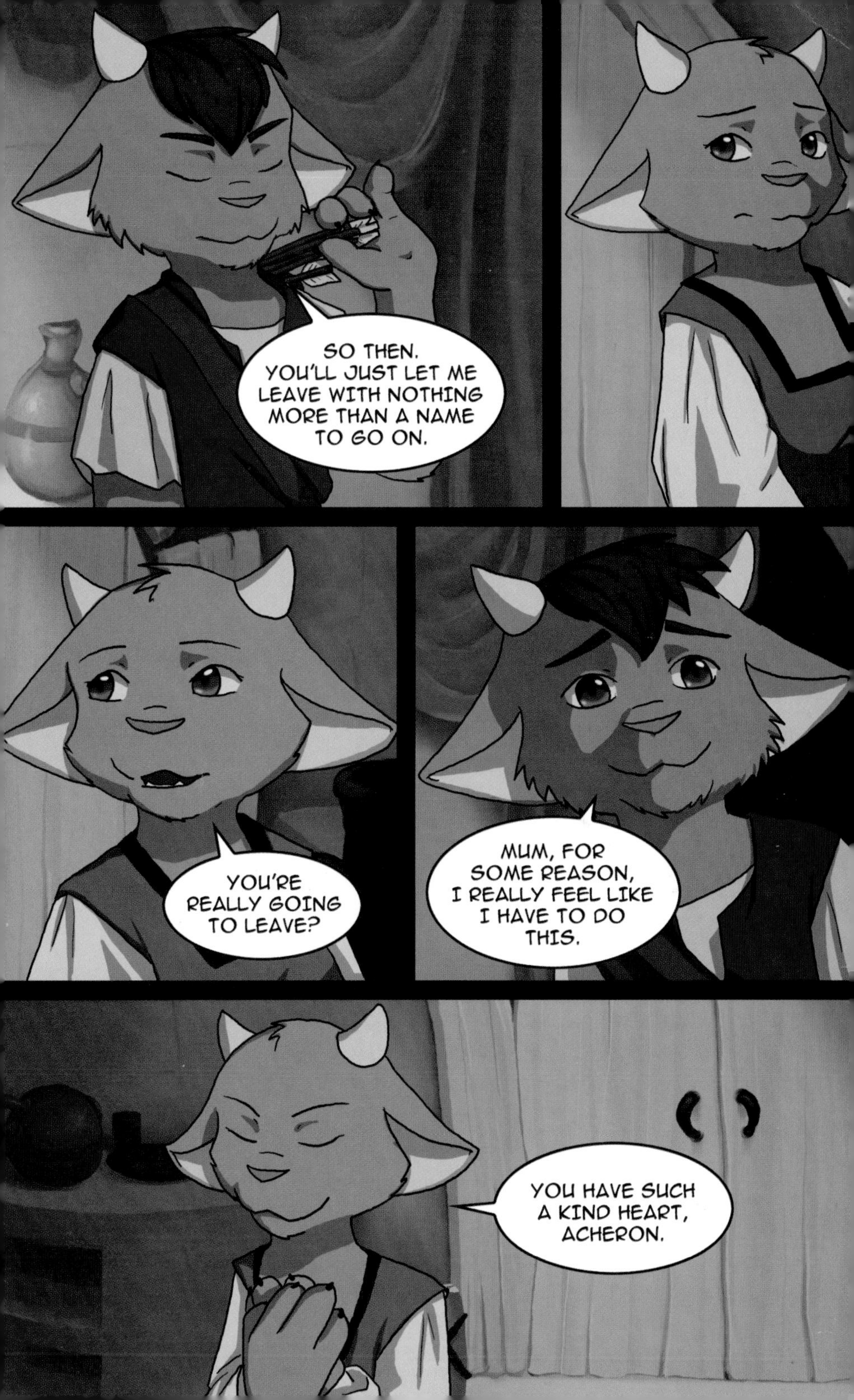
SO THEN. YOU'LL JUST LET ME LEAVE WITH NOTHING MORE THAN A NAME TO GO ON.
YOU'RE REALLY GOING TO LEAVE?
MUM, FOR SOME REASON, I REALLY FEEL LIKE I HAVE TO DO THIS.
YOU HAVE SUCH A KIND HEART, ACHERON.

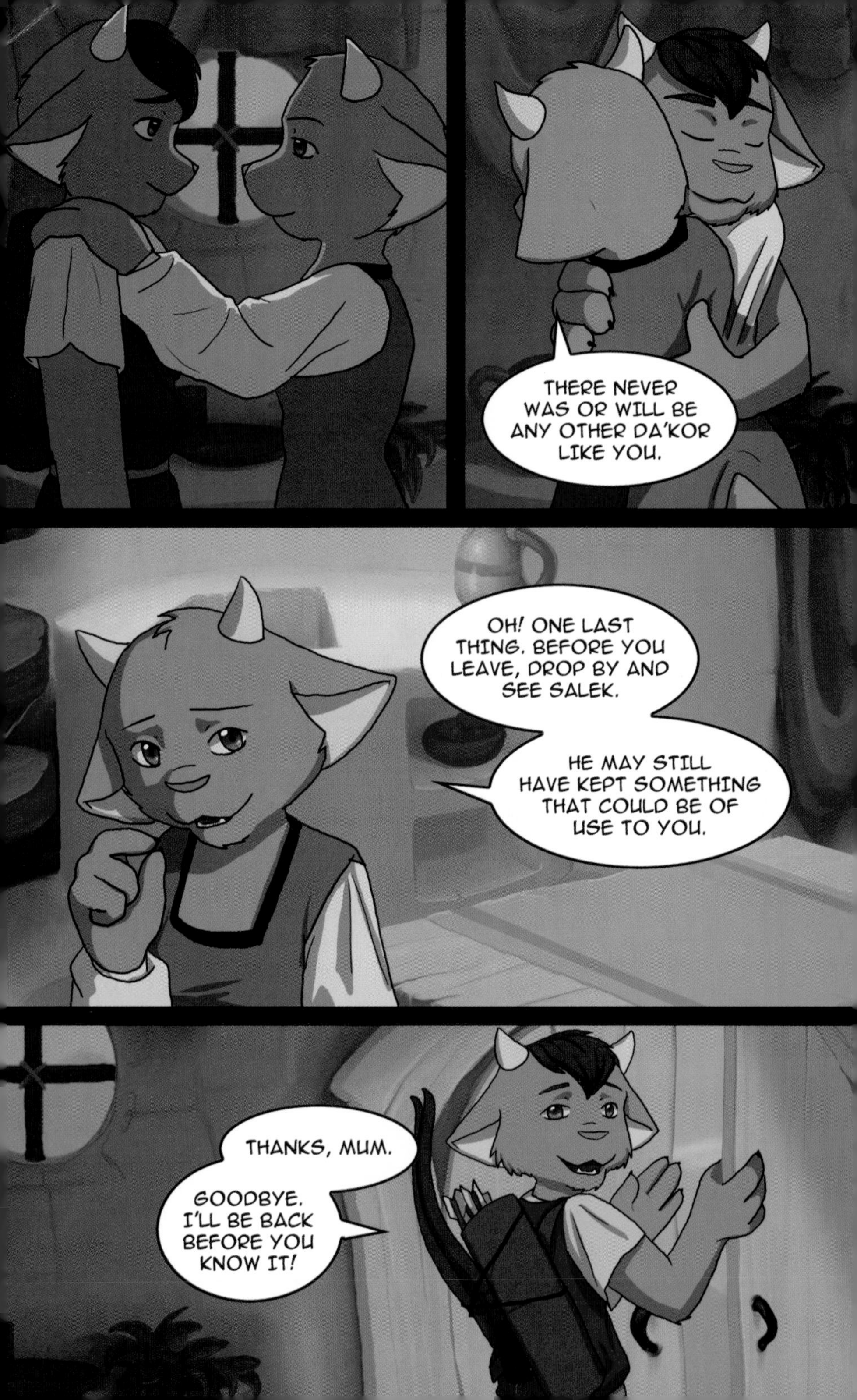
THERE NEVER WAS OR WILL BE ANY OTHER DA'KOR LIKE YOU.
OH! ONE LAST THING. BEFORE YOU LEAVE, DROP BY AND SEE SALEK.
HE MAY STILL HAVE KEPT SOMETHING THAT COULD BE OF USE TO YOU.
THANKS, MUM.
GOODBYE. I'LL BE BACK BEFORE YOU KNOW IT!

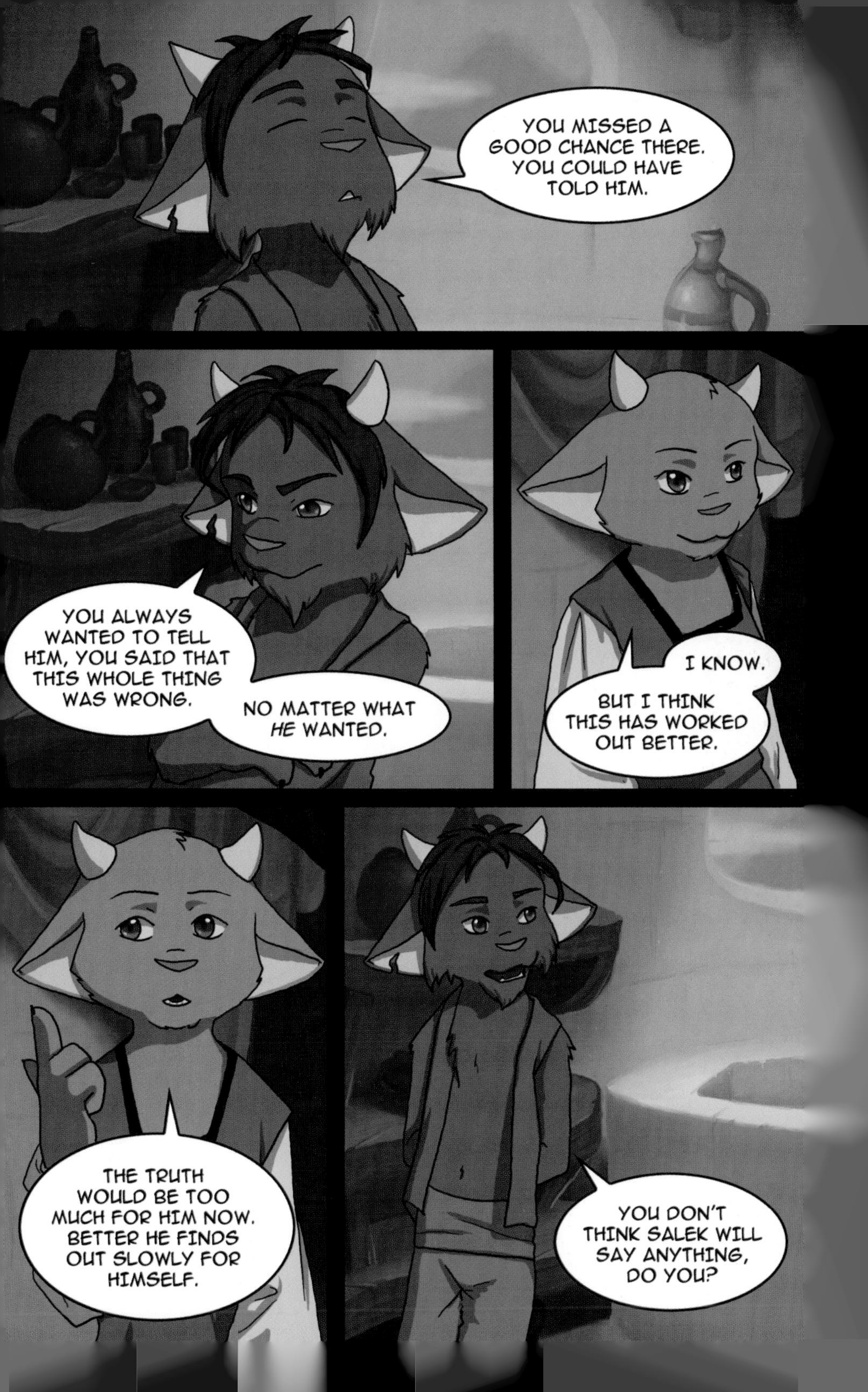
YOU MISSED A GOOD CHANCE THERE. YOU COULD HAVE TOLD HIM.
YOU ALWAYS WANTED TO TELL HIM, YOU SAID THAT THIS WHOLE THING WAS WRONG.
NO MATTER WHAT HE WANTED.
I KNOW.
BUT I THINK THIS HAS WORKED OUT BETTER.
THE TRUTH WOULD BE TOO MUCH FOR HIM NOW. BETTER HE FINDS OUT SLOWLY FOR HIMSELF.
YOU DON'T THINK SALEK WILL SAY ANYTHING, DO YOU?

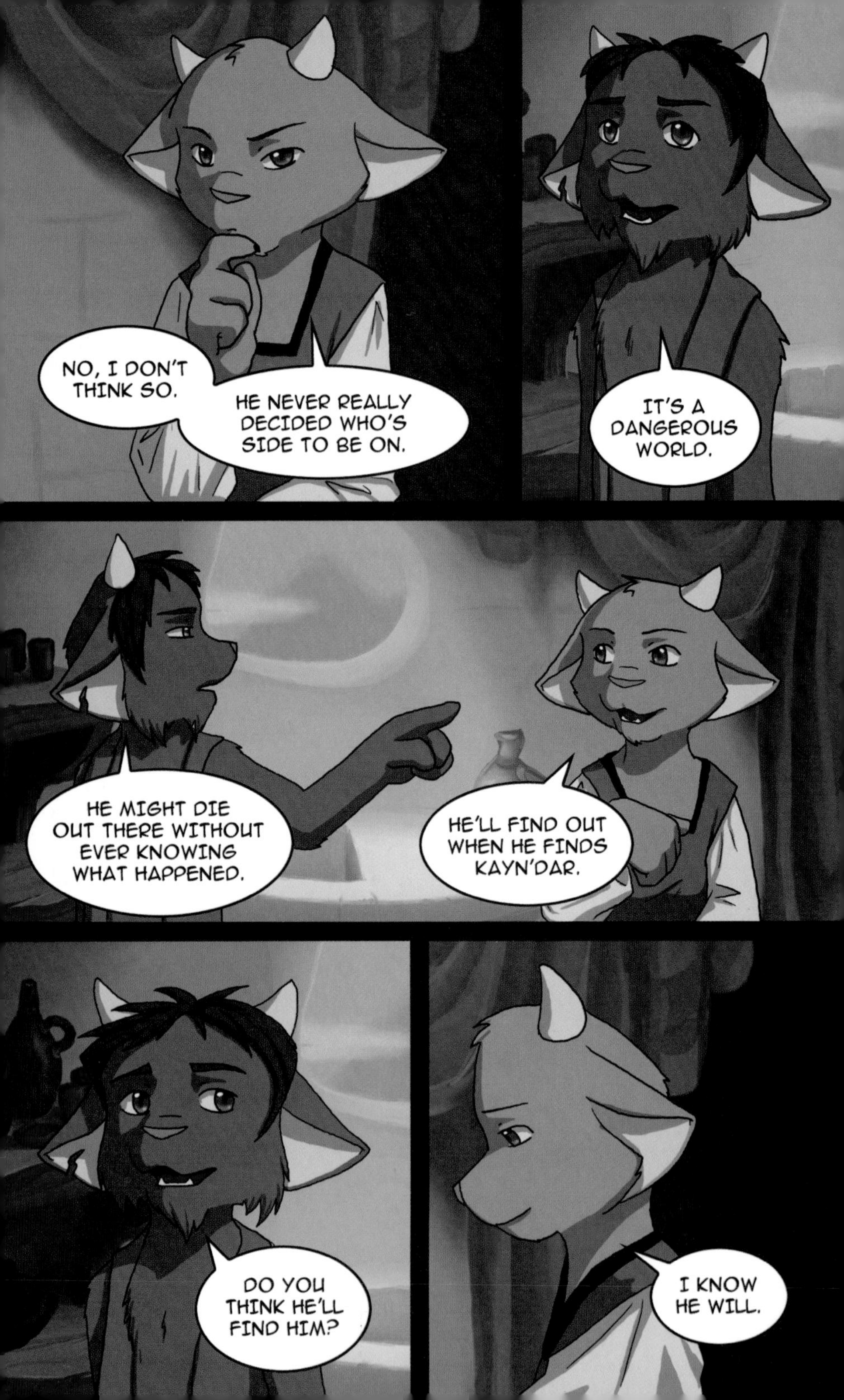
NO, I DON'T THINK SO.
HE NEVER REALLY DECIDED WHO'S SIDE TO BE ON.
IT'S A DANGEROUS WORLD.
HE MIGHT DIE OUT THERE WITHOUT EVER KNOWING WHAT HAPPENED.
HE'LL FIND OUT WHEN HE FINDS KAYN'DAR.
DO YOU THINK HE'LL FIND HIM?
I KNOW HE WILL.

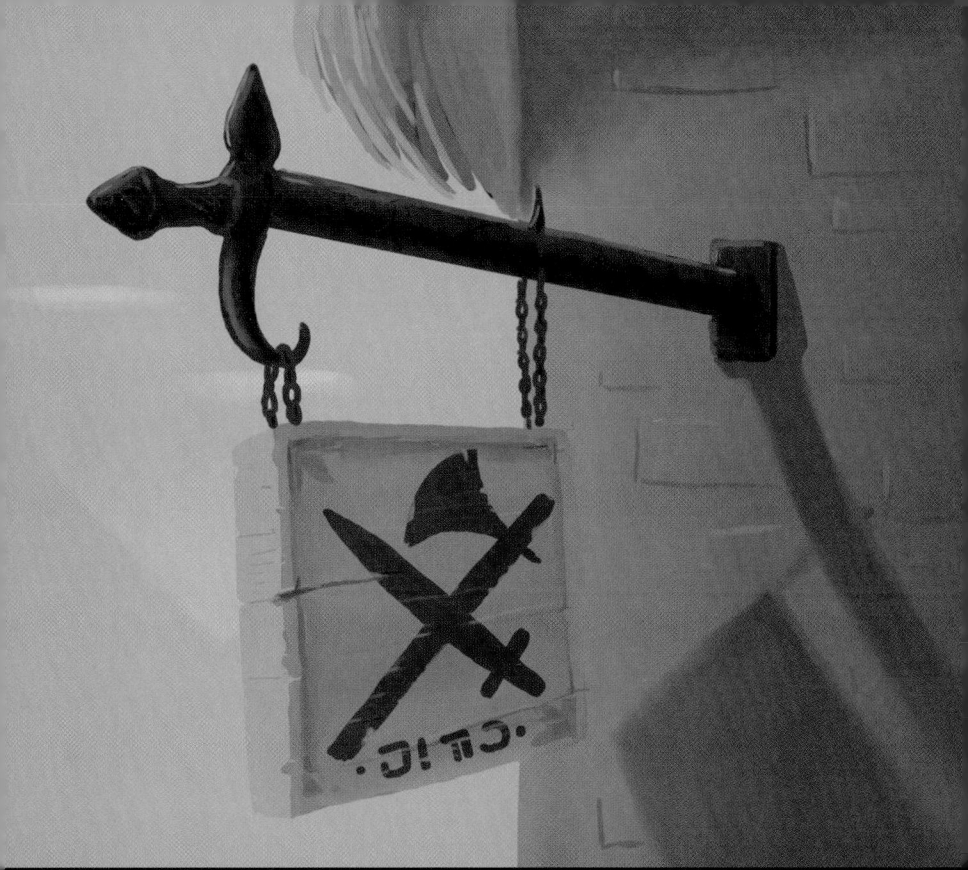

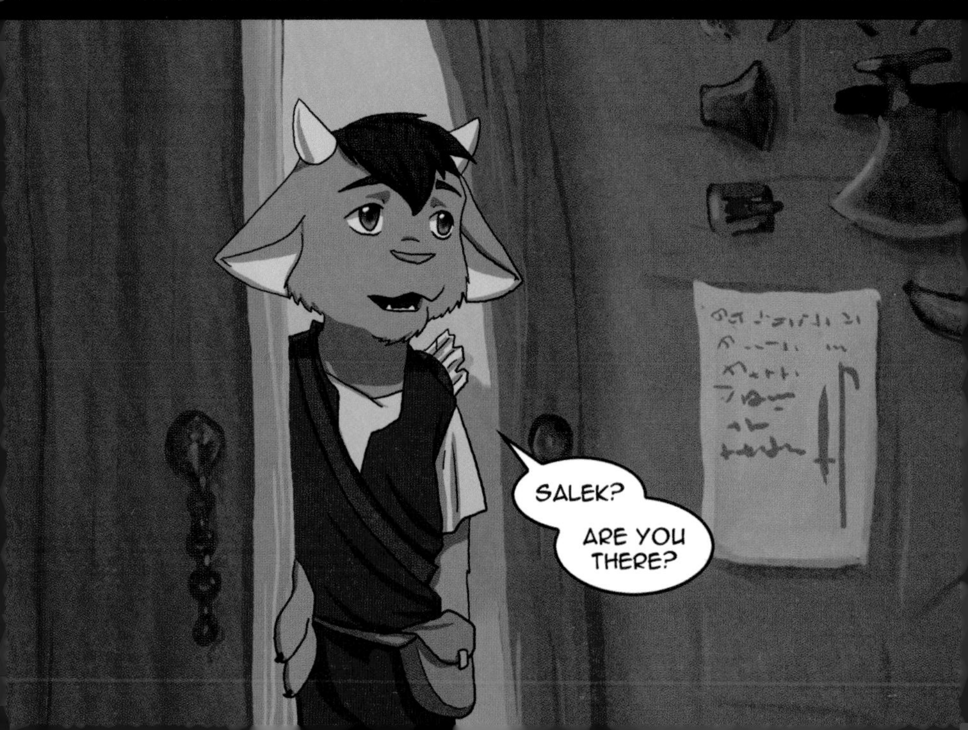
SALEK?
ARE YOU THERE?

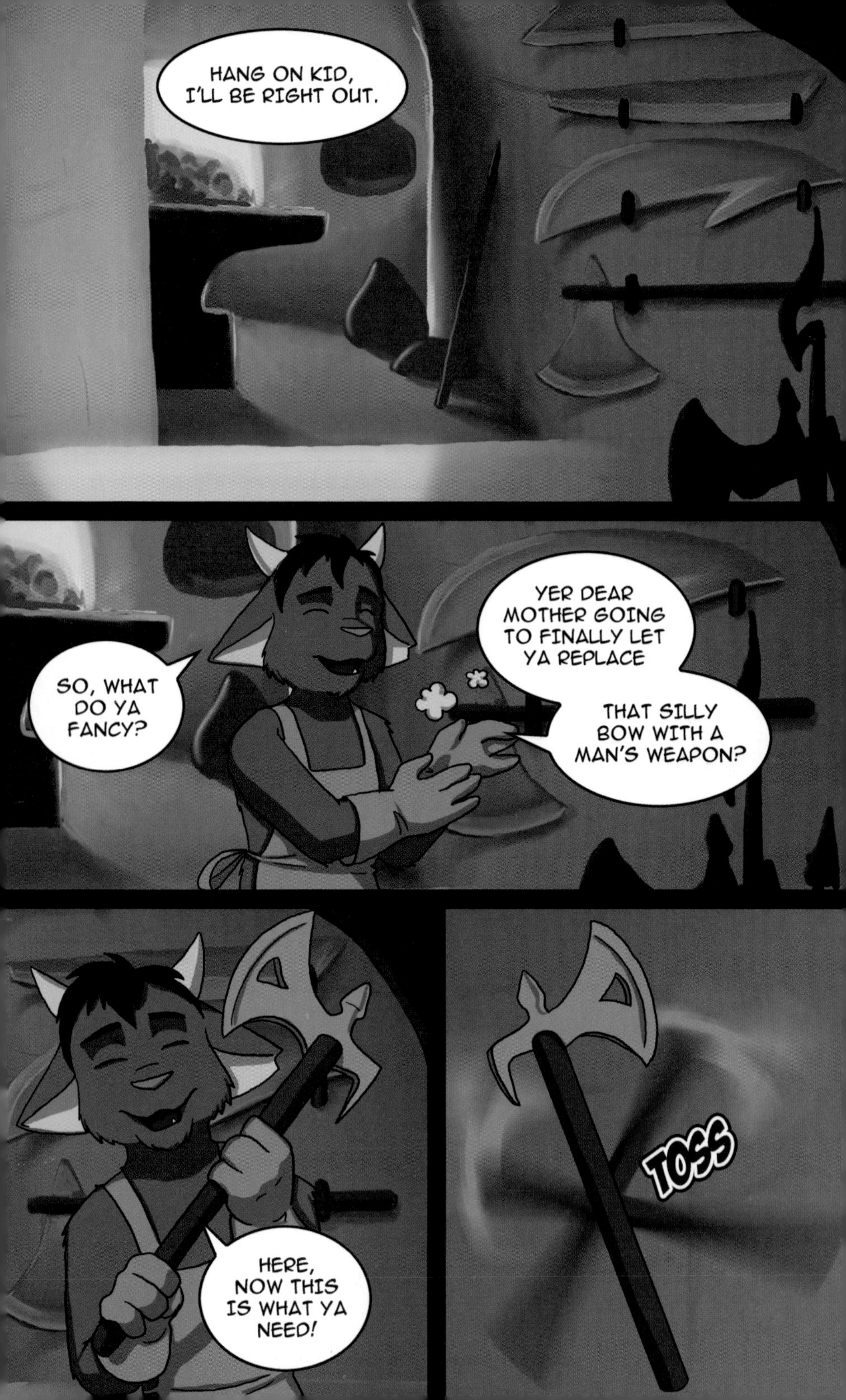
HANG ON KID, I'LL BE RIGHT OUT.
SO, WHAT DO YA FANCY?
YER DEAR MOTHER GOING TO FINALLY LET YA REPLACE
THAT SILLY BOW WITH A MAN'S WEAPON?
HERE, NOW THIS IS WHAT YA NEED!
TOSS

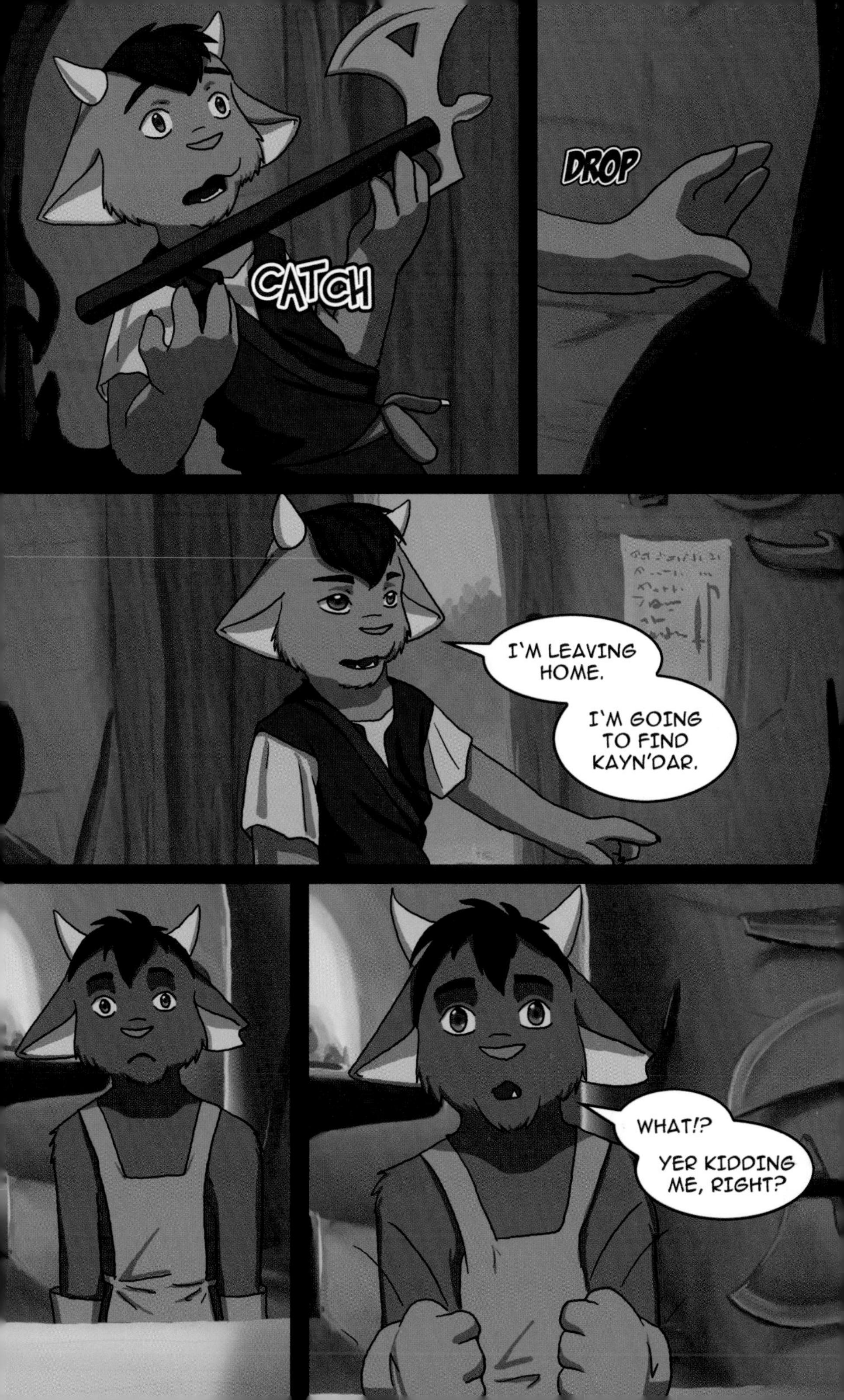
CATCH
DROP
I'M LEAVING HOME.
I'M GOING TO FIND KAYN'DAR.
WHAT!?
YER KIDDING ME, RIGHT?

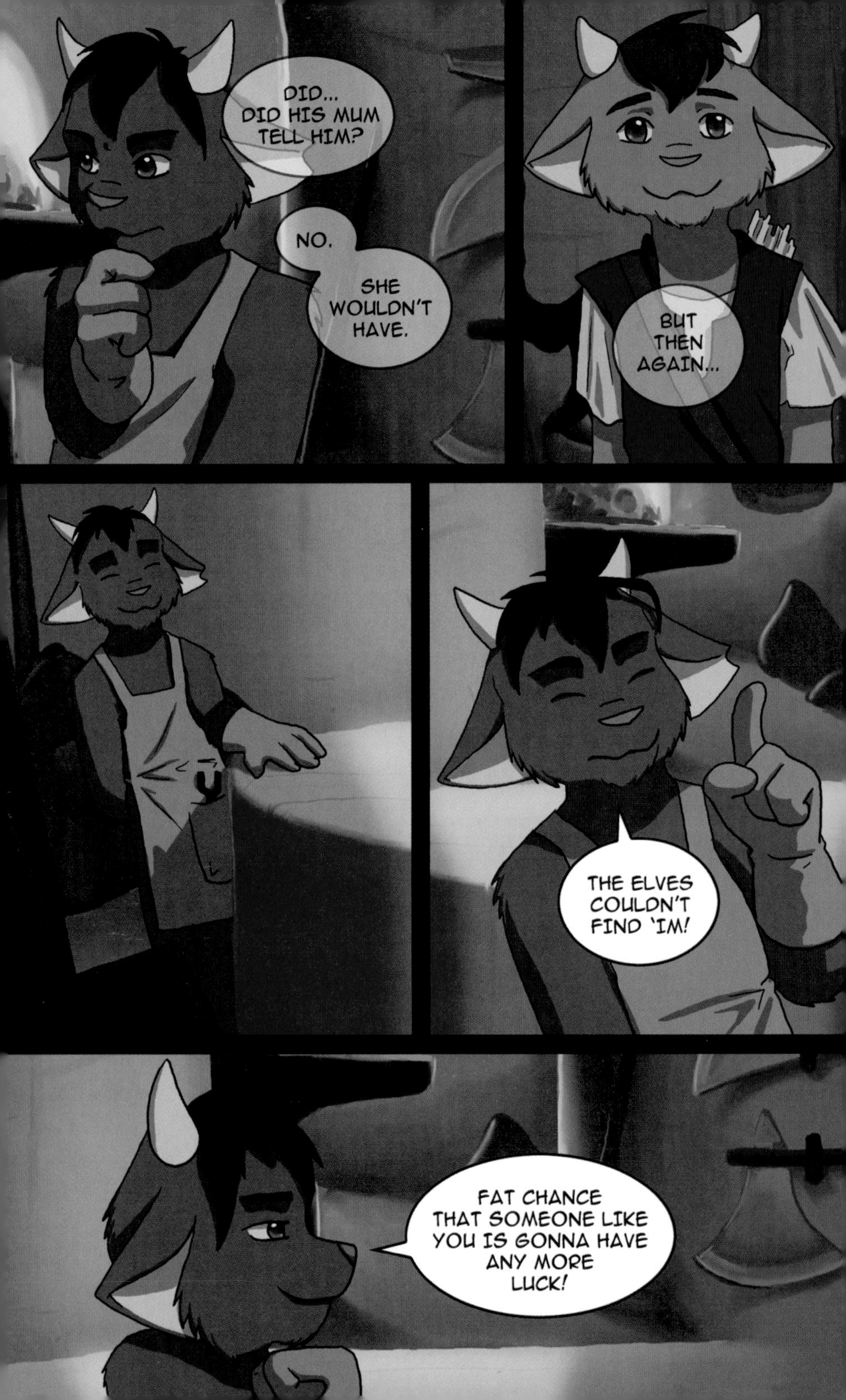
DID...
DID HIS MUM
TELL HIM?
NO.
SHE
WOULDN'T
HAVE.
BUT
THEN
AGAIN...
THE ELVES
COULDN'T
FIND 'IM!
FAT CHANCE
THAT SOMEONE LIKE
YOU IS GONNA HAVE
ANY MORE
LUCK!

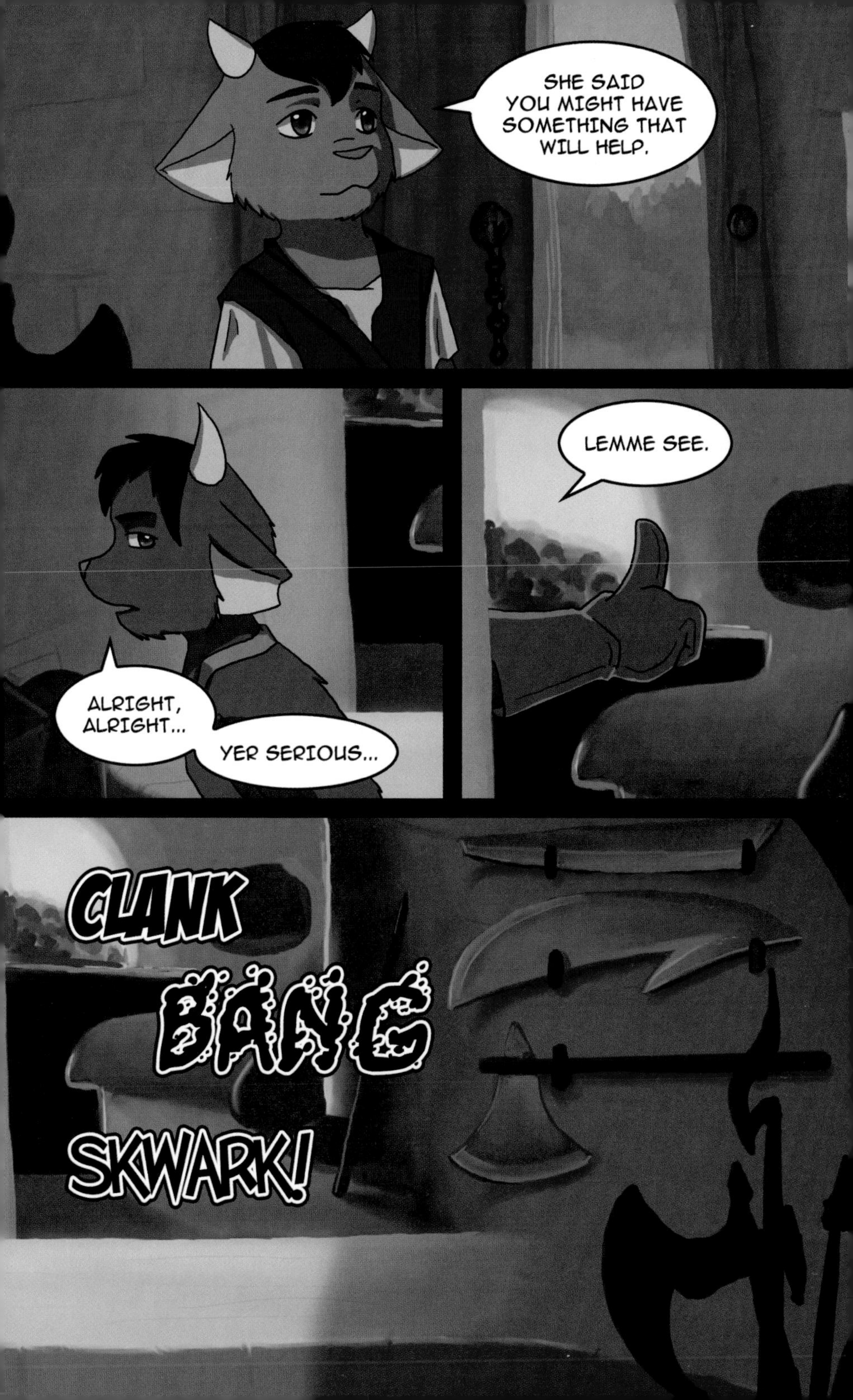
SHE SAID YOU MIGHT HAVE SOMETHING THAT WILL HELP.
ALRIGHT, ALRIGHT...
YER SERIOUS...
LEMME SEE.
CLANK
BANG
SKWARK!

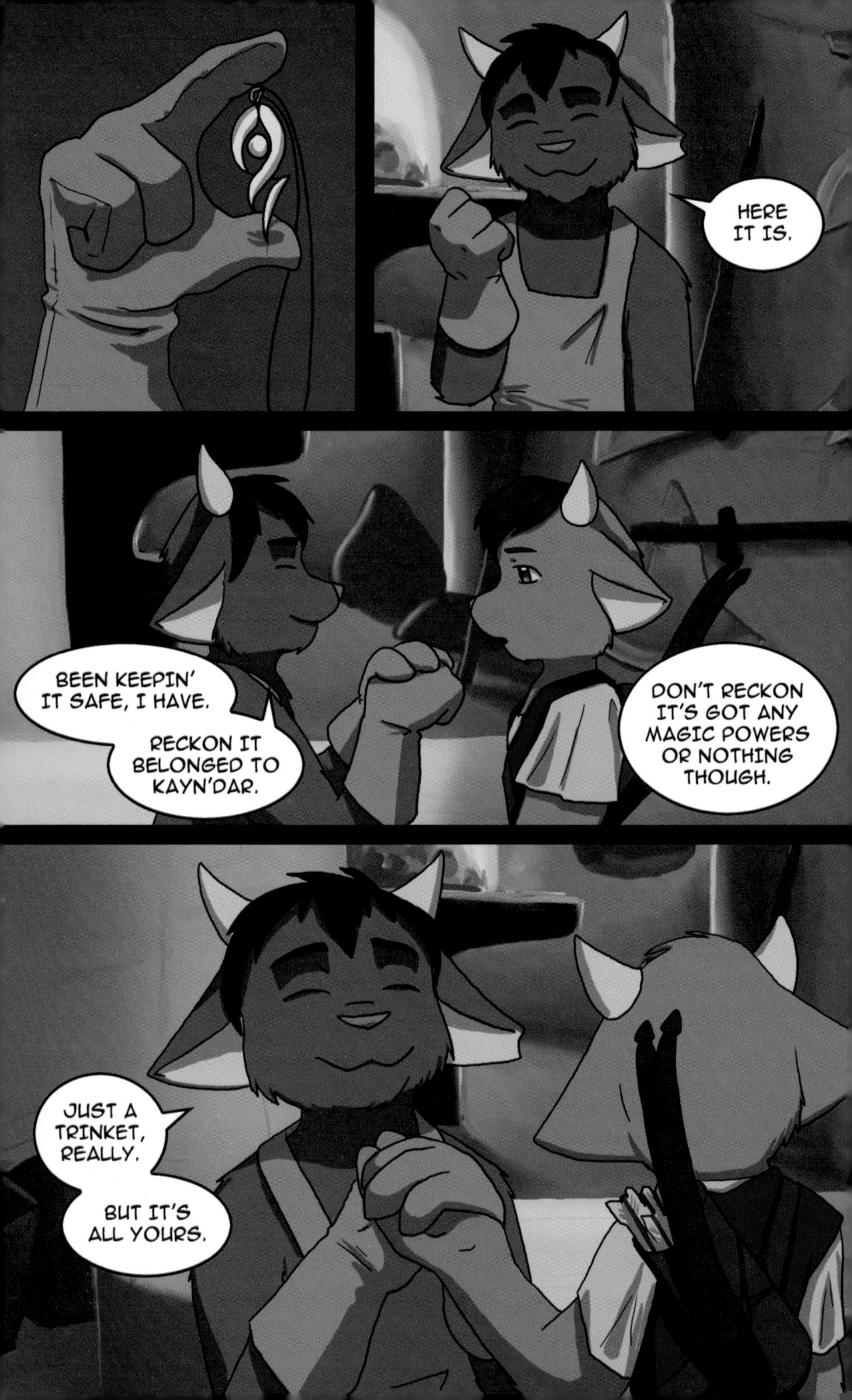
HERE IT IS.
BEEN KEEPIN' IT SAFE, I HAVE.
RECKON IT BELONGED TO KAYN'DAR.
DON'T RECKON IT'S GOT ANY MAGIC POWERS OR NOTHING THOUGH.
JUST A TRINKET, REALLY.
BUT IT'S ALL YOURS.

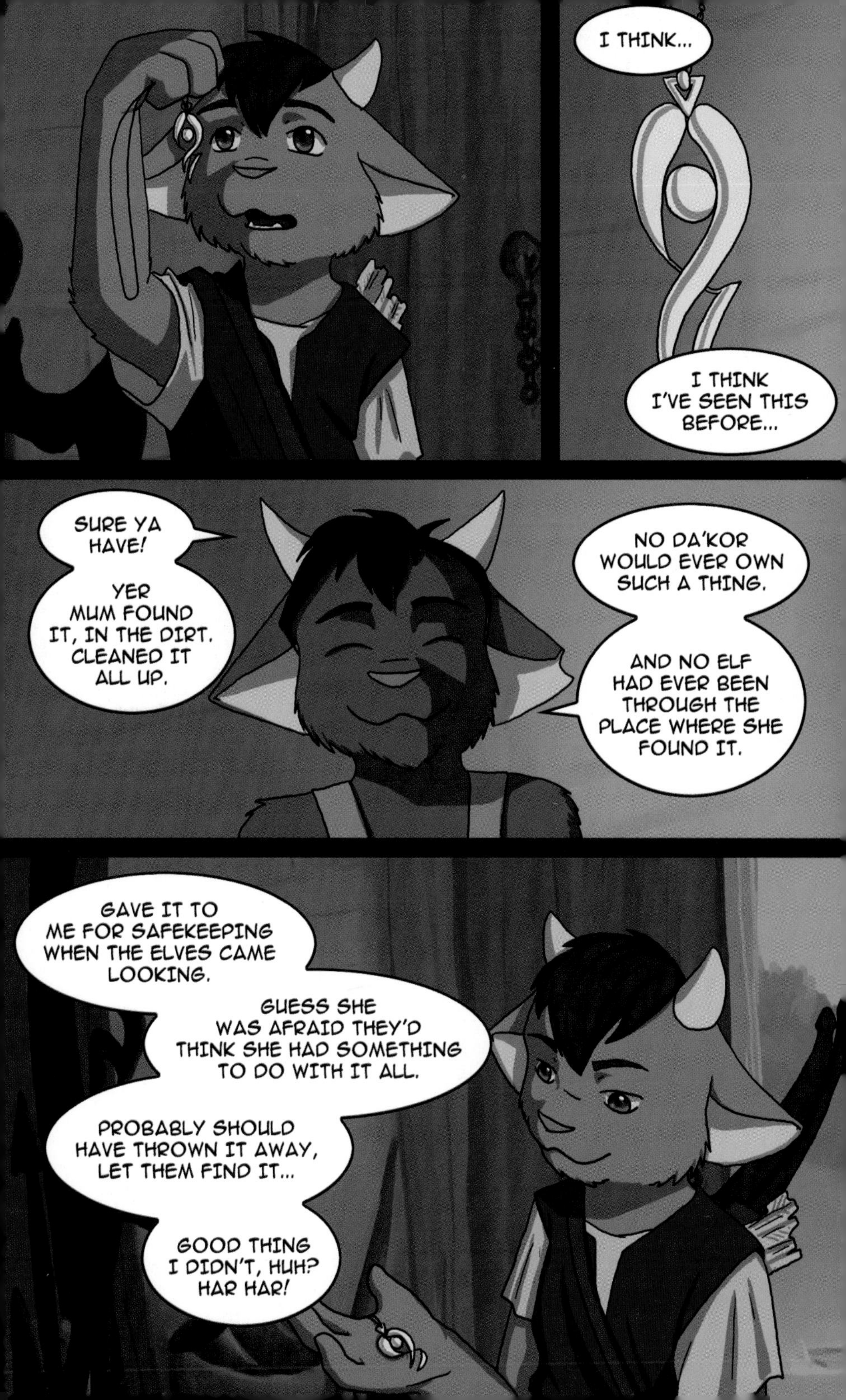
I THINK...
I THINK I'VE SEEN THIS BEFORE...
SURE YA HAVE!
YER MUM FOUND IT, IN THE DIRT. CLEANED IT ALL UP.
NO DA'KOR WOULD EVER OWN SUCH A THING.
AND NO ELF HAD EVER BEEN THROUGH THE PLACE WHERE SHE FOUND IT.
GAVE IT TO ME FOR SAFEKEEPING WHEN THE ELVES CAME LOOKING.
GUESS SHE WAS AFRAID THEY'D THINK SHE HAD SOMETHING TO DO WITH IT ALL.
PROBABLY SHOULD HAVE THROWN IT AWAY, LET THEM FIND IT...
GOOD THING I DIDN'T, HUH? HAR HAR!

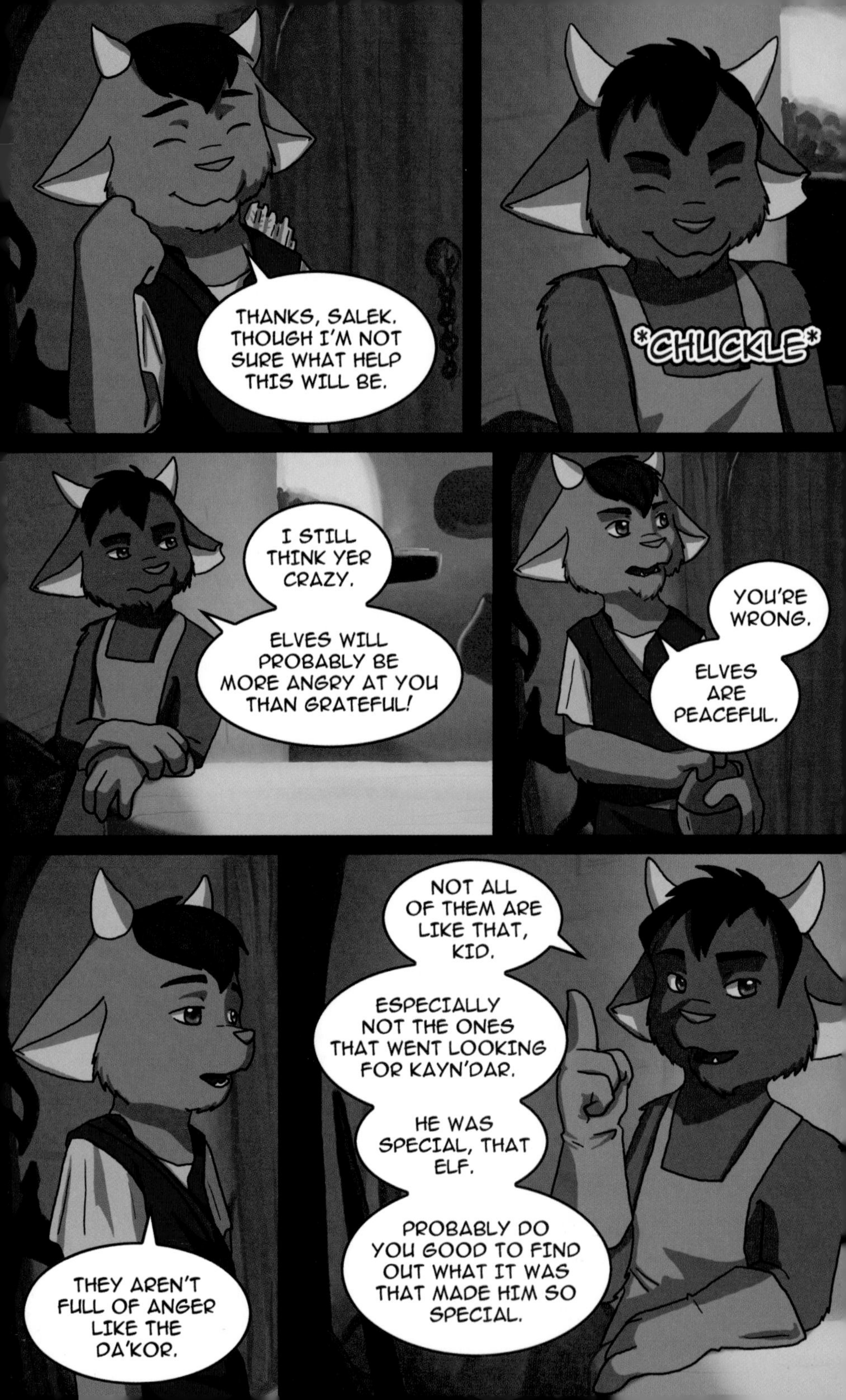
THANKS, SALEK. THOUGH I'M NOT SURE WHAT HELP THIS WILL BE.
CHUCKLE
I STILL THINK YER CRAZY.
ELVES WILL PROBABLY BE MORE ANGRY AT YOU THAN GRATEFUL!
YOU'RE WRONG.
ELVES ARE PEACEFUL.
THEY AREN'T FULL OF ANGER LIKE THE DA'KOR.
NOT ALL OF THEM ARE LIKE THAT, KID.
ESPECIALLY NOT THE ONES THAT WENT LOOKING FOR KAYN'DAR.
HE WAS SPECIAL, THAT ELF.
PROBABLY DO YOU GOOD TO FIND OUT WHAT IT WAS THAT MADE HIM SO SPECIAL.

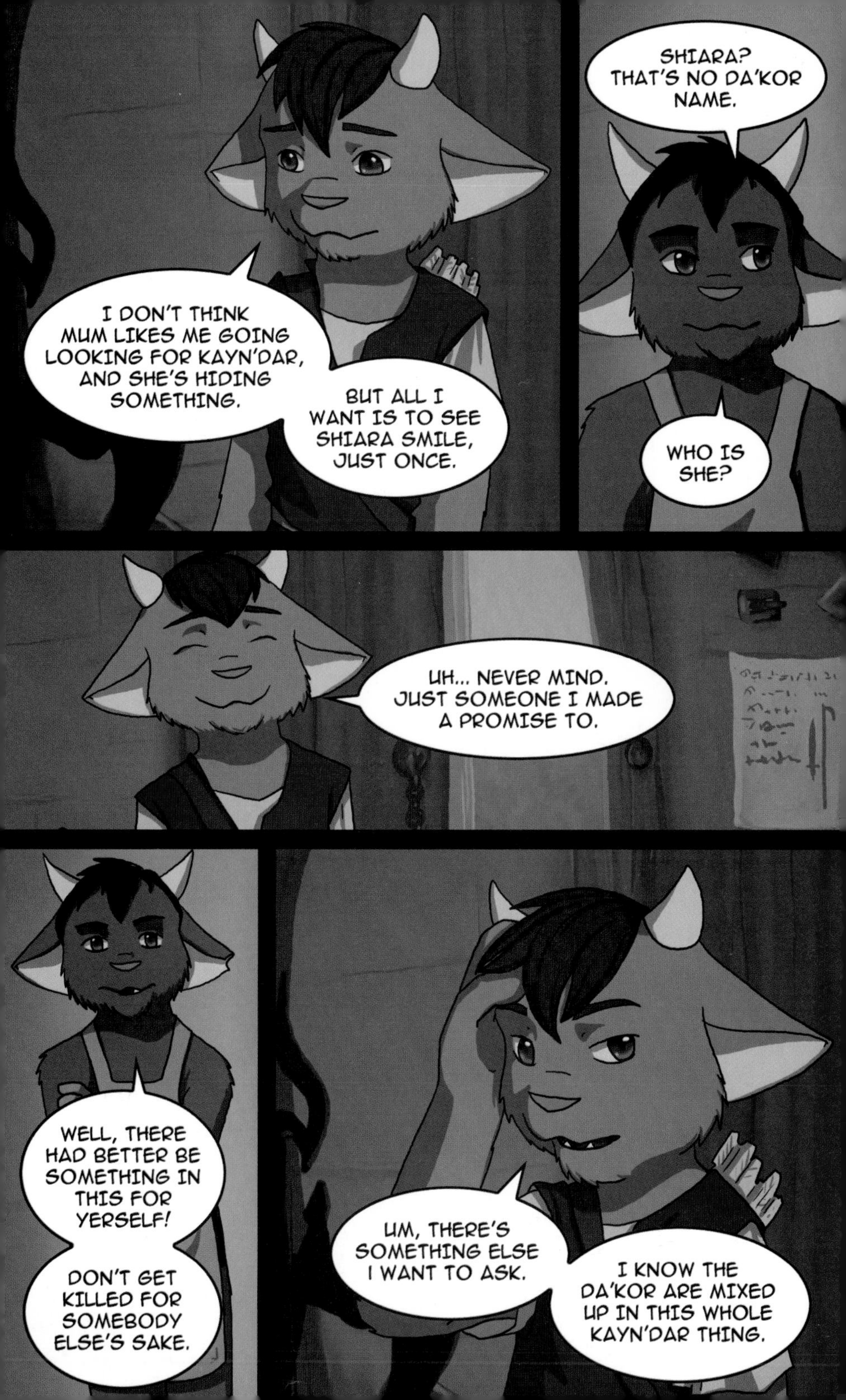
I DON'T THINK MUM LIKES ME GOING LOOKING FOR KAYN'DAR, AND SHE'S HIDING SOMETHING.
BUT ALL I WANT IS TO SEE SHIARA SMILE, JUST ONCE.
SHIARA? THAT'S NO DA'KOR NAME.
WHO IS SHE?
UH... NEVER MIND. JUST SOMEONE I MADE A PROMISE TO.
WELL, THERE HAD BETTER BE SOMETHING IN THIS FOR YERSELF!
DON'T GET KILLED FOR SOMEBODY ELSE'S SAKE.
UM, THERE'S SOMETHING ELSE I WANT TO ASK.
I KNOW THE DA'KOR ARE MIXED UP IN THIS WHOLE KAYN'DAR THING.

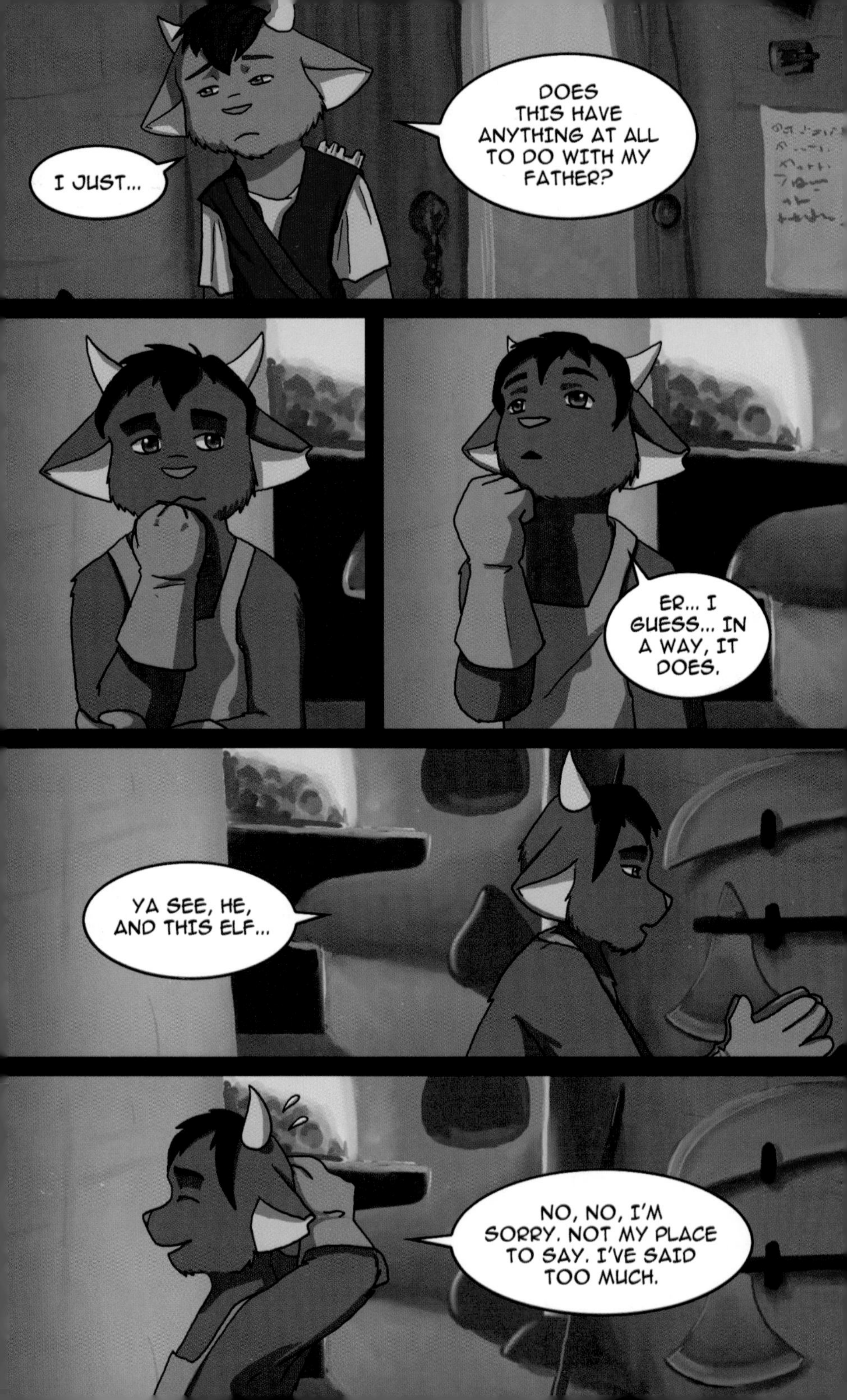
I JUST...
DOES THIS HAVE ANYTHING AT ALL TO DO WITH MY FATHER?
ER... I GUESS... IN A WAY, IT DOES.
YA SEE, HE, AND THIS ELF...
NO, NO, I'M SORRY. NOT MY PLACE TO SAY. I'VE SAID TOO MUCH.

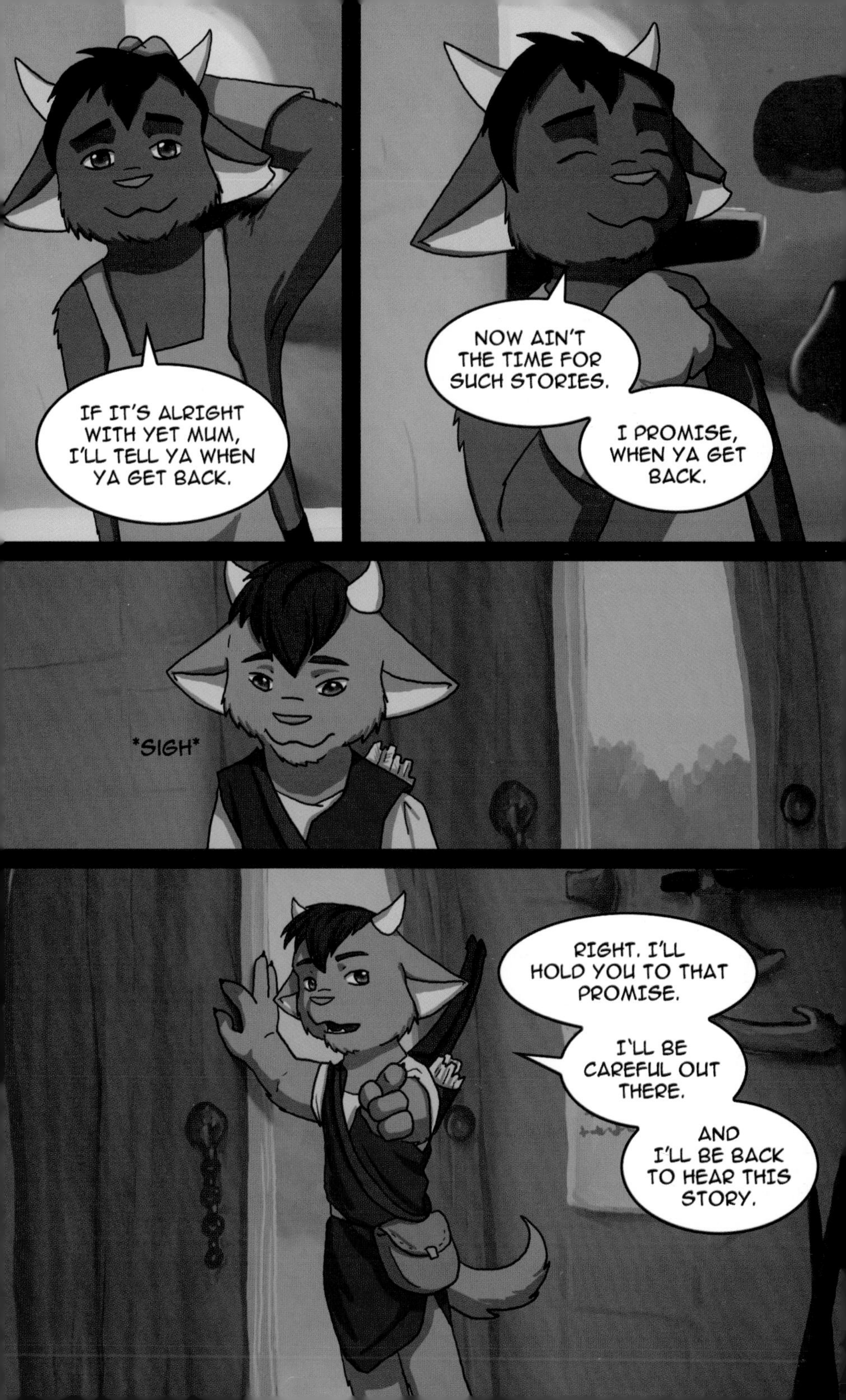
IF IT'S ALRIGHT WITH YET MUM, I'LL TELL YA WHEN YA GET BACK.
NOW AIN'T THE TIME FOR SUCH STORIES.
I PROMISE, WHEN YA GET BACK.
SIGH
RIGHT. I'LL HOLD YOU TO THAT PROMISE.
I'LL BE CAREFUL OUT THERE.
AND I'LL BE BACK TO HEAR THIS STORY.

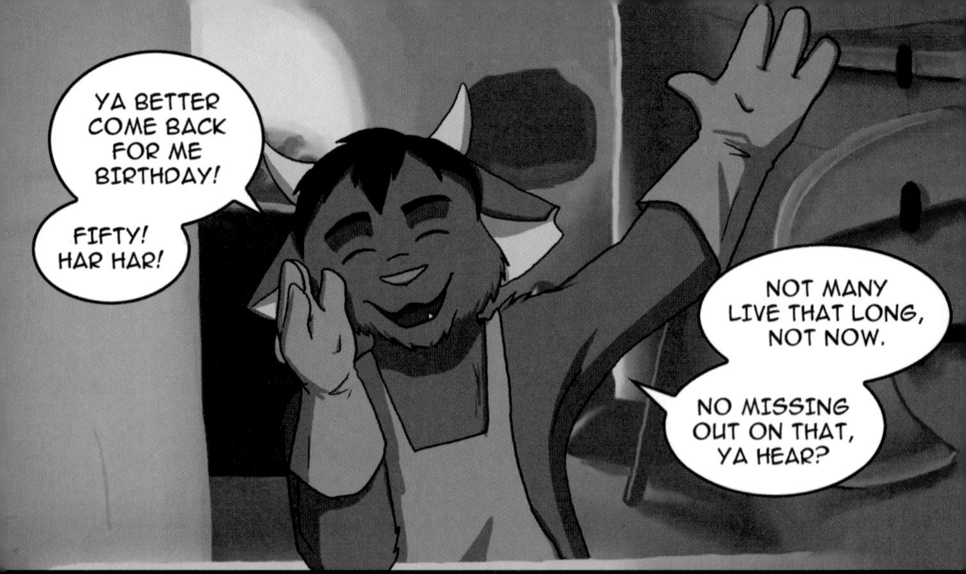
YA BETTER COME BACK FOR ME BIRTHDAY!
FIFTY! HAR HAR!
NOT MANY LIVE THAT LONG, NOT NOW.
NO MISSING OUT ON THAT, YA HEAR?

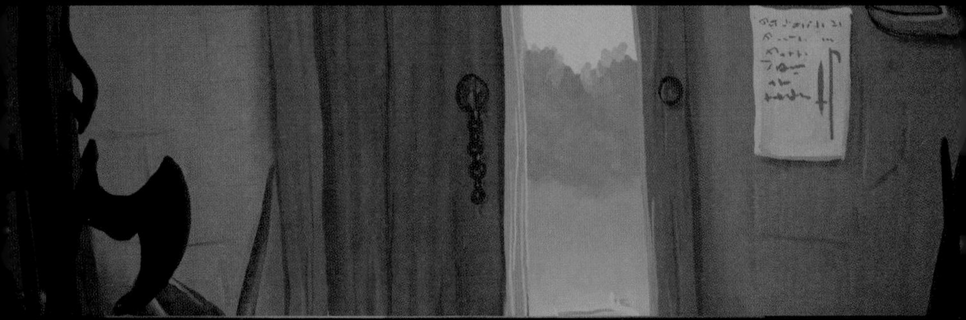

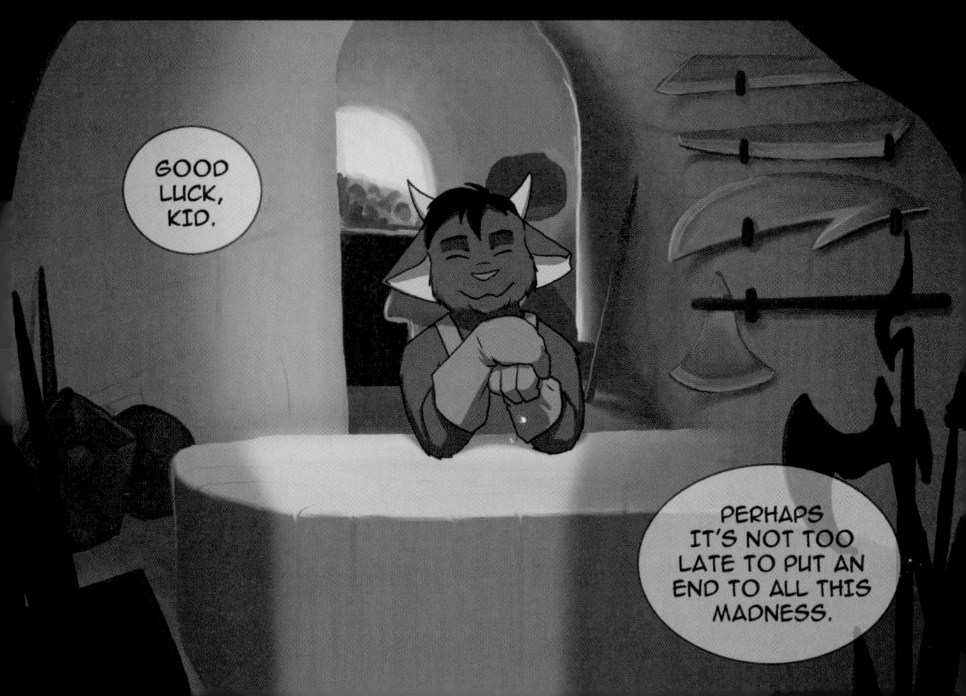
GOOD LUCK, KID.
PERHAPS IT'S NOT TOO LATE TO PUT AN END TO ALL THIS MADNESS.

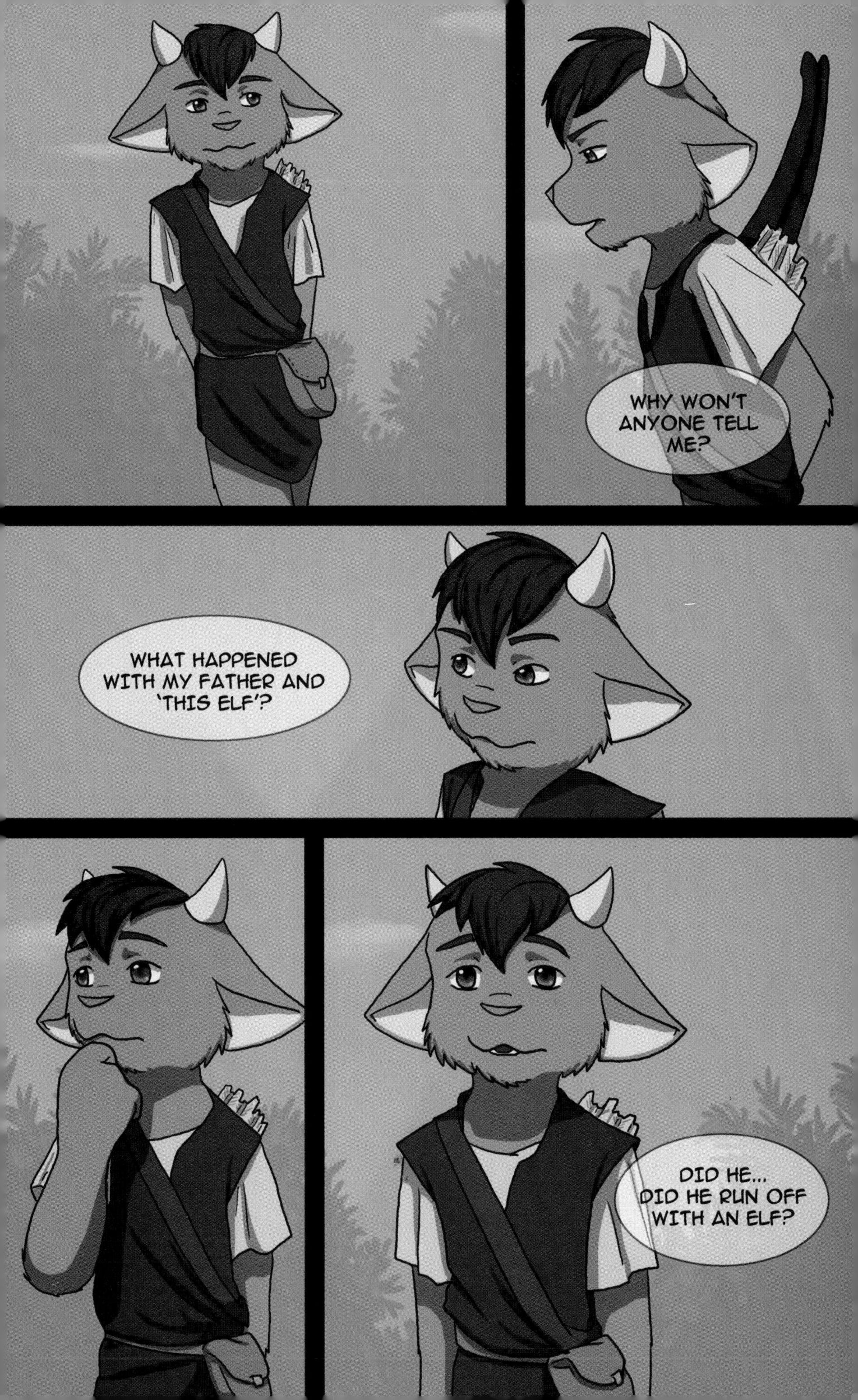
WHY WON'T ANYONE TELL ME?
WHAT HAPPENED WITH MY FATHER AND 'THIS ELF'?
DID HE... DID HE RUN OFF WITH AN ELF?

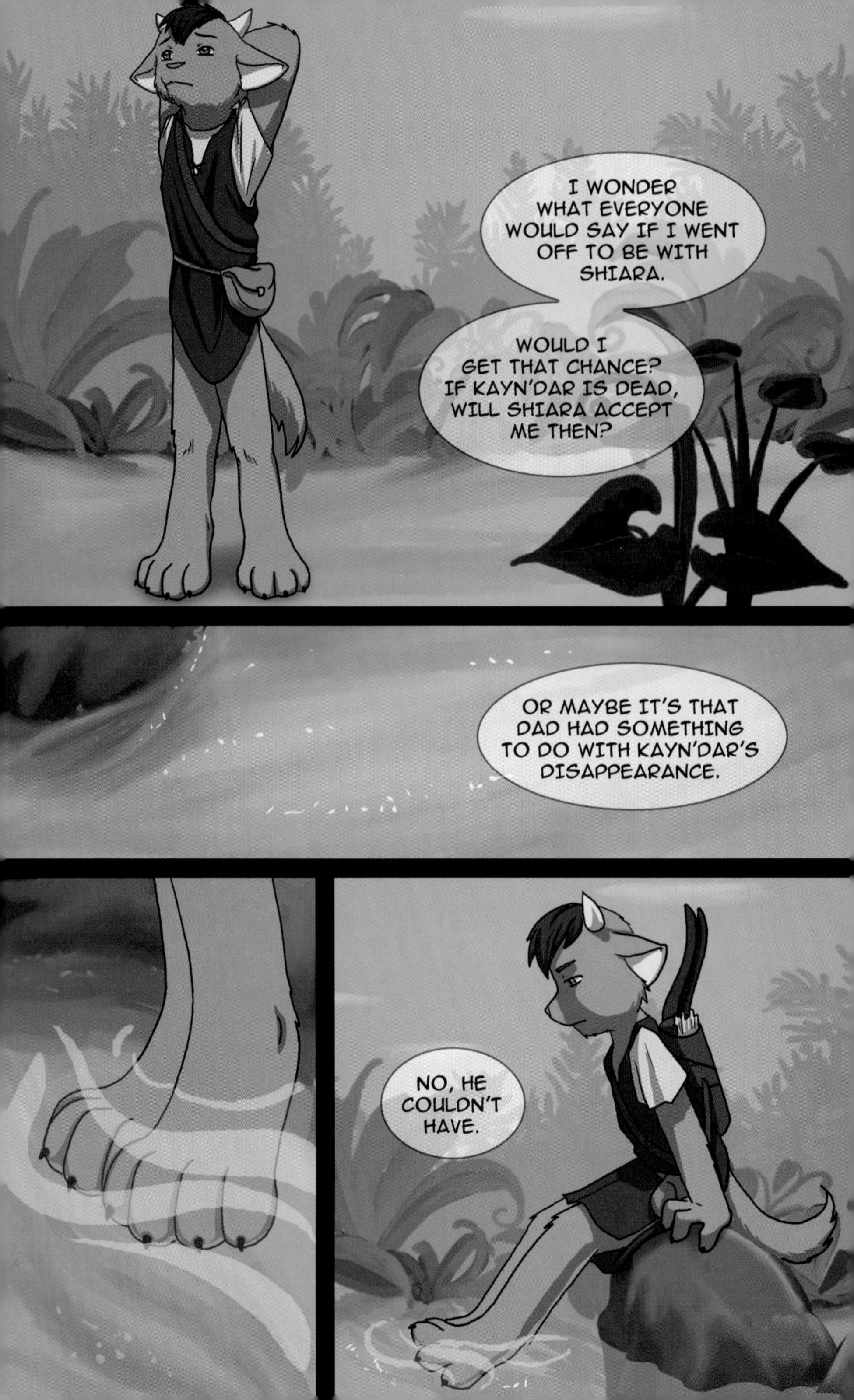
I WONDER WHAT EVERYONE WOULD SAY IF I WENT OFF TO BE WITH SHIARA.
WOULD I GET THAT CHANCE? IF KAYN'DAR IS DEAD, WILL SHIARA ACCEPT ME THEN?
OR MAYBE IT'S THAT DAD HAD SOMETHING TO DO WITH KAYN'DAR'S DISAPPEARANCE.
NO, HE COULDN'T HAVE.

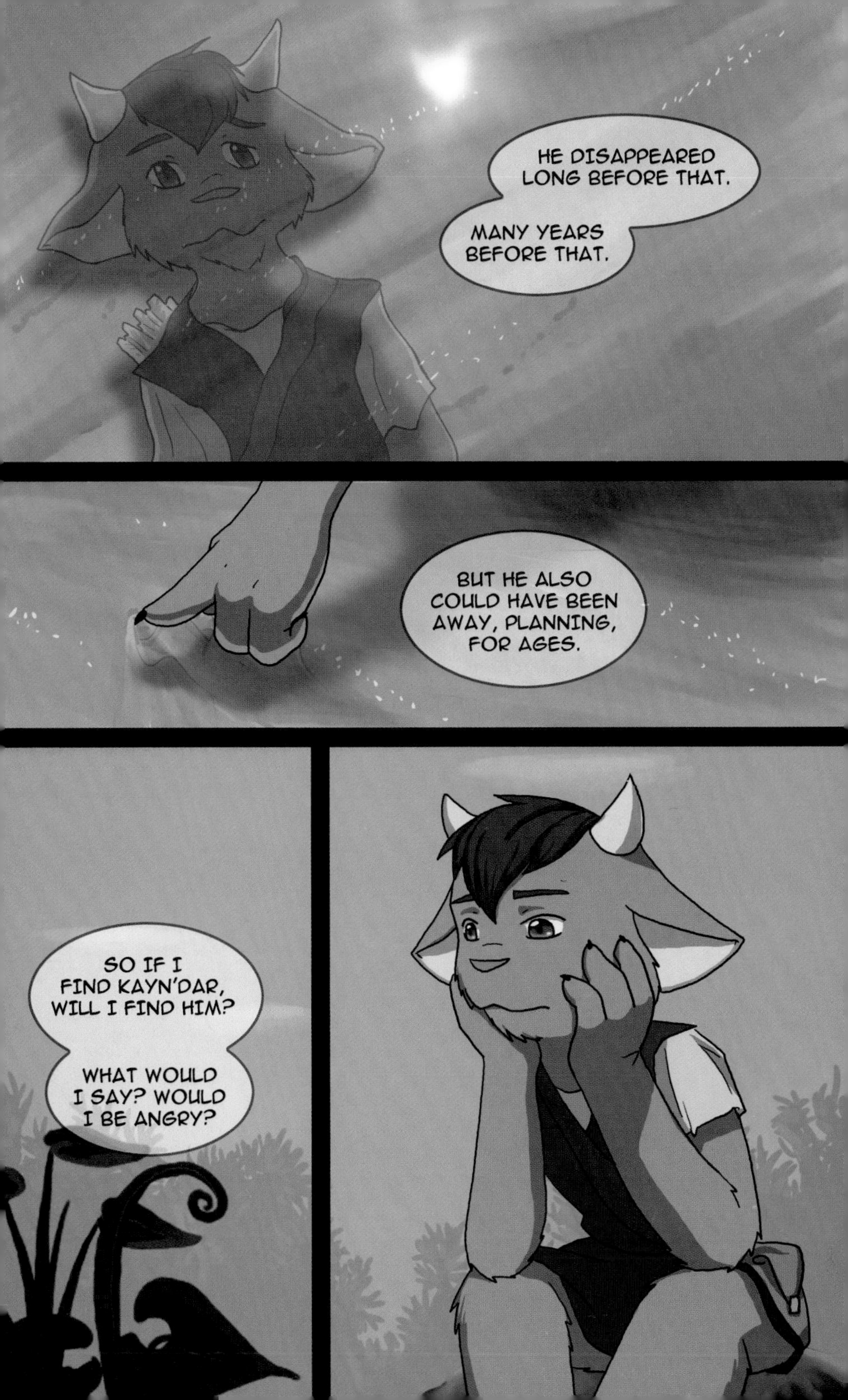
HE DISAPPEARED LONG BEFORE THAT.
MANY YEARS BEFORE THAT.
BUT HE ALSO COULD HAVE BEEN AWAY, PLANNING, FOR AGES.
SO IF I FIND KAYN'DAR, WILL I FIND HIM?
WHAT WOULD I SAY? WOULD I BE ANGRY?

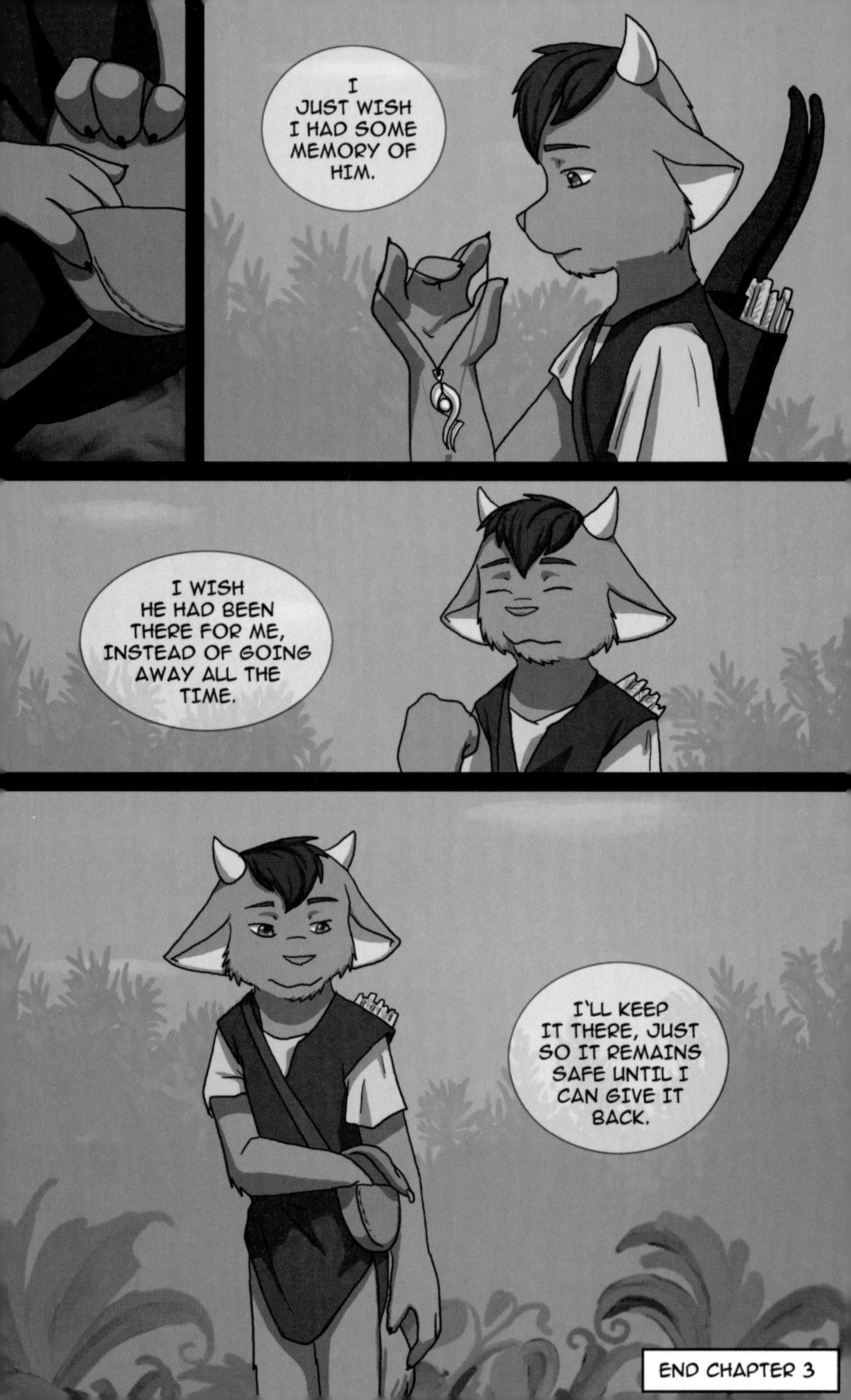
I JUST WISH I HAD SOME MEMORY OF HIM.
I WISH HE HAD BEEN THERE FOR ME, INSTEAD OF GOING AWAY ALL THE TIME.
I'LL KEEP IT THERE, JUST SO IT REMAINS SAFE UNTIL I CAN GIVE IT BACK.
END CHAPTER 3

CHAPTER 4 :JOURNEY'S BEGINNING

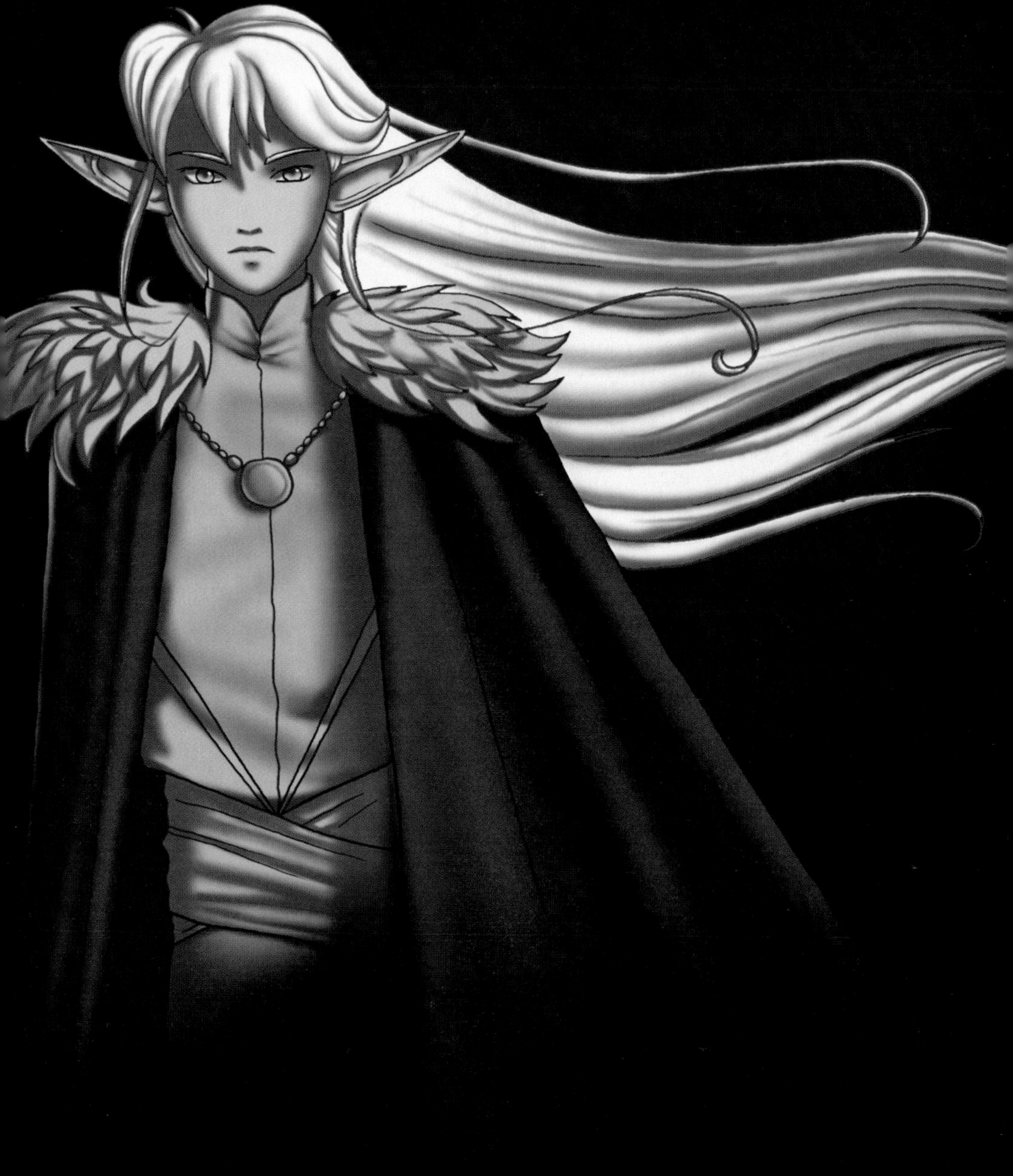

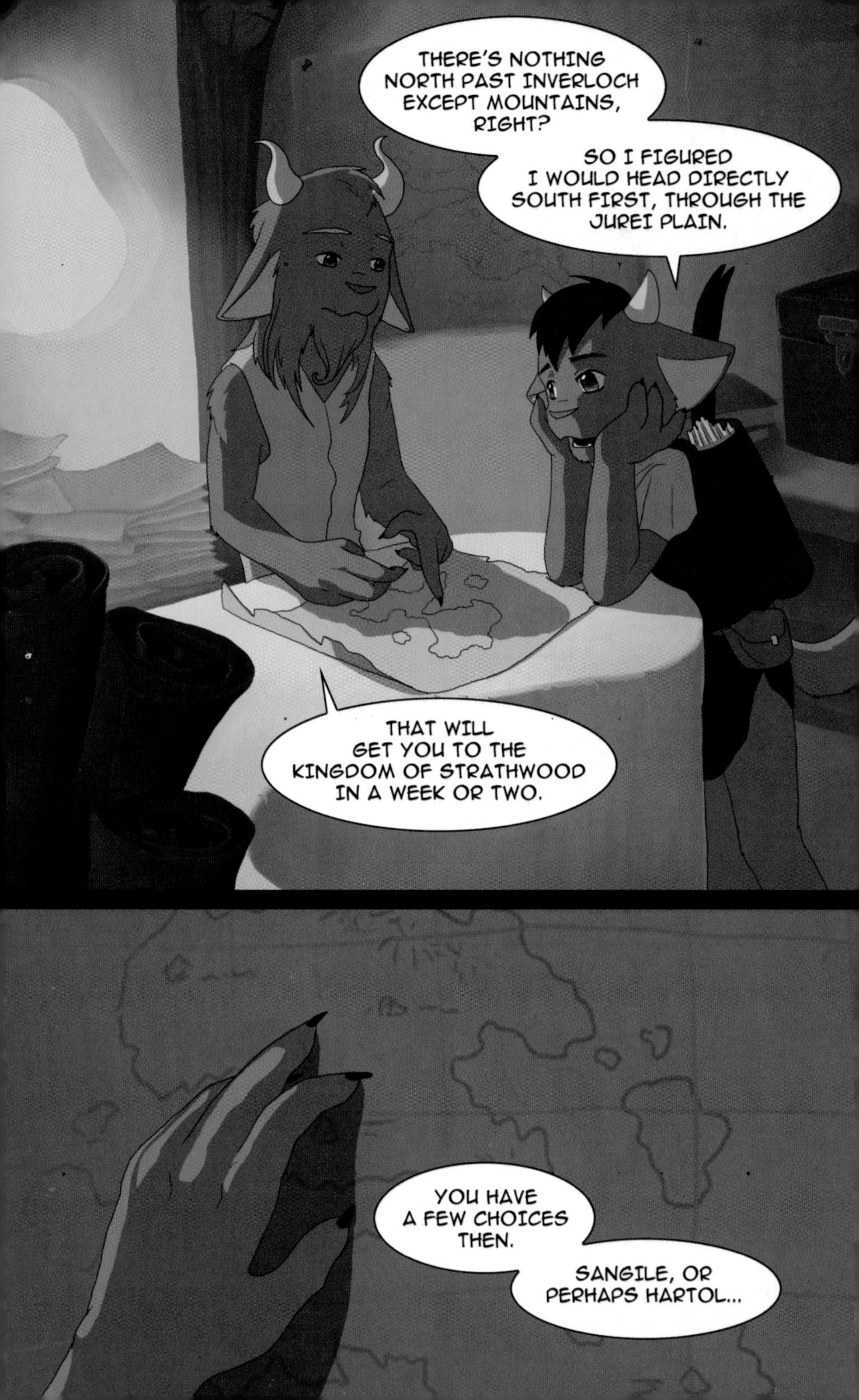
THERE'S NOTHING NORTH PAST INVERLOCH EXCEPT MOUNTAINS, RIGHT?
SO I FIGURED I WOULD HEAD DIRECTLY SOUTH FIRST, THROUGH THE JUREI PLAIN.
THAT WILL GET YOU TO THE KINGDOM OF STRATHWOOD IN A WEEK OR TWO.
YOU HAVE A FEW CHOICES THEN.
SANGILE, OR PERHAPS HARTOL...

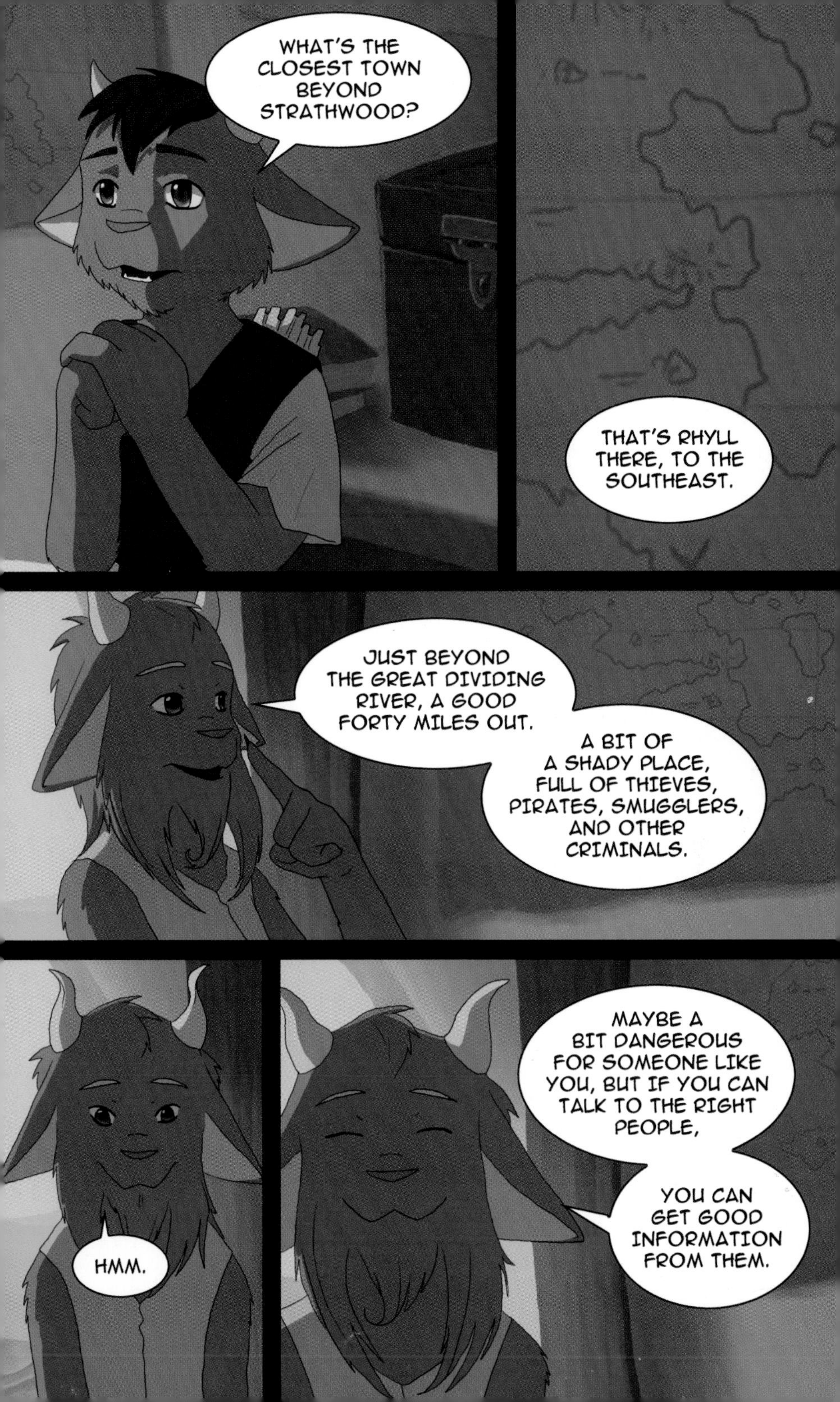
WHAT'S THE CLOSEST TOWN BEYOND STRATHWOOD?
THAT'S RHYLL THERE, TO THE SOUTHEAST.
JUST BEYOND THE GREAT DIVIDING RIVER, A GOOD FORTY MILES OUT.
A BIT OF A SHADY PLACE, FULL OF THIEVES, PIRATES, SMUGGLERS, AND OTHER CRIMINALS.
HMM.
MAYBE A BIT DANGEROUS FOR SOMEONE LIKE YOU, BUT IF YOU CAN TALK TO THE RIGHT PEOPLE,
YOU CAN GET GOOD INFORMATION FROM THEM.

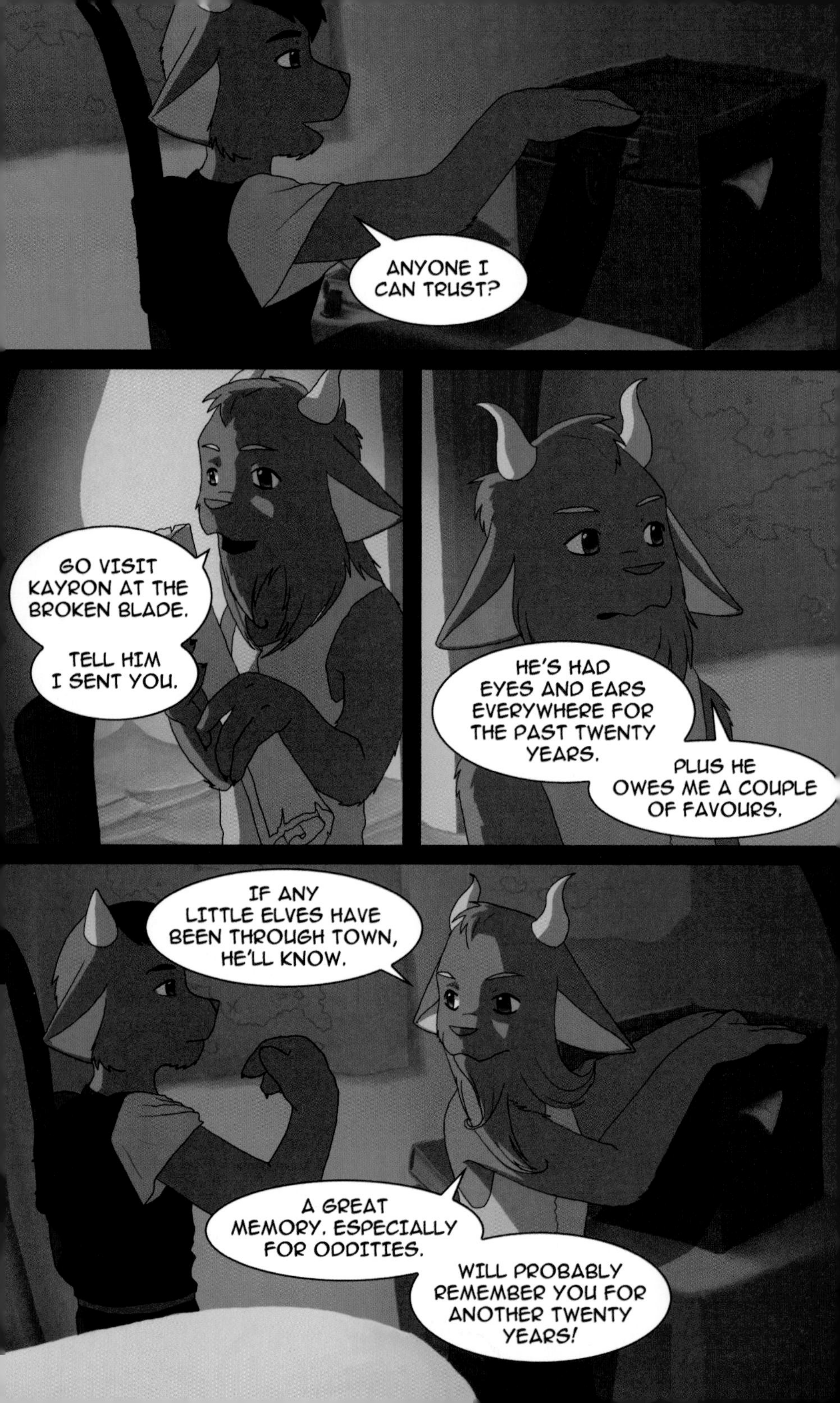
ANYONE I CAN TRUST?
GO VISIT KAYRON AT THE BROKEN BLADE.
TELL HIM I SENT YOU.
HE'S HAD EYES AND EARS EVERYWHERE FOR THE PAST TWENTY YEARS.
PLUS HE OWES ME A COUPLE OF FAVOURS.
IF ANY LITTLE ELVES HAVE BEEN THROUGH TOWN, HE'LL KNOW.
A GREAT MEMORY. ESPECIALLY FOR ODDITIES.
WILL PROBABLY REMEMBER YOU FOR ANOTHER TWENTY YEARS!

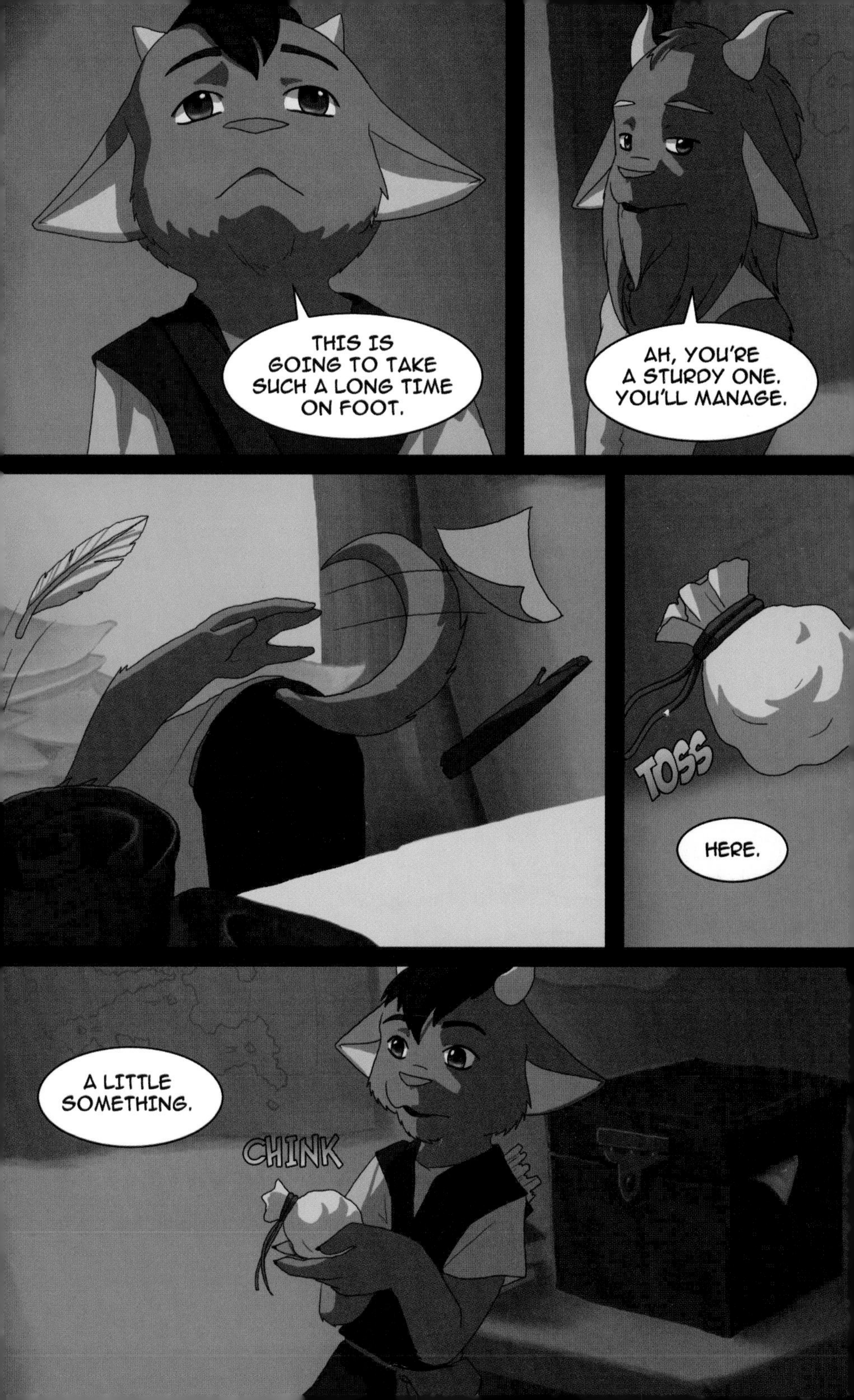
THIS IS GOING TO TAKE SUCH A LONG TIME ON FOOT.
AH, YOU'RE A STURDY ONE. YOU'LL MANAGE.
TOSS
HERE.
A LITTLE SOMETHING.
CHINK

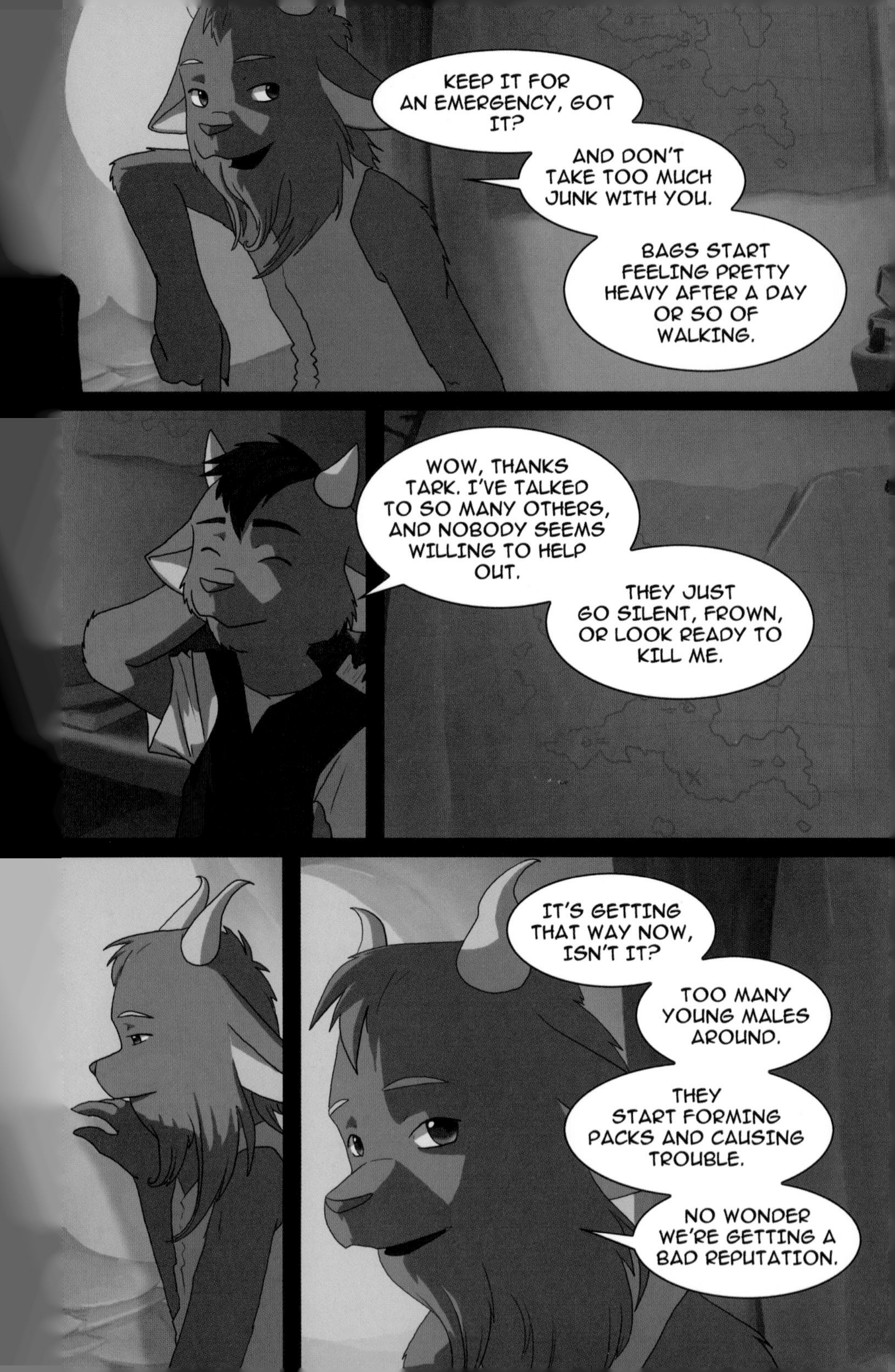
KEEP IT FOR AN EMERGENCY, GOT IT?
AND DON'T TAKE TOO MUCH JUNK WITH YOU.
BAGS START FEELING PRETTY HEAVY AFTER A DAY OR SO OF WALKING.
WOW, THANKS TARK. I'VE TALKED TO SO MANY OTHERS, AND NOBODY SEEMS WILLING TO HELP OUT.
THEY JUST GO SILENT, FROWN, OR LOOK READY TO KILL ME.
IT'S GETTING THAT WAY NOW, ISN'T IT?
TOO MANY YOUNG MALES AROUND.
THEY START FORMING PACKS AND CAUSING TROUBLE.
NO WONDER WE'RE GETTING A BAD REPUTATION.

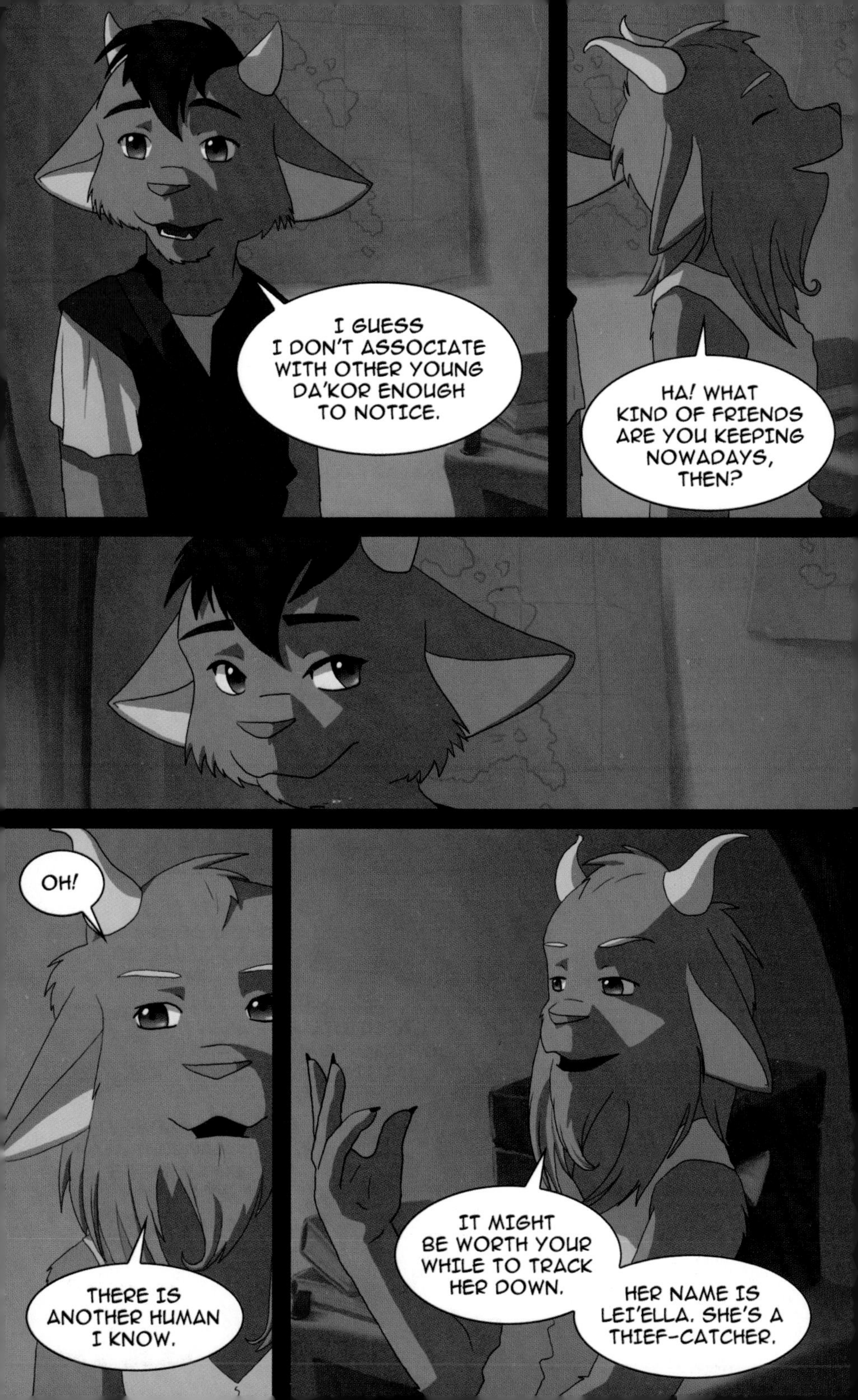
I GUESS I DON'T ASSOCIATE WITH OTHER YOUNG DA'KOR ENOUGH TO NOTICE.
HA! WHAT KIND OF FRIENDS ARE YOU KEEPING NOWADAYS, THEN?
OH!
THERE IS ANOTHER HUMAN I KNOW.
IT MIGHT BE WORTH YOUR WHILE TO TRACK HER DOWN.
HER NAME IS LEI'ELLA. SHE'S A THIEF-CATCHER.

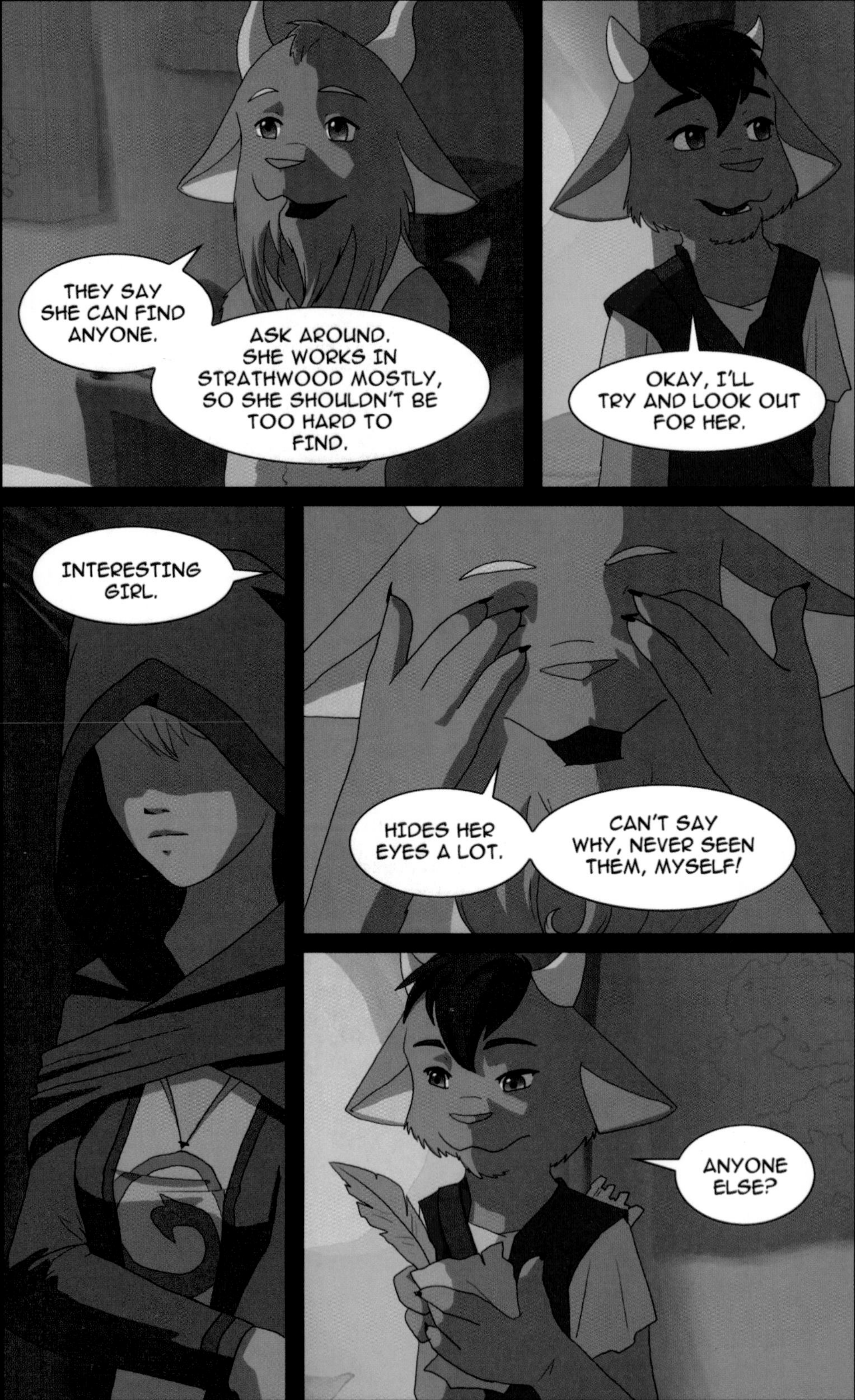
THEY SAY SHE CAN FIND ANYONE.
ASK AROUND. SHE WORKS IN STRATHWOOD MOSTLY, SO SHE SHOULDN'T BE TOO HARD TO FIND.
OKAY, I'LL TRY AND LOOK OUT FOR HER.
INTERESTING GIRL.
HIDES HER EYES A LOT.
CAN'T SAY WHY, NEVER SEEN THEM, MYSELF!
ANYONE ELSE?

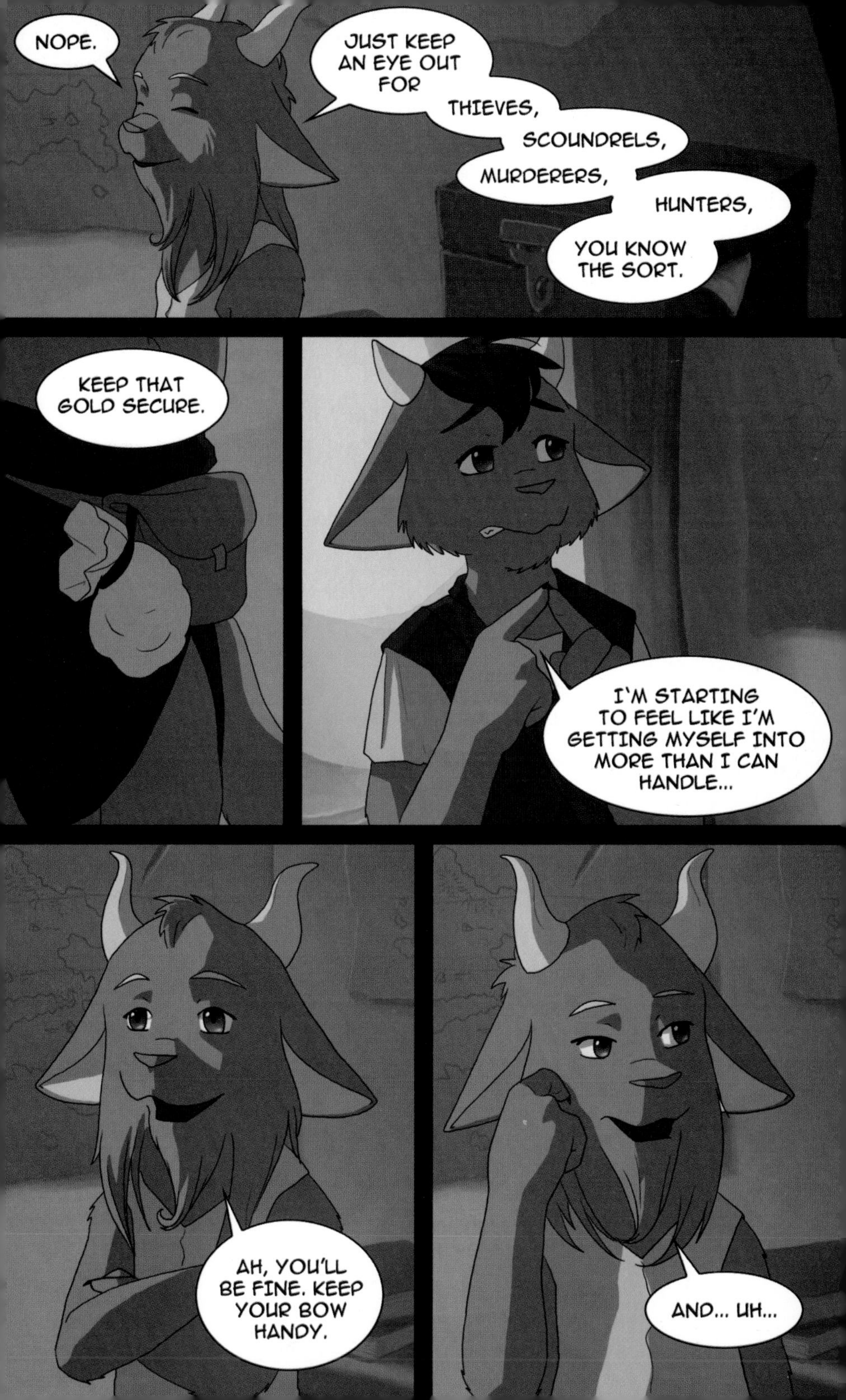
NOPE.
JUST KEEP AN EYE OUT FOR
THIEVES,
SCOUNDRELS,
MURDERERS,
HUNTERS,
YOU KNOW THE SORT.
KEEP THAT GOLD SECURE.
I'M STARTING TO FEEL LIKE I'M GETTING MYSELF INTO MORE THAN I CAN HANDLE...
AH, YOU'LL BE FINE. KEEP YOUR BOW HANDY.
AND... UH...

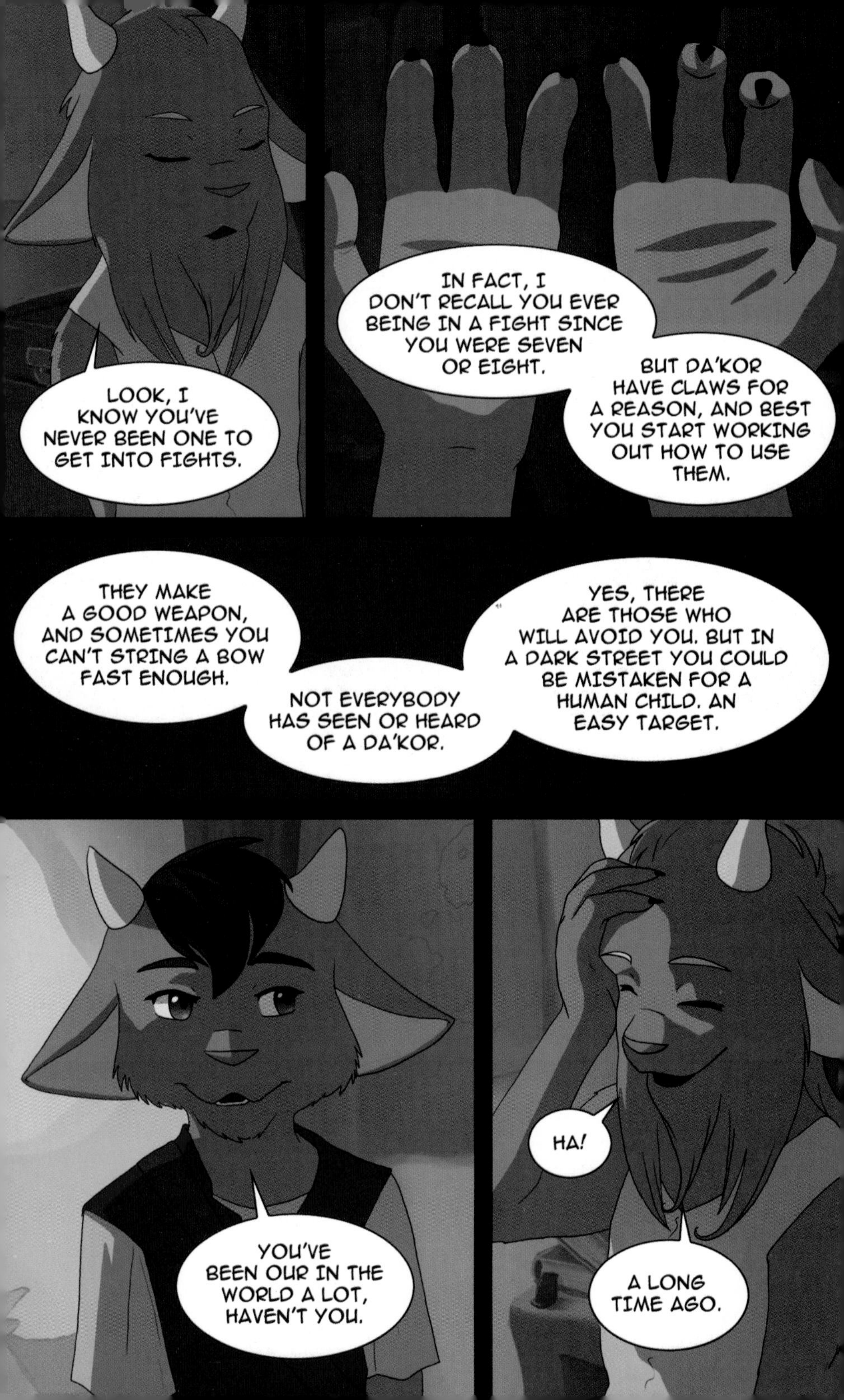
LOOK, I KNOW YOU'VE NEVER BEEN ONE TO GET INTO FIGHTS.
IN FACT, I DON'T RECALL YOU EVER BEING IN A FIGHT SINCE YOU WERE SEVEN OR EIGHT.
BUT DA'KOR HAVE CLAWS FOR A REASON, AND BEST YOU START WORKING OUT HOW TO USE THEM.
THEY MAKE A GOOD WEAPON, AND SOMETIMES YOU CAN'T STRING A BOW FAST ENOUGH.
NOT EVERYBODY HAS SEEN OR HEARD OF A DA'KOR.
YES, THERE ARE THOSE WHO WILL AVOID YOU. BUT IN A DARK STREET YOU COULD BE MISTAKEN FOR A HUMAN CHILD. AN EASY TARGET.
YOU'VE BEEN OUR IN THE WORLD A LOT, HAVEN'T YOU.
HA!
A LONG TIME AGO.

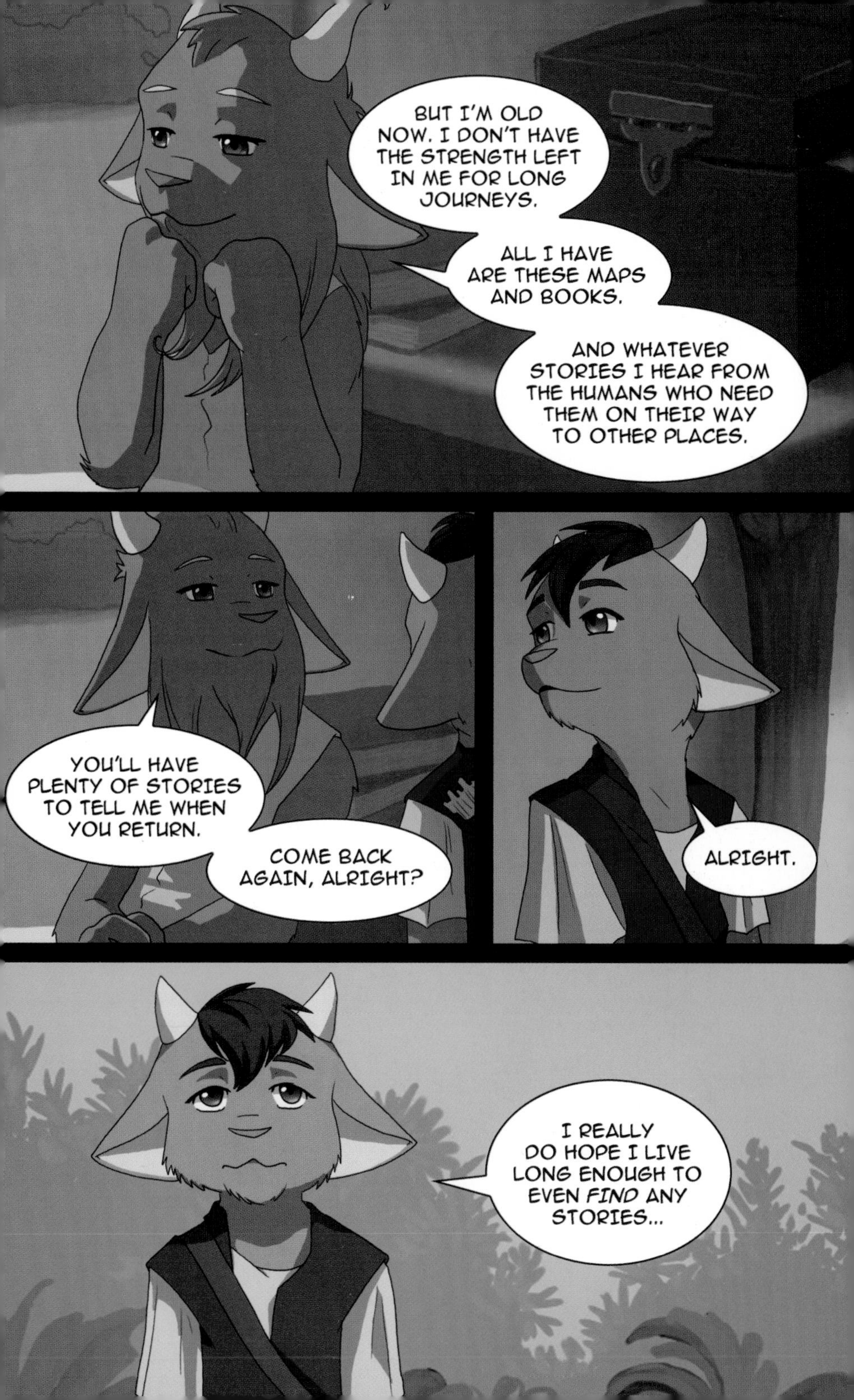
BUT I'M OLD NOW. I DON'T HAVE THE STRENGTH LEFT IN ME FOR LONG JOURNEYS.
ALL I HAVE ARE THESE MAPS AND BOOKS.
AND WHATEVER STORIES I HEAR FROM THE HUMANS WHO NEED THEM ON THEIR WAY TO OTHER PLACES.
YOU'LL HAVE PLENTY OF STORIES TO TELL ME WHEN YOU RETURN.
COME BACK AGAIN, ALRIGHT?
ALRIGHT.
I REALLY DO HOPE I LIVE LONG ENOUGH TO EVEN *FIND* ANY STORIES...

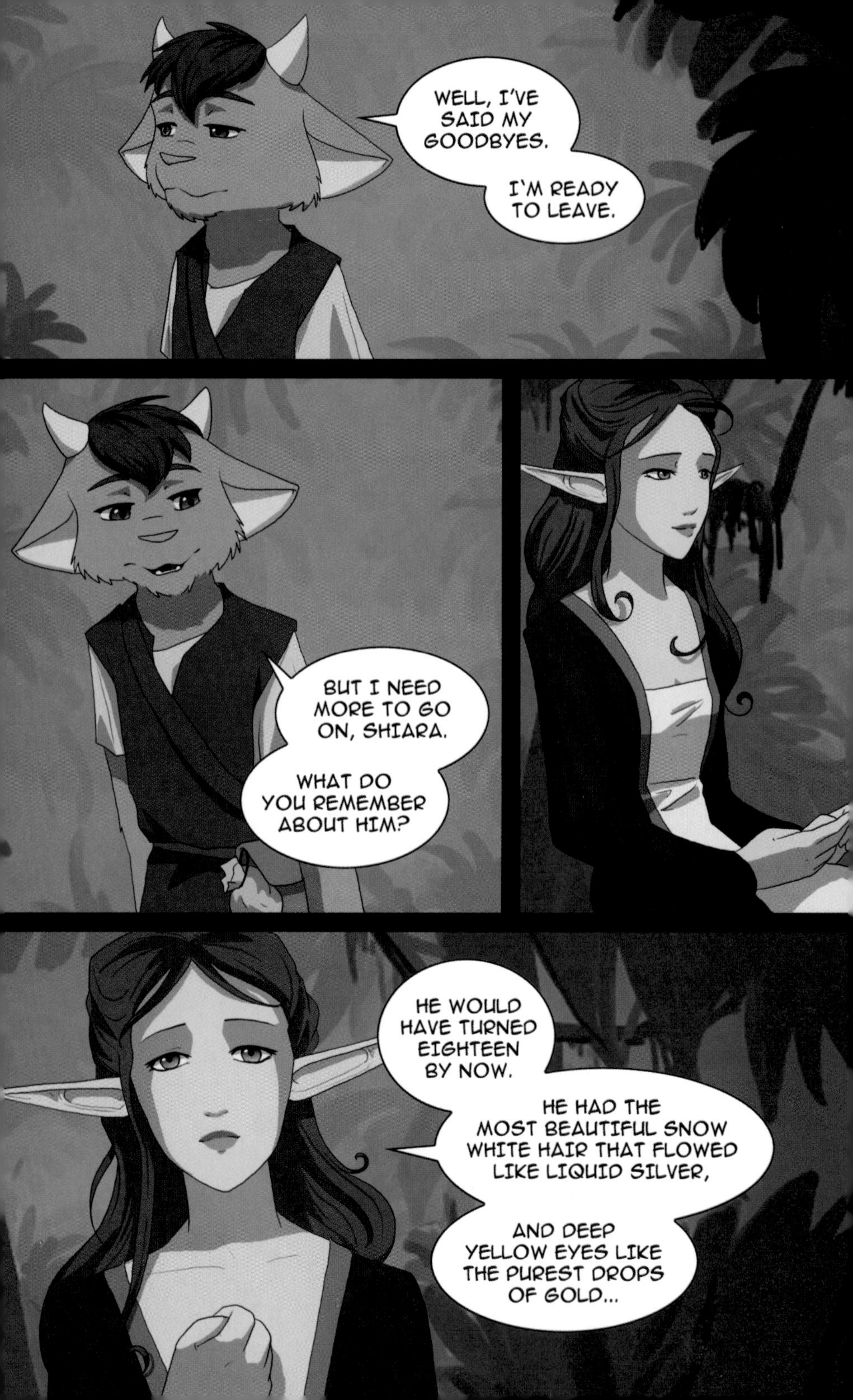
WELL, I'VE SAID MY GOODBYES.
I'M READY TO LEAVE.
BUT I NEED MORE TO GO ON, SHIARA.
WHAT DO YOU REMEMBER ABOUT HIM?
HE WOULD HAVE TURNED EIGHTEEN BY NOW.
HE HAD THE MOST BEAUTIFUL SNOW WHITE HAIR THAT FLOWED LIKE LIQUID SILVER,
AND DEEP YELLOW EYES LIKE THE PUREST DROPS OF GOLD...

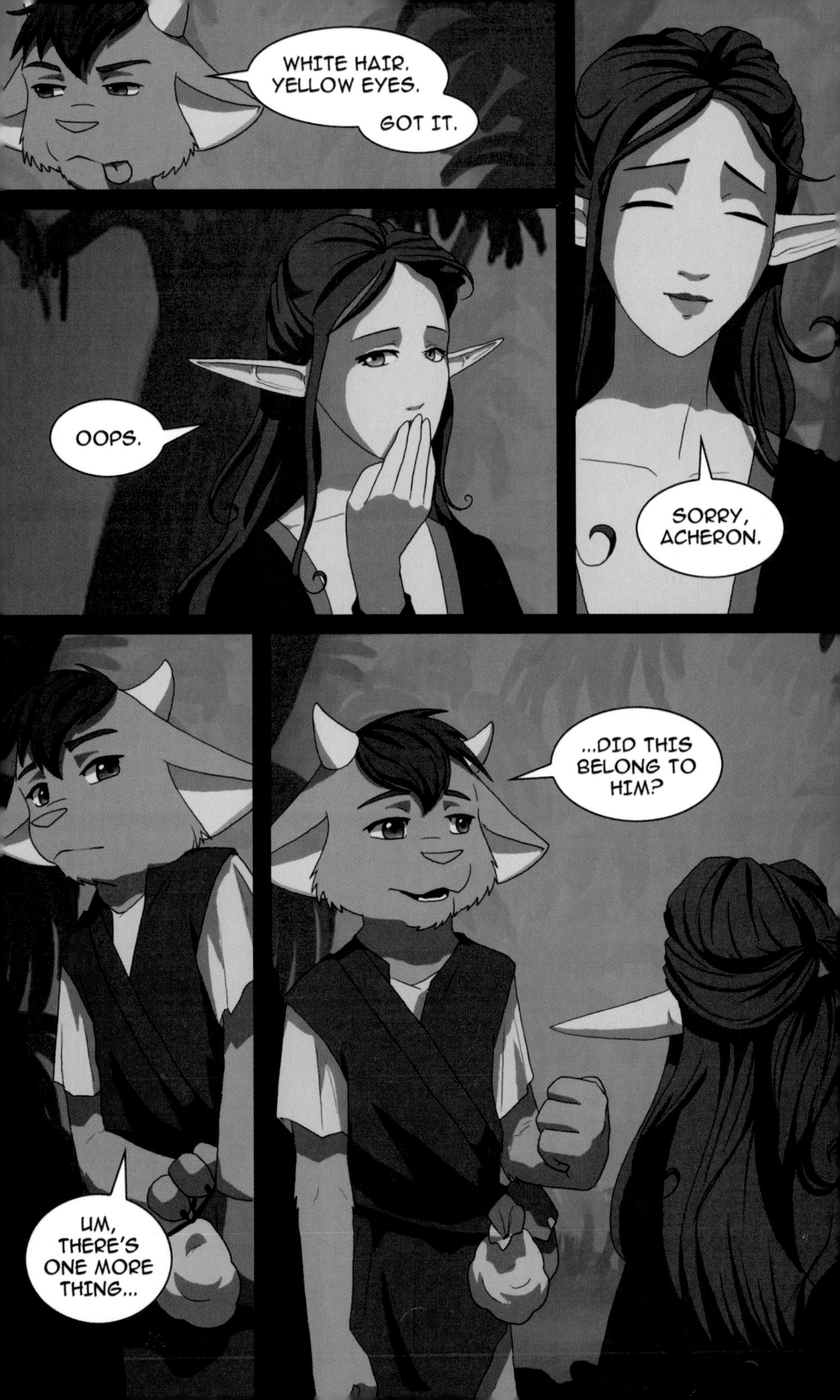
WHITE HAIR. YELLOW EYES.
GOT IT.
OOPS.
SORRY, ACHERON.
UM, THERE'S ONE MORE THING...
...DID THIS BELONG TO HIM?

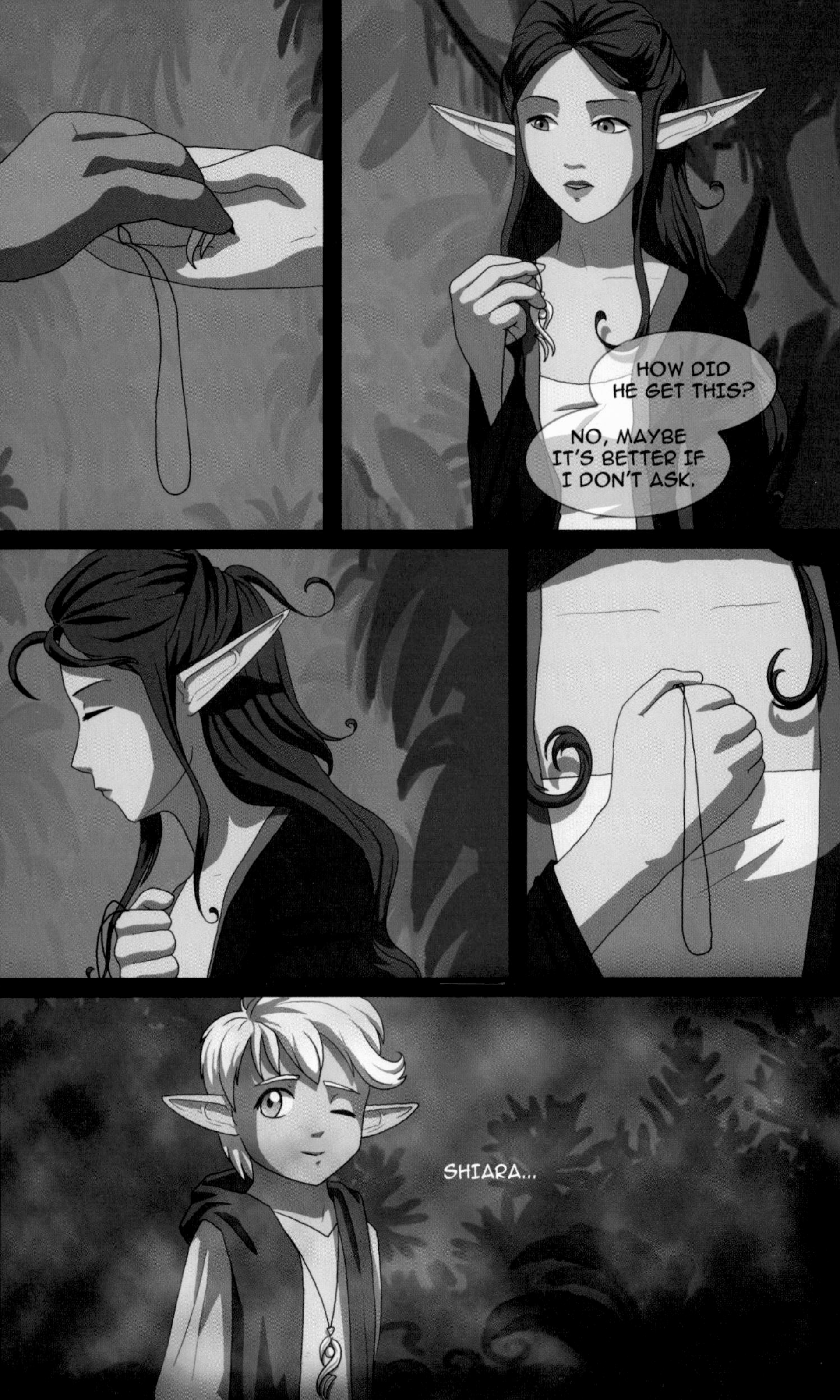
HOW DID HE GET THIS?
NO, MAYBE IT'S BETTER IF I DON'T ASK.
SHIARA...

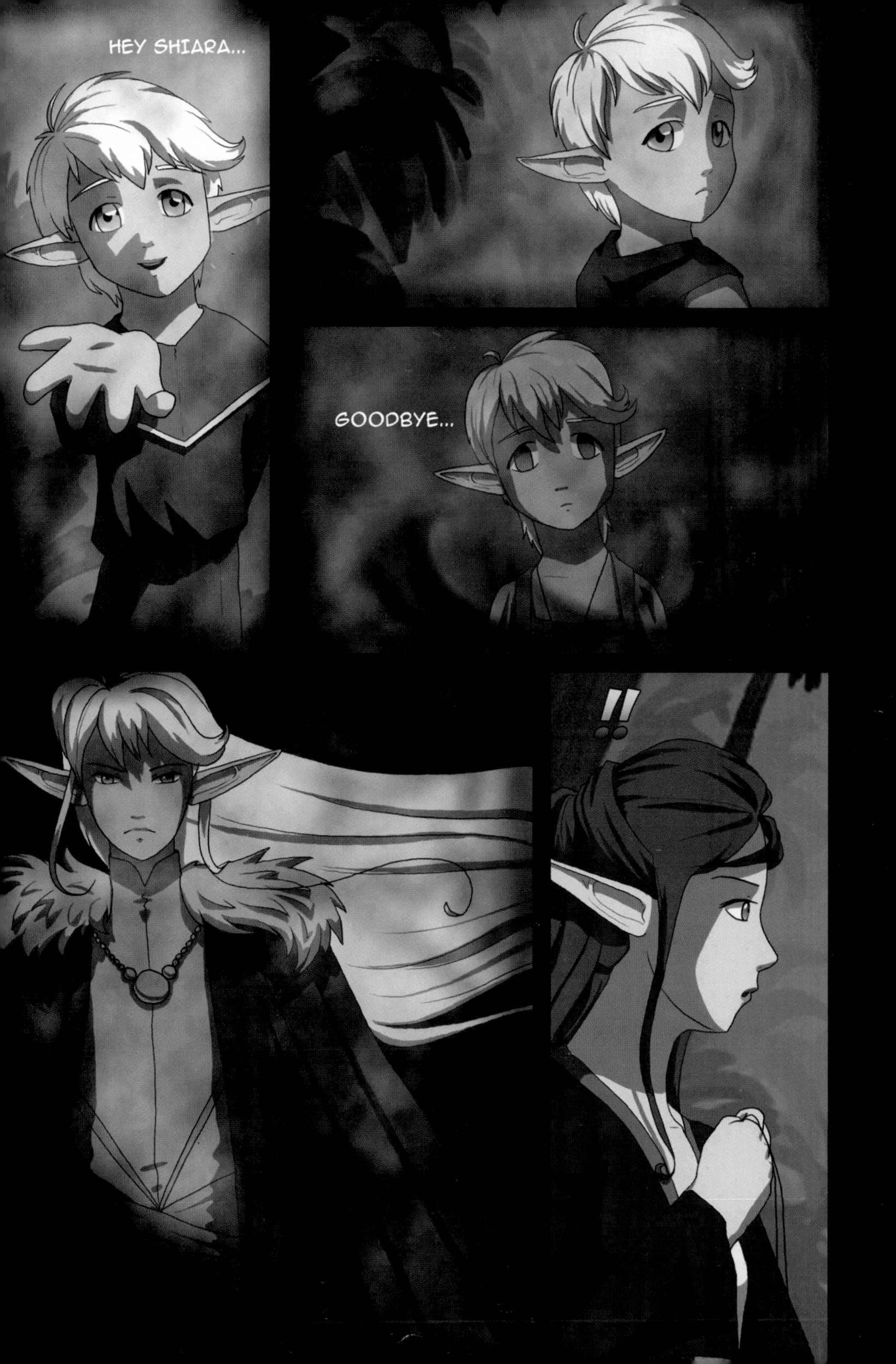
HEY SHIARA...
GOODBYE...
!!

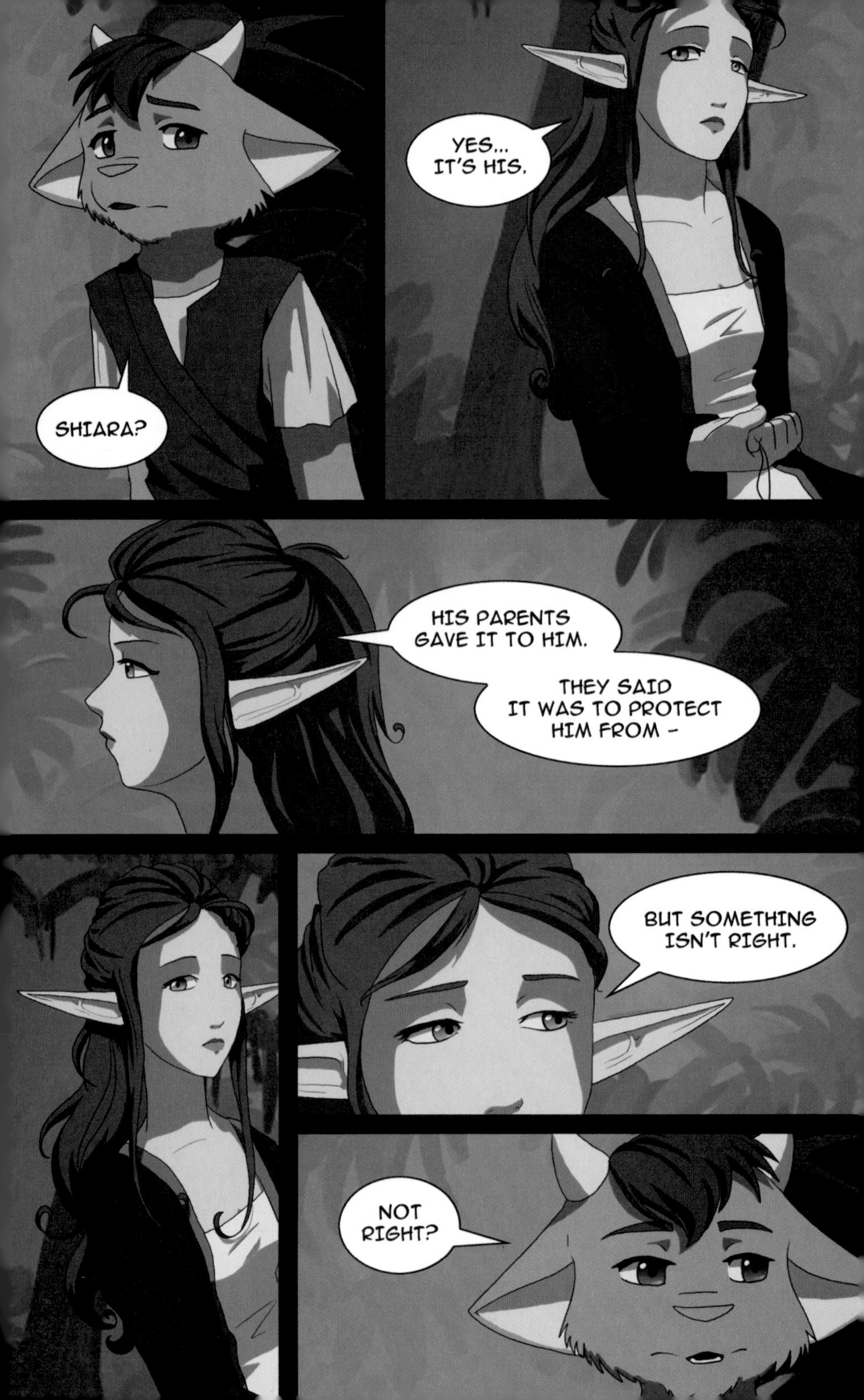
SHIARA?
YES... IT'S HIS.
HIS PARENTS GAVE IT TO HIM.
THEY SAID IT WAS TO PROTECT HIM FROM -
BUT SOMETHING ISN'T RIGHT.
NOT RIGHT?

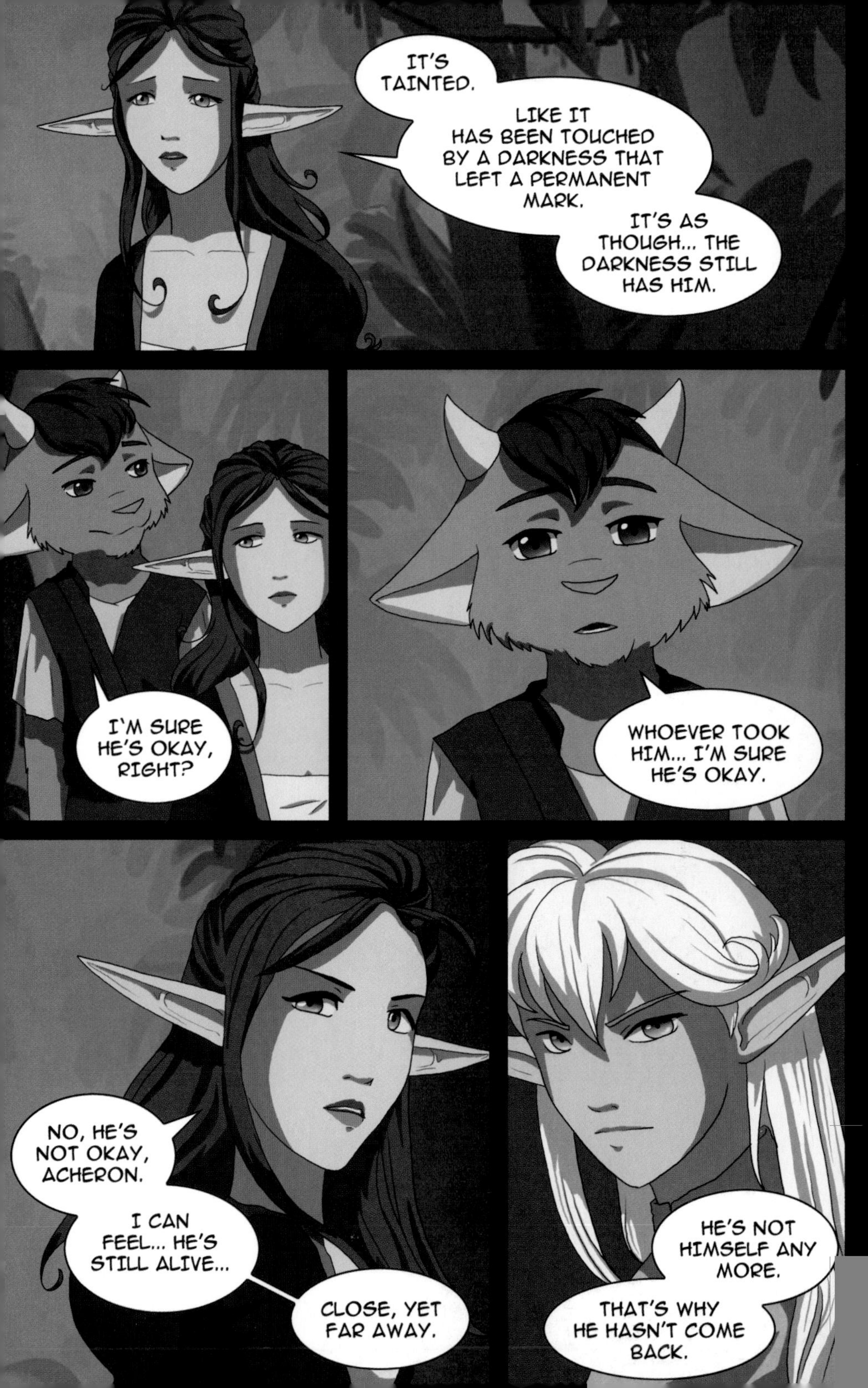
IT'S TAINTED.
LIKE IT HAS BEEN TOUCHED BY A DARKNESS THAT LEFT A PERMANENT MARK.
IT'S AS THOUGH... THE DARKNESS STILL HAS HIM.
I'M SURE HE'S OKAY, RIGHT?
WHOEVER TOOK HIM... I'M SURE HE'S OKAY.
NO, HE'S NOT OKAY, ACHERON.
I CAN FEEL... HE'S STILL ALIVE...
CLOSE, YET FAR AWAY.
HE'S NOT HIMSELF ANY MORE.
THAT'S WHY HE HASN'T COME BACK.

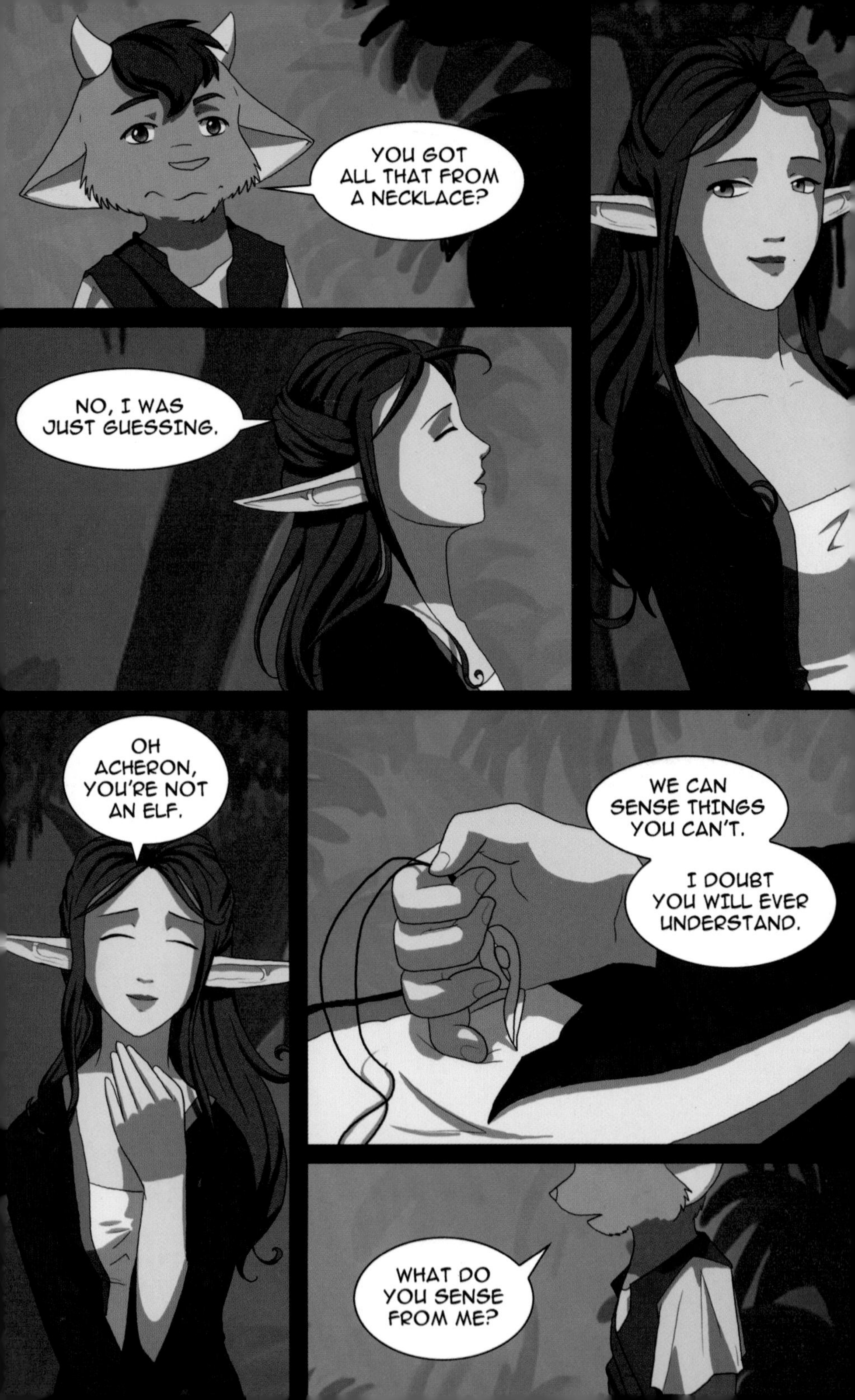
YOU GOT ALL THAT FROM A NECKLACE?
NO, I WAS JUST GUESSING.
OH ACHERON, YOU'RE NOT AN ELF.
WE CAN SENSE THINGS YOU CAN'T.
I DOUBT YOU WILL EVER UNDERSTAND.
WHAT DO YOU SENSE FROM ME?

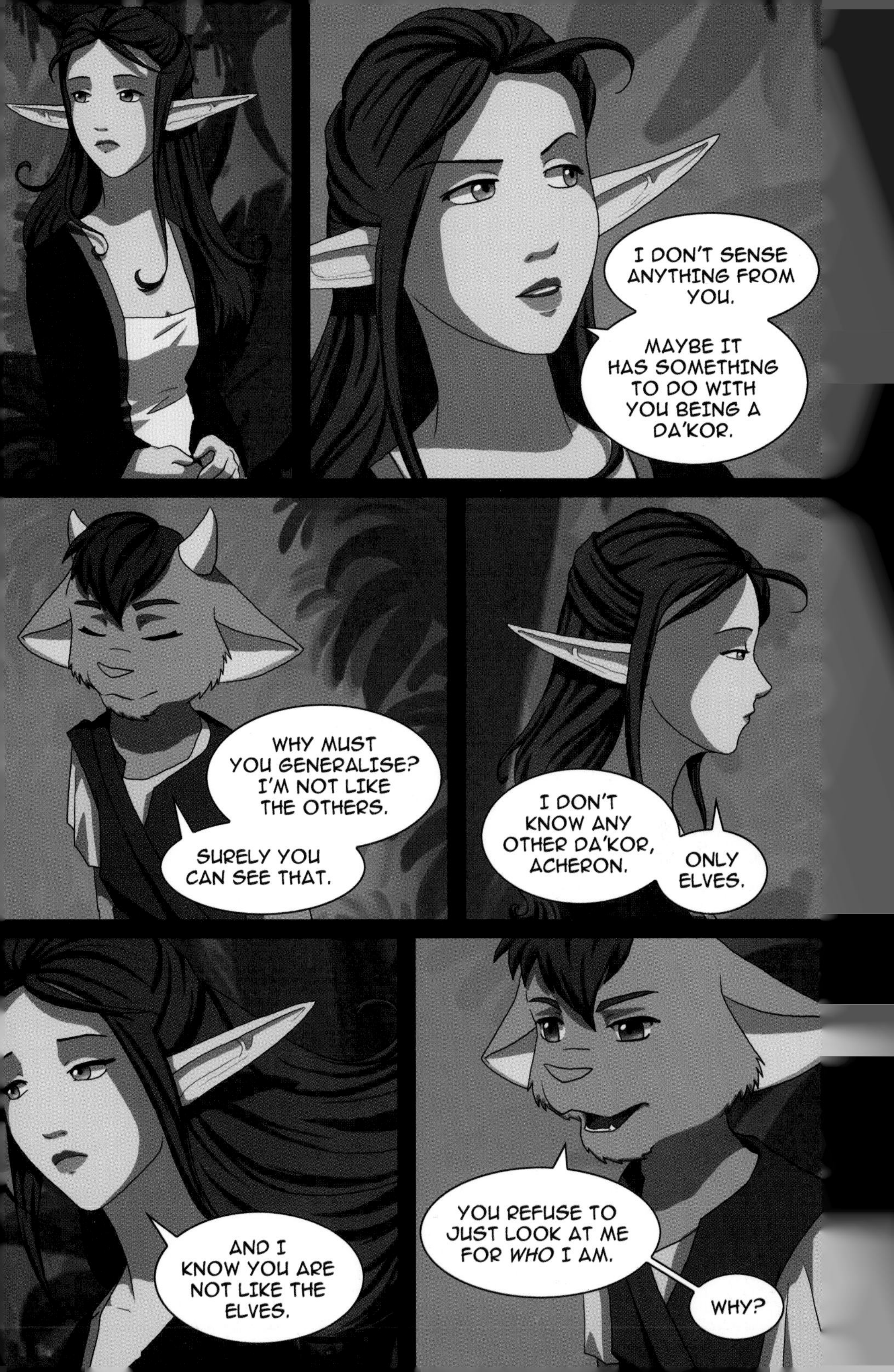
I DON'T SENSE ANYTHING FROM YOU.
MAYBE IT HAS SOMETHING TO DO WITH YOU BEING A DA'KOR.
WHY MUST YOU GENERALISE? I'M NOT LIKE THE OTHERS.
SURELY YOU CAN SEE THAT.
I DON'T KNOW ANY OTHER DA'KOR, ACHERON.
ONLY ELVES.
AND I KNOW YOU ARE NOT LIKE THE ELVES.
YOU REFUSE TO JUST LOOK AT ME FOR *WHO* I AM.
WHY?

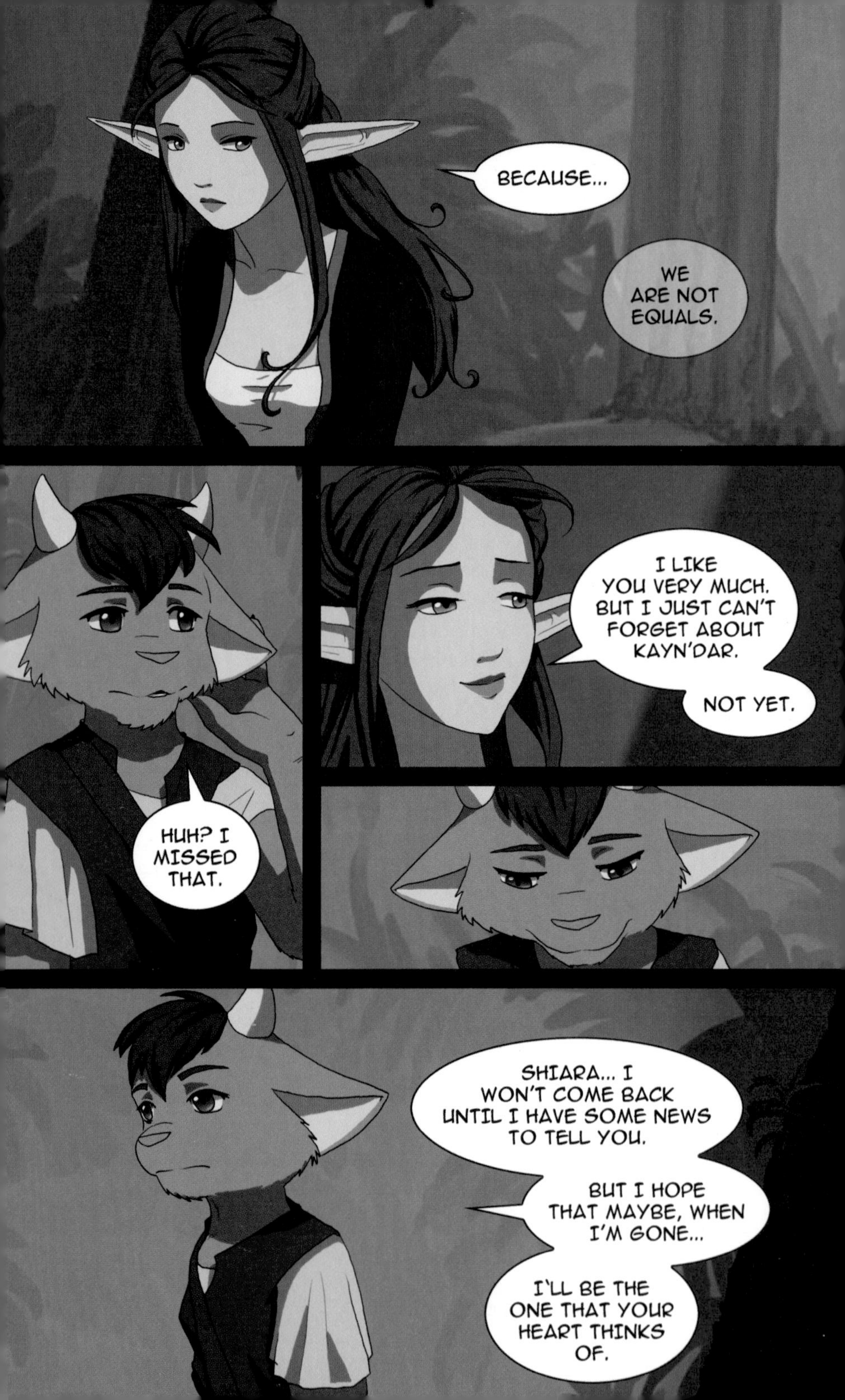
BECAUSE...
WE ARE NOT EQUALS.
HUH? I MISSED THAT.
I LIKE YOU VERY MUCH. BUT I JUST CAN'T FORGET ABOUT KAYN'DAR.
NOT YET.
SHIARA... I WON'T COME BACK UNTIL I HAVE SOME NEWS TO TELL YOU.
BUT I HOPE THAT MAYBE, WHEN I'M GONE...
I'LL BE THE ONE THAT YOUR HEART THINKS OF.

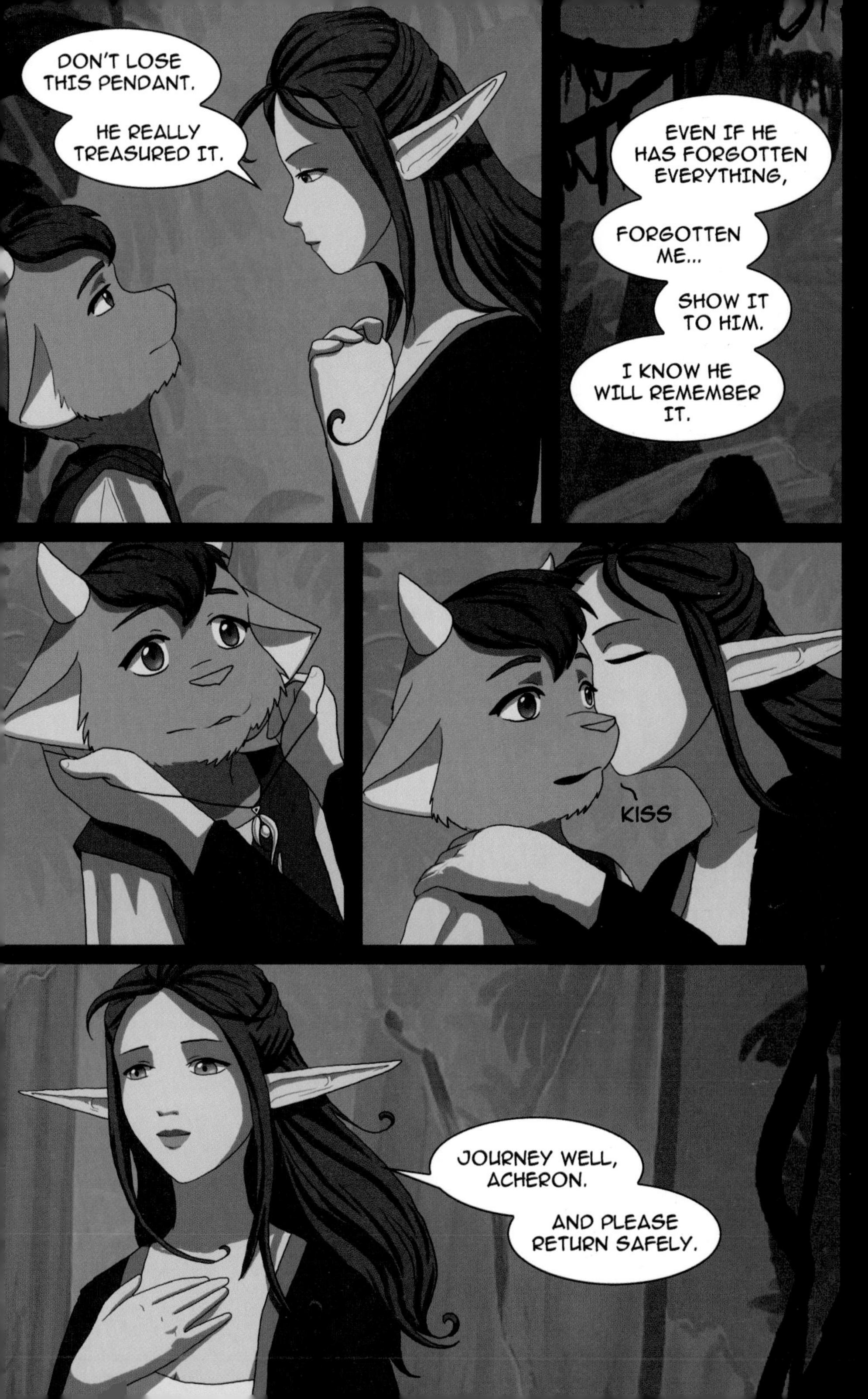
DON'T LOSE THIS PENDANT.
HE REALLY TREASURED IT.
EVEN IF HE HAS FORGOTTEN EVERYTHING,
FORGOTTEN ME...
SHOW IT TO HIM.
I KNOW HE WILL REMEMBER IT.
KISS
JOURNEY WELL, ACHERON.
AND PLEASE RETURN SAFELY.

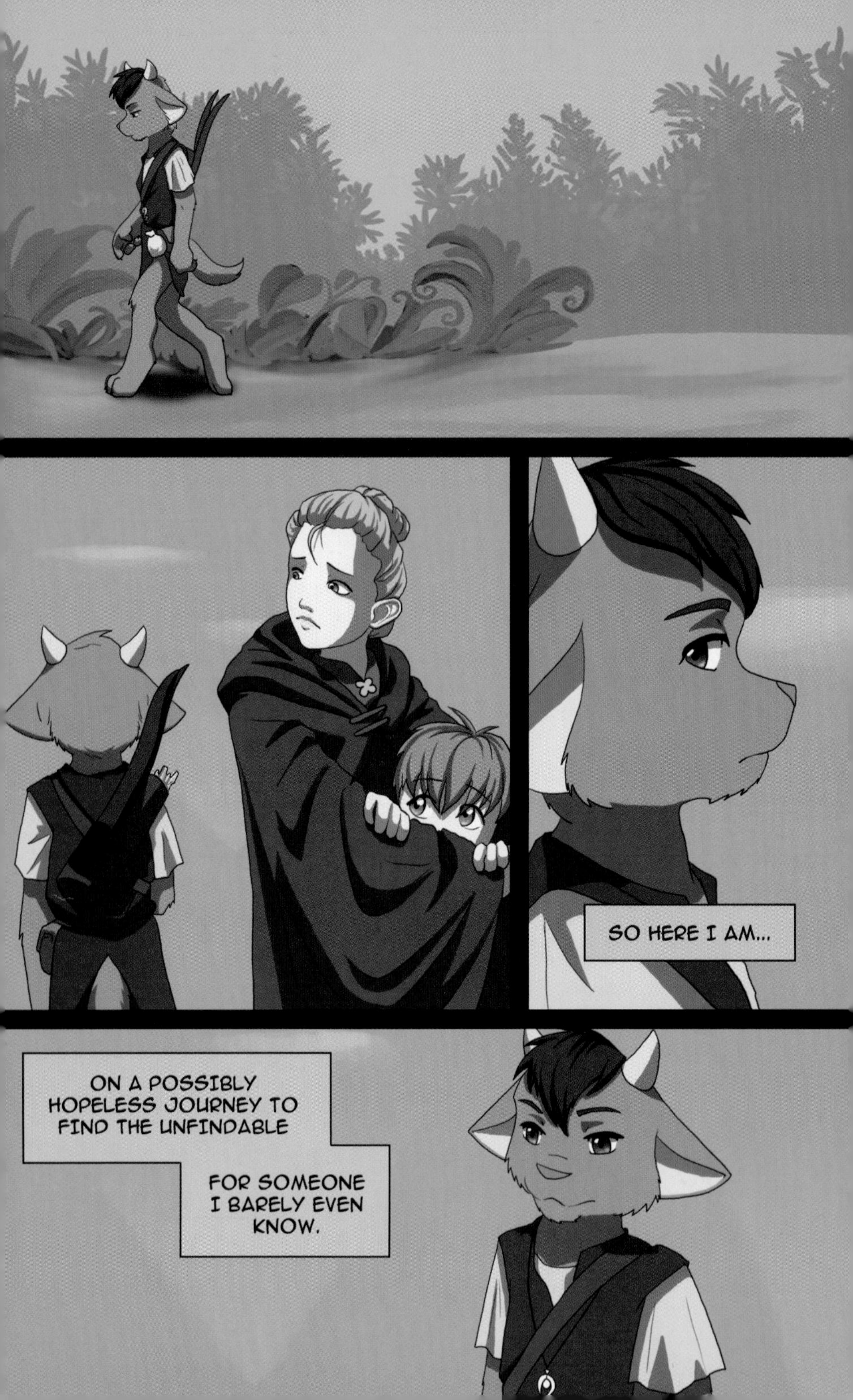
SO HERE I AM...
ON A POSSIBLY HOPELESS JOURNEY TO FIND THE UNFINDABLE
FOR SOMEONE I BARELY EVEN KNOW.

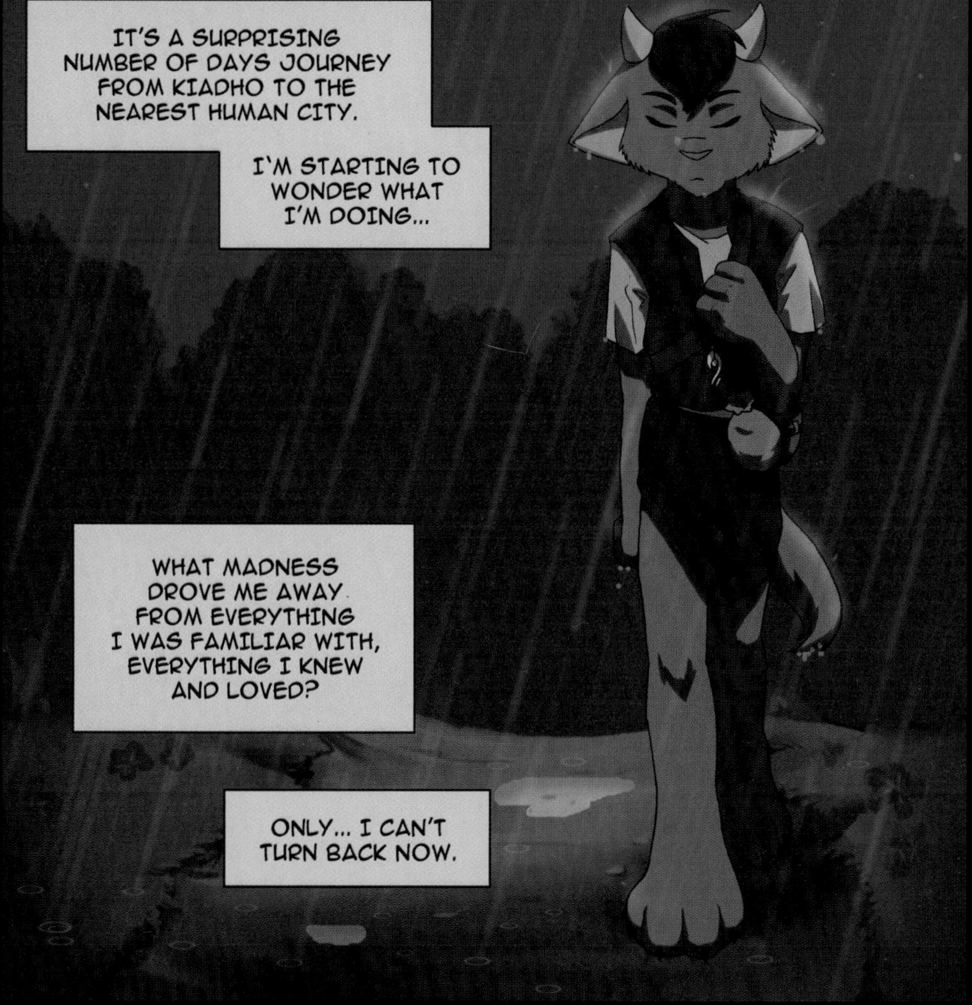
IT'S A SURPRISING NUMBER OF DAYS JOURNEY FROM KIADHO TO THE NEAREST HUMAN CITY.
I'M STARTING TO WONDER WHAT I'M DOING...
WHAT MADNESS DROVE ME AWAY FROM EVERYTHING I WAS FAMILIAR WITH, EVERYTHING I KNEW AND LOVED?
ONLY... I CAN'T TURN BACK NOW.

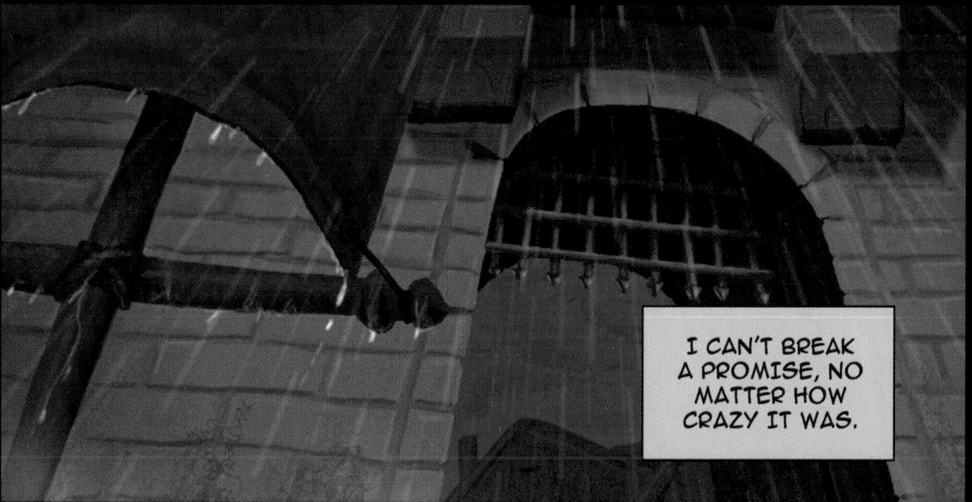
I CAN'T BREAK A PROMISE, NO MATTER HOW CRAZY IT WAS.

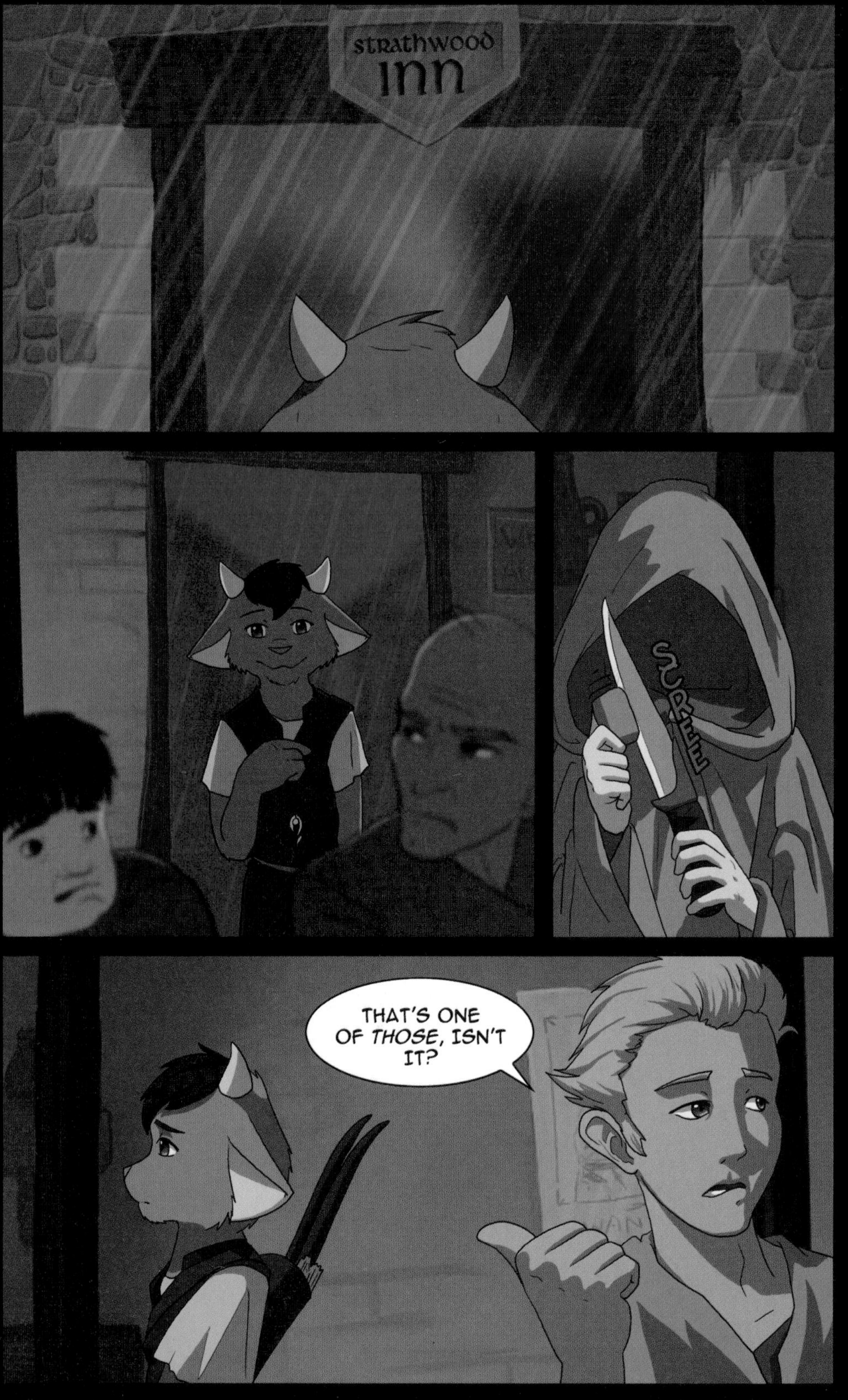
strathwood
INN
THAT'S ONE OF *THOSE*, ISN'T IT?

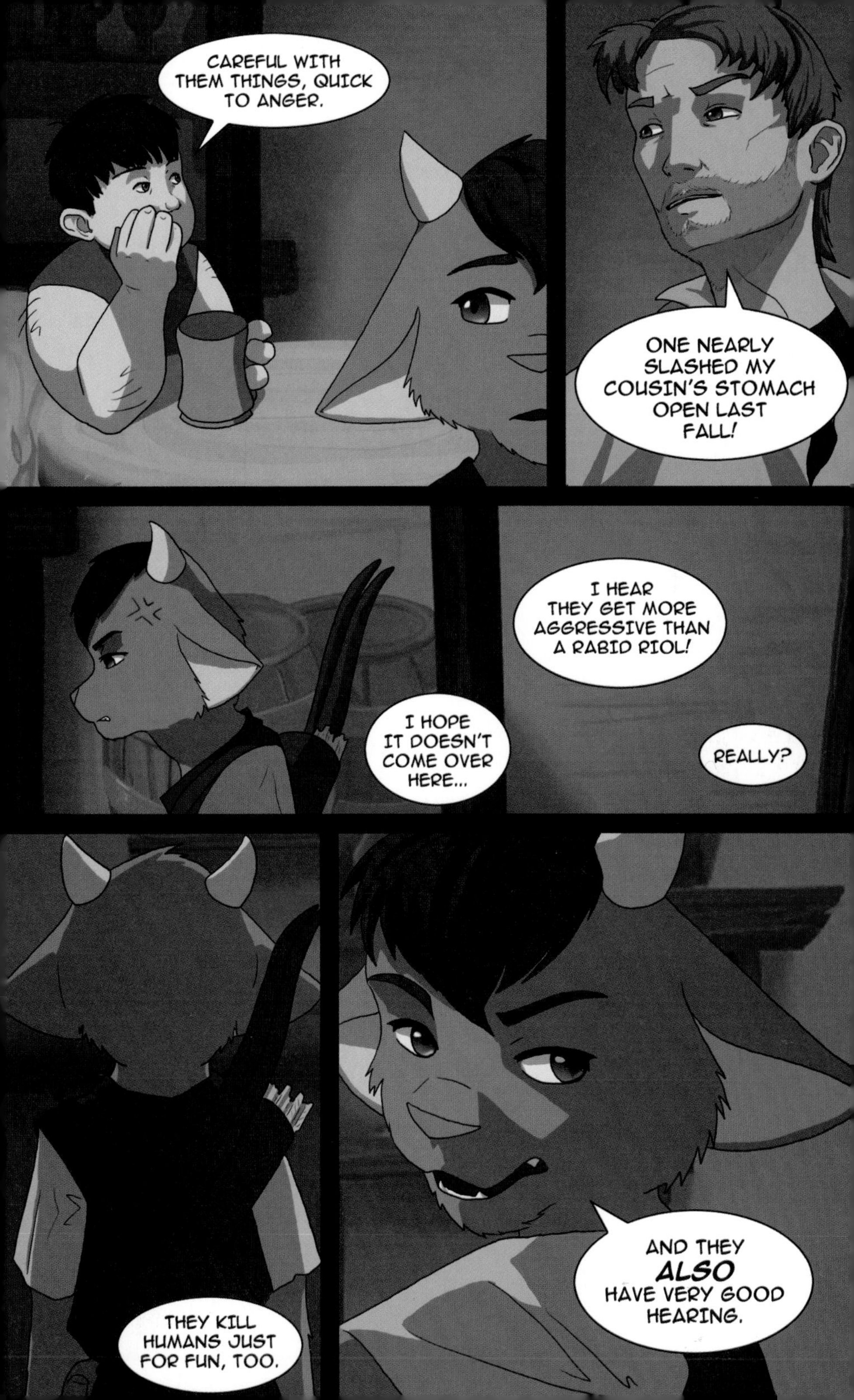
CAREFUL WITH THEM THINGS, QUICK TO ANGER.
ONE NEARLY SLASHED MY COUSIN'S STOMACH OPEN LAST FALL!
I HEAR THEY GET MORE AGGRESSIVE THAN A RABID RIOL!
I HOPE IT DOESN'T COME OVER HERE...
REALLY?
THEY KILL HUMANS JUST FOR FUN, TOO.
AND THEY ***ALSO*** HAVE VERY GOOD HEARING.

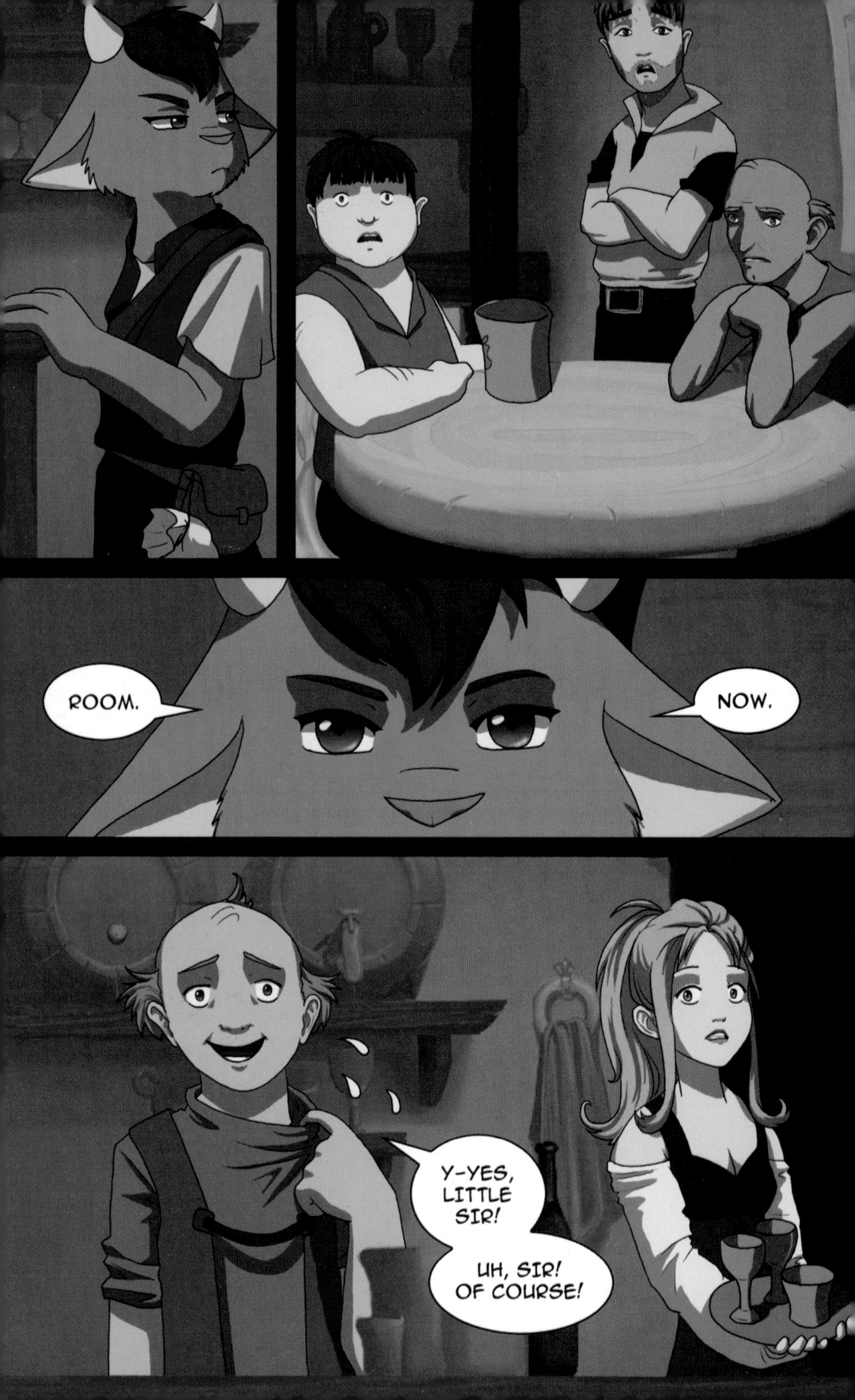
ROOM.
NOW.
Y-YES, LITTLE SIR!
UH, SIR! OF COURSE!

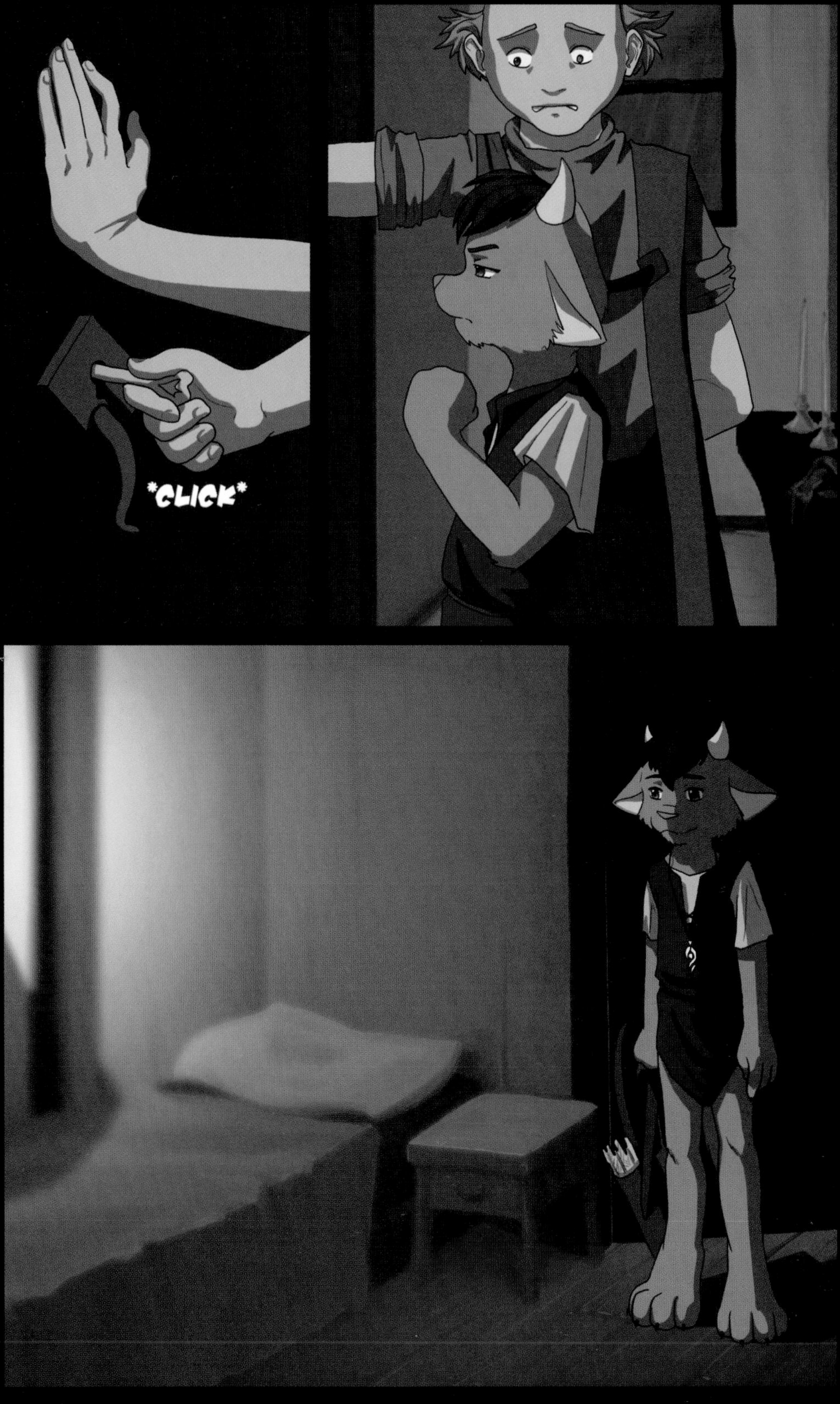
CLICK

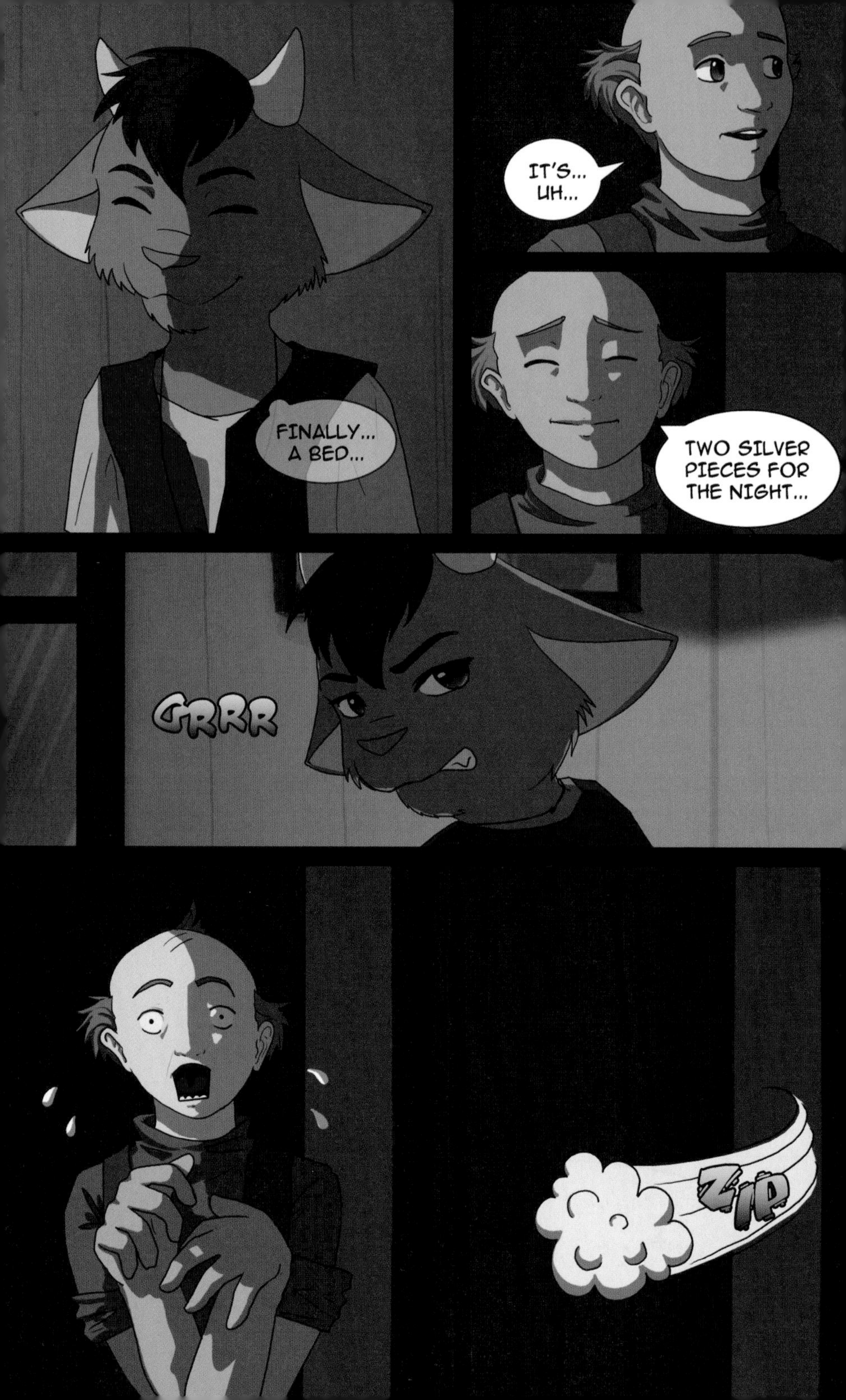
FINALLY... A BED...
IT'S... UH...
TWO SILVER PIECES FOR THE NIGHT...
GRRR
ZIP

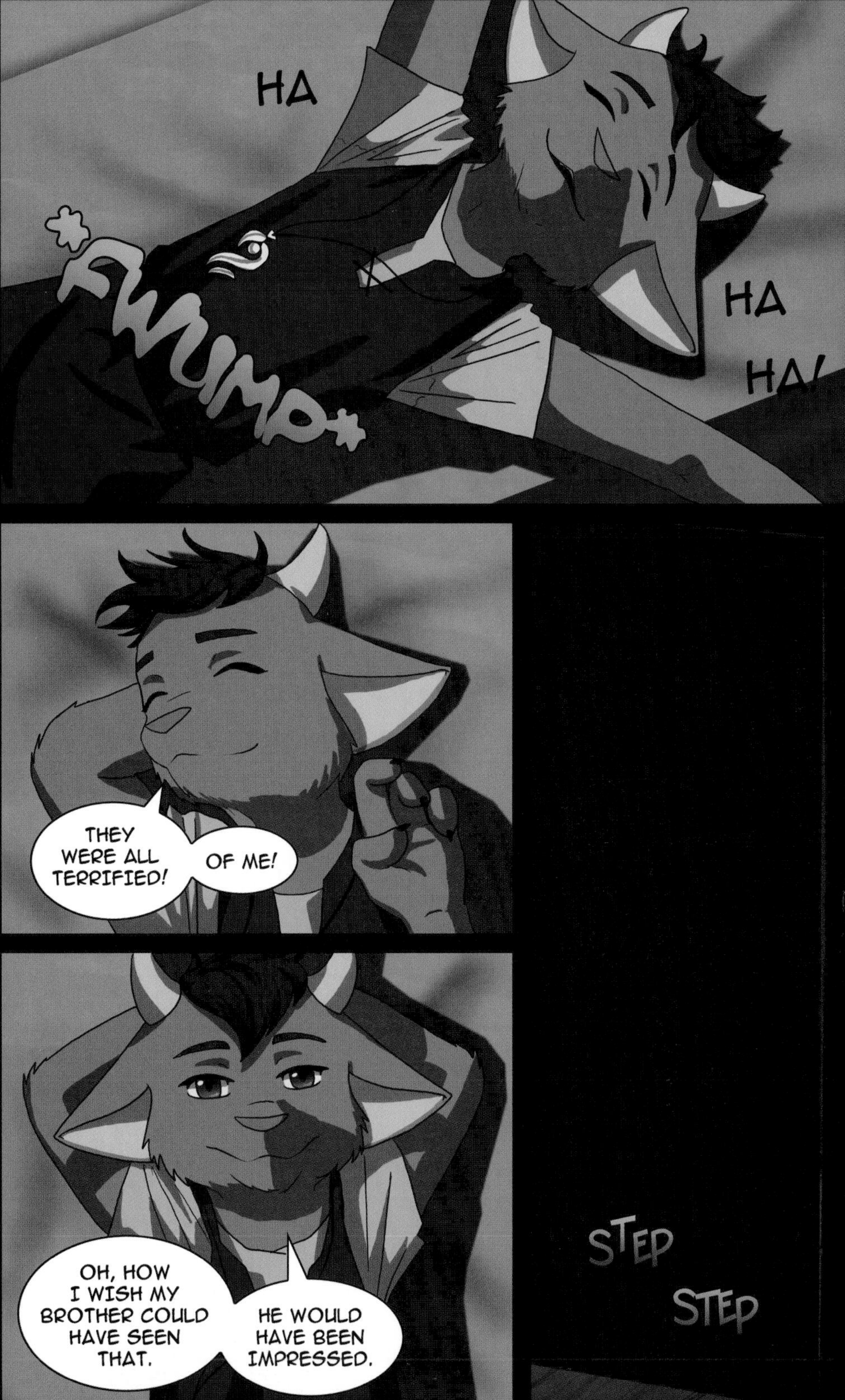
HA
FWUMP
HA
HA!
THEY WERE ALL TERRIFIED!
OF ME!
OH, HOW I WISH MY BROTHER COULD HAVE SEEN THAT.
HE WOULD HAVE BEEN IMPRESSED.
STEP
STEP

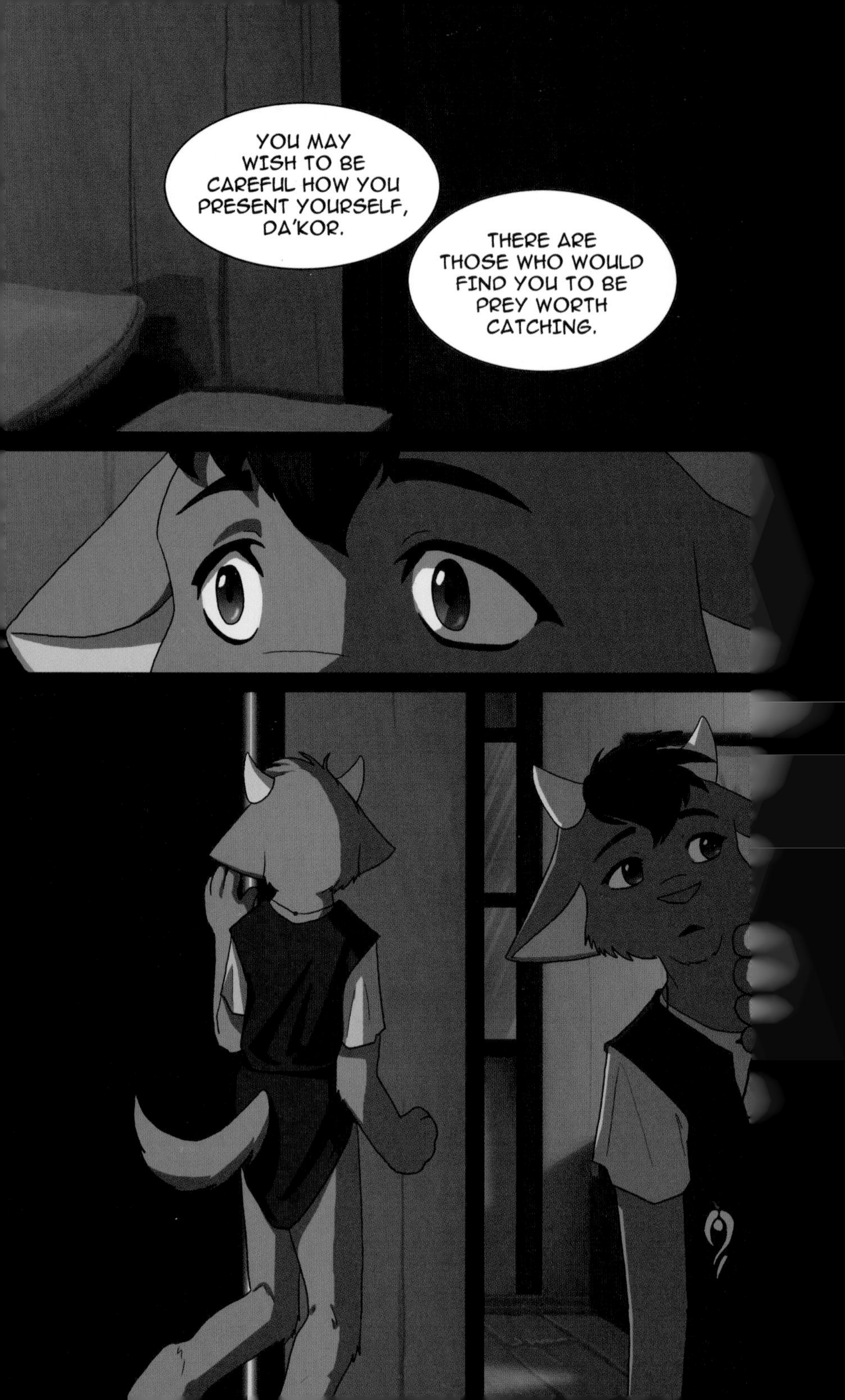
YOU MAY WISH TO BE CAREFUL HOW YOU PRESENT YOURSELF, DA'KOR.
THERE ARE THOSE WHO WOULD FIND YOU TO BE PREY WORTH CATCHING.

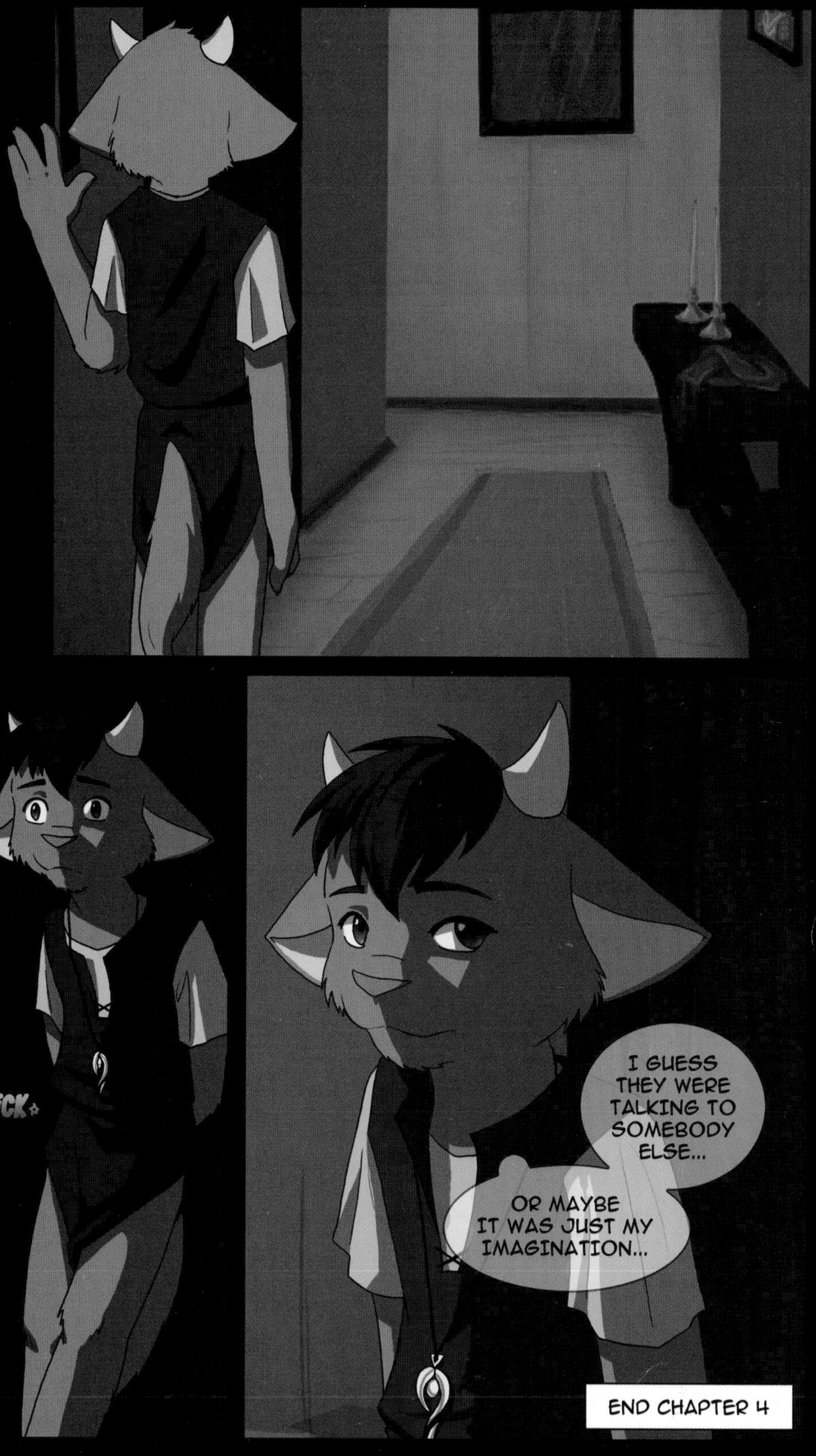
CLiCK
I GUESS THEY WERE TALKING TO SOMEBODY ELSE...
OR MAYBE IT WAS JUST MY IMAGINATION...
END CHAPTER 4

CHAPTER 5 :DISTRUST AND SUSPICION

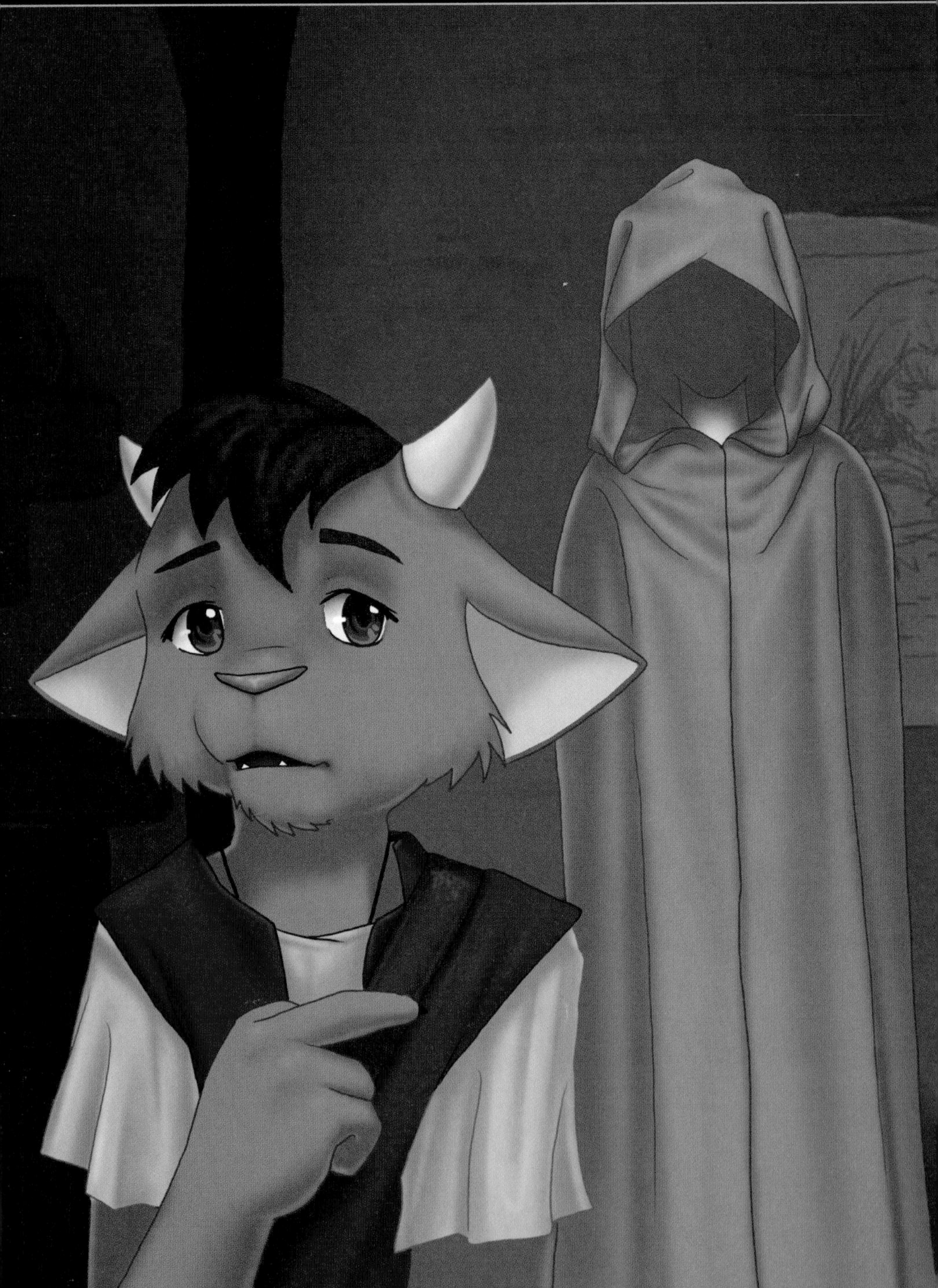

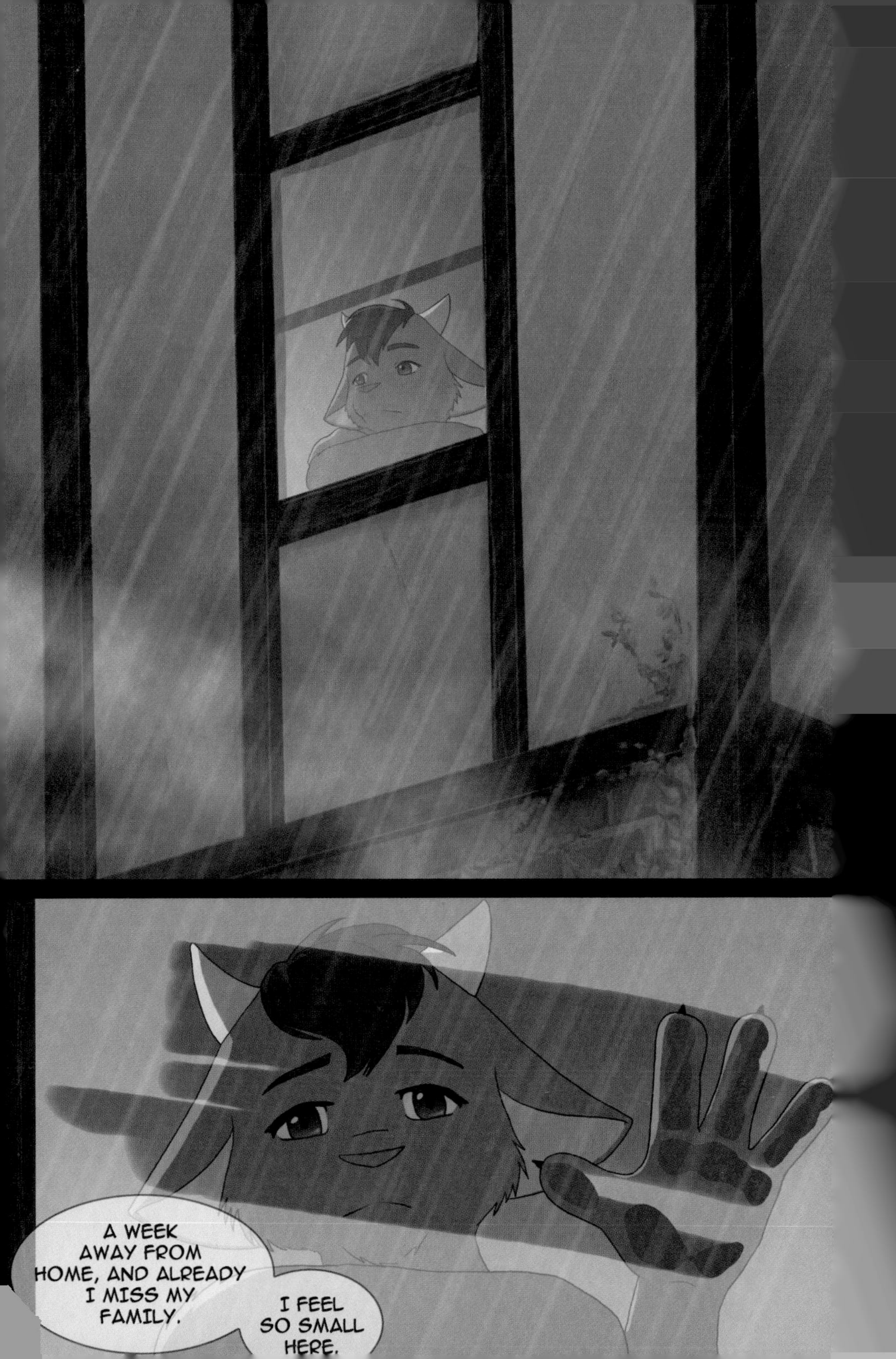
A WEEK AWAY FROM HOME, AND ALREADY I MISS MY FAMILY.
I FEEL SO SMALL HERE.

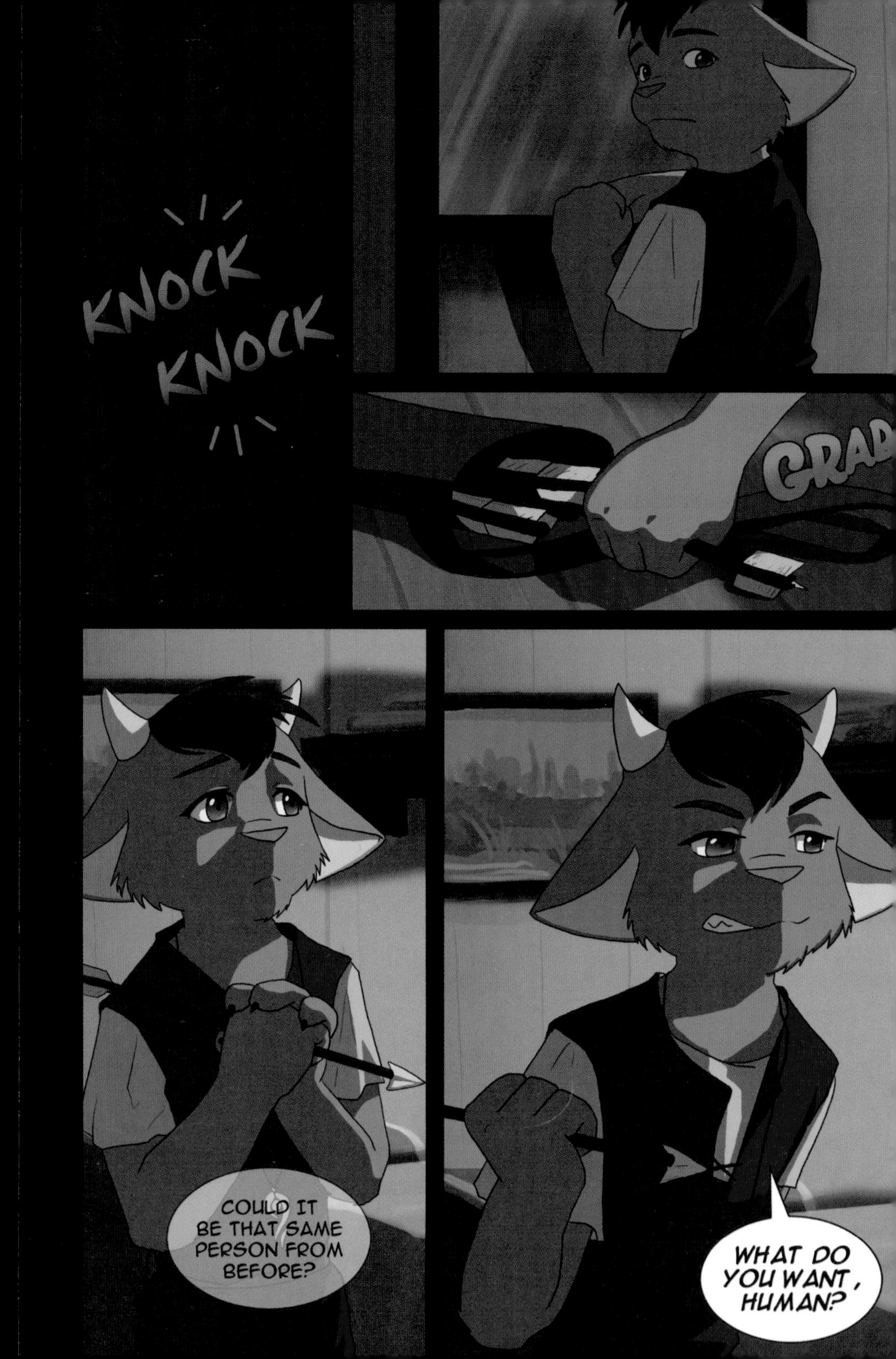
KNOCK KNOCK
GRAB
COULD IT BE THAT SAME PERSON FROM BEFORE?
WHAT DO YOU WANT, HUMAN?

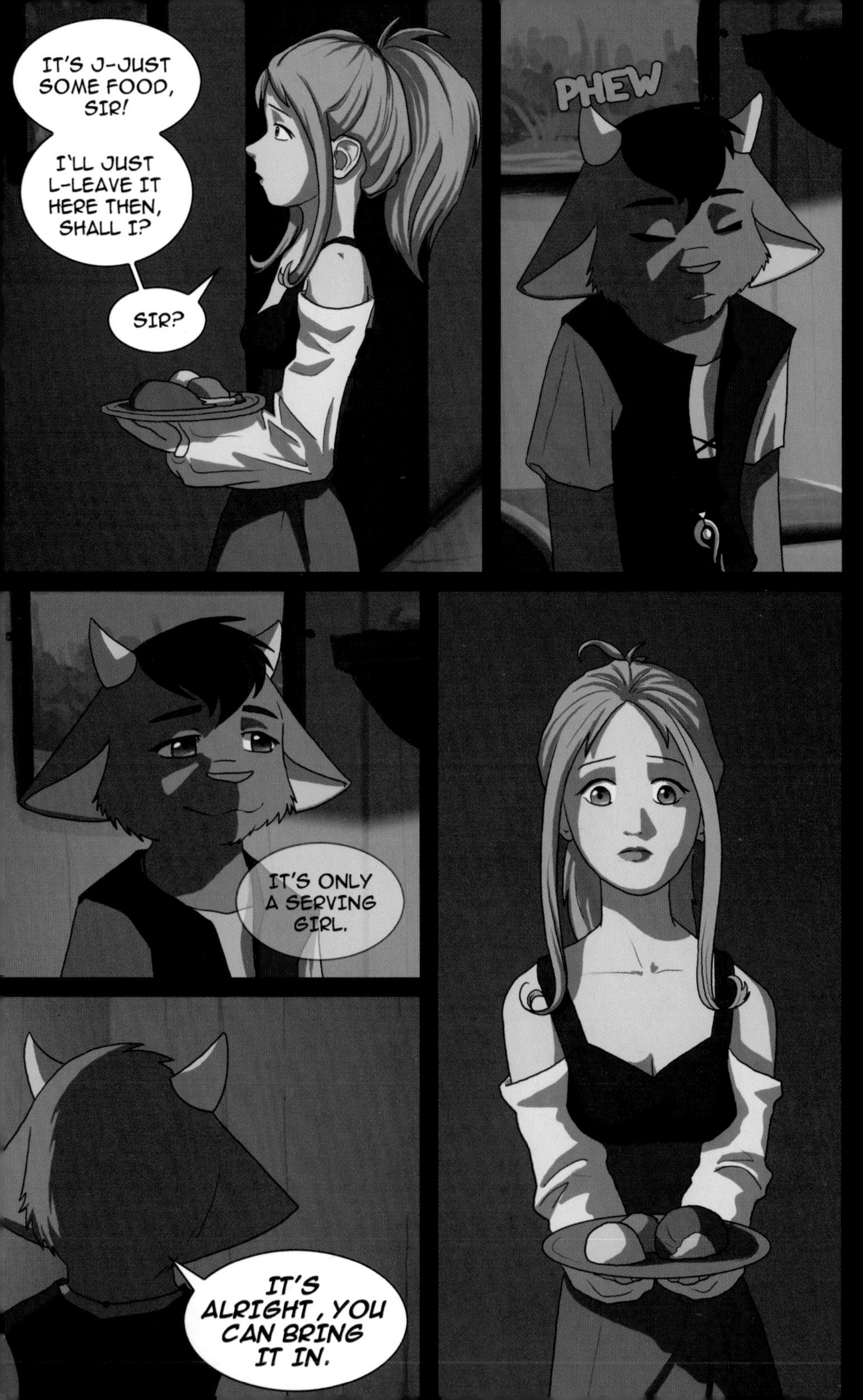
IT'S J-JUST SOME FOOD, SIR!
I'LL JUST L-LEAVE IT HERE THEN, SHALL I?
SIR?
PHEW
IT'S ONLY A SERVING GIRL.
IT'S ALRIGHT, YOU CAN BRING IT IN.

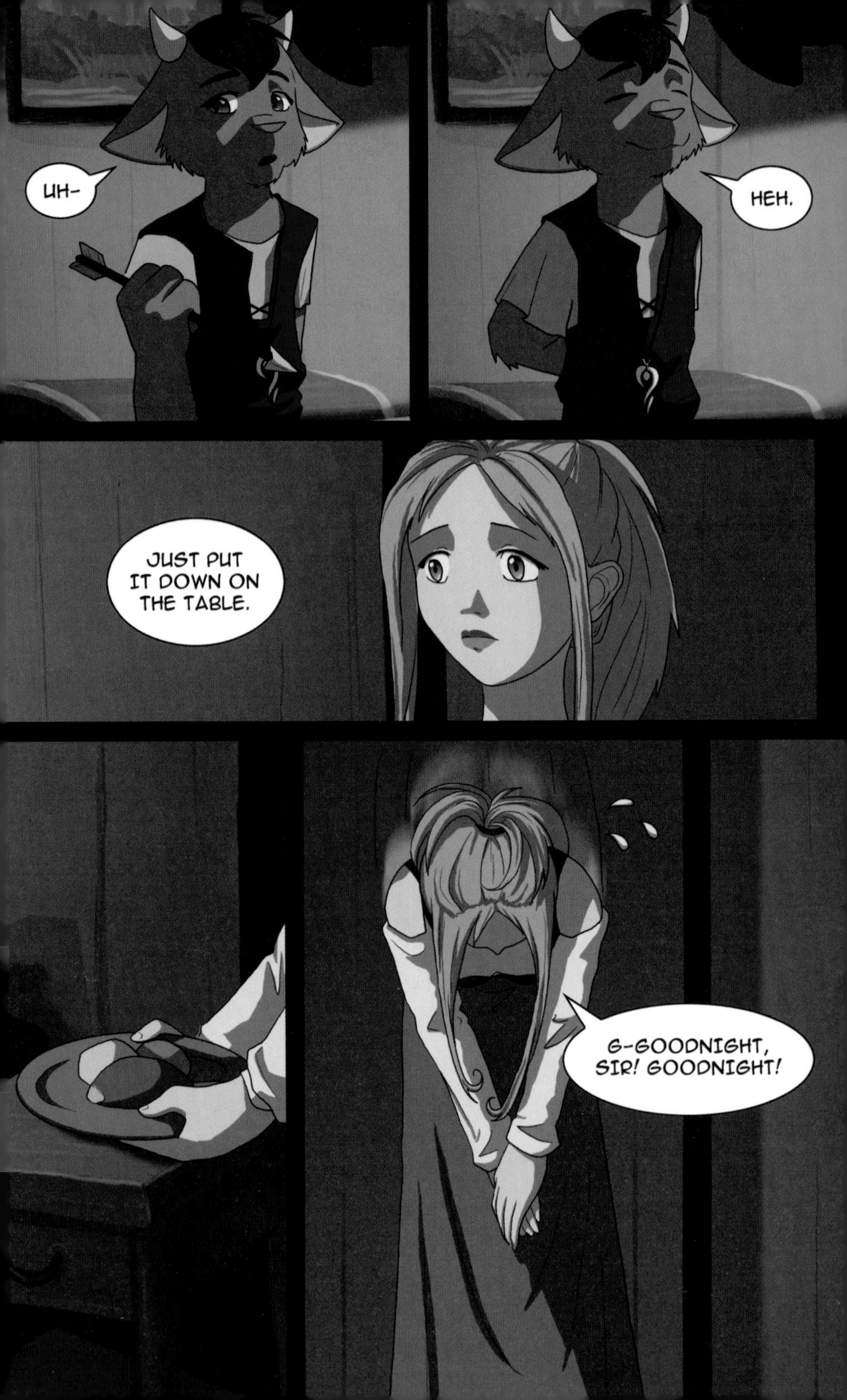
UH-
HEH.
JUST PUT IT DOWN ON THE TABLE.
G-GOODNIGHT, SIR! GOODNIGHT!

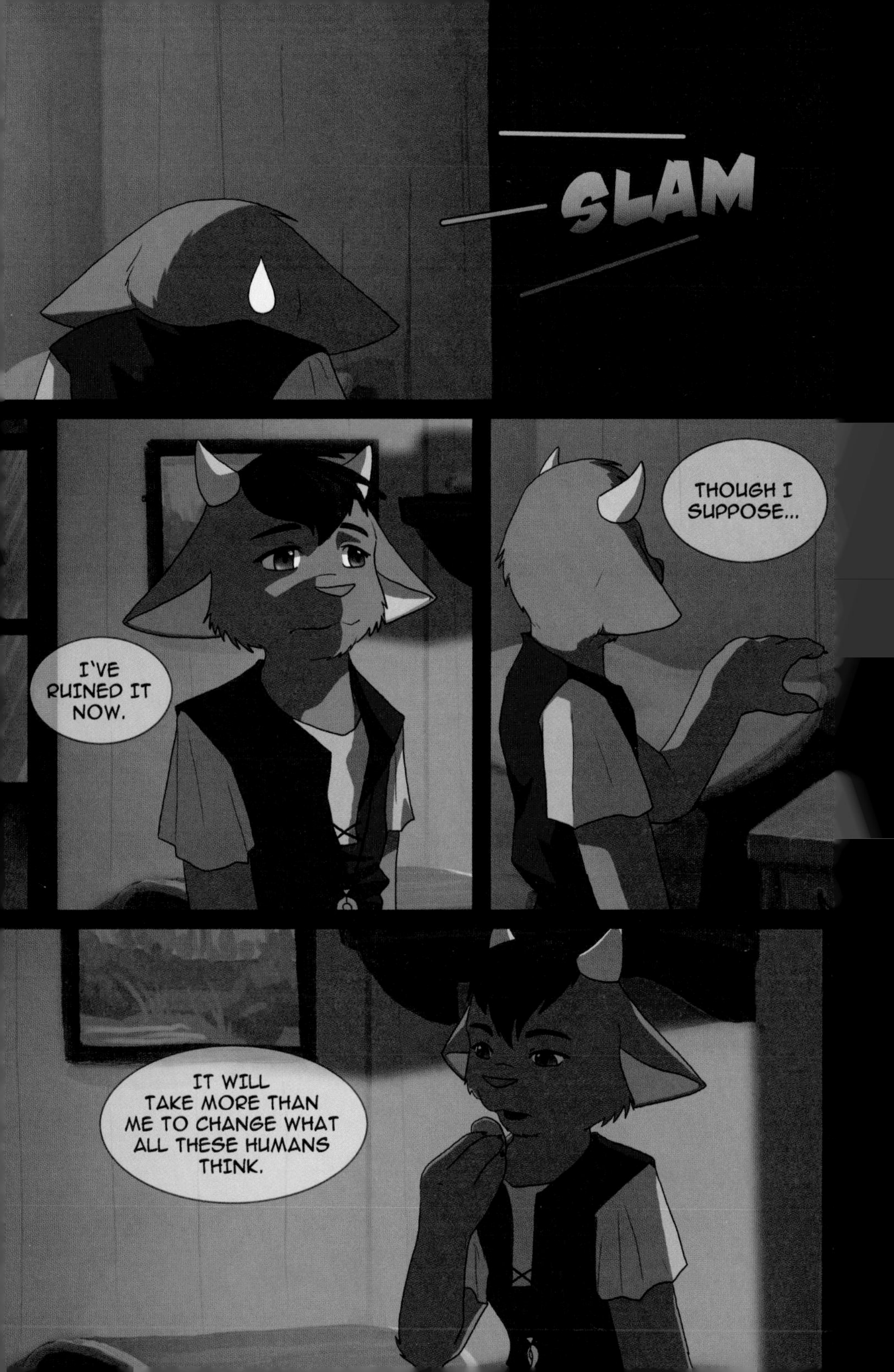
SLAM
I'VE RUINED IT NOW.
THOUGH I SUPPOSE...
IT WILL TAKE MORE THAN ME TO CHANGE WHAT ALL THESE HUMANS THINK.

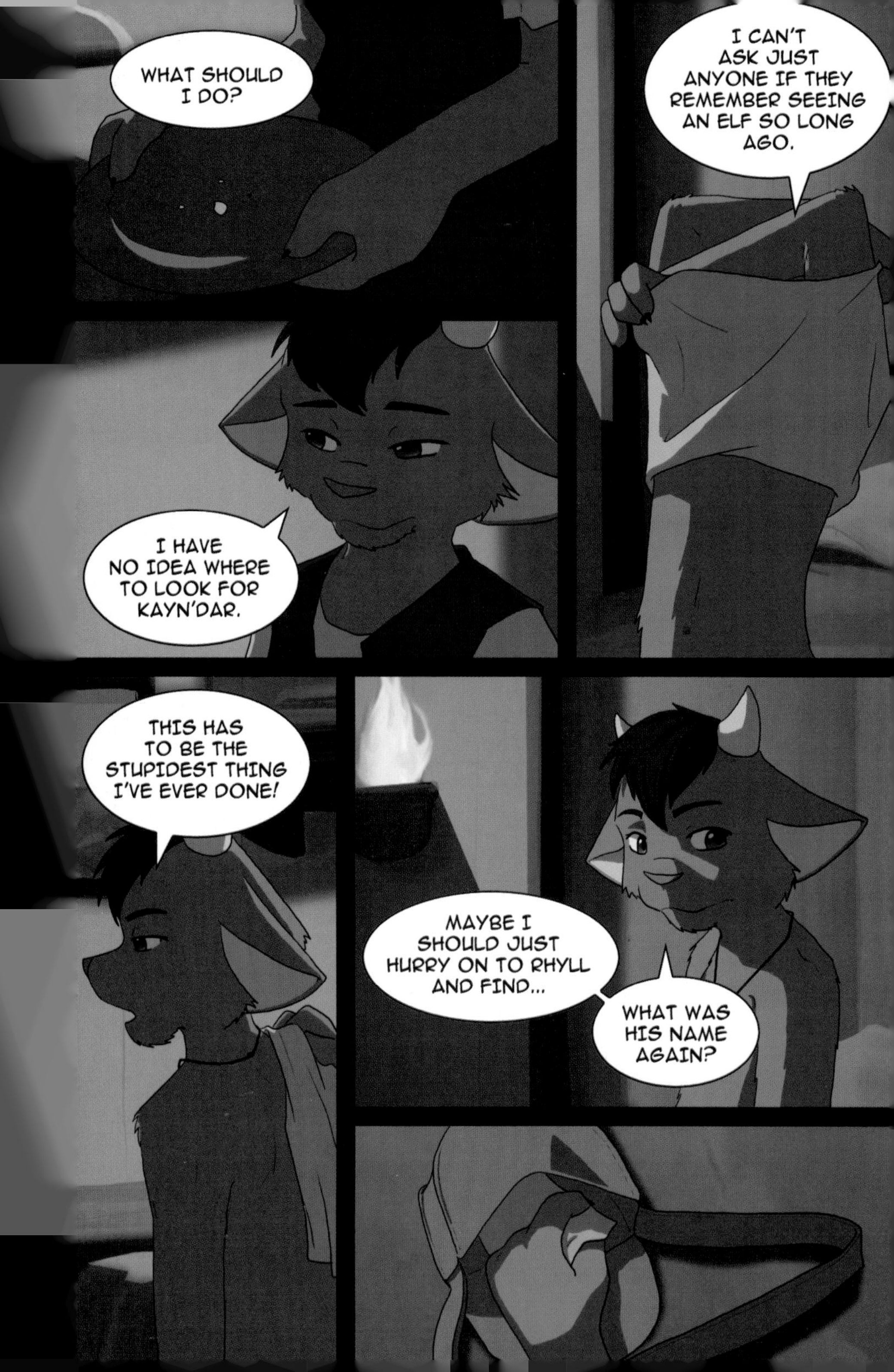
WHAT SHOULD I DO?
I CAN'T ASK JUST ANYONE IF THEY REMEMBER SEEING AN ELF SO LONG AGO.
I HAVE NO IDEA WHERE TO LOOK FOR KAYN'DAR.
THIS HAS TO BE THE STUPIDEST THING I'VE EVER DONE!
MAYBE I SHOULD JUST HURRY ON TO RHYLL AND FIND...
WHAT WAS HIS NAME AGAIN?

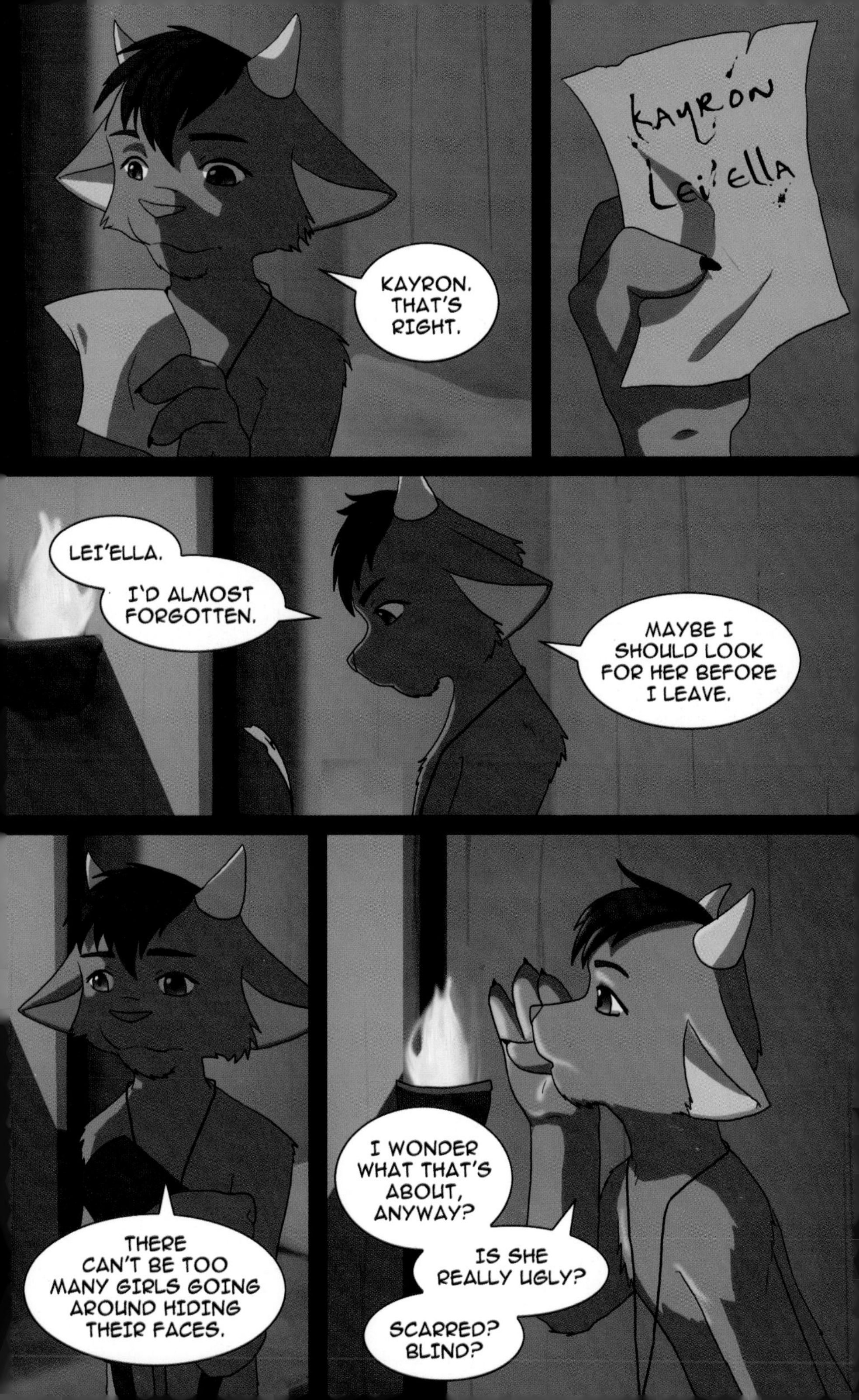
KAYRON. THAT'S RIGHT.
Kayron
Lei'ella
LEI'ELLA.
I'D ALMOST FORGOTTEN.
MAYBE I SHOULD LOOK FOR HER BEFORE I LEAVE.
THERE CAN'T BE TOO MANY GIRLS GOING AROUND HIDING THEIR FACES.
I WONDER WHAT THAT'S ABOUT, ANYWAY?
IS SHE REALLY UGLY?
SCARRED? BLIND?

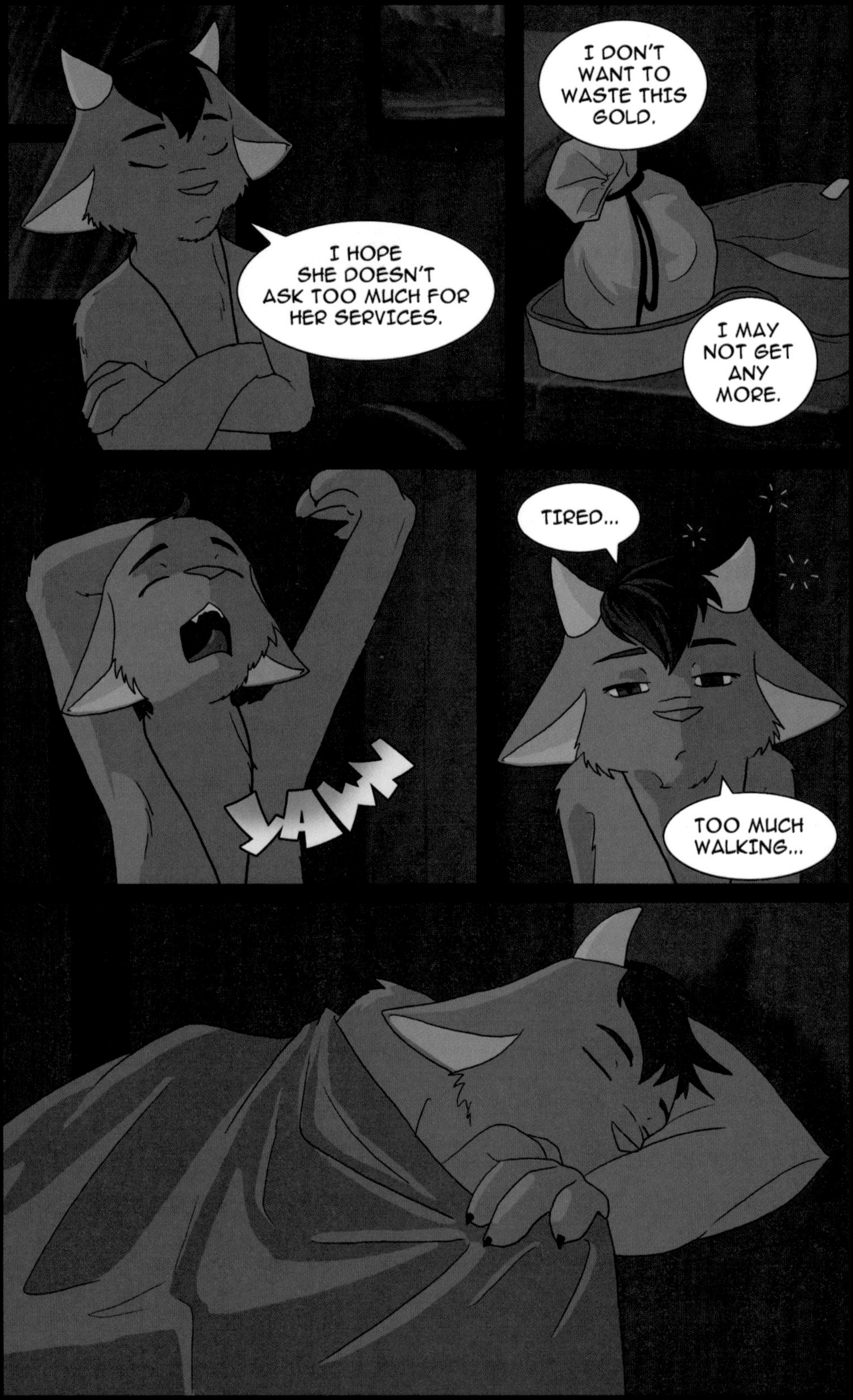
I HOPE SHE DOESN'T ASK TOO MUCH FOR HER SERVICES.
I DON'T WANT TO WASTE THIS GOLD.
I MAY NOT GET ANY MORE.
YAWN
TIRED...
TOO MUCH WALKING...

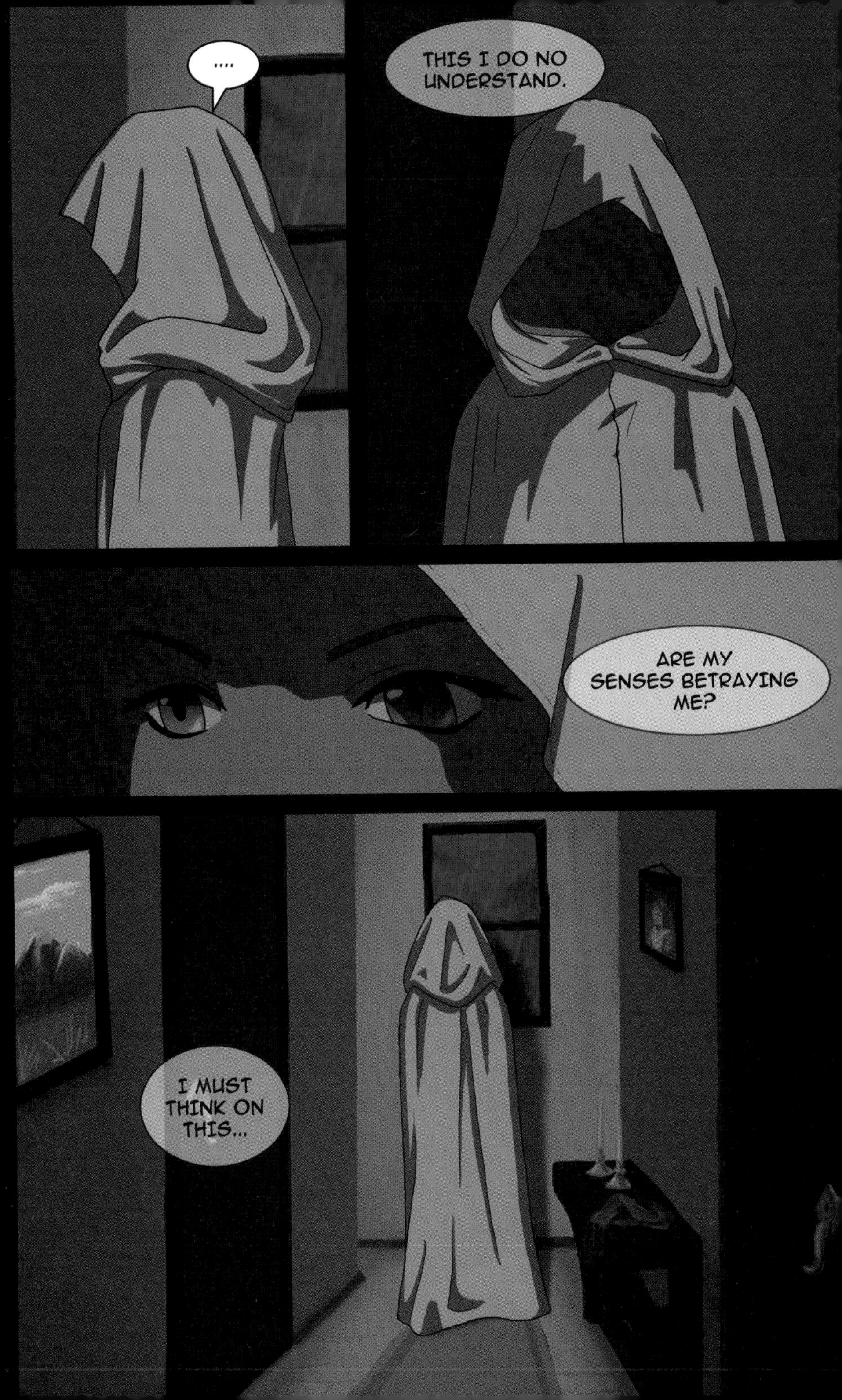
....
THIS I DO NO UNDERSTAND.
ARE MY SENSES BETRAYING ME?
I MUST THINK ON THIS...

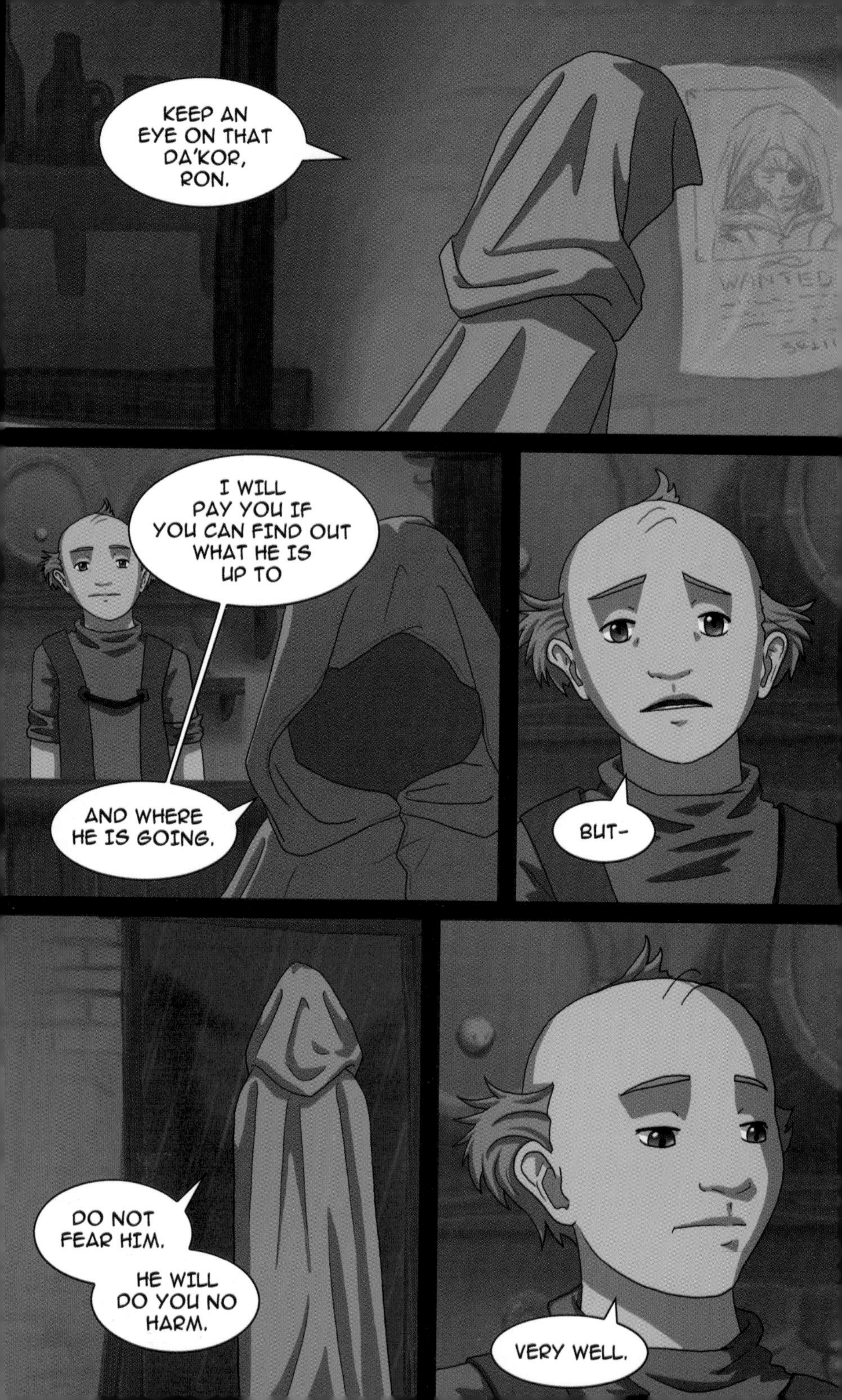
KEEP AN EYE ON THAT DA'KOR, RON.
WANTED
I WILL PAY YOU IF YOU CAN FIND OUT WHAT HE IS UP TO
AND WHERE HE IS GOING.
BUT-
DO NOT FEAR HIM.
HE WILL DO YOU NO HARM.
VERY WELL.

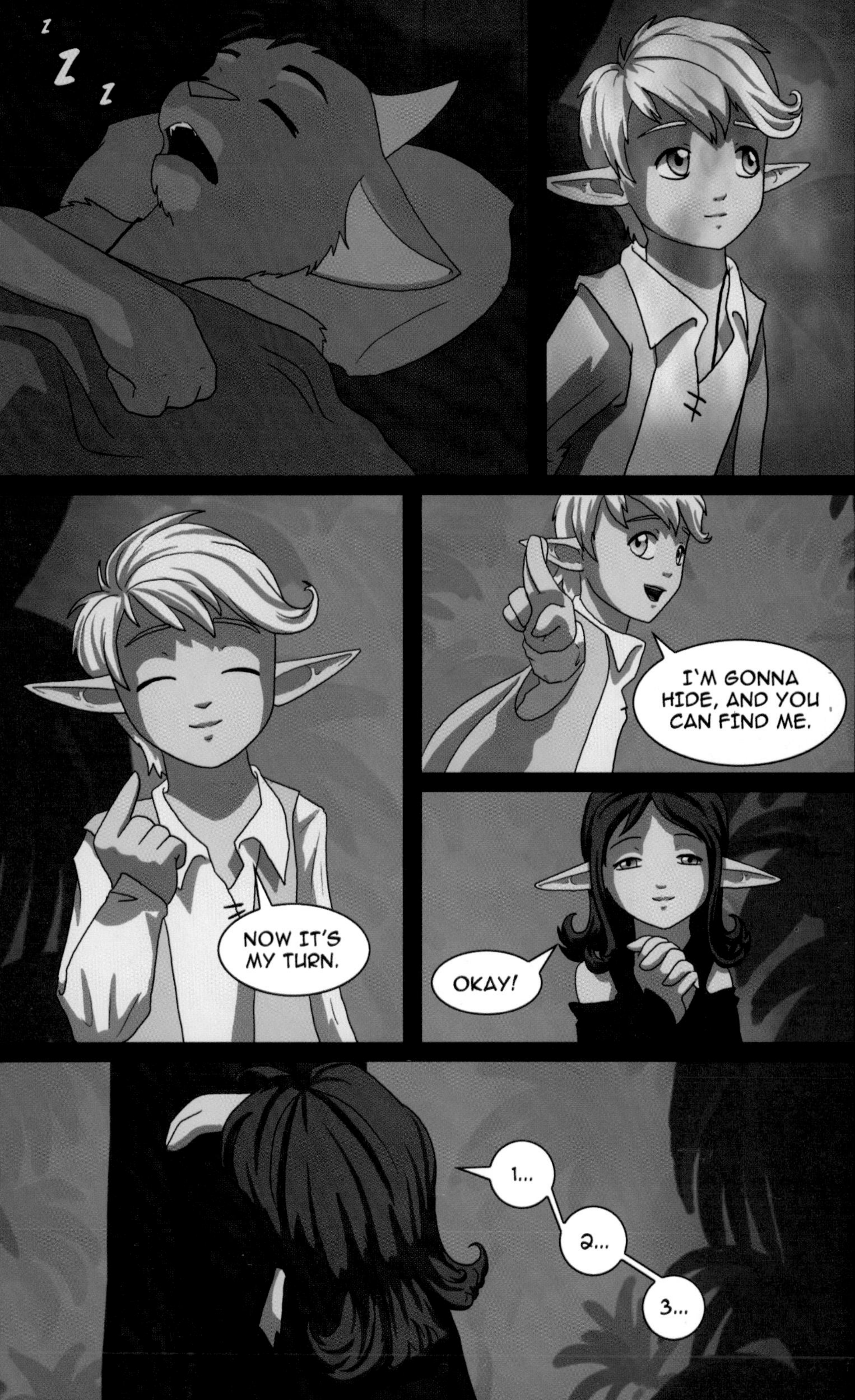
Z
Z
Z
I'M GONNA HIDE, AND YOU CAN FIND ME.
NOW IT'S MY TURN.
OKAY!
1...
2...
3...

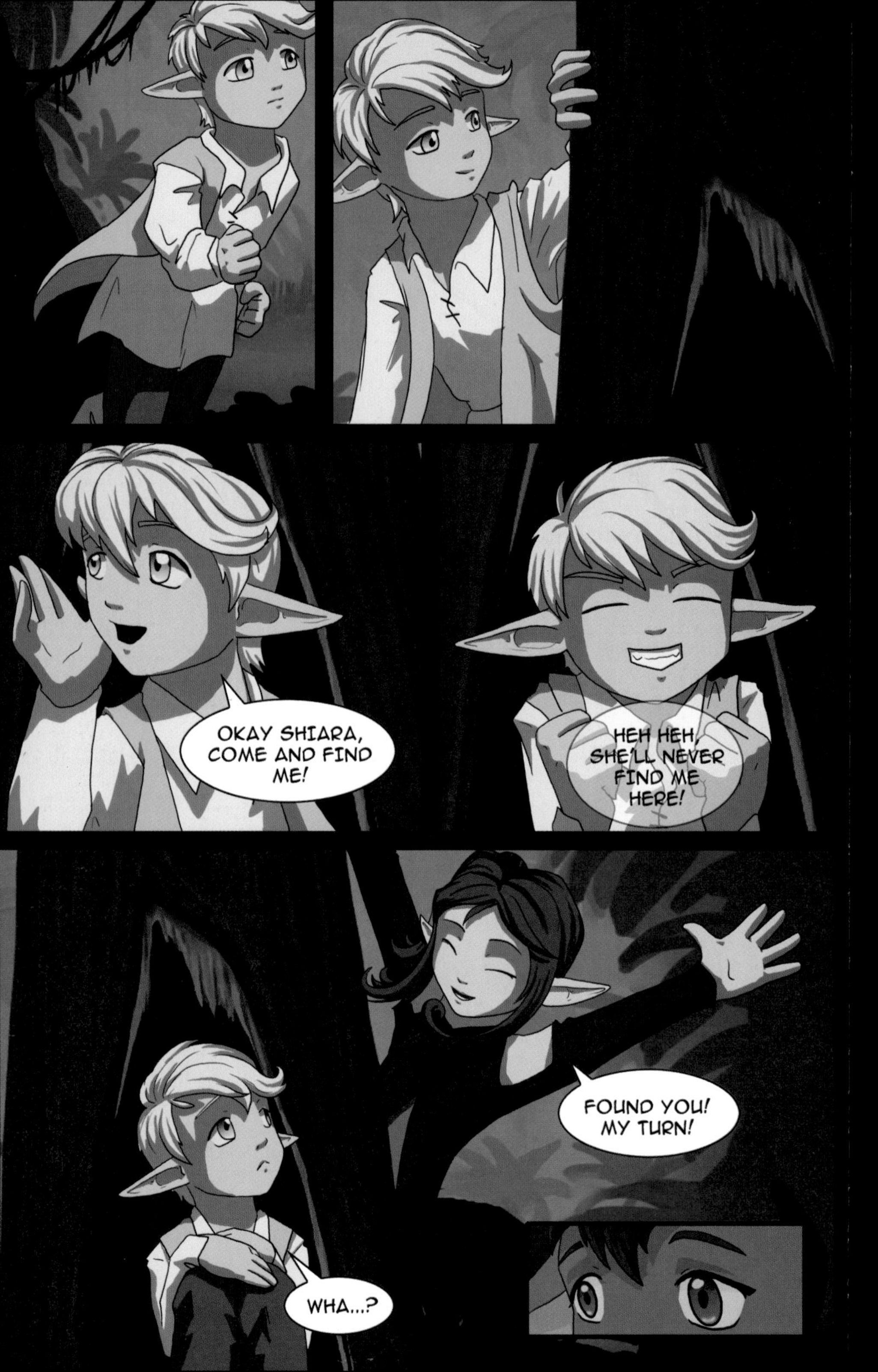
OKAY SHIARA, COME AND FIND ME!
HEH HEH, SHE'LL NEVER FIND ME HERE!
FOUND YOU! MY TURN!
WHA...?

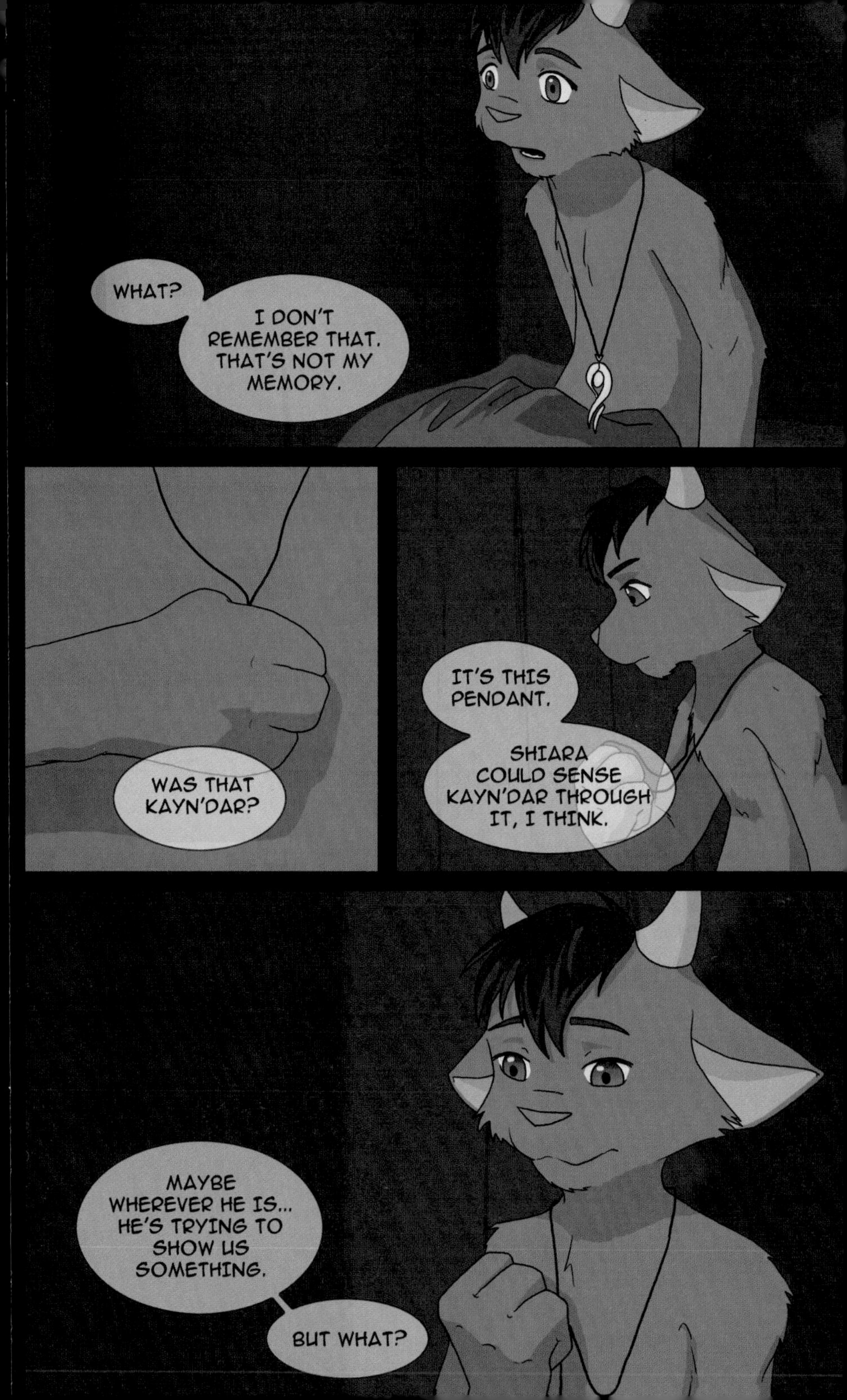
WHAT?
I DON'T REMEMBER THAT. THAT'S NOT MY MEMORY.
WAS THAT KAYN'DAR?
IT'S THIS PENDANT.
SHIARA COULD SENSE KAYN'DAR THROUGH IT, I THINK.
MAYBE WHEREVER HE IS... HE'S TRYING TO SHOW US SOMETHING.
BUT WHAT?

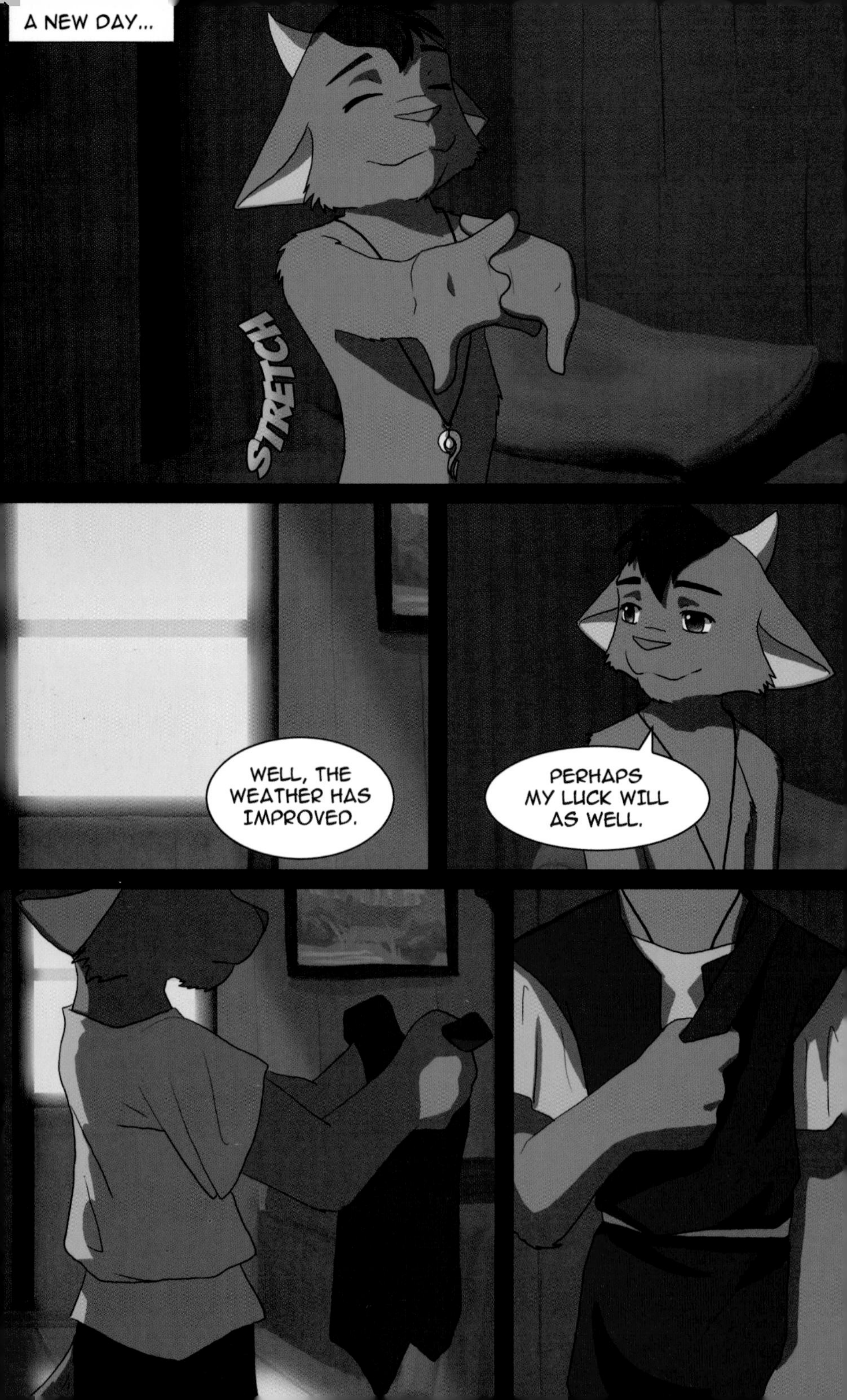
A NEW DAY...
STRETCH
WELL, THE WEATHER HAS IMPROVED.
PERHAPS MY LUCK WILL AS WELL.

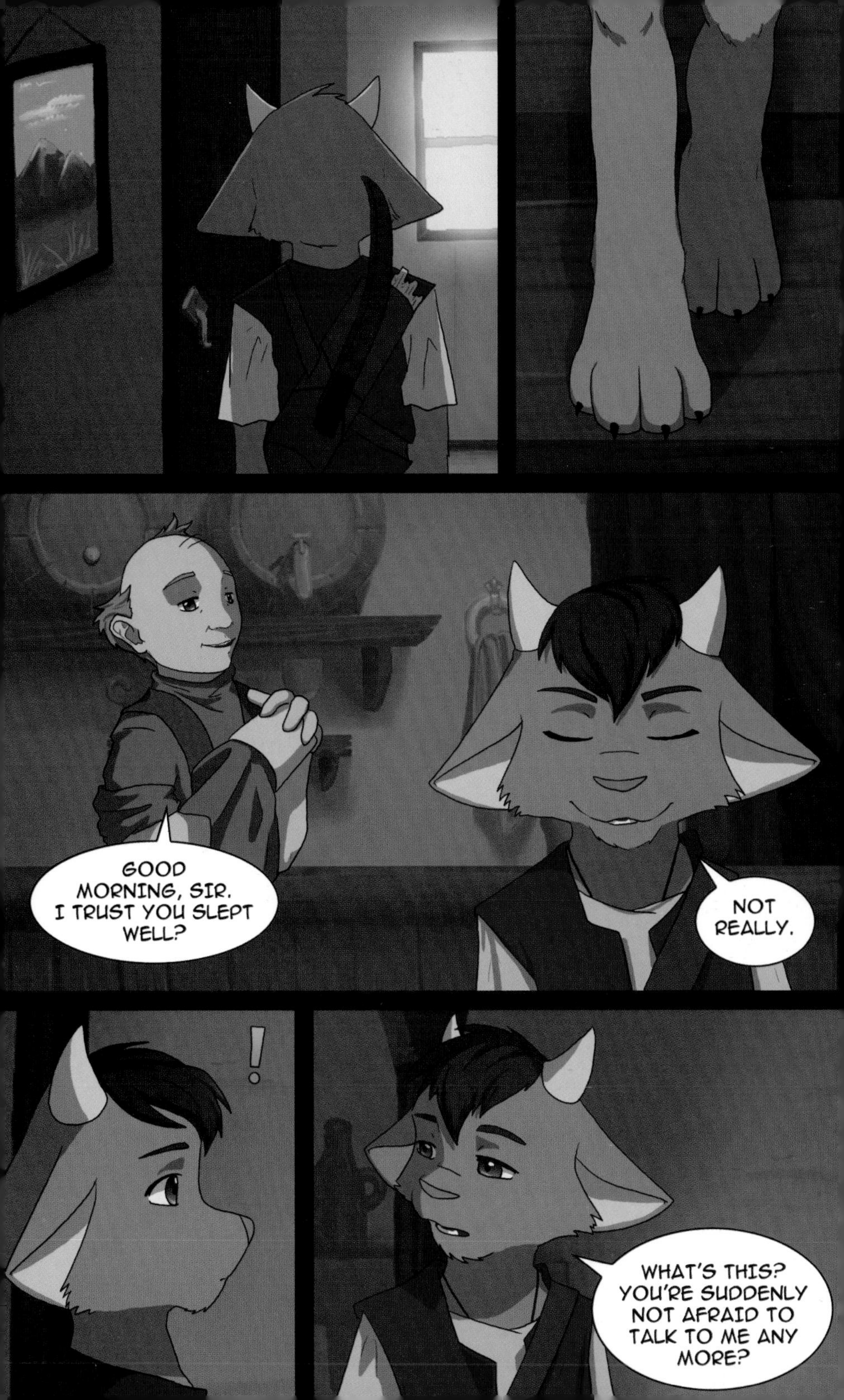
GOOD MORNING, SIR. I TRUST YOU SLEPT WELL?
NOT REALLY.
!
WHAT'S THIS? YOU'RE SUDDENLY NOT AFRAID TO TALK TO ME ANY MORE?

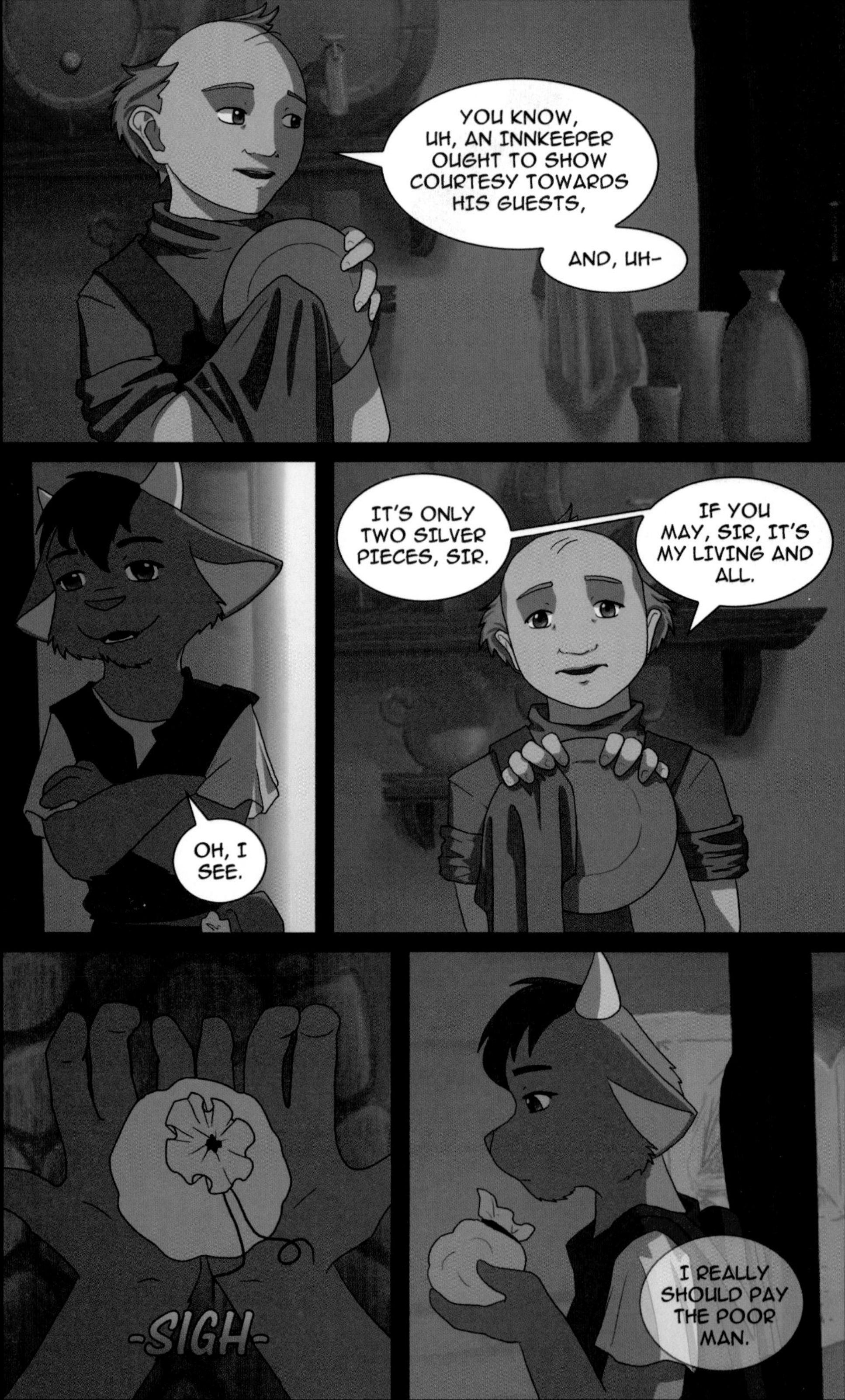
YOU KNOW, UH, AN INNKEEPER OUGHT TO SHOW COURTESY TOWARDS HIS GUESTS,
AND, UH-
OH, I SEE.
IT'S ONLY TWO SILVER PIECES, SIR.
IF YOU MAY, SIR, IT'S MY LIVING AND ALL.
-SIGH-
I REALLY SHOULD PAY THE POOR MAN.

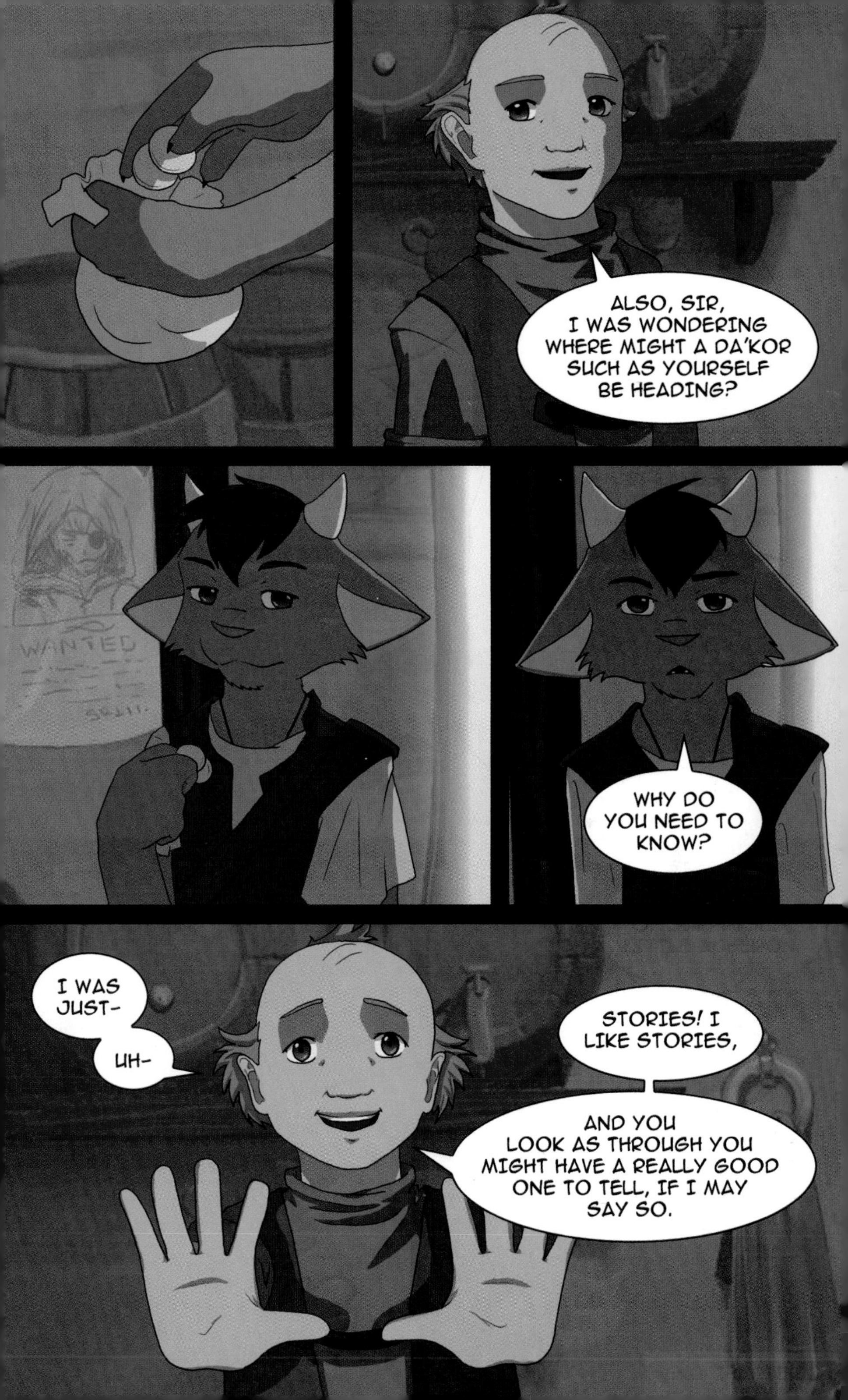
ALSO, SIR, I WAS WONDERING WHERE MIGHT A DA'KOR SUCH AS YOURSELF BE HEADING?
WANTED
WHY DO YOU NEED TO KNOW?
I WAS JUST-
UH-
STORIES! I LIKE STORIES,
AND YOU LOOK AS THROUGH YOU MIGHT HAVE A REALLY GOOD ONE TO TELL, IF I MAY SAY SO.

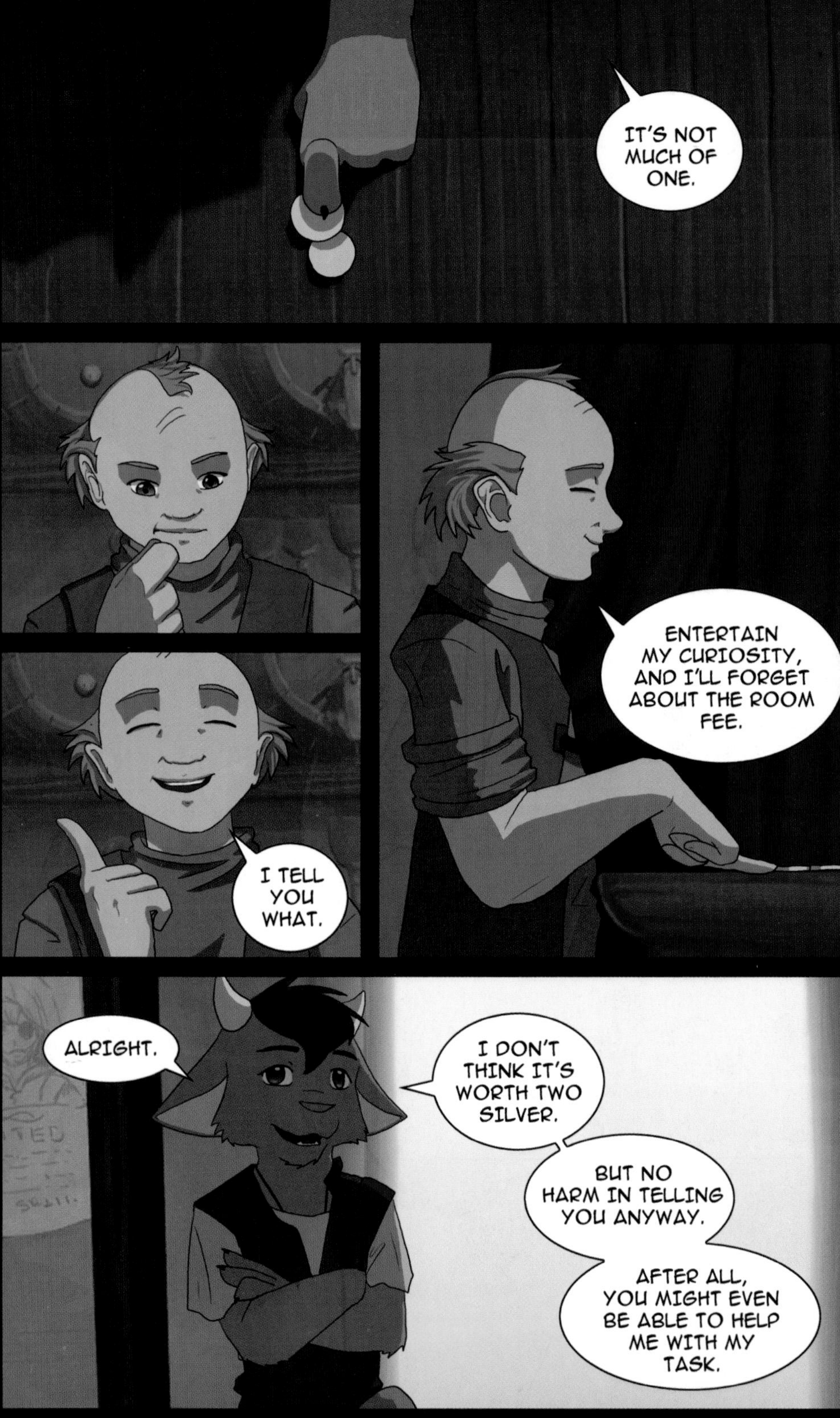
IT'S NOT MUCH OF ONE.
I TELL YOU WHAT.
ENTERTAIN MY CURIOSITY, AND I'LL FORGET ABOUT THE ROOM FEE.
ALRIGHT.
I DON'T THINK IT'S WORTH TWO SILVER.
BUT NO HARM IN TELLING YOU ANYWAY.
AFTER ALL, YOU MIGHT EVEN BE ABLE TO HELP ME WITH MY TASK.

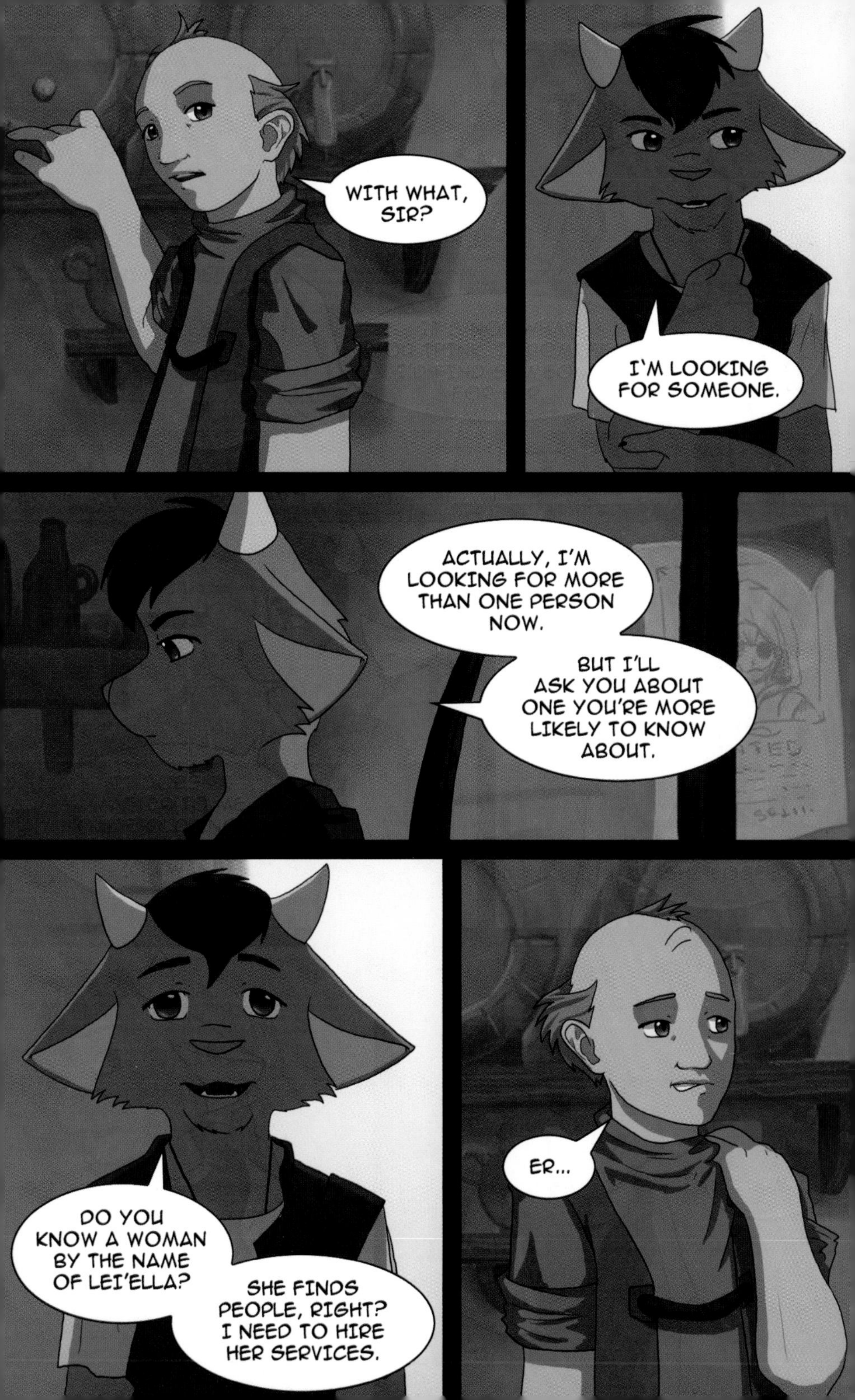
WITH WHAT, SIR?
I'M LOOKING FOR SOMEONE.
ACTUALLY, I'M LOOKING FOR MORE THAN ONE PERSON NOW.
BUT I'LL ASK YOU ABOUT ONE YOU'RE MORE LIKELY TO KNOW ABOUT.
DO YOU KNOW A WOMAN BY THE NAME OF LEI'ELLA?
SHE FINDS PEOPLE, RIGHT? I NEED TO HIRE HER SERVICES.
ER...

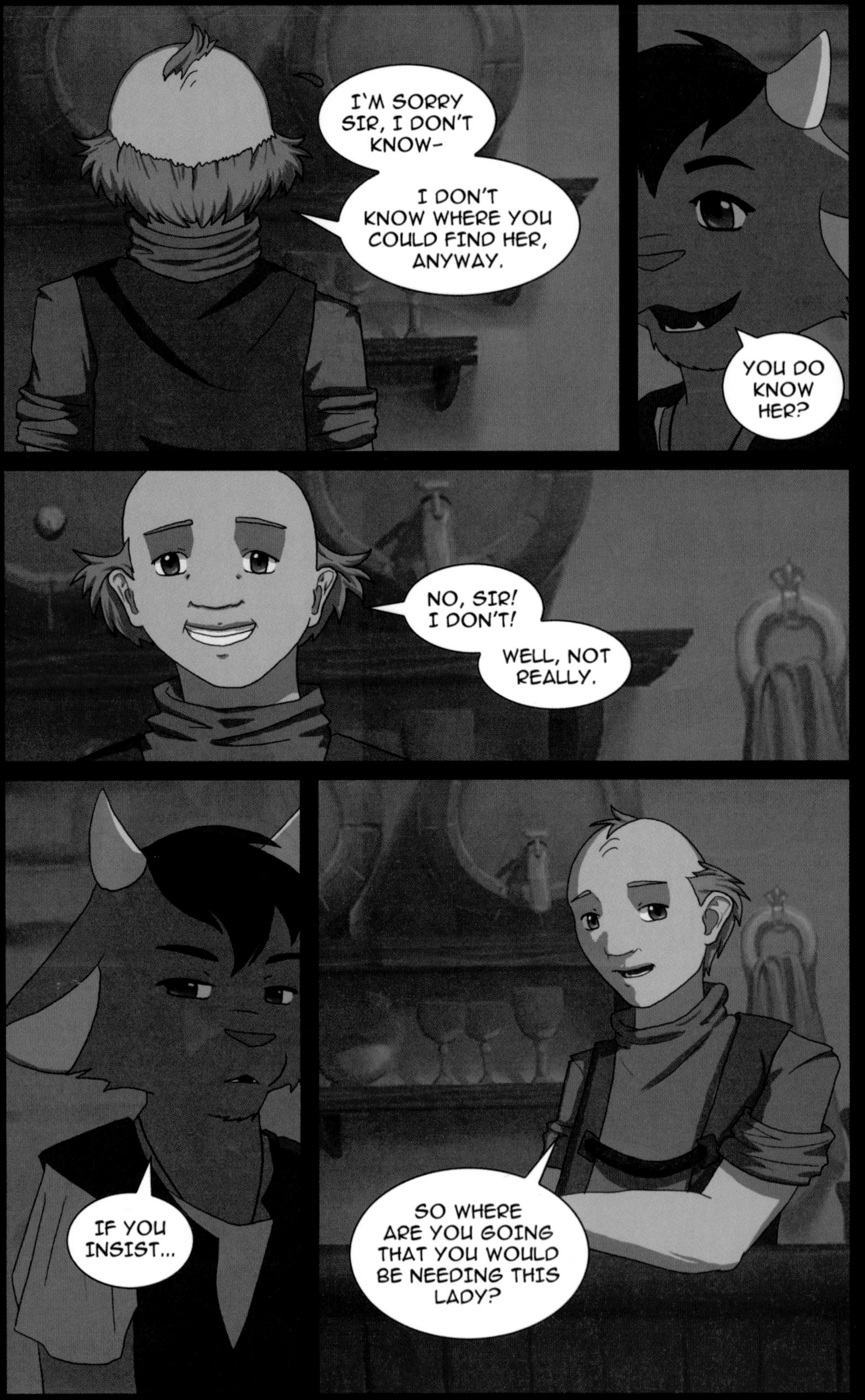
I'M SORRY SIR, I DON'T KNOW-
I DON'T KNOW WHERE YOU COULD FIND HER, ANYWAY.
YOU DO KNOW HER?
NO, SIR! I DON'T!
WELL, NOT REALLY.
IF YOU INSIST...
SO WHERE ARE YOU GOING THAT YOU WOULD BE NEEDING THIS LADY?

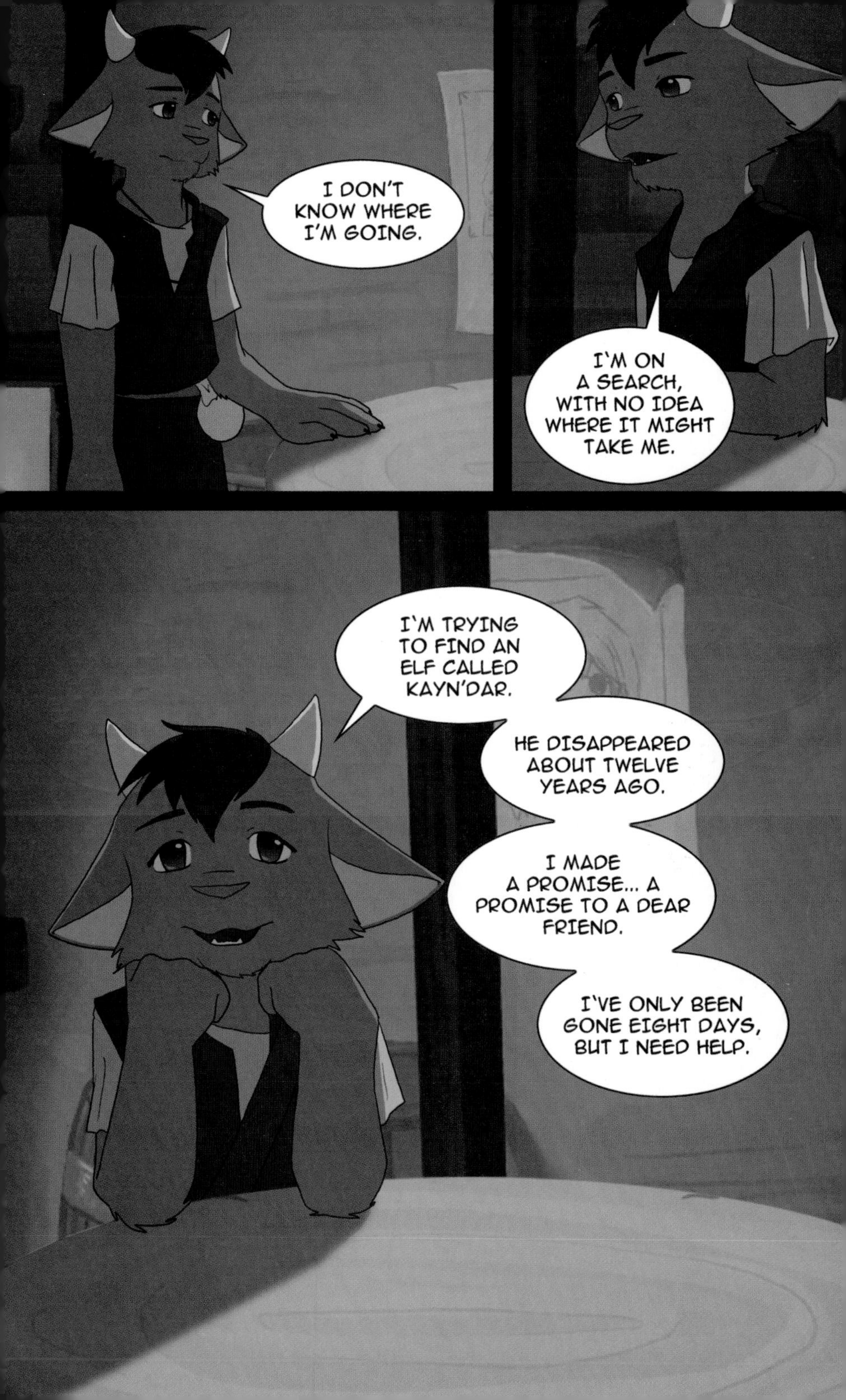
I DON'T KNOW WHERE I'M GOING.
I'M ON A SEARCH, WITH NO IDEA WHERE IT MIGHT TAKE ME.
I'M TRYING TO FIND AN ELF CALLED KAYN'DAR.
HE DISAPPEARED ABOUT TWELVE YEARS AGO.
I MADE A PROMISE... A PROMISE TO A DEAR FRIEND.
I'VE ONLY BEEN GONE EIGHT DAYS, BUT I NEED HELP.

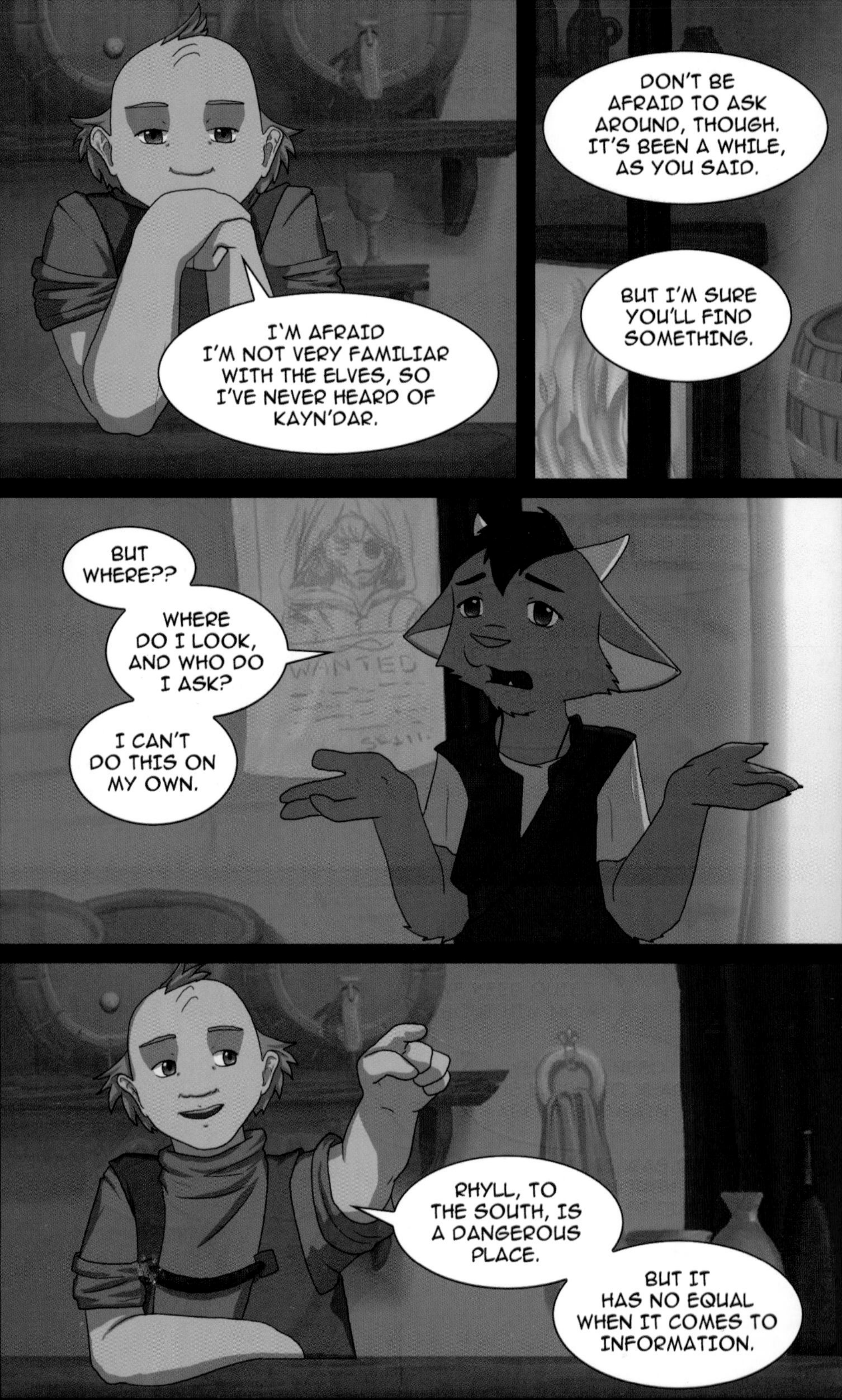
I'M AFRAID I'M NOT VERY FAMILIAR WITH THE ELVES, SO I'VE NEVER HEARD OF KAYN'DAR.
DON'T BE AFRAID TO ASK AROUND, THOUGH. IT'S BEEN A WHILE, AS YOU SAID.
BUT I'M SURE YOU'LL FIND SOMETHING.
BUT WHERE??
WHERE DO I LOOK, AND WHO DO I ASK?
I CAN'T DO THIS ON MY OWN.
WANTED
RHYLL, TO THE SOUTH, IS A DANGEROUS PLACE.
BUT IT HAS NO EQUAL WHEN IT COMES TO INFORMATION.

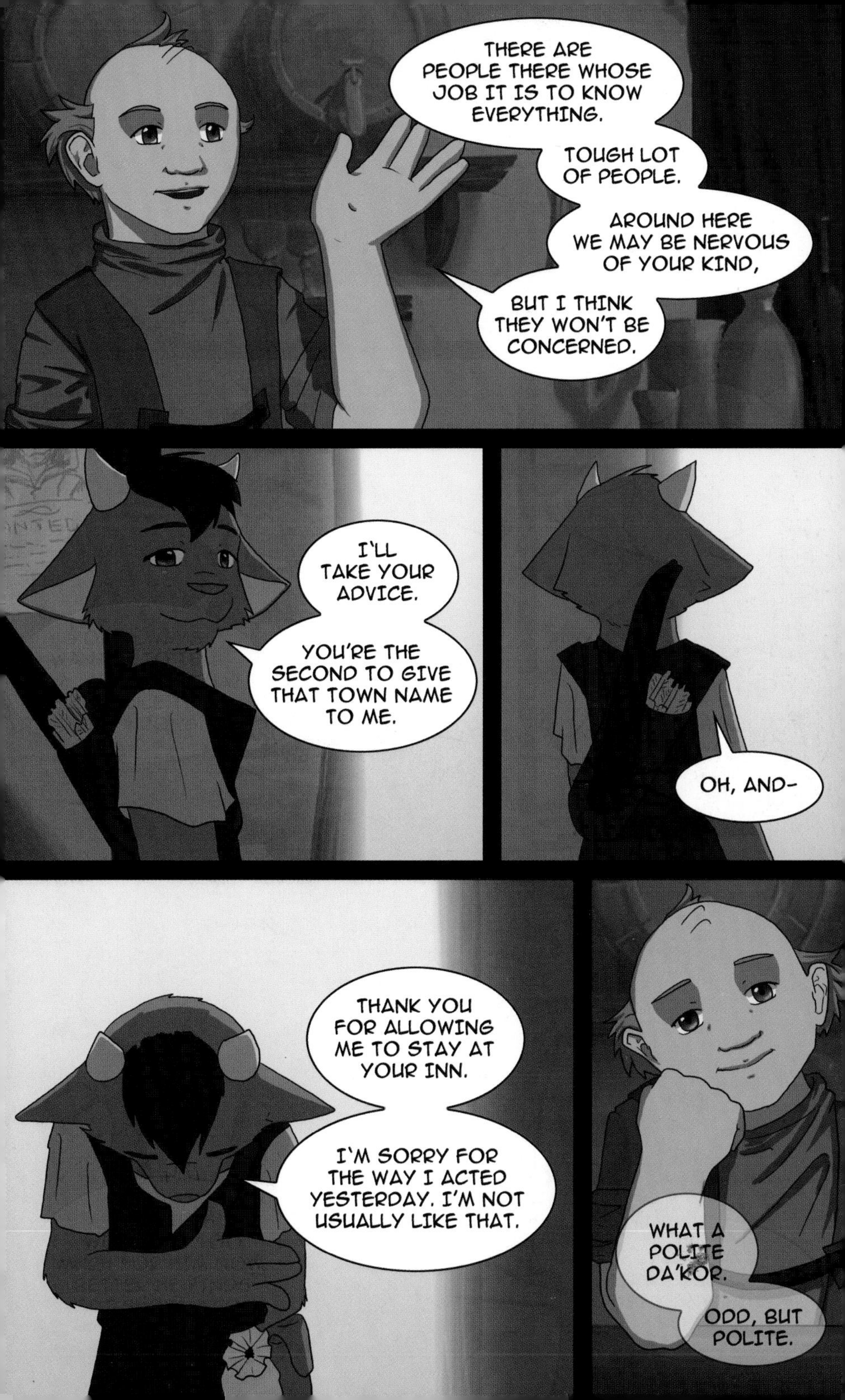
THERE ARE PEOPLE THERE WHOSE JOB IT IS TO KNOW EVERYTHING.
TOUGH LOT OF PEOPLE.
AROUND HERE WE MAY BE NERVOUS OF YOUR KIND,
BUT I THINK THEY WON'T BE CONCERNED.
I'LL TAKE YOUR ADVICE.
YOU'RE THE SECOND TO GIVE THAT TOWN NAME TO ME.
OH, AND-
THANK YOU FOR ALLOWING ME TO STAY AT YOUR INN.
I'M SORRY FOR THE WAY I ACTED YESTERDAY. I'M NOT USUALLY LIKE THAT.
WHAT A POLITE DA'KOR.
ODD, BUT POLITE.

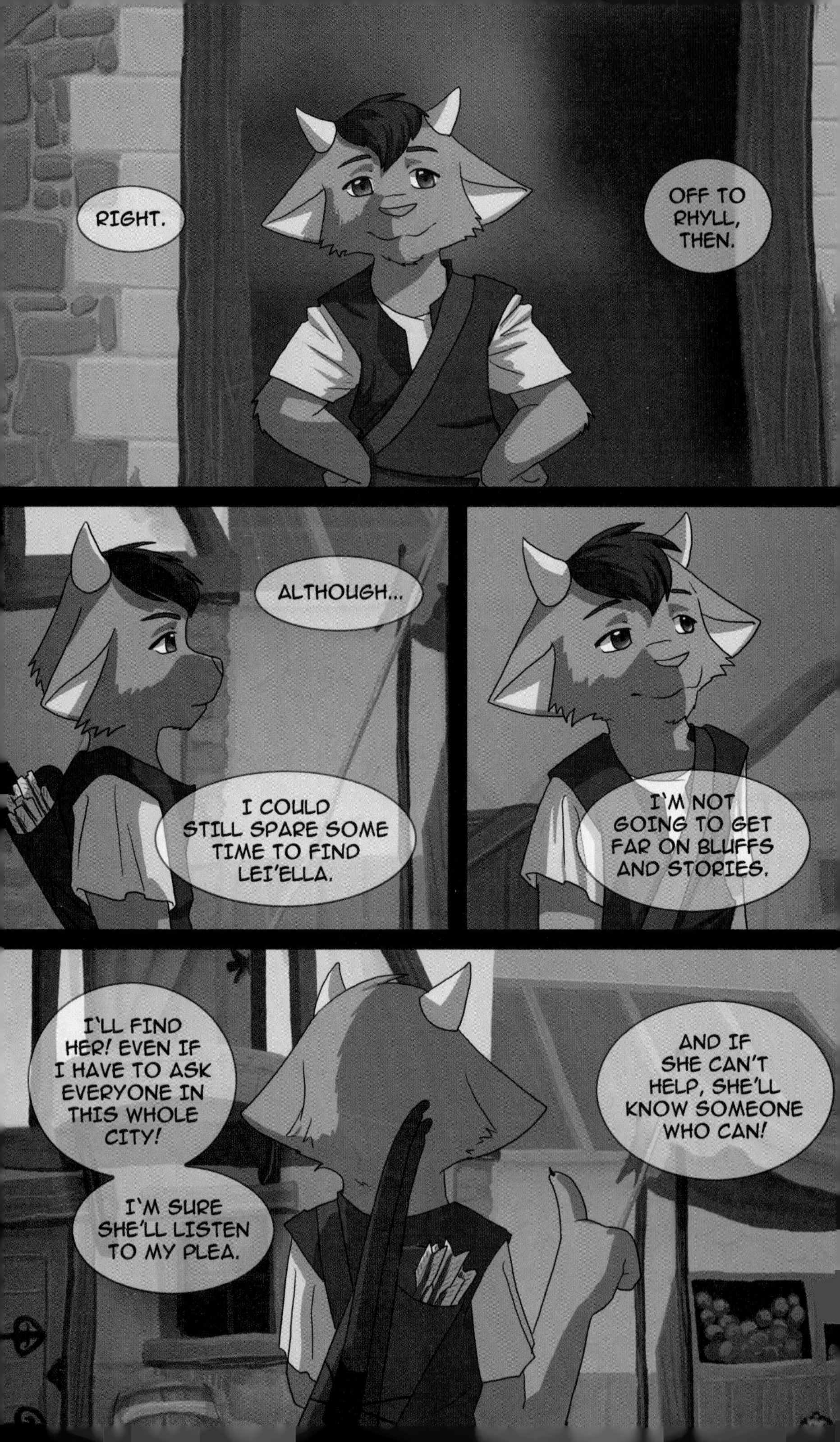
RIGHT.
OFF TO RHYLL, THEN.
ALTHOUGH...
I COULD STILL SPARE SOME TIME TO FIND LEI'ELLA.
I'M NOT GOING TO GET FAR ON BLUFFS AND STORIES.
I'LL FIND HER! EVEN IF I HAVE TO ASK EVERYONE IN THIS WHOLE CITY!
I'M SURE SHE'LL LISTEN TO MY PLEA.
AND IF SHE CAN'T HELP, SHE'LL KNOW SOMEONE WHO CAN!

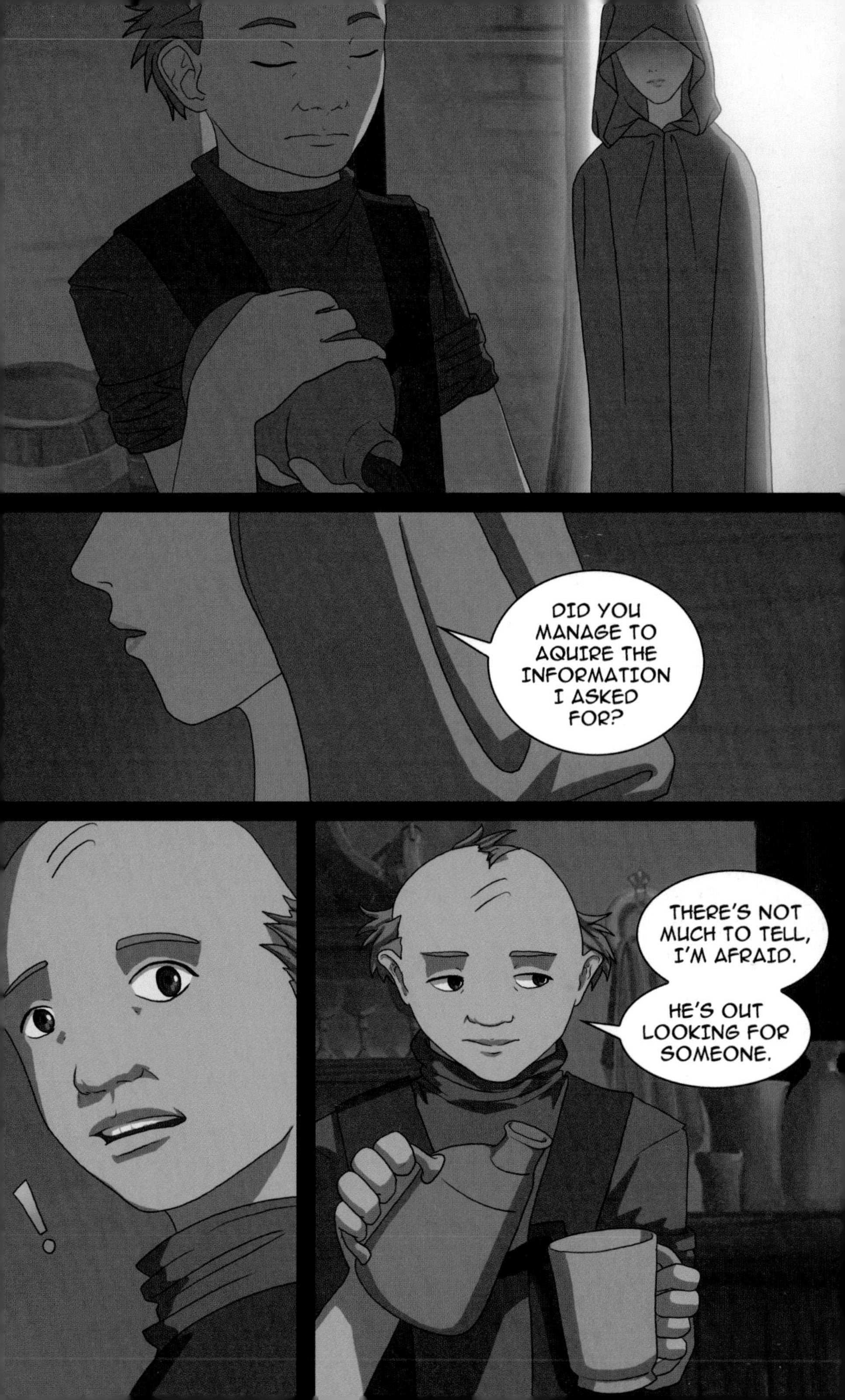
DID YOU MANAGE TO AQUIRE THE INFORMATION I ASKED FOR?
!
THERE'S NOT MUCH TO TELL, I'M AFRAID.
HE'S OUT LOOKING FOR SOMEONE.

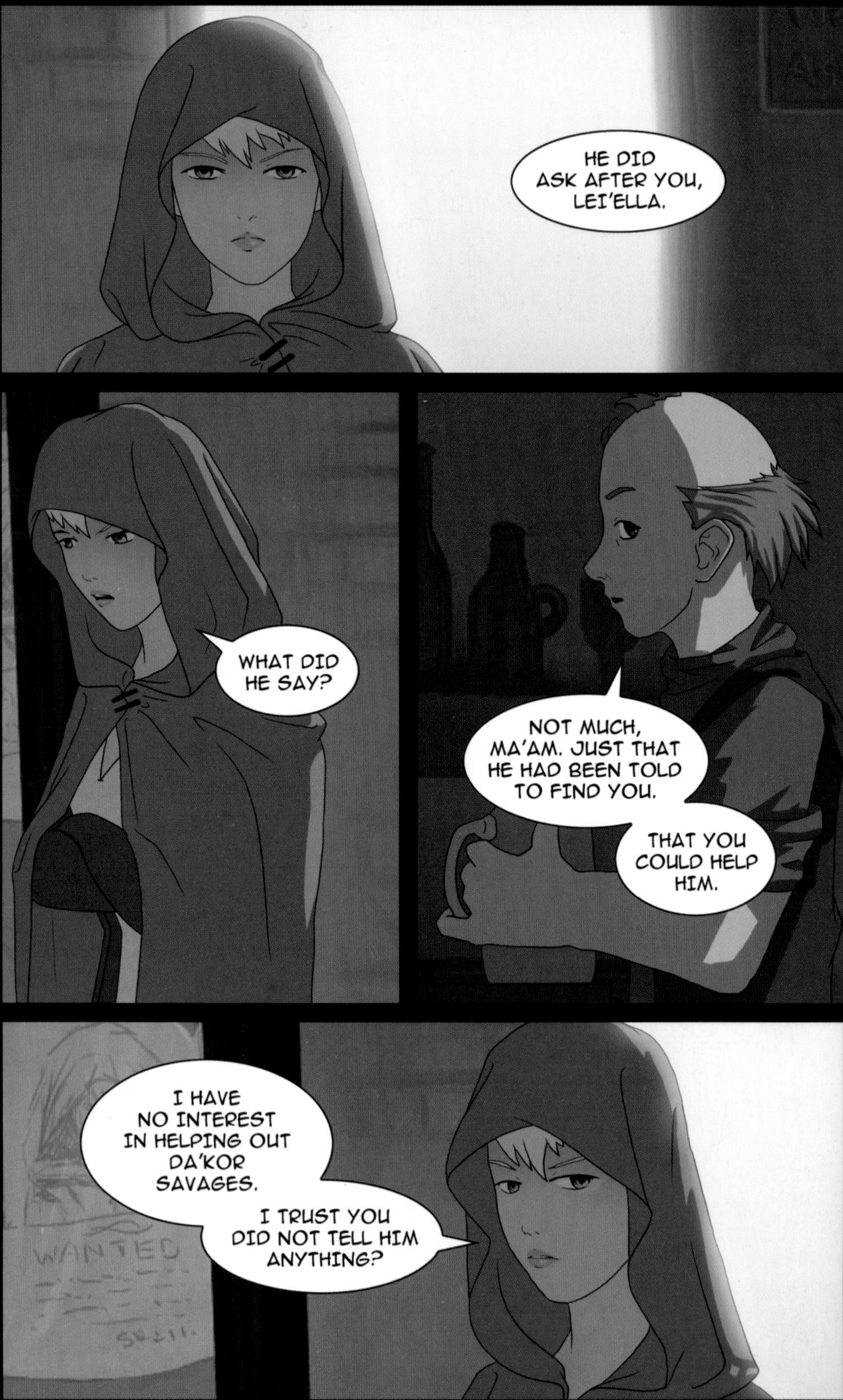

HE DID ASK AFTER YOU, LEI'ELLA.
WHAT DID HE SAY?
NOT MUCH, MA'AM. JUST THAT HE HAD BEEN TOLD TO FIND YOU.
THAT YOU COULD HELP HIM.
WANTED
I HAVE NO INTEREST IN HELPING OUT DA'KOR SAVAGES.
I TRUST YOU DID NOT TELL HIM ANYTHING?

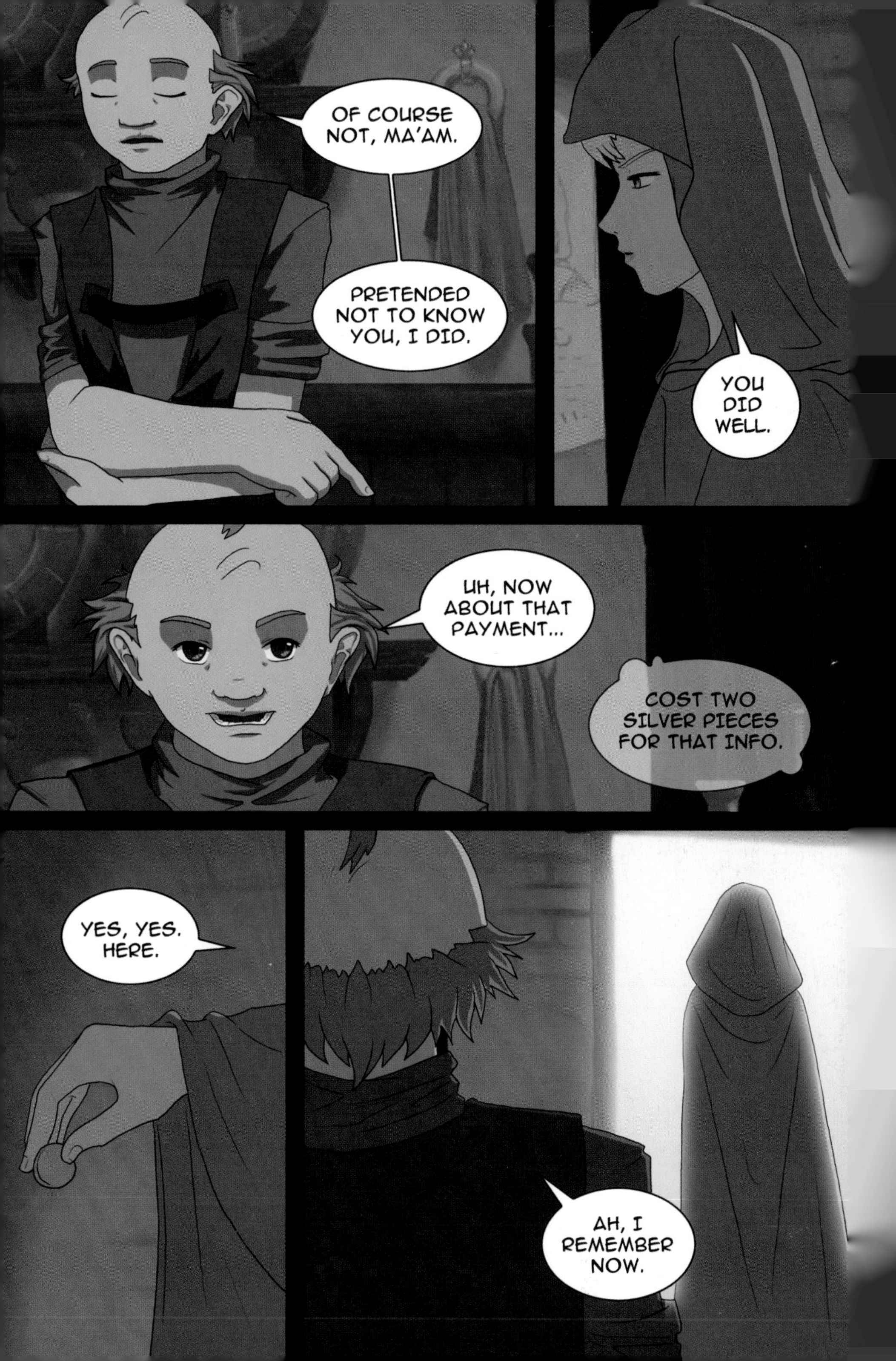
OF COURSE NOT, MA'AM.
PRETENDED NOT TO KNOW YOU, I DID.
YOU DID WELL.
UH, NOW ABOUT THAT PAYMENT...
COST TWO SILVER PIECES FOR THAT INFO.
YES, YES. HERE.
AH, I REMEMBER NOW.

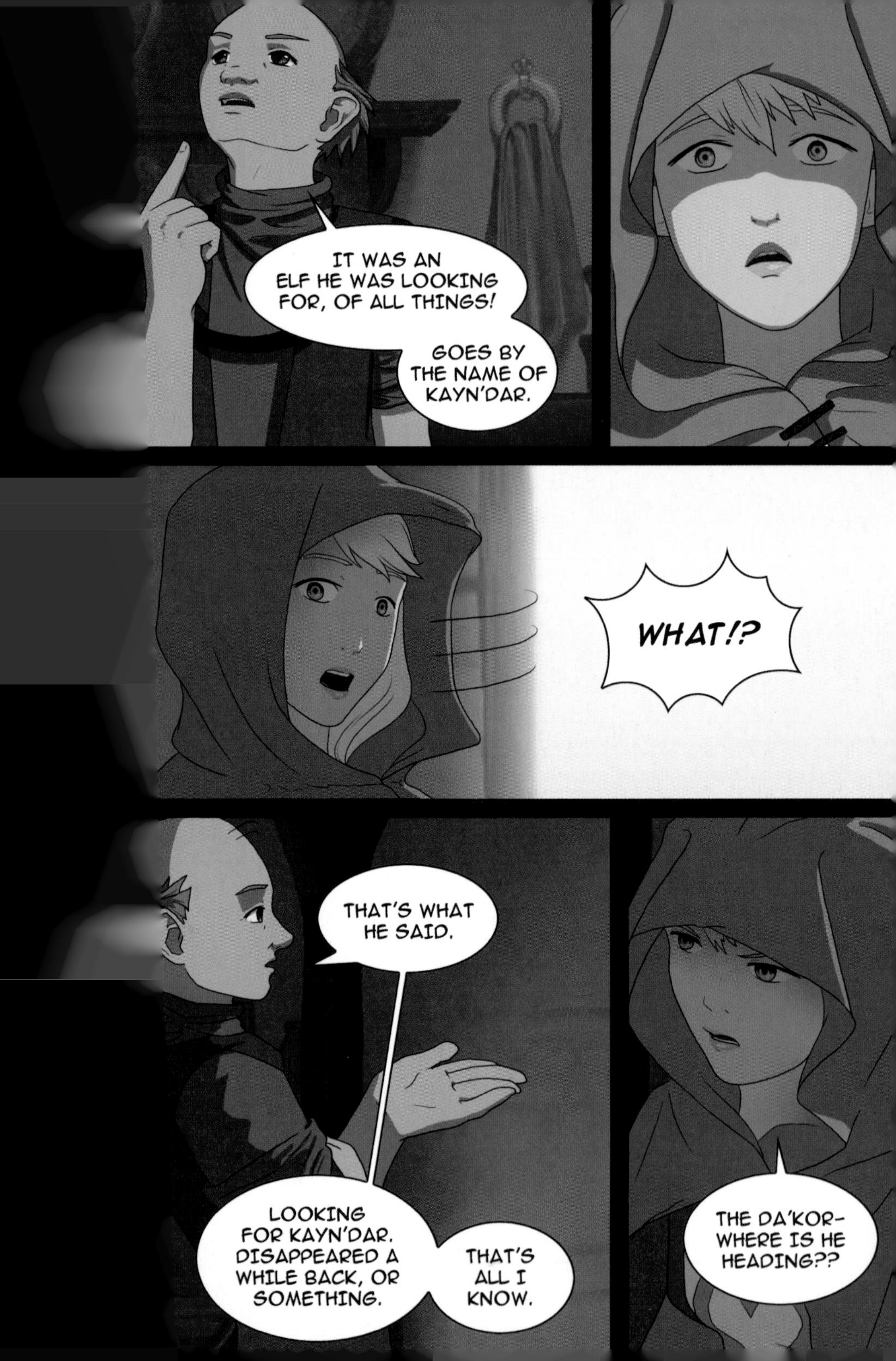
IT WAS AN ELF HE WAS LOOKING FOR, OF ALL THINGS!
GOES BY THE NAME OF KAYN'DAR.
WHAT!?
THAT'S WHAT HE SAID.
LOOKING FOR KAYN'DAR. DISAPPEARED A WHILE BACK, OR SOMETHING.
THAT'S ALL I KNOW.
THE DA'KOR-WHERE IS HE HEADING??

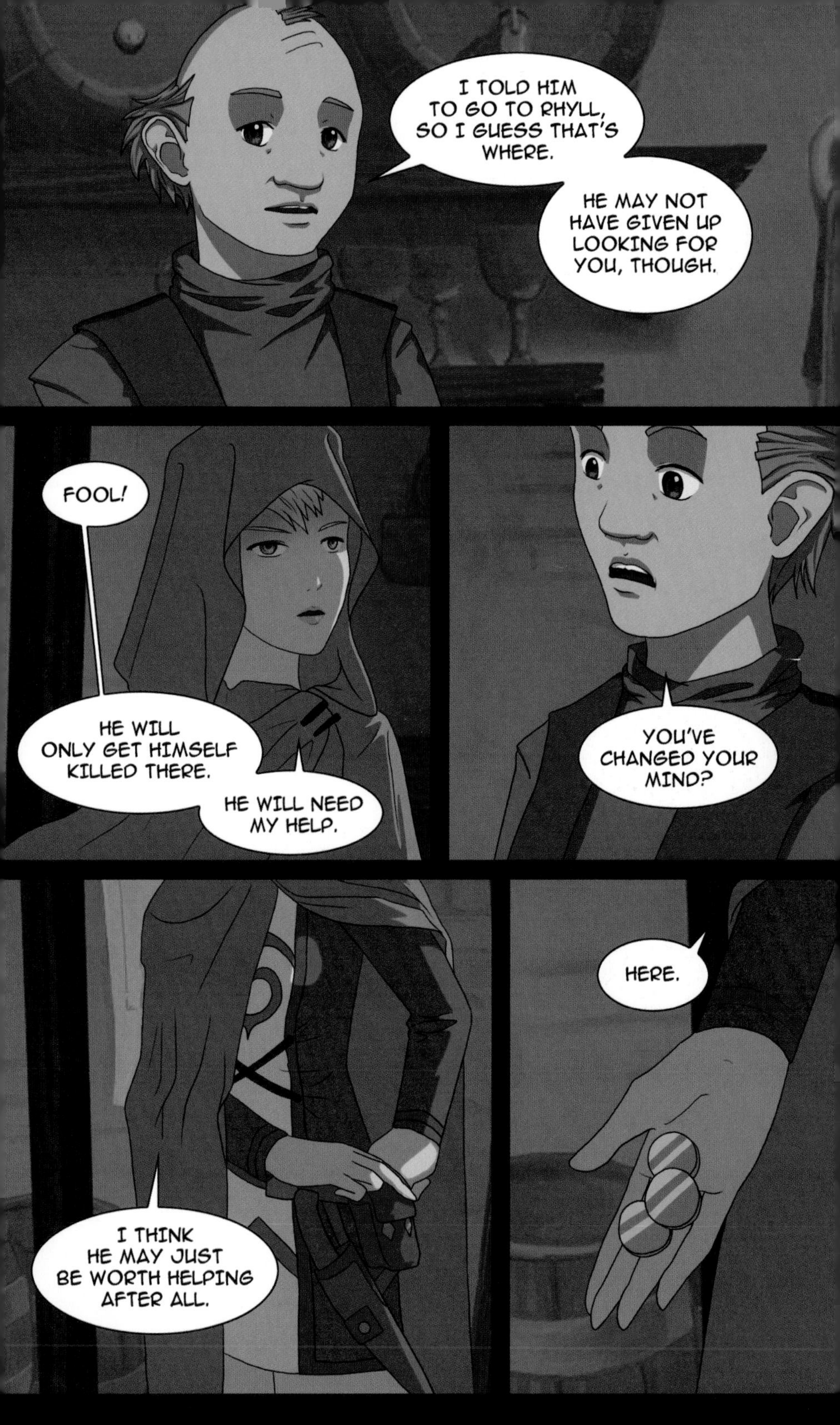
I TOLD HIM TO GO TO RHYLL, SO I GUESS THAT'S WHERE.
HE MAY NOT HAVE GIVEN UP LOOKING FOR YOU, THOUGH.
FOOL!
HE WILL ONLY GET HIMSELF KILLED THERE.
HE WILL NEED MY HELP.
YOU'VE CHANGED YOUR MIND?
I THINK HE MAY JUST BE WORTH HELPING AFTER ALL.
HERE.

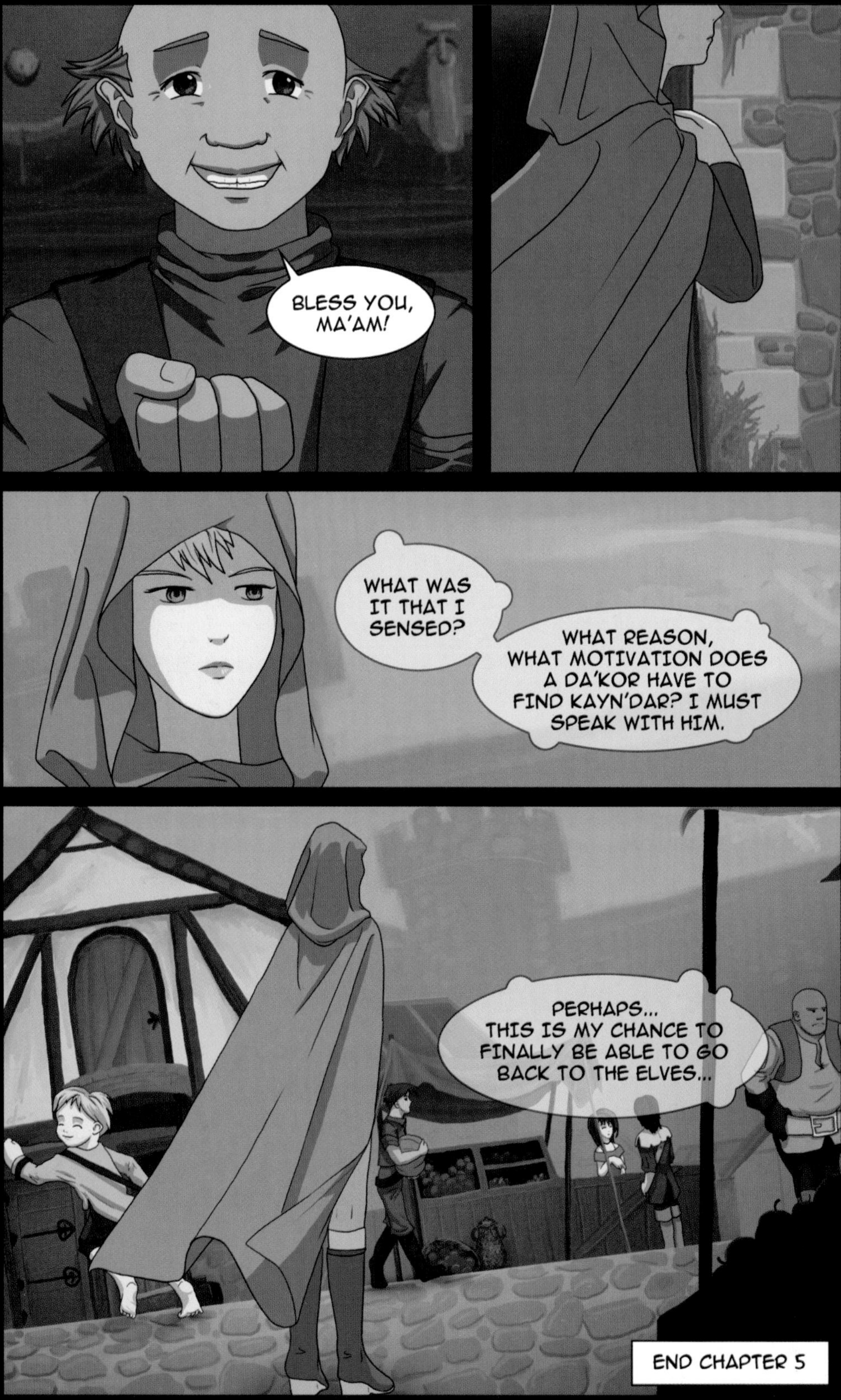
BLESS YOU, MA'AM!
WHAT WAS IT THAT I SENSED?
WHAT REASON, WHAT MOTIVATION DOES A DA'KOR HAVE TO FIND KAYN'DAR? I MUST SPEAK WITH HIM.
PERHAPS... THIS IS MY CHANCE TO FINALLY BE ABLE TO GO BACK TO THE ELVES...
END CHAPTER 5

AUTHOR'S NOTES

When I started drawing the first pages of Inverloch in July 2004, it was nothing more than a hobby with which to fill in my time when not studying for my Information Technology degree, and an outlet for me to develop my skills as a cartoonist. I'd been doing fanart paintings using the computer for several years, but began to tire of drawing other people's characters, and decided I wanted to create my own.

Almost two years and three volumes later, it's practically become a part-time job, with the online version attracting thousands of reader's every day.

Looking back at this first volume, I can't help but wince at how badly it was done. Aside from the script, it was unplanned, with precious few concept sketches and preliminary drawings completed before I began. However, I learned the most during this volume, especially from the feedback I was constantly receiving from readers as I progressed through the pages.

The first five story pages have been redrawn especially for this printed version, with improved character designs, backgrounds, framing, and script. I've often dreamed of completely redrawing the first volume, but I have many other story ideas I'd like to tackle after Inverloch is finished, so it's unlikely to happen.

I hope you enjoyed the first volume of Inverloch as much as I enjoyed drawing it, and hope to see you at our online community at www.seraph-inn.com!

-Sarah Ellerton

DA'KORS

Historically, da'kors are a peaceful species. However, due to constant brutalisation and exploitation by humans, many younger members have begun attacking and killing any trespassers, which only further serves to ruin their reputation. Acheron very quickly learns that the rest of the world doesn't view his people in the same way he does.

Da'kors went through many design changes, from being goblin-type creatures, to reptilians, mammals, then finally to the goat/dog hybrid creature that was finally chosen. People often ask me how I came up with the idea for them; it was an evolutionay process, with many drawings being made, each changed slightly from the previous until I was satisfied with the result. Unfortunately, most of these initial drawings have gone missing.

ACHERON

Acheron lived a very sheltered life, his mother desperately trying to prevent him from becoming a killer like the majority of other males his age. He's rather naive and innocent for the most part, and prefers to talk his way out of trouble rather than risk conflict. He's a bad fighter, and although he knows how to use a bow, he's not very good at it. Having an extremely selfless nature, he much prefers to do things for other people than for himself, even things that may require ultimate sacrifice on his part.

After countless very rough sketches, this was the final pencil design of Acheron made just before I started drawing the comic.

ELVES

Elves are an arrogant race, viewing themselves as being above both da'kors and humans. They have only a small population on this continent, confined to their city Inverloch, sheltered in a large northern forest. They profess to being immortal, and although no elf has ever died of old age, none have ever lived past two thousand years, so this 'fact' is often disputed.

The Inverloch elf design was inspired by those from Record of Lodoss War - I've always been rather fond of their outrageously long ears. To try and add some realism, the Inverloch elves have stiff yet flexible ears, much like those of horses, which can be fully articulated by their owner - which explains how Lei'ella manages to keep hers so carefully hidden inside her hood!

LEI'ELLA

Lei'ella only makes a brief appearance at the end of this volume, but plays a greater part in the rest of the story. She's an elf who, for some reason, is not living im Inverloch with her kin, and shares Kayn'dar's unusual hair and eye colour. Lei'ella is untrusting and very guarded around humans, talkiing very little about herself or her past, but she feels confident opening up to Acheron. She's used to using threats to get what she wants, a necessary part of her job, but is kind and caring beneath the facade.

◀ Lei'ella went through quite a lot of costume designs, ending up with this design which initially belonged to another character from Volume 2.

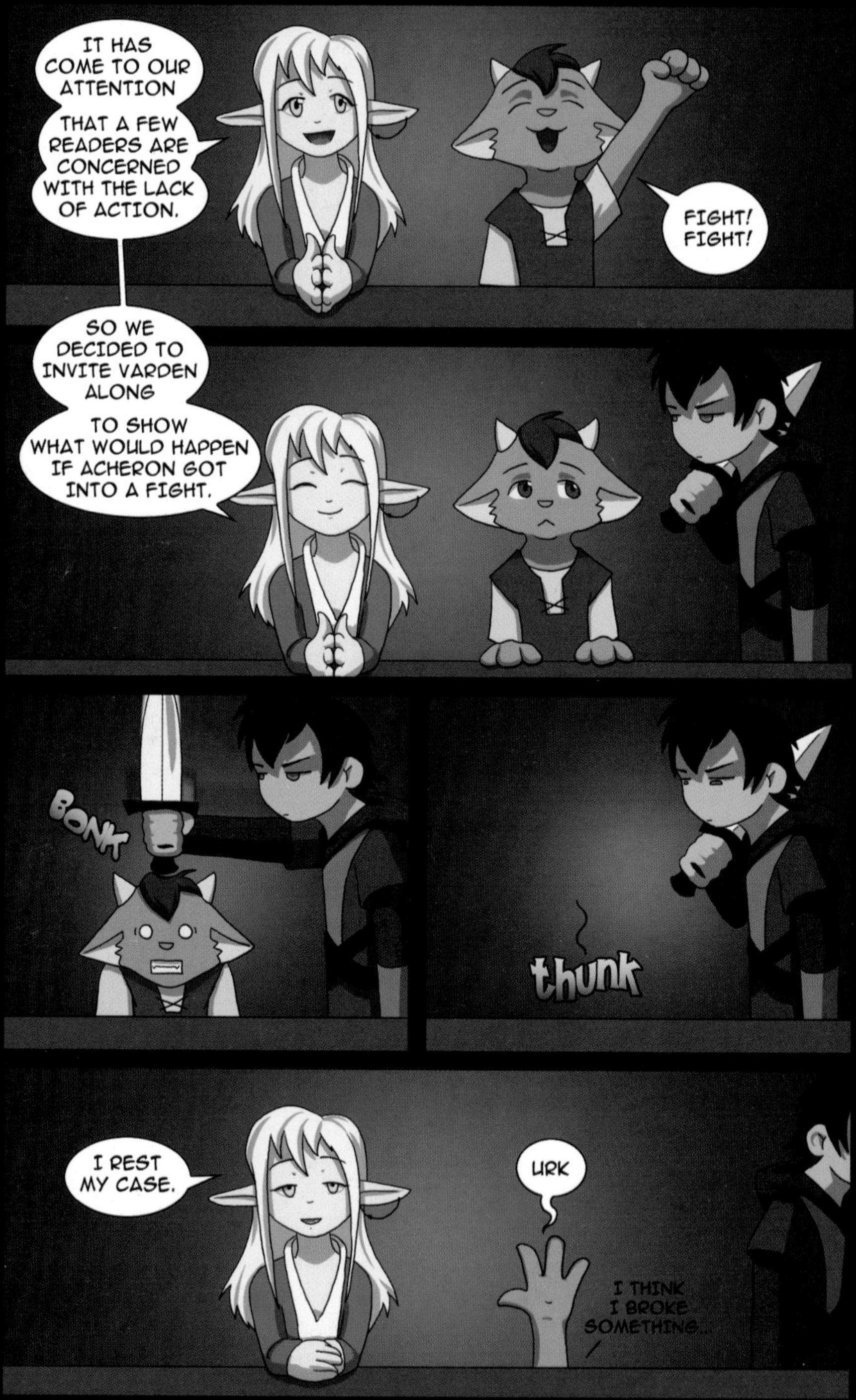
IT HAS COME TO OUR ATTENTION
THAT A FEW READERS ARE CONCERNED WITH THE LACK OF ACTION.
FIGHT! FIGHT!
SO WE DECIDED TO INVITE VARDEN ALONG
TO SHOW WHAT WOULD HAPPEN IF ACHERON GOT INTO A FIGHT.
BONK
thunk
I REST MY CASE.
URK
I THINK I BROKE SOMETHING...

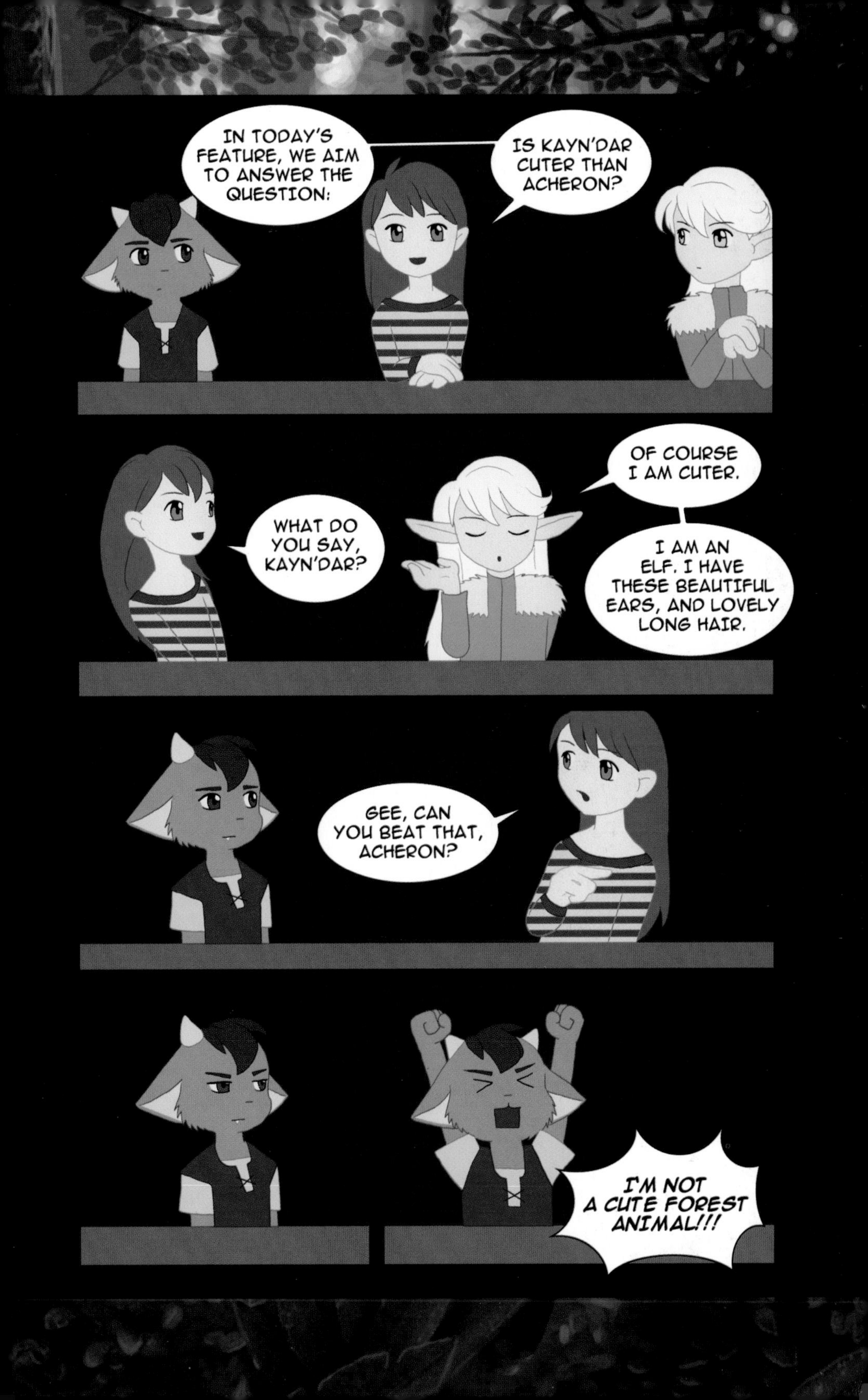
IN TODAY'S FEATURE, WE AIM TO ANSWER THE QUESTION:
IS KAYN'DAR CUTER THAN ACHERON?
WHAT DO YOU SAY, KAYN'DAR?
OF COURSE I AM CUTER.
I AM AN ELF. I HAVE THESE BEAUTIFUL EARS, AND LOVELY LONG HAIR.
GEE, CAN YOU BEAT THAT, ACHERON?
I'M NOT A CUTE FOREST ANIMAL!!!

Coming in VOLUME 2...

His journey now fully underway, it doesn't take long for Acheron to start attracting a little unwanted attention, being one of the few da'kor crazy enough to venture out into human cities alone.

With his new friends Lei'ella the thief-catcher, Varden the thief, and Neirenn the elemental mage, he begins to learn a little more about Kayn'dar's disappearance - but now he also has a da'kor-hunting enemy close on his trail...

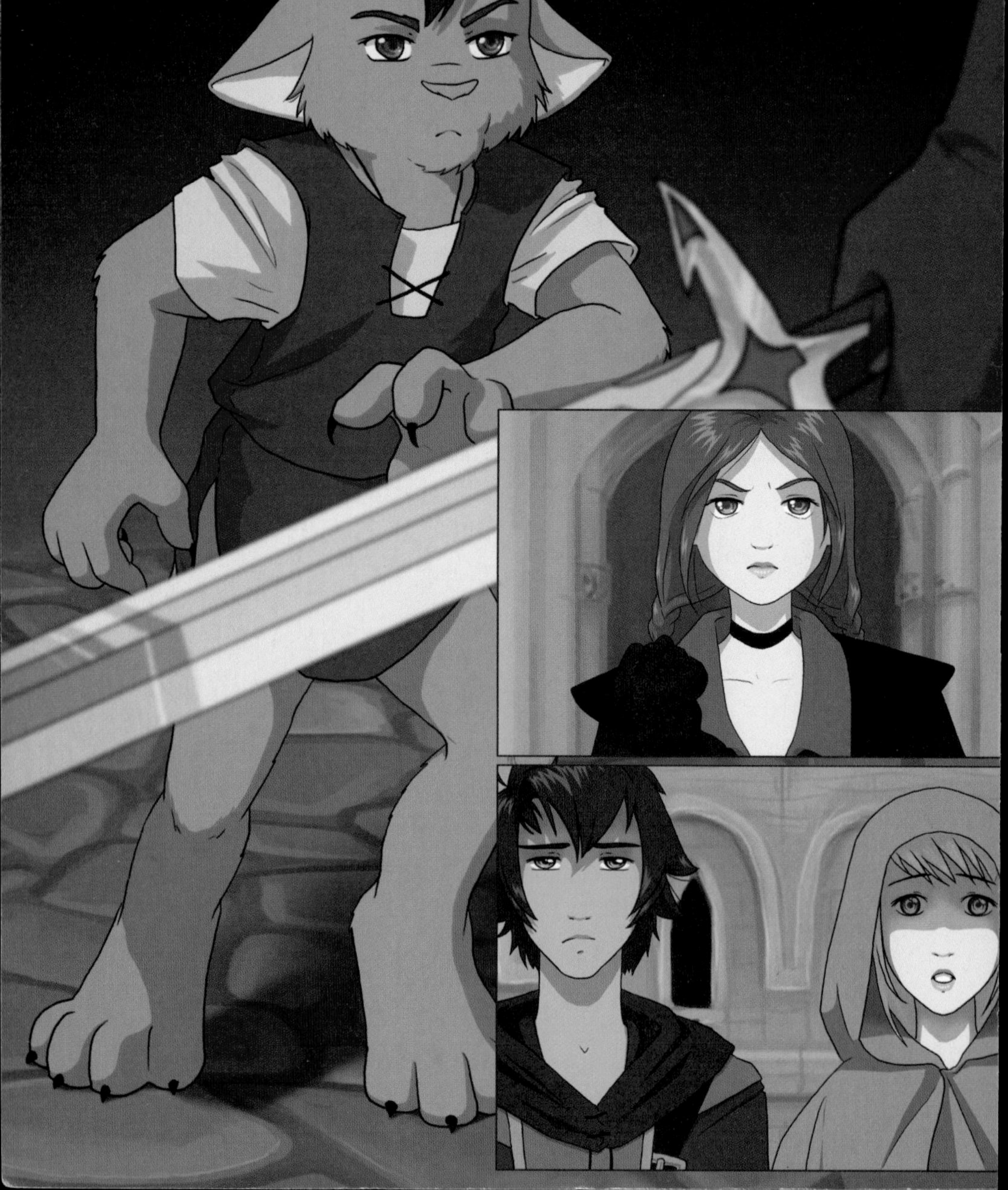

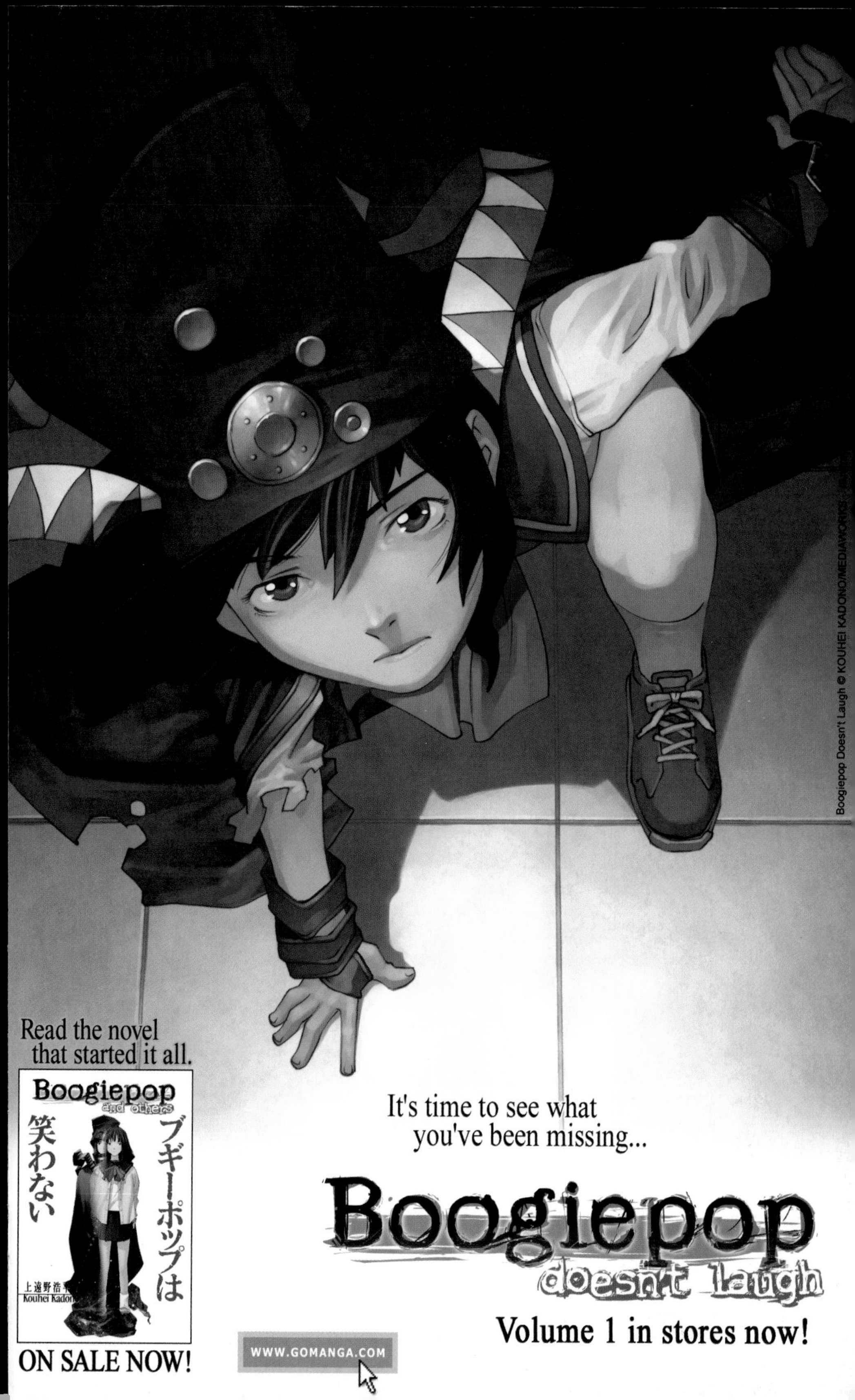

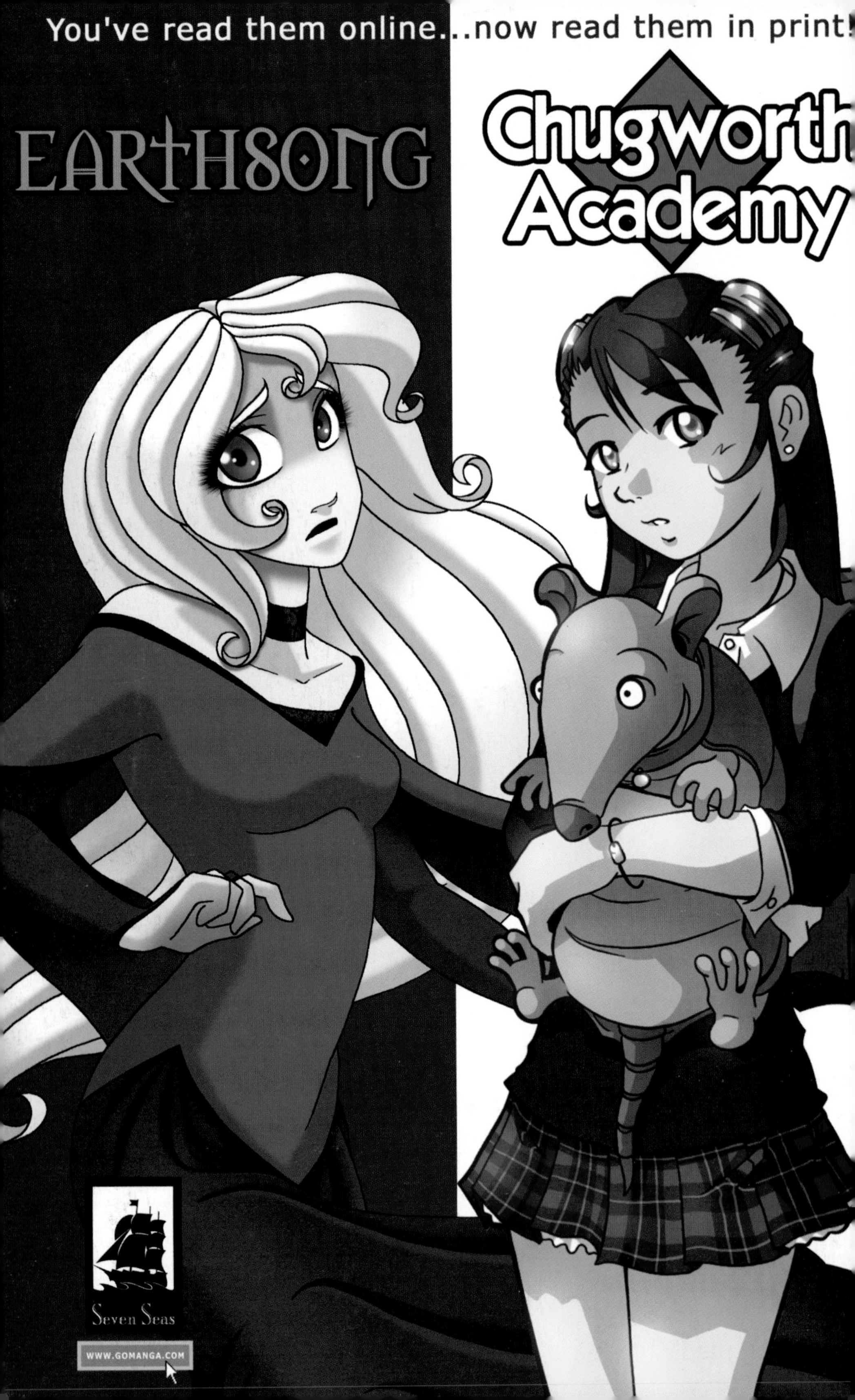
You've read them online...now read them in print!
EARTHSONG
Chugworth Academy
Seven Seas
WWW.GOMANGA.COM

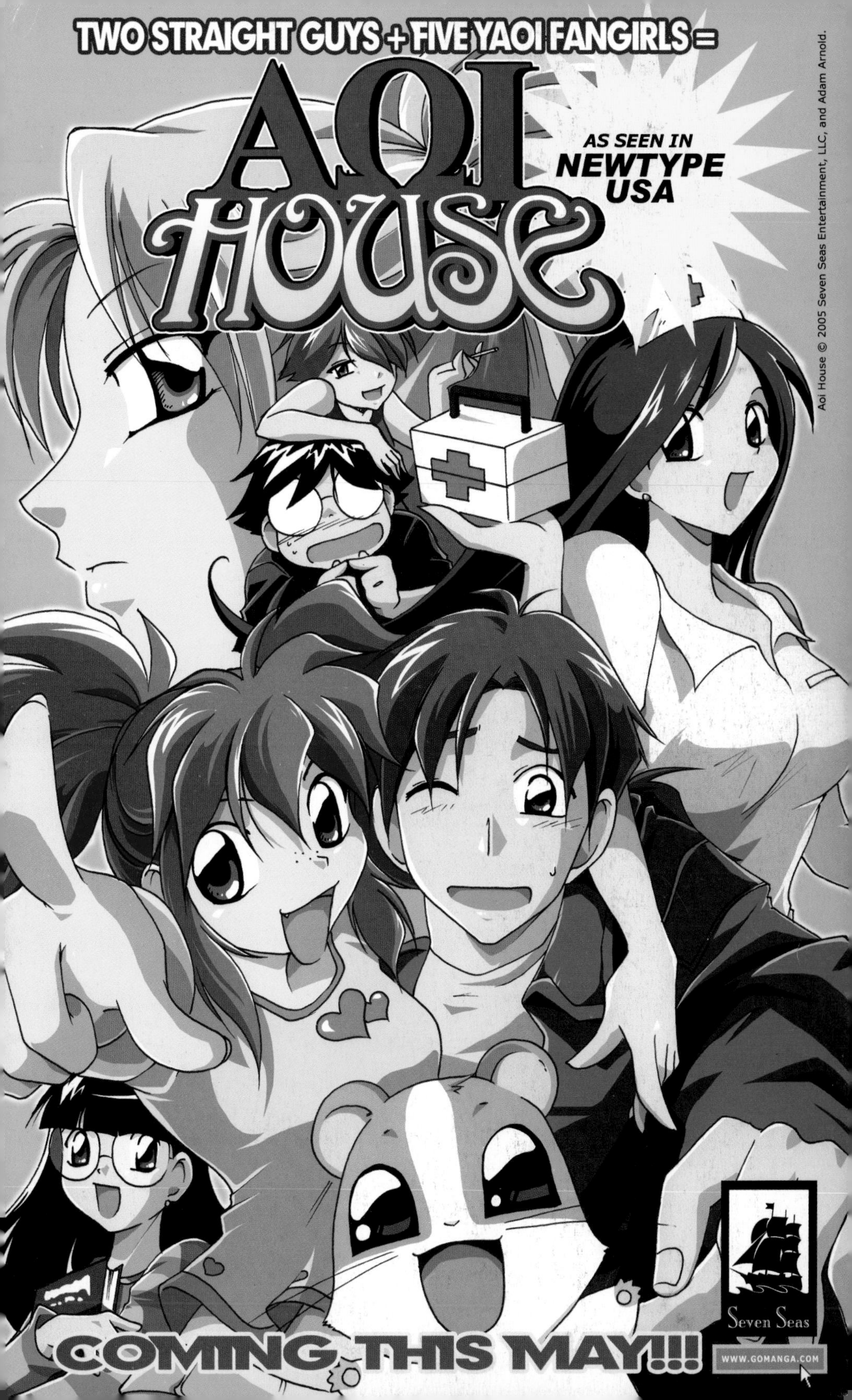

TWO STRAIGHT GUYS + FIVE YAOI FANGIRLS =
AOI HOUSE
AS SEEN IN NEWTYPE USA
Aoi House © 2005 Seven Seas Entertainment, LLC, and Adam Arnold.
Seven Seas
COMING THIS MAY!!!
WWW.GOMANGA.COM

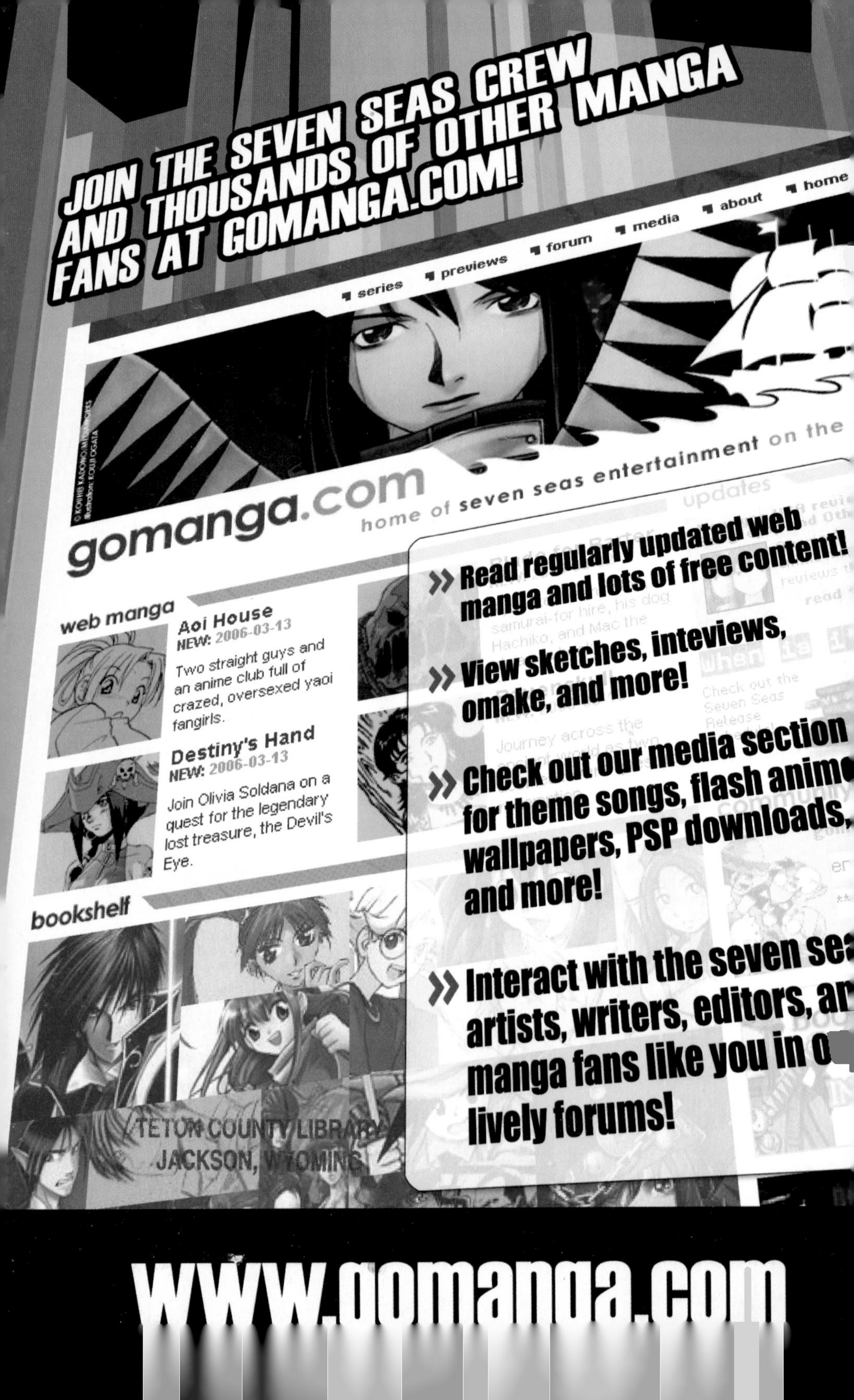
JOIN THE SEVEN SEAS CREW AND THOUSANDS OF OTHER MANGA FANS AT GOMANGA.COM!
series
previews
forum
media
about
home
gomanga.com
home of seven seas entertainment on the
web manga
Aoi House
NEW: 2006-03-13
Two straight guys and an anime club full of crazed, oversexed yaoi fangirls.
Destiny's Hand
NEW: 2006-03-13
Join Olivia Soldana on a quest for the legendary lost treasure, the Devil's Eye.
bookshelf
updates
» Read regularly updated web manga and lots of free content!
» View sketches, inteviews, omake, and more!
» Check out our media section for theme songs, flash anime, wallpapers, PSP downloads, and more!
» Interact with the seven seas artists, writers, editors, and manga fans like you in our lively forums!
www.gomanga.com